FURNITURE *PAST & PRESENT*

Books by Louise Ade Boger

THE COMPLETE GUIDE TO FURNITURE STYLES

(with H. Batterson Boger)
THE DICTIONARY OF ANTIQUES AND THE DECORATIVE ARTS

FURNITURE
PAST & PRESENT

*A complete illustrated
guide to furniture styles
from Ancient to Modern*

By LOUISE ADE BOGER

1966 / DOUBLEDAY & COMPANY, INC., GARDEN CITY, NEW YORK

Library of Congress Catalog Card Number 66–20939

Copyright © 1966 by Louise Ade Boger

All Rights Reserved

Printed in the United States of America

First Edition

CONTENTS

FURNITURE *PAST & PRESENT*

Ancient to Renaissance

To understand the development of domestic furniture and its place in the changing social habits, it is necessary to begin by considering furniture of the ancient world, because the modern is the outcome and inheritor of the ancient, the old visibly influencing the new. Wood, ivory, precious and semi-precious stones, glass pastes, bronze, gold, and silver have been employed since ancient times either in the construction or in the decoration of furniture. Wood played a pre-eminent role, as it does still. Of ancient furniture there are few examples extant, chiefly because there are limits to the endurance of wood and partly because, however great may have been the splendor of ancient civilizations, the amount of furniture was very limited. Chairs, stools, couches, beds, tables, and chests comprised virtually the entire furnishings of the ancients. The Ptolemies of Egypt and the Plantagenets of England, although they lived centuries apart, enjoyed about the same household conveniences. Until the Renaissance, the development in household comfort was negligible.

EGYPTIAN

A history of furniture naturally begins with Egypt, the Egypt of the Pharaohs, whose art history began more than 4000 years before the Christian era. Though a civilization older than Egypt flourished in Assyria and Babylonia, it is Egypt that has given us through her monuments our greatest knowledge of how the ancients lived. Indeed we even possess a more intimate knowledge of the daily life of the ancient Egyptians than of many later civilized people chiefly because of their idea of death. To ensure for the departed a continuance of the golden splendor that was their earthly heritage, the Pharaohs and the enormously rich provided for the after-life either by erecting or excavating vast tombs in which an untold amount of property and treasure were amassed. By bestowing on Egypt an extreme climatic dryness, Nature herself decreed that this

1

elaborate funerary equipment should be preserved. But because of the size and magnificence of the buried treasure, thievery by ancient tomb-robbers was proportionately great. The tomb revealing for the first and perhaps only time an almost undisturbed Egyptian royal burial in all its earthly grandeur is that of Tut'ankhamun, the boy king of Egypt, who lived more than 1300 years B.C. Located in the Valley of the Tombs of Kings, which was some 420 miles south of Cairo and where there are the tombs of more than forty Theban Pharaohs, the tomb of Tut'ankhamun, filled with wonderful royal furniture and funerary equipment, provides an appropriate monument to a great civilization. Tut'ankhamun was one of the last Pharaohs of the XVIII dynasty, which began about 1600 years B.C. During the XVIII dynasty trade developed to an unprecedented extent and the wealth increased proportionately. The arts flourished, and craftsmen in every field produced work of unrivaled splendor and refinement.

Undoubtedly one of the great artistic treasures of Tut'ankhamun's tomb is the throne chair, made of carved wood overlaid with sheet gold and richly adorned with brilliant polychrome decoration in faïence, glass, stones, and silver. The four legs are of feline form, the two front legs surmounted with lions' heads remarkable for their strength and simplicity. The arms are in the form of two crowned and winged uraei, or royal cobra. Three vertical struts support the sloping or raked back. The use of vertical struts for support illustrates a marked feature of Egyptian cabinet-work, that is, sound construction, which imparts to the work an enduring quality. The chair back is enriched with a superb panel inlaid against a background of gold depicting in a charmingly realistic manner an episode in the daily life of the king and queen. The scene is the palace, where the king is sitting upon a cushioned chair, his one arm resting naturally across the back. The queen, standing before him, holds in one hand a small jar of scent or ointment and with her other hand she gently touches the king's shoulder. From the upper part of the panel the solar disk sheds its beneficent rays upon them. The naturalism in the postures, actions, and familiarities of daily life expressed in this panel are typical of the age and considerably soften the earlier cold reserve and severity of Egyptian art. The flesh of the king and queen is of red glass and their wigs of vivid blue faïence; their robes are of silver, and their crowns, collars, and other decorative details are enriched with an inlay of colored glass, faïence, and calcite. The seat of the chair is inlaid with gold, dark and light blue faïence, and calcite. The Egyptian oriental love of vivid color is strikingly revealed in this chair, which in its original state must have been a dazzling sight. The legs are joined about midway with stretchers. Between the seat and the stretchers the traditional openwork ornamental device consisting of papyrus and lotus plants, symbolizing the union of Upper and Lower Egypt, has been almost entirely torn away by thieves.

2

Throne Chair from the Tut'ankhamun Tomb in the Valley of Kings, Thebes, Egypt. Dynasty XVIII. BELOW: Detail of the throne chair showing the back panel. *Courtesy Metropolitan Museum of Art.*

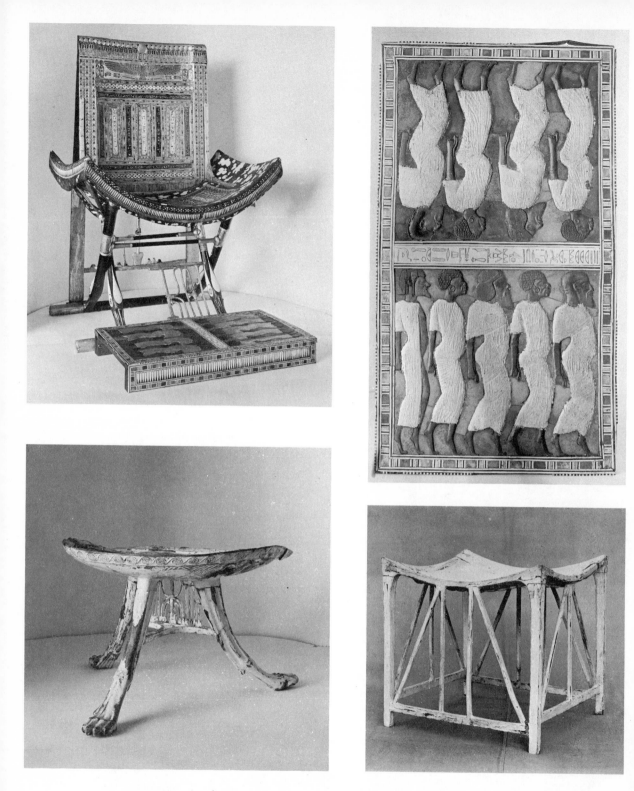

ABOVE LEFT: An ebony stool of X-form made rigid with the addition of a back. The top of the footstool is decorated with captives lying prostrate and bound. From the Tut'ankhamun Tomb. ABOVE RIGHT: Detail of footstool showing the bound and prone captives. BELOW LEFT: Stool of tripod form, painted white. From the Tut'ankhamun Tomb. BELOW RIGHT: Stool painted white. The space between the seat and stretcher is filled in with right-angled triangles. From the Tut'ankhamun Tomb. *Courtesy Metropolitan Museum of Art.*

4

Also possessing great artistic merit is an ebony stool of X-form, but made rigid with the addition of a back. The stool is of austere appearance and elaborately inlaid with gold, ivory, natural stones, faïence, and glass simulating turquoise and lapis lazuli. Because it possesses the character of a chair of state, it is thought to have been Tut'ankhamun's ecclesiastical throne when he was acting as the highest spiritual authority; in many ways it calls to mind the bishop's chair, or faldstool of present-day cathedrals. The ample curved ebony seat inlaid with ivory, in imitation of a piebald hide, is modeled in the semblance of flexible leather and supported on crossed legs formed like the heads of geese, partially bound with thin sheet gold, resting on floor runners. The traditional openwork ornament extends between the stretcher and front floor runner. To make the chair firm and strong, vertical braces are attached to the rear of the chair at the top of the chair back, the seat, and floor runner.

Belonging to the chair is a footstool equally rich in decoration. A favorite subject for the top of royal footstools, captives lie prostrate and bound, so that the king when seated may rest his feet upon them. "Until I make thine enemies thy footstool," chants the Psalmist. Bound and prone captives also supplied the motif for a beaded hassock serving as a footrest for a chair of state.

Many of the features characterizing Egyptian chair and stool design are well defined in these two chairs. Legs adapted from the fore and hind legs of a quadruped were always much favored, and each foot commonly rested on a small solid cylinder or drum which in the more ambitious pieces was sheathed in gold, bronze, or copper. Stools having straight X-form legs terminating on horizontal floor bars or runners and made in many instances to fold up were much in evidence. An unusual painted white stool in this collection is of tripod form, having a dished semi-circular seat supported on three splayed legs terminating in paw feet, the legs being joined about midway with an incurvate stretcher. This form often referred to as the Thebes stool is remarkably comfortable and has served as a model for twentieth-century designers. Especially notable because of their refined simplicity are two oblong stools, one painted white and the other made of redwood having a seat inlaid with white bands of ivory alternating with thin strips of ebony. The seats of both stools incline downward in a graceful curve, and the straight slender legs are joined with stretchers rather close to the ground. To obtain a maximum of strength and lightness, two slender vertical members and two diagonal members forming two right-angled triangles fill in the space between the seat and stretcher. Both stools possess the peculiar charm of the "lighter" Egyptian furniture as distinguished from the furniture with an "enduring" appearance. A certain feeling of simplicity which it pleases us to call modern is found in them, as well as in much of the "lighter" Egyptian furniture.

Of great interest is a folding wood bed painted white, presumably intended for use in traveling or in war, which, in spite of its age, can still be easily folded to one third of its size. The eight legs are adapted from the fore and hind legs of a quadruped; each leg rests on a copper drum. Stretched over the frame is a closely woven linen string webbing also painted white. It has, as is usually the case in Egyptian beds and couches, a foot panel but nothing at the head.

So the treasures go on and on. Curious couches supported on each side by an animal, the elongated body forming the side rail; an ebony bed with a linen string webbing, having a foot panel of ivory, ebony, and gold; headrests of carved ivory; reversible gaming boards marked for two different games; musical instruments, a chest painted white and inlaid with strips of ebony; a red wood chest of elegant simplicity inlaid with ivory and ebony and provided with four movable poles, sliding in rings attached on the bottom, to carry it; richly inlaid caskets; a pedestal of gilt wood enriched with a winged sun, symbol of royal dignity dating from the Ancient Kingdom of Egypt—these are but a few of the priceless relics from this almost incredible collection of tomb furniture.

BABYLONIAN AND ASSYRIAN

A civilization older than that of Egypt flourished in the fertile plains of two rivers, the Tigris and Euphrates, in the sacred land of Mesopotamia. To this district tradition assigns the Garden of Eden. The two great nations of Assyria and Babylonia, which possessed this land, are as difficult to separate historically as geographically. Judging by what we know of their history, the Babylonians and Assyrians were a domineering, aggressive race; sturdy, warlike, and ruthless, delighting in cruel spectacles and inflicting horrible tortures on their conquered enemies.

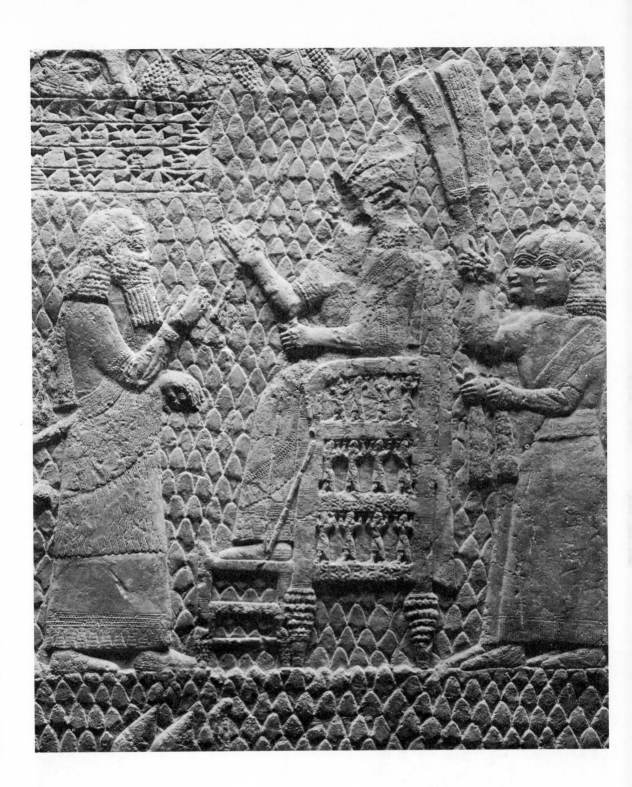

OPPOSITE: A folding wood bed from the Tut'ankhamun Tomb. *Courtesy Metropolitan Museum of Art.* ABOVE: A detail from a stone relief showing the Assyrian King Sennacherib at Lachish sitting on his throne. Rows of captives as supporting figures have been introduced into the side of the chair. The feet of the throne are in the form of inverted pine cones. *Courtesy British Museum.* (*See page 8.*)

Since scarcely a trace of their actual furniture exists, our knowledge is derived almost entirely from bas-reliefs, sculptures, and tablets. Assyrian wall sculptures depict the simplest furniture—chairs, couches, and tables. Much of their ornament suggests Egyptian influence. As in Egypt, here also are found the winged globe, solar disks, lotus plant, and prisoners in the nature of caryatids as decorative supports. Wild animals and beasts of the chase are also carved, the lion, bull, and ram being especially typical. The pine cone, one of the sacred emblems, in an inverted form frequently occurs as a foot for throne chairs and couches. We miss in Assyrian furniture the Egyptian qualities of clearness and exactness. Judging by wall sculptures, their furniture seems clumsy and badly proportioned. The influence of Assyria made itself felt on the one hand in Persia, on the other hand over a great part of Asia Minor. The ruins at the palaces at Susa and Persepolis, Persia's most important relics, suggest that the Persians adopted certain features from the conquered Assyrians.

Detail from a stone relief representing King Ashurbanipal feasting with his Queen in the royal garden after the defeat of Teumman, 660 B.C. *Courtesy British Museum.*

GRECIAN

Practically all our knowledge of the daily life of the ancient Greeks is derived from references in literature and, more importantly, from innumerable scenes of Greek life found on vases and marble reliefs. Unfortunately, furniture used by the Greeks has almost entirely disappeared because of the damp climate, which makes it impossible for wood, the natural material for furniture, to survive. There can be no doubt that the old world empires of Egypt, Assyria, and Babylonia exercised a powerful influence on the early beginnings of Greek art and contributed largely to its development. Egyptian influence, in particular, is still easily discernible in the sixth century B.C. In furniture, such Egyptian legacies as animal legs and feet, stiff and conventional forms, and decorative treatment beneath the seats of chairs and stools are much in evidence.

It was, however, about this time that the aesthetic genius of the Greeks began to emancipate itself from the bondage of tradition in a free and bold quest for the ideal. Gradually, in the course of the sixth century, guided by their natural sense of beauty, this gifted race began to develop a national style, and, in the process of assimilation, they perfected and made their own all the various strands woven into the web of their art from earlier civilizations. In the fifth century B.C., which marks the acme of Greek creative genius, they achieved perfection in every branch of art. The Parthenon and the Erechtheum, two of the most beautiful monuments of Greek art in existence, were built on the Acropolis at Athens. Especially well known is the portico of the Erechtheum, where, as columns, female figures were introduced. To these the name caryatid was given, because they were supposed to represent young maidens carried into captivity by the Greeks in the fifth century B.C. when they destroyed Caryae, a village in Laconia, where a priestess in the temple of the Greek goddess Artemis was called a caryatid. The Egyptians and Assyrians, too, introduced captives as decorative supports in furniture; and, as we know, caryatids figure prominently in the classical styles of furniture.

Representations of furniture painted on vases are remarkable for their refined proportions; the Greek rules of balance and symmetry are carefully observed. A new feeling for form, a new quality of dignity, sobriety, and simplicity came into existence. No piece of furniture is more characteristic of the Greek ideal of beauty—symmetry, rhythm, and balance—than the *klismos,* a variety of light side chair which became the principal inspiration for the Directoire chair in the late eighteenth century. All the curves of the *klismos* are planned with great care to please the eye with their flow. Distinguished by its graceful rhythm and simple dignity, the *klismos* possesses a timeless beauty; every line reveals a subtle symmetry in which both order and freedom are harmoniously combined. The per-

ABOVE: The portico of the Caryatids, Erechtheum, Athens, where in place of columns the architect introduced six female figures to which the ancient Greeks gave the name Caryatids. *Photo Mella.*
LEFT: Detail from an antique Greek vase showing a lady sitting on a *klismos*, which became the model for the Grecian chair at the end of the eighteenth century. *Courtesy British Museum.* (*See page 9.*)

fection of form and quiet beauty seen in the *klismos* is lost in later Greek art when the taste for rich decorative effects prevailed.

ROMAN

From a village on the Palatine Hill, Rome, founded in 753 B.C. according to the legend of Romulus and Remus, spread and conquered until in the time of Augustus it became the center of wealth, luxury, and power of the entire civilized world. All the splendor surrounding the races of antiquity—the Egyptians, Babylonians, Assyrians, Persians, Greeks, and Etruscans—was inherited by the Romans. Even before Greece became a Roman province in 146 B.C., Roman art was dominated by Greek precepts, although it had also previously come under the influence of Rome's Etruscan neighbors, whose art, too, had been influenced by the Greeks. All branches of Greek art are continued in Roman art, because Rome, through her ascendancy, became its logical transmitter. The Romans, whose aim was to dazzle by material greatness and splendor, liked the later Greek art with its rich decorative effects. In the course of adoption, they carried it to a much greater elaboration.

Roman furniture is especially interesting to us, since we borrowed primarily from Roman rather than from Greek furniture. Regrettably, Roman furniture made of wood has shared the same fate as that of Greek. The Romans, however, left records in their literature, fresco paintings at Pompeii and Herculaneum, representations on Roman sarcophagi, and pieces and parts of furniture made of marble or bronze. There are still in existence numerous pieces of bronze furniture, such as tripods, candelabra, and couches provided with fulcra or headrests used for dining and reclining. Latin writers deplore the Roman desire for luxury and their expensive and extravagant tastes, as seen in their lavish use of veneering, plating with gold, silver, or bronze, and inlay work. Exotic woods, tortoise shell, glass, ivory, gold, silver, and bronze were freely employed in inlay work, making their furniture richly colorful.

The most noteworthy Roman seat is the *sella curulis*, having curved legs of X-form, used by the "curule," or the high magistrates and also by the emperor. Like its prototype, the Egyptian folding stool of X-form, it resembles in construction the modern campstool, being in some instances made to fold up. As we shall see, adaptations of this simple but ingenious form have remained in favor throughout the ensuing centuries. The so-called Chair of Dagobert, made of gilded bronze, to which the back and arms were added at a later date, is an early historic example of this kind of seat. Chairs of X-form are also found in China, where they commonly have a yoke-type back.

The Romans made their most valuable contribution to furniture design

LEFT: Detail of a bronze couch and head-rest from Pompeii. The fulcrum terminates in a swan's head, a motif extensively used under the First French Empire. *Courtesy Museo Nazionale, Naples. Photo Mella.* BELOW: A bronze fulcrum inlaid with silver and terminating in a horse's head, from Amiterno. *Courtesy Museo dei Conservatori, Rome. Photo Mella. (See page 11.)* OPPOSITE LEFT: Bronze *sella curulis*, Roman, with gracefully curved legs of X-form. *Courtesy Museo Nazionale, Naples. Photo Mella. (See page 11.)* OPPOSITE BELOW: Table of Saint Gregory, Roman. The very heavy wooden top is supported by marble trestles which are cut in the profile of griffins. *Courtesy Church of Saint Gregory. Photo Mella. (See page 15.)* OPPOSITE RIGHT: Marble tripod, Roman, with lion monopodia for supports. This strange support comprising a head and chest continued by an enormous paw enjoyed a great vogue under the First French Empire and English Regency. From Tavola. *Courtesy Museo Nazionale, Naples. Photo Mella. (See page 15.)*

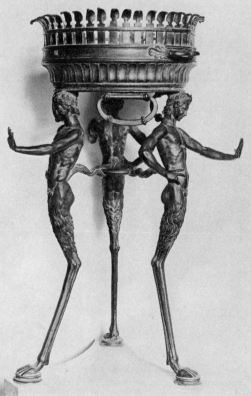

ABOVE: Bronze tripod in the Greek style with supports in the form of a winged male sphinx sitting on the top of a quadruped leg. If we compare this fine example of a quadruped leg with the cabriole leg of the eighteenth century, we can clearly see the relationship between the two curving forms. RIGHT: Bronze tripod from Pompeii resting on a triangular marble plinth. A mixture of parts of living creatures serve as supports. *Courtesy Museo Nazionale, Naples. Photo Mella.*

in the category of tables. No doubt the table with a massive oblong top of wood and marble trestle-end supports, which during the Renaissance became the prototype for the Italian refectory table, is one of the most characteristic. The best decorative employment of the griffin is found in the trestle ends of this class of table, of which there are about two examples in Pompeii and several others in Italian churches and museums. In some examples the head is that of an eagle at one of the trestle ends and of a lion at the other; there is always only one enormous paw. The strong wings are a conspicuous feature; below them the surface is filled in with conventional Greek Foliage.

Next are the tables of tripod form. Especially favored as supports for the tripods with circular tops were either the lion monopodium or legs adapted from those of a quadruped. Of great interest are the slender decorative bronze tripods having circular tops in the form of a basin or bowl very often fitted with three rings serving as handles. Examples of tripods found at Pompeii and Herculaneum were extensively copied in the late eighteenth century when the pursuit of the antique became more exacting. Another interesting group are the many varieties of candelabra, the stands on which ancient lamps were placed. Finally, but by no means the last of relics from Roman antiquity, are the bronze mirrors, familiar articles to the people living in ancient times. They are found wherever Roman civilization spread. With the Roman Empire firmly planted beyond the Alps, the conquered adopted the form and substance of the conqueror's art, as can be seen in the amphitheater at Arles, France.

BYZANTINE

The next period to be considered briefly is that which witnessed the dissolution of the Roman Empire, resulting in the final separation of the Eastern from the Western Empire. It was in Constantine's reign, marked by the adoption of Christianity, that the center of gravity of the empire shifted from West to East. In 330 A.D. Byzantium, or Constantinople, was made a second capital, a second Rome. In the new Eastern Roman Empire the oriental factors, which gradually produced a transformation in Greco-Roman art, triumphed; the result was Byzantine art, reveling in opulence and a profusion of brilliant coloring and gilding, which lasted until the conquest of Constantinople by the armies of Islam in 1453. Byzantium increased in importance, because, as the hordes of northern barbarians encroached more and more on the flourishing provinces of the Roman Empire, a constant emigration took place to the new capital. Noble and patrician families brought with them all their valuable and easily portable possessions, gold, of course, and jewels.

The mode of living became luxurious and splendid, and furniture richly inlaid with precious metals and ivory mirrored the outward grandeur and magnificence of this age. For the Byzantine the Roman Empire never ceased to exist; it survived as glorious as ever along the shores of the Bosporus, centered in Constantinople. Representations of furniture seen in bas-reliefs on the ivory diptychs of consuls show folding chairs of Roman curule form with certain elements of Greek and Egyptian ornamentation, such as lions' heads and paws, dolphins and winged figures of Victory standing on globes, chairs with turned members and chairs with lyre backs, a form known to the Greeks and adopted by the Romans. While the West was decaying, Byzantium remained the sole repository for the arts. Civilization not only was preserved through her efforts, but it grew and spread. Her arts were disseminated through her monks and missionaries who traveled far and wide, through her craftsmen who were forced into exile during the Iconoclastic period, and through her far-reaching commerce. The Italian cities of Ravenna and Venice, the connecting trade links between East and West, were deeply influenced. Byzantine ivories, enamels, and embroideries spread throughout Europe and were imitated in every country. Of major importance was Byzantium's influence on the subsequent development of ornament in the West.

ROMANESQUE

In the five centuries after the fall of Rome, 476 A.D., the art of Western Europe lapsed into a lethargy from which it was aroused briefly by the efforts of Charlemagne in the early ninth century. The period was marked by the incursions of northern barbarian tribes—Goths, Danes, Vandals, Vikings, Franks, and others sweeping through Europe. Gradually the barbarians settled in the lands they had conquered and around the year 1000 practically all the nations of Europe had struggled into existence. Western Europe was awakening from her long sleep. A new life began to manifest itself, crystallizing in the Romanesque style, the name indicating its principal affinity. Apart from its Roman origin, the Romanesque style is permeated with Byzantine influences. The ornament, whether scenes from the Gospel, animals, birds, or foliage scrolls, is bewilderingly rich. It possesses a singular vigor and strength, particularly in the North, undoubtedly resulting from the barbaric temperament of the people who created it. Romanesque architecture, characterized by its roundhead arches and horizontal lines, flourished in Western Europe until around the middle of the twelfth century, when it was gradually supplanted by the Gothic style with its pointed arches and vertical lines.

The Christian Church at this time was the principal source of education and culture and the leading patron of architecture. The papacy had great power. Religious zeal is nowhere shown better than in the imposing cathedral churches and monasteries, which are a more typical outgrowth of this period than the fortified feudal castles. This same religious ardor led to the Crusades and the long warfare between the Christians of the West and the Mohammedans of the East, a contact that further accentuated the oriental elements in Western art. In the eleventh century monastic communities, which had been in existence since the sixth century, were greatly developed. The plans for these monasteries reveal many kinds of buildings. In addition to the church and sacristy, there were the dormitories, the refectory and kitchen, the infirmary, guest lodgings, a library, a scriptorium for writing and illuminating, all kinds of workshops for making furniture, metal and pottery wares, and numerous other buildings. The monks were a powerful influence not only in the development but also in the propagation of medieval art; in fact they provided an incentive to civilizing influences of all kinds.

Domestic architecture reflected the insecurity and instability of the times. The castles of the feudal lords were strongly fortified, for the only relative security was behind thick walls. The people, who lived chiefly in rural communities in cottages generally made of clay matted with straw and twigs, were attached as serfs to the estate of a great nobleman.

GOTHIC

In the 100 years between the thirteenth and fourteenth centuries there was a change in the entire civilized life of Western Europe, animated chiefly by a desire for a freer, more intellectual development. Towns grew in number and in power. They became lively centers of trade. Commerce was expanded and the trade guilds were organized. The power of the Church and feudal lords gradually diminished as the burghers and merchants became more prosperous and powerful. During this period medieval art achieved the acme of perfection. Classical traditions were forgotten everywhere except in Italy. Antique culture was so much a part of life and the Italians so imbued with its spirit that they found it impossible to become sincere enthusiasts of Gothic. The Venetians, who traded constantly with the North, were the only Italians to use the Gothic pointed, intricate traceries on such buildings as the Doge's Palace San Marco. The Italians of the Renaissance were the first to apply the name Gothic to this style of architecture, the only Western style, under the aegis of the Nordic spirit, that did not rely upon Greco-Roman principles to achieve perfection. They used the name derisively, for they regarded Gothic as belonging to the barbarians of the North, the descendants of the Goths who had ravaged the Roman Empire.

Gothic, the style of the age of chivalry and troubadours, began to evolve from the Romanesque around the middle of the twelfth century in the Île-de-France, an old province in northern France with Paris as its capital. Except in Italy, it reigned unchallenged throughout the fifteenth century in all European countries, with national variations much stronger and more obvious than in the earlier Romanesque. Its influence is clearly seen in furniture, which, like all the arts of this period, was made subordinate to architecture, the major art form of the Middle Ages.

In medieval times, when the great nobles changed houses they took all their valuable possessions with them. The furniture was so constructed that it could readily be taken apart for transport; it was made to be transportable, or mobile, as the French word *mobilier* implies. Traveling chests covered with leather or sometimes with canvas glued down and painted were used to transport clothes, tapestries, fabrics, cushions, coverlets, valuable plate, linens, toilet articles, and furniture. These chests or trunks were provided with locks and handles and as a rule were without feet, either to be transported in wagons or more frequently, because there were no roads, hung in pairs across the backs of sumpter horses. Crudely constructed large pieces, such as long dining tables with massive, removable oblong tops supported on trestles that were sometimes of iron that could be folded up; beds, which were little more than boarded boxes surrounded completely by curtains to keep out drafts and to insure privacy, and such built-in pieces as cupboards and benches were left in the castle; they offered no temptation to pillagers, and if stolen their loss would be of no consequence.

Even when times became more secure in the sixteenth century, these nomadic habits of the Gothic period did not disappear. An abundance of fabrics that were easily transportable and a scarcity of furniture, especially costly carved pieces, were characteristic even in the richest French châteaux and English houses. In the furniture inventory belonging to Catherine de' Medici, written in 1589, reference is made to her sumptuous townhouse, where she had the necessary furniture brought in when she desired to eat or remain there, which was frequently, and removed after her departure.

Until the middle of the fourteenth century only carpenters were available to make wood furniture. About that time, however, a new system of construction was developed on the continent which necessitated the use of mortise, tenon, and dowel pins or pegs and was the work of the joiner. No doubt the most important event in the construction of joined furniture was the invention of paneled framing. For example, before this new principle was put to work, a joined chest continued to be made simply of thick boards. Now in place of the full walls of uniform thickness was substituted a system of frames made of uprights and horizontal pieces of thick wood joined with mortise and tenon. The inner edges of the frame were given deep grooves in which were fitted a panel that could be quite

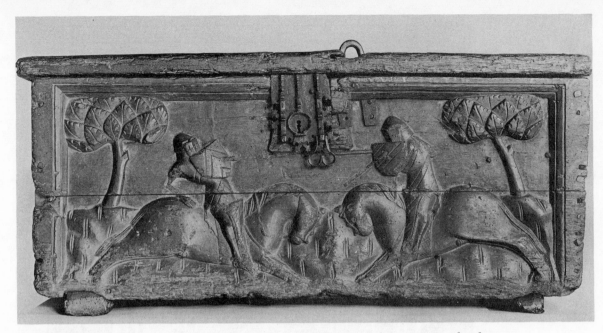

Small oak tilting chest. The front is carved with a representation of two jousting knights; their legs are protected by long tilting saddles. French, c. 1400. *Courtesy Victoria and Albert Museum.*

thin, since it was simply a containing shell and in no manner contributed to the strength. In its slightly loose setting it could expand and contract and thus prevent the danger of splitting, warping, or shrinkage. A chest joined in this way was lighter and stronger and thus more portable; it used less material and so was more economical. In a word, this type of construction, the stout enframement of thin walls, transformed furniture, and the art of joinery was born. In contemporary inventories the term "joined" or "joint" is used to describe furniture so constructed, such as a joined stool or joined table, because joined furniture also meant furniture well made. Paneled framing was introduced into England from the continent in the second half of the fifteenth century, although it did not come into general use until about 100 years later.

Gothic furniture is solid, massive, and severe in character. As a rule, the forms are rectilinear, with emphasis on the vertical, except in Italy where horizontal effects are more characteristic, for instance, the Italian *cassone* as compared with the northern chest. The use of curved lines is limited to the folding chair of X-form, as exemplified in the French *faudesteuil,* the English faldstool, and the Italian *dantesca* and *savonarola*—all borrowed from the Roman chair of curule form. In the northern countries the chief wood employed was oak, a wood of great durability. Walnut was also used in France. Early English furniture lacked the richness and finish found in the contemporary Gothic work in Flanders, France, and Italy. However, from around 1485, when the Tudors supplanted the Plantagenets and the feudal castle yielded to the Tudor manor house, a remarkable advancement in domestic civilization took place.

19

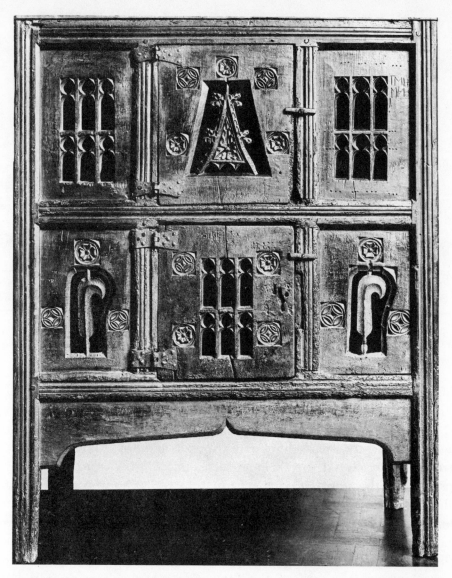

Oak cupboard for food, known as Prince Arthur's cupboard, as it may have belonged to Prince Arthur (d. 1502). The two upper end panels and the lower center panel are pierced in window-like perpendicular tracery. Vestiges of vermilion paint remain. *Courtesy Victoria and Albert Museum.* OPPOSITE: Oak *dressoir* decorated with fragile tracery and carved ornament. French, late fifteenth century. *Courtesy Philadelphia Museum of Art.*

Carving was by far the favorite method of decorating the surface of Gothic furniture north of the Alps. It was bold and vigorous, a manner especially proper for work in oak. The medieval taste for brightly painted woodwork touched with gilding found a natural outlet in the decoration of furniture. Extant rare examples of carved chests painted in vivid primary colors—scarlet, gold, and azure—effectively contrasted with elaborate ironwork give some idea of the brilliance of a medieval domestic interior. There can be no doubt, however, that most of the furniture was simply made of plain heavy wood intended to be covered at all times with either a coat of plain bright-colored paint or fabrics.

The ornament employed in the decoration of furniture, with the exception of a few scenes from romances, deeds of arms, jousts, and even Scriptural incidents, was borrowed entirely from Gothic architecture and duplicated in wood the work of the masons. Foliage was much favored and the plants, selected from native plant life, included maple leaves, parsley, curled cabbage and cress leaves, and, above all, vine leaves with bunches of grapes. Arcades of fragile tracery, copied from the magnificent tracery windows, enjoyed a great vogue and were freely lavished on the paneled cupboard doors of dressers and the façades of chests. However, by far the favorite decoration for paneled furniture is the linen-fold motif,

22

which lent itself to an infinite number of variations from the simple to the complex.

From the Middle Ages to the time of the Industrial Revolution the development in furniture has been from simple to complex, from scarcity to plenty, and from crudely made to skillfully wrought. Extant furniture from medieval times is exceedingly rare. We gain most of our knowledge from illuminated manuscripts, carved reliefs in wood, ivory, or stone, and contemporary accounts and inventories. Medieval rooms depicted with such minute detail in manuscript books of the time give us a good idea of what these rooms were like. Tables and forms, benches, settles, a chair for the master, chests, a cupboard of some nature as a food cupboard, perhaps a buffet or dresser for the display of valuable plate and other treasures comprise the furniture in the hall, the chief living room in the house used primarily for dining and entertaining. Colorful fabrics are draped over the furniture and cushions are placed on the seats to provide a little comfort and some feeling of luxury. The furnishings of the other rooms are equally meager and consist of a bed, chest, *prie-dieu,* and perhaps a table, cupboard, or press and bench. In houses of wealth, beds with their rich stuffs often cost more than all the rest of the furniture. As in ancient Roman times, the wardrobe or garderobe for the reception of clothes and other possessions is a small room adjoining the master's apartment.

The chair in medieval times was regarded as a symbol of authority and its use was restricted to the master of the house and distinguished guests. (The tradition of "the chair" is still observed when the person who conducts a meeting is referred to as the chairman.) The richest castles seldom had more than two chairs. Benches fixed to the wall, movable forms either with or without backs, chests and settles were the ordinary seats. It is generally accepted that the typical medieval chair was evolved from a chest by the addition of a paneled back and sides. Since chairs were an appanage of state, it is only natural that this massive seat of box-like form was richly carved. According to contemporary French records, each chair also had its own *bouge* or trunk of leather made expressly for it. For convenience in traveling, however, seats of X-shaped framework, a lighter type of chair fitted with straps of leather and fabric for seat and back, were the best solution—they folded and if necessary were quickly taken apart. This was fully appreciated, for we see kings and great

OPPOSITE ABOVE: Medieval interior with settle and dresser surmounted by a coved canopy paneled with linen-fold. The settle has the usual chest beneath the hinged seat and is also furnished with a foot rail. The lady is seated on a stool, while a chest serves as a table for the chessboard. From an illuminated manuscript of *Les Trésors des Histoires* (Cotton Augustus, V, f. 334 b), c. 1470. *Courtesy British Museum.* OPPOSITE BELOW: Banquet. From a fifteenth-century French illuminated manuscript, *Repas des noces de Béatrix de Cologne avec Guérin de Metz. Courtesy Bibliothèque Royale de Belgique.*

ABOVE: A bedroom of the time of Henry VI. The tester is suspended from the ceiling. At one corner the curtain is looped up, bag-like, its usual position when not shielding the bed from view. A dresser, usually with a covering of white damask, displaying valuable plate, was sometimes placed as shown here in the lying-in chamber where the lady received her friends. From *The Metrical Life of Saint Edmund, King and Martyr: The Birth of the Saint.* Executed c. 1433 by Lydgate for Henry VI. *Courtesy British Museum.* RIGHT: Walnut "joyned" chair of box-like form. It has linen-fold panels and a top panel pierced with tracery; beneath the hinged seat is the customary chest. French, fifteenth century. *Courtesy Metropolitan Museum of Art. The Cloisters Collection (Purchase 1947).* (See page 23.)

24

nobles sitting in *X*-shaped chairs, usually with curving legs and richly draped with fabric.

Another early chair—a variety of great antiquity and wide geographical distribution, being found in Germany, Flanders, Italy and England, perhaps of Byzantine origin—is the so-called turned chair, having the entire structure turned, the seat being triangular. (A chair of this type has been used by the president of Harvard University when giving degrees since the eighteenth century and is referred to as the Harvard chair.) Once again, as in ancient times, articles of tripod form, that is, three-legged, preceded those with four legs for two very good reasons—tripods do not require the precision work to make one that does not wobble and they are firm and steady on uneven flooring. The insecurity of the early three-legged stools, crudely constructed with the splayed legs simply wedged into sockets, probably suggested the simple "worldis wele is lyke a III-foted stole, it faylyt a man at hys most nede" from the *Castle of Perseverance* written about 1425. From this period the few oak stools that have survived are mostly of trestle form, having solid splayed end supports connected by a deep underframing. In the medieval house the chest or coffer was of primary importance. No other article of furniture was able to take its place, and it was capable if necessary of supplanting all others. Apart from its use as a case for storing and transporting every kind of personal possession, it also served as a seat, bed, or table and in the kitchen it became the *huche* or hutch in which the bread was kneaded and, when baked, stored.

Finally a few words about a type of buffet that was made simply of superimposed shelves (*gradins* in French) intended to show beautiful and costly gold and silver plate—cups, dishes, bowls, vessels, and the like. In the medieval hall it commanded a position of importance because on the days of great banquets the shelves, with their lavish display of plate, were one of the most convincing of all signs of the host's wealth. On the continent the buffet was occasionally built to towering heights and in France the number of shelves was strictly regulated according to etiquette. Buffets were often painted in color and gilt; others were entirely concealed under rich stuffs.

Sometimes the buffet was a temporary structure of shelves, taken down and removed from the hall after the banqueting. In this case, correctly speaking, it was not a true piece of furniture. A banquet given by Henry VII in the hall of Richmond Palace describes such a piece "sete thereup of IX or X stages." To keep the guests from handling the costly objects, occasionally it was enclosed by a barrier. We read that when Wolsey was host to the French ambassadors after the signing of the Treaty of Hampton the dresser "was barred in round about that no man might come nigh it. . . ." These buffets, or *dressoirs* (at this period there was little or no

LEFT: A project for a buffet by Matteo de Domenico (Bolognese, flourished 1625–75). The heavily scrolled outline is typically baroque. *Courtesy Cooper Union Museum.* BELOW: Painting by Francesco Zugno (1709–87), a follower of Tiepolo, showing an immense buffet loaded with gold and silver plate. *Courtesy Museo Civico Correr, Venice. Photo Mella.* (See page 25.)

distinction made between the two terms; to add to the confused terminology, it was also sometimes called in England a cupboard, that is, a "borde" to set cups upon), afforded a striking background for a profusion of plate and crystal; their appeal still lingered well into the seventeenth century. No doubt the craze for oriental porcelains prolonged their existence. Other types of buffets, or *dressoirs*, were in use in medieval times, and new forms were evolved during the Renaissance; however, regardless of their form, they all had one feature in common, that is, one or more flat spaces or shelves for the display of plate.

Italian

MEDIEVAL

Individuality of expression received an early impetus in Italy due to the social and political life of the democratic communes and free towns. At least from the twelfth century, nobles and burghers lived together within the walls of the city. In this manner the interests of both classes were identified, and the feudal lord learned to regard society from a different perspective than that of his mountain castle. The Italians benefited from extensive trade relations, a deadly foe to feudalism, which brought great wealth to Italy. As early as the fourteenth century the Italian nobleman enjoyed a life of domestic comfort and refinement far in advance of the nobleman living in the northern countries. Contemporary records around 1280 mention the prosperity and refinement of the Florentines. Venice was in her glory in the Middle Ages, when her ships controlled the richest trade routes in the world. Venetian noblemen and merchants in the fourteenth century lived in fanciful and picturesque Gothic castles built along the canals. Fine goldsmith work, paintings on wood panels, drawings, bronze medals, manuscripts, and remains of antique sculpture were included in their furnishings. The social and domestic life in northern Italy was far less developed. At this time Siena contributed considerably to the development of a more gracious and worldly manner of living. Her palaces, perhaps second only to those of Venice, were furnished with Gothic furniture remarkable for its decorative and artistic qualities.

RENAISSANCE

As the Gothic terminates the Middle Ages, so the Renaissance marks the beginning of the modern era. Freed from the bonds that elsewhere impeded progress in Europe, the Italians were the first of the modern people to discover the outside world, to see it and feel it as something beautiful. To this discovery they added a still greater achievement, the discovery and development of man as an individual. Ever since the fourteenth century the civilization of Greece and Rome exerted a powerful hold on Italian life as the basis, purpose, and ideal of existence, and because of the special genius of the Italian people they were able to mold their enthusiastic devotion for antique culture into an art movement that conquered the Western world. Essentially the fifteenth century, generally referred to as the Early Renaissance, was an intellectual age of preparation and experimentation. Ruins within and outside of Rome were zealously scrutinized, as the material knowledge of ancient Rome increased steadily by excavations. The so-called grotesques, that is, the mural decorations of the ancients, were discovered under Pope Alexander VI, 1431–1503. In architecture the Five Orders were reintroduced, having been in abeyance for almost 1000 years. The great change Renaissance art made in architecture is exemplified in furniture.

The Renaissance begins in Florence early in the fifteenth century, and in the course of the century sculpture, painting, architecture, and furniture were transformed by an overwhelming enthusiasm for antique culture. Florence was pre-eminent in all the arts in the fifteenth century; the Medici family—first Cosimo the Elder, then Lorenzo the Magnificent—renowned for its leadership in the culture of the age, was largely responsible for her enviable position. Apart from Florence, Milan, Ferrara, Mantua, and Urbino excelled as art centers. The spirit of the Renaissance, the genuine enjoyment in living, is captured with extraordinary felicity in the private study or studiolo of Federigo Da Montefeltro, Duke of Urbino. This very small room, sumptuously decorated with *trompe l'œil* intarsia, was the most beautiful room in the Ducal Palace at Gubbio. It was the duke's own private room to which he retired for contemplation and studious pursuits. It is unlikely that the small chamber ever contained more than a table and a chair or two. The intarsia displaying numerous musical instruments, arms, and books reminds us of the many-sided personality of an enlightened Italian prince. Built about 1479–82, the room acclaims to all of us the cultural superiority of the Italians at this time; their enthusiasm for beauty, their belief that life was well worth living.

Gay and festive Venice, the fabulous city of the lagoons, resplendent with color, was second only to Florence as an art center. In Beatrice Sforza's *Venetian Letters,* 1493, she mentions façades emblazoned with frescoes and interiors of variegated marbles or inlaid with mosaics bedecked in tapestries, oriental carpets, and gilded and painted *cassoni* and chairs. Luxury and splendor became the Venetians; they were never stifled by it. When Leonardo da Vinci visited Venice late in the fifteenth century, he was not prepared for the pageantry and extravagance of the Venetian scene, accustomed though he was to court life at Florence. To a Florentine it was a little too dazzling.

In the High Renaissance, culminating in Rome early in the sixteenth century, perfection was achieved in every branch of art, the first three decades being the most celebrated period of Italian art and one of the great periods of all times. Because of her ardent pursuit of antique culture, strengthened by her ever-increasing wealth, Rome became the mecca for great artists—Bramante, Raphael, Michelangelo, and other men of genius were invited to her court.

Worldly Venice was more magnificent and sensuous than ever before. Venetian fetes and festivals attracted patricians from all parts of Italy. An enjoyment of life and its pleasures was in the air and it sparkled in every piece of Italian art. This brilliant zest for life was brought to a sudden halt by the sack of Rome in 1527, when the imperial and Spanish army plundered the city for eight days. The spontaneity and vitality, the intellectual zest and aesthetic inventiveness which made the Early and High Renaissance such a brilliant and creative period were dimmed in the Late Renaissance. The hold Spain was to retain on Italy and the renewed strength of the papacy, with its broader implications of the moral and anti-classical impact of the Counter Reformation, had a telling effect. However, if these blemishes of a baroque character, which became

30

Scene depicting life in a villa at Treviso, Venetia, by Ludovico Toeput, called Pozzoserrato (flourished late sixteenth century). The lady is seated in a *dantesca. Courtesy Museo Luigi Bailo, Treviso. Photo Mella.* OPPOSITE: Private study of the Duke of Urbino. From the Ducal Palace at Gubbio (c. 1479–82). Probably designed by the Sienese artist, Francesco di Giorgio, and executed under the supervision of the Florentine woodworker, Baccio Pontelli. One of two rooms decorated with *trompe l'œil* intarsia; the other is still in Urbino. *Courtesy Metropolitan Museum of Art. Rogers Fund, 1939.* (*See page 29.*)

increasingly evident as the sixteenth century progressed, mar the gilded picture, they by no means destroy it. Only Venice remained free from the influence of Spain and the papacy; she still retained the worldly brilliance of the High Renaissance.

The Renaissance in Italy was colorful, extravagant, and spectacular. It was an age of pageantry—the pageantry of festivals. A marriage of convenience between patrician families, the functions of trade guilds offered numerous popular occasions for display. Orders and citizens in brilliant and sumptuous costumes, caparisoned cavalry, colorful pennants and banners with coats of arms became the accents of such spectacles. No less spectacular were the stately Renaissance palaces and magnificent villas, their outside walls often incrusted with antique and rare bas-reliefs and statues, built by Popes, princes, and aristocratic families. The gardens of these houses were incredibly beautiful. There were statues, fountains perhaps in the form of a Hercules, whose club yields a shower of water falling into a great shell, or in the posture of a laundress wringing water out of a piece of linen into a vast basin, grottoes with walls richly composed of coral and shells or representing artificial rain with roofs of brilliant mosaics, fish ponds, aviaries, and sometimes vivariums. In brief, an elysium of delight. The palaces were literally storehouses of paintings, tapestries, statues, and vases of porphyry, oriental alabaster, and other rare materials, antique arms and armor, manuscripts, rare medals, enamels, ivories, and sumptuous walnut furniture. Draperies and cushions of cut silk velvets, carved and gilded chandeliers, candelabra and candlesticks, pedestals and wall brackets for the reception of bronze and marble sculptures, mirrors, bronze andirons, services of silver and gold plate, fine linens, exquisite Venetian point laces, delicate Venetian glass vessels, Della Robbia plaques, lustered majolica, and brilliant oriental carpets contributed to the splendor of the furnishings. In a word, as the introuvable John Evelyn wrote in his diary in 1644 after visiting the palace of Prince Doria in Genoa, "The house is most magnificently built without, no less gloriously furnished within."

Only the Romans and the French under the Bourbon monarchs ever achieved such splendor. Evelyn, during his sojourn in Italy in 1644–46, portrays so vividly in his diary the overwhelming richness of the furniture in the houses he visited. He writes of "whole tables and bedsteads of massy silver, many of them set with agates, onyxes, cornelians, lazuli, pearls, turquoises, and other precious stones . . . huge tables of porphyry. . . . There is another [cabinet] which had about it eight Oriental columns of alabaster, on each whereof was placed a head of Caesar, covered with a canopy so richly set with precious stones, that they resembled a firmament of stars. . . . Here were divers tables of *pietra commessa*, which is a marble ground inlaid with several sorts of marbles and stones of various

ABOVE: Project for a table top to be inlaid with several kinds of colored marbles. Black chalk, pen and ink with watercolors (Italian, probably Florentine, c. 1600). *Courtesy Cooper Union Museum.* RIGHT: Carved walnut *dantesca* (second half of the sixteenth century). This chair form is derived from the Roman X-form seat and resembles the modern camp stool in construction. *Courtesy Metropolitan Museum of Art. Gift of Benjamin Altman, 1913.* BELOW: Carved walnut refectory table (Florentine, c. 1500–50). The fan-shaped trestle-end supports indicate an imitation of ancient Roman trestle-end tables. *Courtesy Frick Collection, New York.* (*See pages 34–35.*)

colours, representing flowers, trees, beasts, birds and landscapes . . . [a] cabinet supported by twelve pillars of oriental agate and railed around with crystal. . . . The fabric of this cabinet was very ingenious, set thick with agates, turquoises and other precious stones. . . . The next chamber had a bedstead all inlaid with agates, crystals, cornelians, lazuli, etc. . . . but for the most part, the bedsteads in Italy are of forged iron and gilded, since it is impossible to keep the wooden ones from the cimices. . . ." *Pietra commessa,* being the proper invention of the Florentines, was so commonplace in these houses that Evelyn writes: "Here are also divers cabinets and tables of the Florence work." Much more interesting to Evelyn are "a whimsical chair, which folded into so many varieties, as to turn into a bed, a bolster, a table, or a couch . . . a conceited chair to sleep in with the legs stretched out, with hooks, and pieces of wood to draw out longer or shorter" and "a chair that catches fast any who sits down in it, so as not to be able to stir out, by certain springs concealed in the arms and back thereof, which on sitting down surprises a man on the sudden, locking him in by the arms and thighs, after a true treacherous Italian guise."

In order to understand why Italy had so many art centers, it is necessary to realize the underlying spirit of the Italian race, that is to develop an individual or free personality, one unafraid of singularity, of being and seeming unlike his neighbors. As early as 1390, the men of Florence no longer followed any prevailing fashion of dress; each preferred to dress in his own way. This wealth of individuality which the Italian has always set forth provides the explanation for the different art centers that, in spite of the national spirit of their art, maintained at all times a certain amount of independence that varied according to circumstances. For example, Venetian furniture offers an interesting contrast to Tuscan or Florentine furniture, for while the latter is severe and correct, the former is more rich and graceful. The furniture of Liguria, with its intricate and elaborate carved decoration, as that of Piedmont and Savoy, shows a close relationship to that of France. A close artistic bond always existed between northern Italy and France, which resulted in a frequent exchange of cultural influences. The furniture of Rome was affected by her own classical ruins and antique masterpieces that were constantly being excavated. Remarkable for its grandeur, her furniture was inclined to be ponderous; the spell of Rome was omnipotent—even her *cassone* resembled an ancient sarcophagus. The differences in the various art centers go on and on.

Practically all fine Italian Renaissance furniture is made of walnut. It is massive, dignified, imposing, and essentially rectilinear in form, with emphasis on horizontal effects. Occasionally curved lines are introduced, as in the *dantesca* and *savonarola.* It is easy to see that the Italians borrowed heavily from Roman antiquity in such adaptations as the *savonarola* and *dantesca,* the *cassapanca* with a fulcrum-shaped arm and the

The Dream of Saint Ursula by Vittore Carpaccio (Venetian School, c. 1450–1522). This paint-ing gives an intimate glimpse of a chaste interior. *Courtesy Accademia d'Arte, Venice. Photo Mella.*

richly decorative refectory table with ornately shaped and elaborately carved trestle-end supports. Owing to the desire for comfort and luxury, new forms such as writing cabinets with fall fronts, chests of drawers, tables with draw tops, slant-front bureaus, and credenzas were introduced. However, in comparison with eighteenth-century standards, the number of pieces in the different categories is still very limited and offers little comfort. A good idea of an Early Renaissance bed mounted on a *predella*, or dais instead of legs, which are a sixteenth-century innovation, is given in Carpaccio's *The Dream of Saint Ursula*. As a rule, the top of the *predella* is hinged so it can serve as a chest for storage. It also served as a seat in the same manner as a chest.

35

ABOVE: Carved and molded sacristy cupboard (Tuscan, c. 1490–1500). The doors are flanked by fluted pilasters with Ionic capitals and bases. *Courtesy Metropolitan Museum of Art, Rogers Fund, 1916.* RIGHT: Walnut dolphin table, carved and parcel gilded (Tuscan, early sixteenth century). The octagonal top is supported by four dolphins resting on an X-form base. The fan-shaped outline derives from the trestle-end supports of ancient Roman tables. BELOW: Richly carved walnut credenza (Florentine, second half of the sixteenth century). The stiles are carved in high relief with two male and two female terms draped below the waist; there is a gadrooned base on lion-paw feet. *Courtesy Parke-Bernet, from the collection of Myron C. Taylor.* OPPOSITE: The central salon at the Villa Caldogno (now Nordera) at Caldogno, Vicenza. The frescoes by G. A. Fasolo (sixteenth century) show a race of caryatidal supermen, a taste bred in the wake of Michelangelo's heroic figures. *Photo Mella. (See page 38.)*

Everyone was at home in antiquity. The cabinetmakers proclaimed their enthusiasm for antique culture not only by borrowing their infinitely rich and varied ornament from Roman antiquity but also by incorporating into their furniture designs such classical architectural features as moldings, pediments, cornices, columns, and pilasters which they skillfully adapted to the scale and purpose of decorative furniture. Italian furniture made in the early sixteenth century retained all the simplicity and dignity of the Early Renaissance, but greater care was given to the refinement of detail. This goal of classical purity and harmony in design to the smallest detail imbued early sixteenth-century cabinetwork with an artistic reserve or restraint that is one of its most striking features. The influence of Raphael, whose art epitomized the refinement and elegance of the Renaissance, is seen in the fanciful grotesques with their graceful classical details of real and fantastic figures of every kind and in every imaginable variation—dolphins, swans, griffins, sphinxes, satyrs, sirens, tritons with their conch-like trumpets, cherubs, human figures, birds and beasts.

Of all the great masters in Rome, Michelangelo stands out, for he inaugurated a new school of art that marked the beginning of baroque. His influence on architecture and furniture, which was much in evidence by the middle of the sixteenth century, became more pronounced as the century progressed. It is seen in boldly modeled moldings, occasionally of

an exaggerated scale, forcefully modeled caryatids that largely supplanted fluted pilasters, which, when used, were often tapered, a prominence of human figures of a sculpturesque quality, a more vigorous type of ornament displaying a greater intricacy of curved forms, breaking of the entablature and base moldings around the order or pilaster, very often a profusion of useless ornament—in brief, a bold departure from the designs of Bramante and Raphael.

Other dissonances of the "mannerist" tradition, which usually are no more than indulgences in deviation from the classicism of the High Renaissance, are grimacing masks and grotesques of less pleasing composition. However, in spite of all these "blemishes" introduced by Michelangelo and his followers which dominated Late Renaissance art and ultimately evolved into the baroque, the eye is still charmed by the richness of the decoration and the general excellence of form. Running parallel with this taste is the work of Andrea Palladio, perhaps the most gifted of Bramante's successors. Although Palladio's work displays unmistakable baroque characteristics, it has grandeur and dignity. Late Renaissance cabinetwork influenced by Palladio, such as the credenza, is in a general sense austere; it is characterized by a more sparing and concentrated use of ornament and by undecorated moldings and heavy bases.

Perhaps no piece of furniture shows more clearly the gamut in architectural features and ornament from the early days of the Renaissance to the end of the sixteenth century than the credenza. Raphaelesque grotesques, tapering pilasters, and numerous other features fix the date of a credenza at first glance. In fact, all the furniture exhibits at least some of these changes with remarkable clarity. For instance, the progression of carved ornament from paucity to exuberance is aptly displayed in the *sgabello* and in the typical Renaissance armchair of rectangular form with an upholstered velvet seat and a velvet back panel stretched between the two uprights, characterized in the later models by an ornately carved and prominent broad front stretcher slightly beneath the seat rail. The taste for decorative sculpture, which was pushed to its limit in the Late Renaissance, is seen on the stiles of writing cabinets and chests of drawers embellished with several tiers of figures carved in the round. The use of decorative sculpture divorced from form and function is also clearly expressed in a *cassapanca,* though on the whole the design is austere, bearing the arms of the Orsini family. On each of the two scrolls surmounting the back of the *cassapanca* reclines a sensitively carved nude female figure. The position of these figures, so superficially adapted to the situation, is exemplary of the "mannerist" tradition of the late sixteenth century.

The great change in Venetian furniture occurred after the arrival of the Italian sculptor Sansovino from Rome in 1527, when the earlier preference for gilded gesso and painted furniture with fanciful designs modeled in

LEFT: Carved walnut *sgabello* (Urbino, c. 1500). *Courtesy Metropolitan Museum of Art. Gift of Annie C. Kane, 1926.* RIGHT: Ornately carved walnut *sgabello* (Ligurian, second half of the sixteenth century). *Courtesy Parke-Bernet.* CENTER: Carved walnut cabinet mounted on a cupboard (Florentine, second half of the sixteenth century). The stiles of both sections are carved with several pairs of full and undercut nude figures standing in tiers. *Courtesy Parke-Bernet, from the collection of Myron C. Taylor.* BELOW: Carved walnut *cassapanca* with scroll-shaped arms that are an imitation of ancient Roman fulcra (Florentine, third quarter of the sixteenth century). The two cartouches below the seat enclose grimacing masks. *Courtesy Metropolitan Museum of Art. Purchase Fund, 1958.*

low relief yielded to natural wood richly carved in high relief touched with gilt. Sansovino's decoration, with its rich and graceful elegance tinged occasionally with boldness, appealed to the Venetians and provided the initiative for a new style of carved ornament for furniture in which putti, caryatid-like figures terminating in volutes, scrolls, and other motifs of a sculpturesque character played an important role—in short, a harbinger of Venetian baroque. However, even when the baroque was manifesting itself, Venice preferred grotesques and masks of pleasing composition.

Rich and colorful surface decoration—painting, gilding, *pastiglia*, intarsia, *certosina, pietra dura*, and carving—distinguishes the furniture of this epoch. Although intarsia, generally treated as a true inlay of one or more woods upon a lighter or darker ground but sometimes worked as a marquetry, was used primarily for the decoration of stalls and lecterns in the church choirs, it was also employed on a smaller scale to ornament furniture, as *cassoni* and cabinets. The subjects are usually either arabesques or panels of "picture" intarsia of gardens, buildings, or cupboards with different articles upon the shelves, seen through partly open doors often of latticework, represented in an elaborate perspective treatment for which there was a veritable craze at that time. Tuscany and Lombardy were both important centers, and such renowned artists as Raphael sometimes provided the designs for intarsia, which achieved its highest artistic merit from about 1475 to 1525, when it was delineated with such extraordinary perfection that it rivaled the finest paintings. A marquetry of ivory, tortoise shell, mother-of-pearl, brass, and other metals, ebony and fruit woods, essentially a later development of intarsia, came into vogue around 1600. It answered the demand for more sumptuous surface decoration that characterized Italian taste around the beginning of the seventeenth century.

Another beautiful form of inlaid decoration is *certosina*, which reveals Islamic influence in its intricate arrangement of geometrical and conventionalized patterns worked in minute pieces of ivory. Extant examples of *cassoni*, cabinets, and X-form chairs decorated with *certosina* suggest how splendid were the furnishings of the *Quattrocento* made in Italy when exotic influences were blended with native Italian art. *Pietra dura*, a fine variety of *pietra commessa* (inlaid mosaic) in which hard and precious stones—agate, cornelian, turquoise, amethyst, and the like—are used in relief embodies with extraordinary felicity the temper and taste of the Italians of the late sixteenth and first half of the seventeenth century, when they loved above everything else a glittering display of rich materials and a luxury that was more showy than refined. Tables, beds, and particularly cabinets adorned with *pietra dura* enjoyed a great vogue in the first half of the seventeenth century, when it was almost de rigueur for every elegant house in Europe to possess at least one example.

Carving was by far the favorite decorative medium for enriching the surface of furniture in the sixteenth century, and it was always the work of accomplished craftsmen. No piece of furniture exhibits the carver's skill more advantageously than the *cassone*, especially the marriage *cassone*, on which not only carvers but also celebrated painters, such as Botticelli, Signorelli, and others of equal renown, lavished their skill. It is important to remember that for the first time, during the fifteenth century in Italy, furniture came to be regarded as a work of art in itself, and eminent artists were employed in its design and ornamentation. Vasari, in his writings on Italian art, considered the subject worthy of notice, as he remarks about sixteenth-century carved furniture, "Admirable ornaments in walnut . . . are to be seen. When they are in good Walnut which is black they might pass for bronze." He also expresses warm admiration for painted *cassoni* in the possession of Florentine patrician families. Many paintings adorning museum walls at the present time were originally the painted front panels on *cassoni*. The subjects for these panels are countless. Allegories,

ABOVE: Walnut armorial marriage *cassone*, carved and parcel gilded (Venetian, second half of the sixteenth century). The panel above the bold gadrooning represents the Procession of the Triumph of Bacchus; it is mounted on a base carved with strapwork and pleasing masks. The stiles are carved with caryatids finishing in animal paws. *Courtesy Metropolitan Museum of Art. Gift of Mrs. Ralph K. Robertson, 1945.* CENTER: Scene from the life of Florentine aristocracy: the Adimari nuptials. From a *cassone*, c. 1420. *Photo Mella.* BELOW: Marriage *cassone* decorated in gilt gesso partly enriched with color (Florentine, first half of the fifteenth century). The figures modeled in low relief represent a procession with the bride and groom advancing to meet each other attired in the elegant costumes of the period. *Courtesy Victoria and Albert Museum.*

42

historical and religious themes were favored, but it was the scenes from mythology, stories fresh and fascinating to the Italians of the Renaissance, of which the carver and painter never tired. Then, too, the constant pageants and processions were a familiar illustrative theme in Italian art; thus, favorite subjects for the marriage *cassoni* were a wedding feast or a bridal procession and, owing to the great popularity of Petrarch's *Trionfi,* the Triumph of Love was a favorite subject.

RÉSUMÉ—BAROQUE, ROCOCO, AND NEO-CLASSICISM

Rome is the fountainhead of baroque art and is referred to as the baroque city. The word baroque, from the Italian *barocco,* a misshapen pearl, was given to this style by later critics because it violated the principles of pure classicism. Italian baroque, essentially a continuation of late sixteenth-century Italian art, reached its culmination about the middle of the seventeenth century when, and particularly in France, a strong classical counter-movement arose that resisted the exaggerations of the baroque without surrendering its high artistic values. To gain some understanding of baroque it is necessary to keep in mind the Counter Reformation, which brought about the predominance of a religion whose chief preoccupation was to overwhelm and to dazzle. The interiors of churches were transformed into dramatic displays of decoration full of ecstasy and rapturous splendor. Baroque art aims at effect. For example, to create an effect of excitement, restlessness, and movement, which are typical baroque features, Bernini, the representative par excellence of the Jesuit style and thoroughly familiar with all the resources of his art, treated the draperies on his stone sculptures in a writhing, whirling manner rather than in soft, classical folds. The Roman Church kindled the baroque spirit, and the style spread into other European countries, Catholic countries being the chief fields for baroque art. In France it was so homogeneously developed under the aegis of Louis XIV that toward the end of the seventeenth century, when French art became pre-eminent in Europe, Italy, along with other European countries, found herself accepting the French interpretation of her own baroque style. However, her native influence still continued to contribute characteristically to the prevailing style.

Furniture of the seventeenth century made in Italy until it was tempered by French influence displays many of the features found in the late sixteenth century. The ornament, of a heavily plastic quality, comprises all the classical Renaissance forms, but is marked by exaggerated movement and dramatic planning and contrast. The Venetians made the finest baroque furniture, rich with riotous ornament—half figures of a caryatid nature terminating in foliated scrolls, putti, shells, cartouches, and highly dynamic and decorative scrolls sometimes ending in volutes and often so extended that they are scarcely recognizable. In spite of all its violations, Venetian baroque furniture is not without charm. When the exuberance of baroque ornament is restrained, as is evident in the Louis XIV style and also in some later Italian and Venetian baroque moderated by French taste, it possesses a stately and sweeping rhythm that is entirely pleasing.

Once again, as in baroque, the new impulse for rococo, which differs essentially from the former in its lightness and its use of asymmetry and is marked by anomalous designs suggested by shell forms, rocks, and waves, came from Italy. Its origins can be traced to those examples of ornamental treatment expressed in the grottoes first developed in Italian gardens in the latter part of the sixteenth century. The rococo as perfected in France provided an appropriate monument to the special genius of the French artists who were skillfully able to adapt Italian novelties of a baroque character to the French conception of art. So the new style with an entirely different approach returned to its Italian birthplace to be received as something foreign or exotic by the Italians, who then developed it in a variety of ways.

Our first thought in considering Italian rococo furniture is Venice, which produced not only the most original creations but also the most exquisite ones—charming for the fantasy and vivacity of their decoration, expressed in colorful, artistic delicacy and in delightful sculptural detail. Bearing in mind the Venetian love of color, which is the salient point in all her arts, it is easy to understand that their so-called lacquered furniture of the eighteenth century, reveling in its original and capricious interpretation of rococo, would be most acceptable to Venetian taste. Lacquer arrived in Venice as elsewhere as a kind of imitation of the true lacquer of the Far East. In Venice it was essentially simply paint and varnish. The surface was prepared with several layers of gesso, dried and rubbed down; then it was painted with tempera colors and protected with a layer of varnish to simulate oriental lacquer.

Of all the painted Venetian furniture, the commodes are especially choice and delicious. Some are decorated with *chinoiseries* that painters such as Tiepolo loved to use in their large schemes of decoration comprising Chinese figures, bamboo and pagodas, surrounded by gay rococo frames, sometimes partially gilded so that the work will seem more precious, with the scenes in very low relief as though applied to the ground, which is often yellow or green. Later the *chinoiseries* yielded to pastoral and rustic scenes and landscapes with small figures, perceptibly related to the style of the contemporary fashionable painters, such as Zuccarelli. However, far more numerous are the commodes with painted decoration selected from plant life, in particular, flowers—delicate and minute flowers arranged borderlike, and bunches of flowers gracefully arranged in the larger areas such as drawers—painted in lively colors on a plain ground.

Carved gilt console table (first half of the eighteenth century). With its putti, caryatids, acanthus scrolls, and trophies, it represents an enchanting phase of Venetian baroque. *Courtesy Palazzo Rezzonico, Venice. Photo Mella.* BELOW: Carved and painted commode of *bombé* and serpentine contour (Venetian, mid-eighteenth century). *Courtesy Museo Civico Correr, Venice. Photo Mella.*

LEFT: *Secrétaire à abattant* of palissander and rosewood (Lombardian, last quarter of the eighteenth century) mounted in gilt bronze and decorated with marquetry. By Giuseppe Maggilioni, whose best work was in the Louis XVI style. *Courtesy Palazzo Reale, Genoa. Photo Mella.* RIGHT: Antique Etruscan marble chair. The form of the back hollowed to about one half of a cylinder was imitated in chair design in the closing years of the eighteenth century. *Courtesy Palazzo Corsini. Photo Mella.* OPPOSITE: Project for a chair and three tripods. Aquarelle (Italian, probably Rome, 1775–1800). The chair back hollowed to about one half of a cylinder, the snake twisted around the tripod, the slender, ram-headed uprights recall the form and ornament of the classic originals. *Courtesy Cooper Union Museum.* (See page 48.)

Rococo, the period of indulgence in caprice and fancy, was rapidly approaching its end owing to a newly awakened enthusiasm for classical remains stimulated by excavations commenced in 1738 at Herculaneum and Pompeii. It is important to remember, however, that this classical revival was countenanced also by a reverence for antiquity which was dormant but not dead during the rococo. So once again Italy became the scene of archaeological activities, and, as in the Renaissance, Rome was the center of this research and abounded with scholars from every country in Europe. The entire period received lively support from literature and the theory of art of such men as Goethe, Lessing, and Winckelmann.

This overwhelming enthusiasm for antique art afforded a new and powerful impetus that transformed the character of furniture—symmetry was re-established, cornices and other architectural details were again prominent, sinuous rococo curves yielded to severe and simple classical

47

lines, tapered and fluted supports, of baluster shape and occasionally rectangular, supplanted cabriole legs. This transformation, however, was not quickly effected, and the introduction of classical motifs, expressed in the lighter form of the eighteenth century, preceded any major structural change. Undoubtedly Italy's finest contribution to early classicism is her so-called Louis XVI style, which displayed a wide range of varying expressions according to local receptiveness, the purest expression being found at Piedmont, especially at Turin. Although lacking the pedantic perfection of the French Louis XVI, the Italian Louis XVI, through its artful blending of Pompeian, Etruscan, and Roman antique ornament with Raphaelesque arabesques and the antique fantasies of Piranesi, possesses a spontaneity, a singular freshness that recall the traditions of the *Quattrocento.*

A more pronounced taste for the antique and its closer imitation became evident in the later eighteenth century, resulting in the Directoire style that logically evolved into the Empire style, the second phase of classicism. In comparison with the Louis XVI and Empire styles, the Directoire is not an independent and finished style in itself, but is, in essence, the ending of one and the herald of the other. Sanctioned by fashion, artists and cabinetmakers turned to direct classical sources for their inspiration and began to reproduce exact forms where examples existed, and for those pieces unknown to the ancients, the great majority, to formulate designs consonant in character. The general conception of the Directoire style is aptly expressed in chairs, settees, and tripods chiefly inspired by the remains of ancient Greece. The principles of the Empire style were forecast in Italy before it was established in France by Fontaine and Percier. However, as in the previous eighteenth-century styles, the Empire style was not adopted in Italy until after it had been accepted in France. Nowhere outside of France was the Empire style more successfully interpreted than in Italy, where the cabinetmakers, while revealing their allegiance to the French Empire, modified the style with sufficient freedom to dispel the grandiose severity inherent in the French work. Chairs and stools of simple design, depending for decoration on their gracefully curving *X*-form supports, borrowed from antique Roman seats of curule form, frequently painted in the fashionable white and gold color scheme, effectively display the creative charm embodied in the Italian Empire.

Spanish

MEDIEVAL

Spanish art in medieval times was distinguished by the coexistence of two schools of art—Christian and the impersonal ornament of Islam. Spain was occupied by the Moors, followers of Mohammed, from the early eighth century till their final defeat in 1492, and even then many still remained in certain sections, chiefly along the southern coast, where they constituted an important urban element, until their final expulsion in 1607. Moorish occupation had a dominating effect on Spanish ornament and design, as may be seen in the style of decoration called Mudéjar, a combination of Moorish and Christian art. Islamic art, like all art in ancient times, was the expression of the religious feelings of a people, and, faithful to the teachings of the Koran, the Mohammedans proscribed all natural images in their art. This fundamental principle, almost invariably followed, led to making symmetrical designs from forms devoid of positive meaning. The Alhambra at Granada, with its exuberant and wonderfully imaginative geometric patterns of infinite variety and interlacements of exquisite foliage and floral forms conventionally disguised, combining also Arabic inscriptions, all in relief, rich in the fanciful combination of natural colors, profusely embellished with gold, displays almost endless examples of Moorish decoration in its greatest splendor.

Moorish influence persisted long after the Moors had vanished. The tutelage of the Moors, who were highly accomplished in the craft of woodwork, is clearly perceptible in Spanish furniture—in ornament, design, and methods of construction. At the same time, Spanish furniture was greatly influenced by Moorish habits of life. For instance, articles of furniture brought into Spain from the Near East, such as chests and cabinets originally intended to be placed on the floor or at a low level, were mounted on stands designed for that purpose, giving a distinctive character to

Spanish furniture. Even after the "European" policy of Ferdinand and Isabella and their successors became operative in the arts, this combination of Hispano-Moresque culture remained a distinguishing feature.

RENAISSANCE

The sixteenth century marked the most brilliant era in Spanish history. Ferdinand and Isabella, through the voyages of Columbus, had acquired title to the New World with its promise of untold wealth and opportunity. Fabulous amounts of gold and silver bullion poured into Spain through the exploits of Spanish traders and navigators. This growing prosperity, plus the increased security resulting from the cessation of racial wars after the fall of Granada, provided the initiative for the aristocratic families and wealthy middle class to build town palaces and fine houses in such leading cities as Madrid, Seville, and Barcelona. Early Spanish Renaissance domestic architecture generally mirrored the influence of the earlier Moorish work, which enhanced the value of rich decorations in the patios, galleries, doorways, and windows by contrasting them against plain walls. Magnificent wrought-iron grilles, sometimes enriched with gilding, used at the windows and openings, and also decorative wrought-iron handrails, were a distinguishing feature of these houses. The most prominent feature, however, were the colorful and exuberant built-in decorations that seemed even more striking against the simplicity of plain, smooth, white plaster walls. The most exotic interiors were found in the south of Spain, where Moorish influence survived the longest. These built-in decorations based on Mudéjar principles—polychrome tiles (*azulejos*), painted wooden ceilings (*artesonado*), and plasterwork or stucco (*yesería*)—used in the great majority of Spanish interiors made them completely different from those found in any other part of Europe.

The Moorish love for colorful and ingenious craftsmanship in the adjuncts to their furniture, such as hangings and carpets, rather than in the furniture itself, of which they had very little, was also inherited by the Spanish, as may be seen in the houses of the aristocracy where the walls were adorned with silk velvet or damask hangings, generally scarlet, frequently exquisitely embroidered or appliquéd with armorial bearings and embellished with gold braid and deep fringe with straight gold threads. Equally favored were finely woven Renaissance tapestries, paintings in richly carved massive frames, hangings of leather with elaborate designs embossed and frequently tooled in part, brilliantly painted and gilded, and tiled wall pictures painted with pictorial representations extending over a large number of tiles, made in obvious imitation of tapestry, and embroidered altar frontals. Magnificent cut-pile Spanish carpets, Moorish rugs and mats with interlacements of pure arabesque design, and

50

Stairhall with floor and wainscot of polychrome tiles. Seville, Palace of the Duke of Alba. Illustrated in *Spanish Interiors and Furniture* by Arthur and Mildred Byne. *Courtesy William D. Helburn.*

51

Ground floor *salón* with painted, heavily beamed ceiling and carved plasterwork frieze (sixteenth century). In the drawing, furniture of the period has been introduced: a *papelera* mounted on a stand with splayed trestle-end supports and a decorative wrought-iron brace, a brazier and a *sillón frailero*. Seville, Palace of the Duke of Alba. Illustrated in *Spanish Interiors and Furniture* by Arthur and Mildred Byne. *Courtesy William D. Helburn.* (*See page 50.*)

Main *salón* of the principal story with ceiling of oiled pine, carved plasterwork frieze, and sanded stone floors (sixteenth century). In the drawing, furniture of the period has been introduced: *sillones fraileros,* chests, a stool, a small box on the table, and a *sillón de tijera* or X-form chair; the fashion for the latter did not last through the Renaissance. Seville, Palace of the Duke of Alba. Illustrated in *Spanish Interiors and Furniture* by Arthur and Mildred Byne. *Courtesy William D. Helburn.* (*See page 50.*)

glowing Hispano-Moresque lustered drug jars, deep dishes and large plates were also employed with great richness of effect. In this atmosphere of rich color, the Spanish formally arranged a few pieces of furniture, chiefly walnut, which they preferred to place against the wall. Traditionally Moorish was the prevailing fashion for heavy draperies and canopies, ingeniously designed decorative nailheads (*chatones*), fringes, braids and tassels, the many small boxes and cushions as seats.

Spanish Renaissance furniture was essentially rectilinear, with the exception of the *sillón de tijera,* an X-form chair of ancient Roman curule form. A pronounced feature of Spanish furniture design was the marked absence of architectural detail, such as pediments and pilasters, which were so characteristic of Italian Renaissance furniture. Much of the furniture was even devoid of moldings. Owing to the efforts of Charles V and Philip II to make effective the "European" policy in the arts, the court furniture developed along lines remote from native Hispano-Moresque art. Nowhere is the difference between these two types more strikingly revealed than in the traditional Spanish table with a plain oblong top devoid of moldings and an ornamental underbrace connecting the two splayed, open and

53

turned trestle-end supports, also frequently of lyre form, and the rare Spanish copy of the massive Italian Renaissance table with its heavily molded oblong top and elaborately carved, ornately shaped, solid trestle-end supports. The intrinsic charm of traditional Spanish Renaissance furniture is not in any great elegance or finished craftsmanship, but rather in its simplicity, its boldness of design and vigorous lines. The forceful simplicity peculiar to the structural design of this cabinetwork was in harmony with the simple structure of Spanish rooms. A unique feature of its construction was the frequent use of decorative wrought-iron underbraces for tables, stands, and benches. These distinguishing features, together with its unrivaled metal mounts and the originality of composition of its ornament— motifs of Gothic, Renaissance, and Arabic origin—give this furniture a singular beauty that achieved for it enduring renown in the history of European cabinetwork.

The limited number of pieces in Spanish furniture no doubt stems from the scarcity of portable Moorish furniture, comprising chiefly small low tables primarily used for dining, with cushions serving as seats and all kinds of box-like pieces intended to be placed on the floor or at a low level. Even in later centuries, when the Spanish were aware of the almost endless number of new forms introduced in the different categories by French cabinetmakers, they always seemed satisfied to a large extent with the basic pieces. There was a general dearth of seat furniture, both in variety and comfort, even according to Renaissance standards. The chair, stool, and bench comprised all the seating facilities in a Spanish Renaissance house. The *sillón frailero,* or monk's chair, of simple rectangular form with quadrangular supports, distinguished by its broad front stretcher, was the favorite and principal Renaissance armchair. The seat and back panel were of leather, sometimes either embossed or stitched in a geometrical pattern, stretched between the side rails and uprights respectively and secured with large decorative nailheads. Occasionally in the more elegant models the leather was covered with velvet and enhanced with gold braid and fringe. In a similar fashion, when used in a more elegant setting, the wood bench, the great majority of which were without arms, was covered on back and seat in either leather or velvet, often quilted or stitched in geometrical patterns and fastened with ornamental nailheads to the solid wood back and seat. Otherwise, the wood back was enriched in a variety of ways—by metal plaques, carving, or an openwork design comprising a

OPPOSITE ABOVE: Walnut table with splayed and turned trestle-end supports and a decorative underbrace of ironwork (seventeenth century). *Courtesy Hispanic Society of America.* CENTER: Walnut table (seventeenth century) in the Italian manner, richly carved and molded; with solid trestle-end supports, a colonnaded traverse, and an H-form base. *Cathedral of El Pilar, Larger Sacristy, Saragossa. Photo Mas.* BELOW: Walnut table with splayed lyre-shaped trestle-end supports, a wrought-iron underbrace, and a frieze provided with four drawers carved on both sides (seventeenth century). The two center drawers pull out on one side, and the two end drawers on the opposite side. *Courtesy Hispanic Society of America.*

55

Walnut bench with carved lyre-formed trestle-end supports (seventeenth century). The gilt metal plaque set into the back bears the arms of Pedro Álvarez de Acosta, Bishop of Osma (1539–63). Detail of the above, showing gilt metal plaque. *Courtesy Hispanic Society of America.* BELOW LEFT: Folding *sillón frailero* of walnut (sixteenth century). As in many early examples, the frame can be dismounted. *Museo Episcopal, Vich, Barcelona. Photo Mas. (See page 54.)* BELOW RIGHT: Walnut chair carved with conventional floral and geometric designs (seventeenth century). The back has a row of arches with turned piers. *Courtesy Philadelphia Museum of Art.*

row of arches with turned piers, the latter being especially characteristic of the low back of a wood side chair. Arcades were often introduced in Spanish furniture design; nowhere is their use more typical than the broad arcaded stretcher distinguishing the *puente* stand.

Other principal pieces of Spanish Renaissance furniture are the beds completely concealed by heavy draperies, tables, chests, *vargueños*, and *armarios*. Apart from the table with wrought-iron underbraces and splayed trestle-end supports, which is the most popular and characteristic of all Spanish Renaissance tables, especially typical are the many diminutive tables reproducing in miniature the larger ones. The idea for these, no doubt, was inspired by the indispensable tiny Moorish table about twenty inches in height. An absolutely necessary piece of Spanish furniture is the brazier, a metal basin filled with charcoal, to provide heat.

Just as the *sillón frailero* is the typical chair of the Spanish Renaissance, so the *vargueño* is the characteristic cabinet. Unrivaled for the superb skill displayed in its colorful and exuberant decoration, the *vargueño*, in the form of an oblong cabinet provided with a hinged drop front that opens to reveal an interior of small drawers and compartments and serves as a writing board, is Spain's choicest piece of furniture. The *vargueño* is mounted on various forms of stands especially designed for it. The interior, and frequently the exterior, of the early *vargueño* is generally skillfully inlaid with light-colored woods and ivory, stained in vivid colors or un-colored, worked in designs often combining Christian themes, such as a representation of animals entering the ark, with the impersonal ornament of Islam, such as interlacements of foliage of arabesque design. Later such typical Renaissance motifs as grotesques *à candaliere* (developed, cande-labrum-like, symmetrically above a vertical axis) intermingled with winged cherubs and foliage scrolls in the Italian fashion were frequently favored. This general class of *vargueño* with inlaid decoration sometimes entirely of ivory, correctly mounted on either a *puente* stand or a stand with splayed trestle-end supports and a decorative wrought-iron underbrace, illustrates with remarkable felicity the Moorish special genius for clearly defined and distinct ornament.

Another distinctive class of Renaissance *vargueño*, but essentially a type more closely identified with the seventeenth century, displays an archi-tectural façade glowing with gold and rich colors, incorporating pediments and spirally turned colonnettes made of either ivory or wood. The small drawers and doors, with metal drop handles in the form of exquisitely wrought miniature shells, were richly inlaid with ivory lozenges and similar motifs worked in geometric patterns and often etched in black with stylized flowers, foliage, and scrolls, indicating the vitality of Moorish precepts. Sometimes the façade was further enlivened with touches of red and blue paint. The exterior of the drop front of these *vargueños* was

LEFT: Brass brazier with fluted gilt wood columns (seventeenth century). The brass-covered top and shelf bear in *repoussé* the arms of Castille, Castille and León, Navarre, France, and the Robles family. An inscription on the top reads: "Zarragoza 1641 Conde de Robles." *Courtesy Hispanic Society of America.* RIGHT: Walnut *vargueño* decorated with an inlay of various woods and ivory in the Mudéjar style (sixteenth century). It is mounted on a *puente* stand, distinguished by its broad arcaded stretcher. *Museo Arqueológico Nacional, Barcelona. Photo Mas.* (*See page 57.*)

decorated with large wrought-iron appliqués, filled with delicately pierced stylized designs, generally backed with scarlet velvet, and an elaborate lock, hasp and pulls with drop handles at each end. This *vargueño* was properly mounted on a *taquillón.* The *papelera,* closely akin to the *vargueño,* but designed with ball or bun-shaped feet and without a drop front, embodies the same kind and quality of decoration, all of which rarely lacked some elements of Moorish influence.

In Spain, as in all countries, chests were of primary importance, but unlike other countries, where they were gradually supplanted by more specialized pieces, as chests of drawers, their popularity continued long after the Renaissance. The carved and painted decoration adorning early Spanish chests was in Gothic, Moorish, or Mudéjar taste. Later, classical Renaissance motifs were introduced which became more "Italian" in concept, as the influence of the Renaissance gradually became more effective. The linen-fold and flamboyant tracery reflecting French influence, and

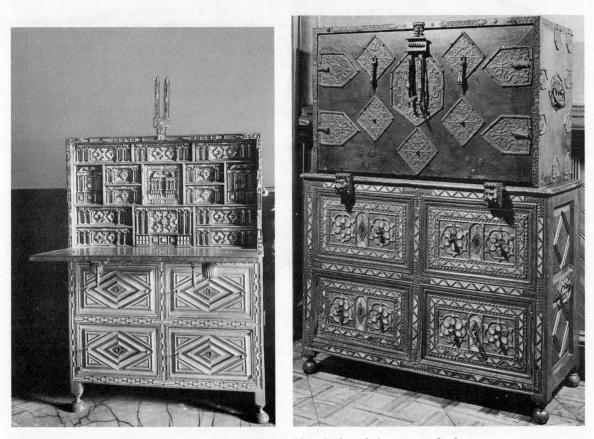

LEFT: Walnut *vargueño* (seventeenth century). It is richly inlaid, and the interior displays an architectural façade; it is mounted on a *taquillón. Museo de Arte de Cataluña, Barcelona. Photo Mas.* RIGHT: Walnut *vargueño* (seventeenth century). The exterior is decorated with pierced wrought-iron appliqués backed with scarlet velvet; it is mounted on a *taquillón. Instituto Amatller, Barcelona. Photo Mas. (See page 57.)

later with some infusions of Flemish and German Gothic, were favorite Spanish Gothic motifs. Also popular subjects were Christian themes and heraldic devices with spirited and vigorous birds and beasts executed in the stylized animal forms of Near Eastern art. Walnut chests in the Moorish taste displayed a distinctive style of inlaid decoration, not unlike Italian *certosina* and notable for its geometric precision, comprising minute pieces of ivory worked in a rich mosaic of typical Levantine designs of stars, circles, rosettes, quatrefoils, and hexagons.

Distinctively Spanish are the chests covered with leather, plain or embossed and often tooled, or velvet often embellished with nailheads in geometric patterns. The exquisite wrought-iron lock plates and decorative bands of jewel-like quality used on these chests well explain Spanish preeminence in metalwork. Other chests, in particular bridal chests, were decorated on the inner side of the hinged lid. This chest was usually provided with another plain lid, which permitted the top lid to rest against

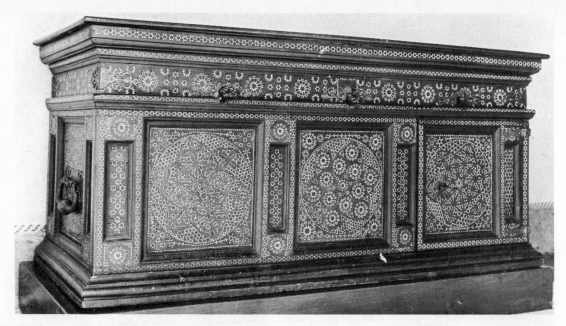

ABOVE: Walnut chest decorated with an ivory inlay of typical Moorish design (sixteenth century). *Museo Lázaro, Madrid. Photo Mas.* BELOW LEFT: Detail of metal mounts on a chest upholstered in crimson velvet (fifteenth century). The convex lid is banded with Gothic tracery, and the two single-hasped shell locks are decorated with turreted pinnacles and geometric designs of dots. *Courtesy Hispanic Society of America.* (*See page 59.*) BELOW RIGHT: Mudéjar door panel (fourteenth century). Door panels of this kind, employing Moorish methods of joinery to form striking surface designs, were also used to close in a recessed wall cupboard. *Courtesy Hispanic Society of America.* OPPOSITE: Walnut bridal chest, carved and polychromed (sixteenth century). The inside of the lid is painted with the Annunciation. The bride's chest often had a door on one side of the front, which, when opened, revealed a nest of drawers. *Museo de Arte de Cataluña, Barcelona. Photo Mas.*

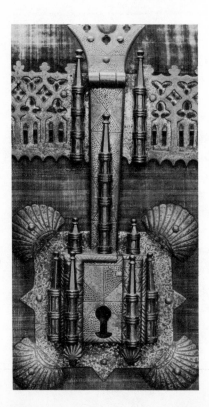

the wall in order to display its decoration. The Spanish taste for all kinds of chests may be seen also in the elaborate miniature boxes and chests, generally less than twelve inches in length, which the Spanish profusely placed on tables. As elsewhere during the Middle Ages, small chests in the form of Gothic tombs, having a lid resembling a hipped roof, were also found in Spain. The love for colorful and over-all minute and delicate surface decoration, inlaid, carved in low relief, and painted—an outstanding feature of Hispano-Moresque art—is illustrated in the *vargueño* and chest, the two pieces selected by the Spanish for a lavish display of their artistic skill.

Because of the popularity of the chest, the tall movable *armario*, or cupboard, either single or double-bodied, was a relatively scarce article of Spanish domestic furniture prior to the seventeenth century, the earlier ones being chiefly sacristy cupboards. Domestic cupboards were often built into the walls and enclosed with doors that resemble the woodwork in a traditional Moorish carved and painted ceiling. A typical decoration for paneled cupboard doors is to divide each door equally into two or more rectangular panels, enclosing within a molded circle or diamond as large as the space will permit, and then in true Moorish taste to fill in all kinds of delicate ornament, inlaid or carved in low relief. In one type of double-bodied *armario* the rectangular panels in the upper body are filled in with

LEFT: Walnut *armario*, probably a sacristy cupboard (sixteenth century). The panels in the upper portion are filled with turned spindles; the treatment of the panels in the lower portion is typically Moorish. *Museo de Artes Decorativas, Madrid. Photo Mas.* (*See page 61.*) OPPOSITE: Walnut bed with spirally turned posts (seventeenth century). The headboard comprises two rows of arches with turned piers and is surmounted with an ornately carved and pierced cresting. *Museo Episcopal, Vich, Barcelona. Photo Mas.* BELOW LEFT: Charles IV chair painted white with gilt enrichments (eighteenth century). It has a decorative bentwood underbrace. *Museo Romantico. Photo Aprodisio Aguado, S.A.* BELOW RIGHT: Slat-back chair with baluster-turned uprights and front legs, rush seat (eighteenth century). It is painted red with gilt decoration. *Museo Episcopal, Vich, Barcelona. Photo Mas.* (*See page 64.*)

turned spindles. (Spindles long or short were much used in Spanish doors.) Turning was always a favorite Spanish method for working wood; it was widely employed in the seventeenth century, when perhaps the most popular piece for the cabinetmaker's lathe was the bed, with its turned posts and headboard. Occasionally the headboard designed with rows of turned spindles surmounted with a delicate and elaborate cresting resembled the wrought-iron *reja,* the church screen separating the public from the choir. Although many kinds of turning were used, spiral turnings, interrupted by disk-like turnings, and knob turnings, with some of pronounced girth resulting in a bulbous outline, were among the most frequently found in the early seventeenth century on bedposts as well as on the legs of tables.

LATER CABINETWORK

It is beyond the province of this book to dwell upon foreign taste in Spanish furniture which invaded Spain first from Italy and then especially

63

from France. Baroque art found a congenial territory in Spain, and, owing to the peculiar temperament and character of the Spanish, it never completely died out. The resultant bold quality is distinguishable in well-designed pieces as grandiose simplicity and in pieces of inferior design as overelaboration and heaviness. Since Spain was governed by the Bourbons in the eighteenth century, it is only natural that French art and customs should prevail. Following the dictates of fashion, Spanish cabinetmakers working in the large cities in order to satisfy their wealthy patrons tried to erase all those traditional features indigenous to Spanish furniture which stemmed from the Hispano-Moresque culture and won for Spain its eminence in furniture design.

The Charles III style essentially corresponds to the Louis XV, while the Charles IV style may well be regarded as the Spanish parallel of the Louis XVI. The royal workshop at Madrid, established by Charles III, was instrumental in developing these styles in Spain. Most of the seat furniture, of carved wood, was either gilded or painted white with gilt enrichments. Some of these pieces display a refreshing interpretation of the French styles. An extant Charles IV open-back side chair, of marked originality, is particularly interesting because it clearly retains an Hispano-Moresque flavor in its decorative underbrace of bent wood and in the simple and vigorous treatment of the open back, having an almost diamond-shaped band boldly interlaced between the flaring uprights and crest rail. The Fernandino (Ferdinand VII) style is the Spanish representative of the French Empire; less elegant than its prototype, it frequently substituted mounts of carved wood for those of bronze. The Isabellino (Isabella II) style, identified with nineteenth-century romanticism, with its conspicuous middle-class air, reflects the fashion of an epoch rather than an independent style. It copies the prominent ogival arches of the Gothic style, the neo-classicism of Louis XVI, Empire, and Biedermeier, but above all its most characteristic pieces descend from Louis XV, a revived rococo marked with exaggerated curves.

In the provinces removed from the French court, sturdy furniture continued to be made along traditional lines. Typical of this taste is a slat-back chair generally made of pine, gilded and painted red, green, ivory, or black, having a rush seat. This model with its striking design and brilliant color appealed to the Spanish taste and became very popular during the eighteenth century.

Dutch and Flemish

GOTHIC

The Low Countries, comprising what is now known as Holland and Belgium, are pressed closely between countries inhabited by Teutonic and Latin races. This dual influence has been reflected through the centuries in their religion, politics, and arts. In a broad sense, Belgium was influenced by France and Holland by Germany. The history of this section of Europe is very checkered, and attempts to fit in all the different influences contributing to its art is like solving a jigsaw puzzle. Dynastic events first united the Netherlands in the fourteenth century with Burgundy and finally with Spain under the Emperor Charles V, 1519–58, whose reign was destined to be filled with the uproar of the Reformation.

In the Gothic period, towns like Bruges and Ghent became thriving art centers, abounding with the most skillful of craftsmen. Beautifully wrought gold plate, enamels, laces, embroideries, silk velvets, tapestries made at Tournai, embossed and tooled leather, an art learned from the Spanish Moors, and wrought brass and copper wares, or *dinanderie* made at Dinant, were all included in Flemish achievements. The fame of the Flemish wood carver spread far beyond his own domain. His carvings borrowed from Gothic stone sculptures ornamented Flemish Gothic furniture, which was similar to that found in the rest of Christian Europe. Paintings by Van Eyck and his contemporaries convey the atmosphere of a late Gothic interior with notable success. Perhaps the perfect example is Van Eyck's *Giovanni Arnolfini and His Wife* with its exquisitely painted details. The frame of the mirror decorated with miniatures, the one lighted candle in the brass chandelier, the carved details on the furniture, and the canopy of the bed with its valance apparently fixed to the ceiling, since there are no end posts, the one curtain of the bed knotted up out of the way, which was the customary daytime practice at this time, become almost tangible in this enchanting example of beautifully finished art.

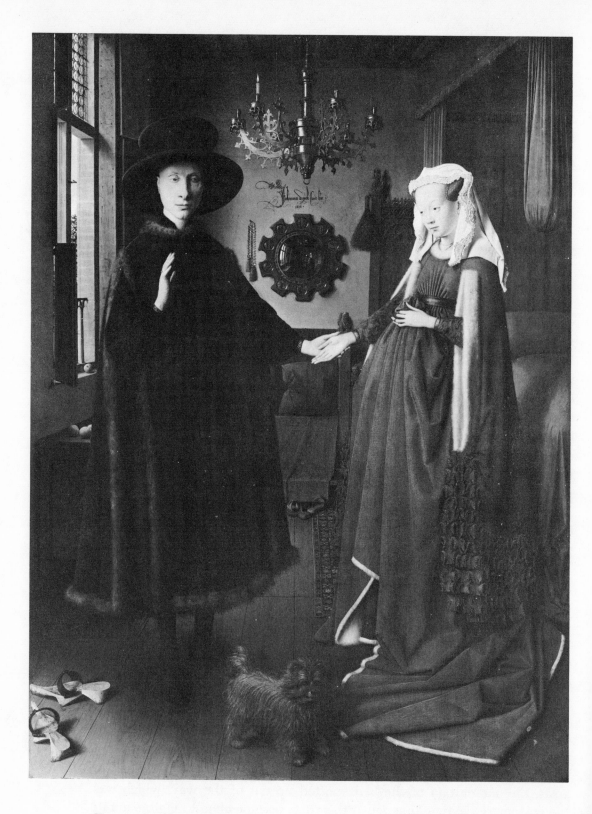

Giovanni Arnolfini and His Wife (Flemish, signed by Jan van Eyck and dated 1434 above the mirror). *Courtesy National Gallery, London.* (*See page 65.*)

RENAISSANCE

During the sixteenth century the commerce and industry which had enjoyed such an auspicious beginning in the Gothic period prospered so prodigiously that the Netherlands earned the reputation as the beehive of Europe. Its busy cities, such as Lille, Antwerp, Ghent, Amsterdam, and scores of others, excited the wonder and envy of all Europe, not only because of their wealth but also by reason of the culture of their citizens. However, from one source, the Reformation, a deepening shadow had begun to fall across the land, which finally broke out in open revolt, with the southern Catholic Netherlands remaining loyal to the Spanish Crown. The seven northern Protestant provinces, which were destined to be a great maritime and commercial power, continued their struggle against Spain until their independence was formally recognized in 1648. Thus the Lower Meuse separated two different civilizations—Flanders, which remained Spanish and Catholic, and Holland, which was free and Protestant. This is a fact which must always be considered in any comparative study of Dutch and Flemish arts. It becomes patent in the early seventeenth century when Flanders completely accepted the painter Rubens, whose work, typifying the sensuous, worldly essence of Catholicism, made him the representative par excellence of the baroque movement in Catholic Europe.

Italian Renaissance ornament, imitated more or less from the antique, was carried north of the Alps either directly or via the Netherlands. In the beginning, the only change noticeable in furniture was in the style of ornament which was grafted on late Gothic forms. In a word, the chair still has its box-like form, but the back, for example, now has pilasters for the uprights, while the Gothic linen-fold motif is replaced by Renaissance grotesques combined with strapwork in the style of the Dutch ornamentists Cornelis Bos and Cornelis Floris. Brussels, Antwerp, and Liége, as in the preceding Late Gothic period, were leading centers for furniture carved with Early Renaissance motifs. In the course of the sixteenth century, Italian Renaissance ornament was adopted and transformed by the artists and ornamentists of Northern Europe, especially in Germany and the Netherlands, who developed an independent style in which strapwork, cartouches, and grotesque masks played an important role. This distinctive ornamental style of Northern European Renaissance is found repeatedly in the pattern books of such Dutch and German artists as De Vries and Dietterlein. Numerous Flemish pattern books such as the one by De Vries were published in the second half of the sixteenth century. These books of engraved ornamental designs were circulated among and influenced carvers and furniture makers throughout the North. Their influence was strongly evident in Burgundy, long connected by both political and artistic ties to the Low Countries, and in Renaissance England. For instance, in Burgundy the furniture designs of Hugues Sambin patently reveal the influence of these pattern books. French furniture displaying this style of decoration is as a rule notable for its vigorous yet restrained carving (see French Chest page 86).

Flemish Renaissance furniture, like their Renaissance architecture, was overburdened with a surfeit of ornament that almost amounted to riotous extravagance. The composition of the ornament lacked the clarity and purity for which the Italian craftsmen of the High Renaissance were unsurpassed, and which was seldom if ever found in the work north of the Alps. However, in spite of these as well as other infringements, there is much in the best Flemish Renaissance work that silences all adverse criticism with its general beauty of effect. Because the Flemings were fundamentally decorative and picturesque in outlook, it is difficult to determine when the Late Renaissance evolved into baroque. It seems from existing examples that until around the mid-seventeenth century the furniture is essentially a continuation of Late Renaissance rectilinear forms. An excellent general idea of Flemish Renaissance work is embodied in De Vries' pattern book, published in 1577, which displays not only the extravagances of the style, such as his designs for testered beds with figural supports and for tables supported by female sphinxes or crouching animals, but also its more practical aspects, as his designs for cupboards. De Vries' influence continued until around the mid-seventeenth century. Late Flemish work followed the current French styles, and, like all their furniture it bore the stamp of opulent Flanders.

The Flemish, like all other European countries, produced chairs of X-form, where they retained their popularity well into the seventeenth century, as may be seen in Dutch and Flemish engravings. Chairs of the French type called *caquetoire* were also found in the Netherlands. It is only to be expected that the close relationship existing between Spain and the Netherlands at this period led to the adoption of certain Spanish ingredients in their furniture design. For example, some chairs with open backs designed with one or more rows of arches and turned piers recall a similar treatment in Spanish chair backs. A touch of Spanish influence is seen in the principal Late Renaissance Flemish upholstered chair of "square" pattern, often regarded as an Antwerp innovation, having a seat and back panel of leather fastened to the frame with ornamental nailheads and finials in the form of a lion holding a coat of arms. This chair with a rectangular back and seat, displaying a family resemblance to the Spanish *frailero,* may be regarded as the principal model for the first half of the seventeenth century, when it enjoyed a great vogue in the North European countries. Because turning was so fashionable at that time, it is only natural that the chair displayed turned members. In a typical late six-

Carved oak cupboard (Flemish, c. 1560). It is notable for its rich variety of Renaissance motifs; the two doors carved in high relief with strapwork enclose oval medallions of nude figure subjects. The cupboard is interesting as a Flemish prototype of the Elizabethan hall and parlor cupboard. *Courtesy Parke-Bernet, from the collection of Charles E. F. McCann.* BELOW: Engraving by Pieter Serwouters (1586–1657) showing a typical Dutch interior. An X-form chair, a chest, and a testered bed are part of the furnishings. *Courtesy Metropolitan Museum of Art. Elisha Whittelsey Collection, 1952.*

teenth- and early seventeenth-century example, the legs are of turned balusters and blocks. The legs were turned out of pieces of wood square in section and this square form was left intact in parts where the maximum strength was required, that is to say, at the joining points of the stretchers. Since this model has two rows of stretchers, with the lower edge of the bottom row being notched, there are two blocks in each leg. Fortunately, as almost always happens, a pleasant shape was evolved out of this technical necessity. The most pleasing are chamfered, with the faces left plain. Many square upholstered chairs at this time were made without arms, a practice accounted for by the extravagant dimensions of the ladies' skirts. Hence, the upholstered version in France is known as a *chaise à vertugadin* and in England as a farthingale chair. Chairs of this related design displayed different kinds of turnery, with either knobbed or spiral, mortised and tenoned into retangular sections, being much in evidence. Knobbed turning is the most rudimentary form and was widely used in England during the Commonwealth, while spiral turning, which is by far the most frequent, is especially characteristic of the Louis XIII walnut chair and its contemporary Flemish walnut model. Small bun feet are typical for this entire class of chairs of the so-called "square" pattern.

Around 1650 this low-back chair gradually began to yield to a new ornate type of tall "caned" walnut armchair with spirally turned members

OPPOSITE ABOVE LEFT: Carved palissander chair (North Netherlands, first half of the seventeenth century). The back is filled in with arches and turned piers. (*See page 68.*) OPPOSITE ABOVE RIGHT: Palissander chair of "square" pattern (North Netherlands, first half of the seventeenth century). *Courtesy Rijksmuseum, Amsterdam.* OPPOSITE BELOW LEFT: Walnut armchair with spirally turned members. (Flemish, first half of the seventeenth century). *Courtesy Philadelphia Museum of Art.* OPPOSITE BELOW RIGHT: Carved walnut armchair with spirally turned members (North Netherlands, second half of the seventeenth century). It has the fashionable caned back panel and seat. LEFT: Carved walnut armchair with scrolled supports (North Netherlands, latter part of the seventeenth century). *Courtesy Rijksmuseum, Amsterdam.* (*See page 73.*)

71

Ebony cabinet with painted panels (probably made at Antwerp, first half of the seventeenth century). The stand has supports in the form of African Moors. BELOW: Interior of an ebony cabinet with panels painted in the manner of Rubens (probably made at Antwerp, first half of the seventeenth century). *Courtesy Rijksmuseum, Amsterdam.*

and bun feet, distinguished by a broad front stretcher, cresting, and a back panel that were developed into decorative areas. The fashion for these caned walnut chairs spread from France and Flanders to Holland, and from there to England where it became the popular Restoration chair. The general form of these chairs was widespread in Northwest Europe, and they were rendered with a distinctive idiom in each country. As a rule, those having oval caned-back panels are of continental origin. The redundant carved ornament adorning the decorative areas was thoroughly baroque in conception. Gradually the preference for curves, a pronounced baroque feature, began to assert itself in the form, as legs of scroll form with armposts forming complementary curves supplanted the spirally turned legs and armposts, and the *H*-form spiral stretcher yielded to a heavy X-form stretcher composed of four consoles arranged in an arched manner to display their scroll-shaped profile. Down scrolling open arms that turn outward and terminate in massive volutes are typically baroque and characteristic of this chair. The Flemish development of this caned chair with its heavily plastic scrolls and ornament is familiarly referred to in furniture literature as the "Flemish" chair. There was also an upholstered version having a padded seat and back, though by no means as typical as the caned variety.

The cabinet veneered in ebony, mounted on a stand, possessed the greatest artistic merit of all Flemish Renaissance furniture. Sculptors, painters, stone and ivory cutters, *marqueteurs*, enamelers, carvers and metalworkers lavished their skill on its decoration. These luxury cabinets having their provenance in Italy were later found at Antwerp, Augsburg, and Nuremberg in Germany, and at Paris. Those made at Antwerp in the seventeenth century were often decorated with painted panels of religious, historical, and mythological subjects executed in the grandiose manner of Rubens, depicting in rich and glowing colors a sensuous world with female nudes of billowy opulence. Some of the stands having supports in the form of African Moors in colorful costumes bring to mind the early Louis XIV *guéridon* in the form of a young Moor. Another class of ebony cabinets were decorated with carving, a medium in which the Flemings triumphantly excelled. Their carved reliefs adorning these cabinets elicited the highest praise throughout Europe, and the French king, Henri IV, sent his cabinetmakers to Flanders to learn the art of carving in ebony. Hence, the French name *ébéniste*, later given to the French cabinetmaker, was derived from *menuisier en ébène,* or joiner in ebony.

DUTCH

In the early years of the seventeenth century a new national cultural period began in Holland, during which an indigenous style of Dutch furniture was evolved, side by side with the rise of the Dutch genius in painting and architecture. This divergence in Dutch and Flemish furniture, with the latter following the current French styles and the former developing into a national style, dates from around 1640. It must be remembered, however, that the Dutch style was by no means divorced from the French style, for later in the century, due to the revocation of the Edict of Nantes in 1685, many highly skilled French craftsmen sought refuge in Holland, the foremost among whom was Daniel Marot, French architect, designer, and engraver of ornament. Although Marot's work was in the style of Louis XIV, his later designs, after residing in Holland, showed a curious blending of Dutch and French influences. His books of engraved designs exerted great influence on contemporary English taste, and he was undoubtedly responsible for introducing into England new forms and style of ornament from abroad. The result was a similarity between contemporary Dutch styles and the English styles of William and Mary and Queen Anne.

Owing to the close ties between England and Holland, English furniture during the second half of the sixteenth and seventeenth centuries was more influenced by Holland than by any other European country. At certain periods these ties were intensified; in such a time of political confluence as the reign of William and Mary, furniture developed along almost parallel lines. English walnut and marquetry furniture from the time of the Restoration in 1660 until about 1700 bears the unmistakable imprint of Dutch influence, and although Dutch influence persisted in England as long as walnut remained the fashionable wood for cabinetwork, the influence was less marked from around 1700. The finest Dutch furniture was made from around 1660 to 1690. As a rule, the Dutch furniture of that period was more elaborately ornamented than the English, which usually revealed more restraint in the general character of its design and decoration. Dutch carved ornament very often had more intricate detail than similar English specimens. A peculiar heaviness and overelaboration which characterized so much of the seventeenth-century Dutch furniture was also apparent in their eighteenth-century work. Much of the early eighteenth-century Dutch furniture was similar to the English Queen Anne and Early Georgian styles, while their later work essentially follows the prevailing French fashions. Undoubtedly their best work in furniture, as in their architecture, lies in examples of marked simplicity rather than specimens on a grander scale with rich ornament, for unfortunately the Dutch did not possess the special talent for integrating ornament, with the result that it was often heavy, excessive, and obvious.

The lucrative Dutch trade with the Orient, stemming from the Dutch East India Company founded in 1602, afforded a powerful impetus in developing Chinese influence not only on the Dutch arts of decoration but on all European countries. Japanese and Chinese lacquer wares were

Veneered walnut secretary cabinet with a slant front (North Netherlands, 1753). The *bombé* shape of the lower portion (the so-called kettle base) was introduced from Holland into England under William III. BELOW: Center table of carved and gilt wood (North Netherlands, first quarter of the eighteenth century). The top is supported by female busts ending in scrolls. The carved ornament shows extravagant Venetian baroque exuberance. *Courtesy Rijksmuseum, Amsterdam.*

brought into Europe by Dutch traders from the beginning of the seventeenth century. Oblong cabinets with two doors, which when opened revealed an interior of small drawers and doors, mounted on carved gilt wood stands, were particularly fashionable. Screens obtained in China were occasionally used as paneling in smaller rooms. The popularity of Chinese porcelain and Japanese Imari was an important incentive for Delft faïence, which developed so handsomely from about the middle of the seventeenth century. All kinds of shelves, brackets, and special articles of furniture, such as china cabinets with glazed doors, were designed for the display of china. Then there was an infinite variety of curios—jades, ivories, and bronzes.

Another interesting feature resulting from the contact with the Orient was the social custom of drinking tea; inspiring designs for all forms of tea equipage, from tea tables to teapots. Apart from the direct influence of imported wares was the more curious interest in the Far East, to which may be attributed the fantastic *chinoiseries*, with their fanciful compositions depicting an imaginary world of pseudo-Chinese figures and scenes.

Travel books, chiefly Dutch, purporting to portray the life and customs of the Chinese, published from about the third quarter of the seventeenth century, were an important source for disseminating Chinese taste. Numerous engravings by Peter Schenck of Amsterdam at the end of the seventeenth century, and several German houses, inspired some of the earlier *chinoiseries* in the late baroque taste.

In chair design the arrival of Daniel Marot and numerous other French refugees proved a stimulating influence. This may be seen in the so-called Marotesque chair, a tall walnut chair chiefly characterized by a back either filled or almost filled in with ornate pierced carvings and having an elaborate arched cresting, as a rule with baluster turned legs, stretchered and mounted on bun feet. Toward the end of the century the Dutch cabinetmaker introduced a number of novel features, resulting in an

OPPOSITE LEFT: Walnut chair (North Netherlands, c. 1690–1700). The richly carved cartouche-shaped back is in the manner of Daniel Marot. OPPOSITE RIGHT: Walnut chair (North Netherlands, first quarter of the eighteenth century). This type of chair, introduced from Holland into England, served as the model for the Queen Anne splat-back chair. ABOVE LEFT: *Blomverk* cabinet (North Netherlands, last quarter of the seventeenth century) decorated with beautiful polychrome floral marquetry in the Dutch style. ABOVE RIGHT: *Kast* or cupboard of palissander and ebony (North Netherlands, c. 1650). The heavily molded base breaks around the orders in typical baroque fashion. *Courtesy Rijksmuseum, Amsterdam.* (*See page 78.*)

entirely new and distinctive type of walnut chair, the Anglicized version of which became the graceful Queen Anne splat-back chair, the most pleasing of all English chairs. This new Dutch chair displayed a slender leg of cabriole form, stretchered and terminating in a cloven-hoof foot. The uprights of the back are curved; a shoulder is formed on the uprights, which join into the cresting and approximate a hoop shape. The splat follows the curve of the occupant's back, and the outline of the splat suggests a vase. Later, for the first time, the splat joins the seat framing. The resemblance of this class of chairs to Chinese Ming splat-back chairs is too marked to be accidental. Undoubtedly the answer lies in the close relations existing between China and several European countries. Later English models sometimes even display a slight concave in the center front of the crest rail that served as a neck rest in the Chinese yoke-type model.

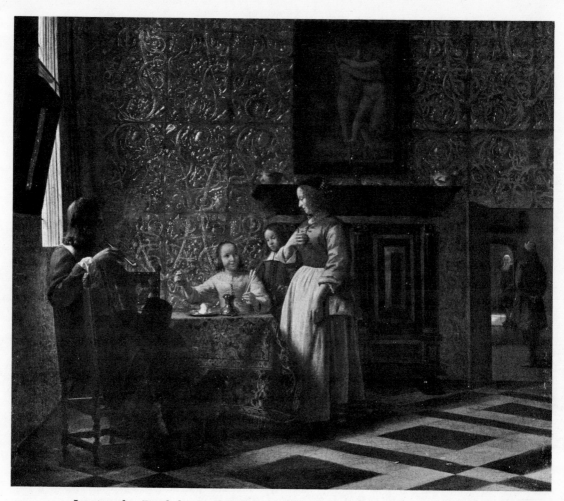

Interior of a Dutch house (by Pieter de Hooch, Dutch School, 1629–77). Against the embossed leather wall stands an imposing Dutch cupboard; the table is covered with the customary carpet or cloth. *Courtesy Robert Lehman Collection.*

The Dutch cabinet was designed with large plain surfaces, so that the Dutch *marqueteur* could display his skill on its decoration. There were the so-called star cabinets, with ingenious compositions of stars and circles worked in various colored woods, and the *blomverk* cabinets with superb polychrome floral marquetry; the latter well explain why the Dutch *marqueteur* was much sought after in Paris and London to instruct in this process. Other typical expressions of Dutch baroque are tables with S-scroll supports, and above all the massive cupboards distinguished by heavily molded projecting cornices, molded bases breaking around the orders, and large flattened ball feet. Because the cupboard was an important part of a Dutch interior, it was often made of such costly materials as palissander or ebony. The single-bodied type provided with two long doors often divided and flanked by free-standing columns, fitted with a row of drawers in the molded base, was much favored.

French Renaissance

FRANÇOIS I STYLE

Just as Gothic architecture took but a feeble hold on Italy, so that of the Renaissance was not quickly accepted north of the Alps, owing to the still lingering vitality of the flamboyant Gothic style. When the Renaissance did spread into Europe, which was during the second half of the fifteenth century, it was first felt in France, a country always receptive to any new ideas in artistic expression. In France, as in Flanders and Germany, the new art was introduced by princes and nobles. Thus it was devoted more to secular than to ecclesiastical architecture. The oldest monuments of the French Renaissance are the magnificent châteaux built in the valley of the Loire during the reign of François I, 1515–47. They retain the high sloping roofs, the towers and turrets of medieval times. It is only in the ornament, especially that of pilasters, that the Italian Renaissance influence is evident. The masterpiece of this hybrid union of Gothic and Renaissance, in which Gothic forms are clearly perceptible under the veil of Renaissance ornament, is Chambord, a fairy apparition with its profusion of turrets, pinnacles, and dormer windows that decorate the roof of this 440-apartment château.

In like manner, the furniture of the François I style keeps its Gothic forms, but abounds in charming Italian Renaissance elements that had been completely Frenchified. The medallion is highly characteristic of François I, although it was already in use under Louis XII. Designed as the head or bust, in profile or full face, of a man or woman, carved in varying degrees of relief, it is set in a frame, generally round, composed of a wreath of foliage or a turned molding. Occasionally the female head is enframed in a lozenge, the heraldic attribute of a woman. The entire family of ornament known as grotesques, inspired by the Loggie frescoes of Raphael in the Vatican, invaded the decorative areas of paneled furniture, as on the façade of chests or chairs of box-like form, supplanting

79

Oak door panel carved with a fanciful grotesque (early sixteenth century). Similar grotesque compositions were carved on the back of the Gothic chair during the François I period. *Courtesy Metropolitan Museum of Art. Bequest of George Blumenthal, 1941.* BELOW: Oak chest with an arcaded façade (first half of the sixteenth century). The panels and pilasters are carved with grotesques. In the two end panels, medallion heads are part of the composition. *Courtesy Victoria and Albert Museum. (See page 79.)*

the linen-fold, tracery, and other popular Gothic motifs. All the ornament is varied, vivid, and fanciful; it was adapted so happily to French taste.

HENRI II STYLE

This delightful period of Franco-Italian art came to a close toward the end of the reign of François I, when a purification of the style took place, resulting in the Henri II style of 1547–89. The structure of the furniture is modified in accordance with Renaissance principles, and the ornament is perfected. Pilasters are no longer decorated with grotesques but are properly fluted and display a capital and base. The chair, which under François I kept its massive paneled form, began to grow somewhat lighter, as the chair of box-like form gradually yields to the chair with an open frame. First the side pieces were removed, freeing the arms (records began to mention *chaise à bras*, the early French word for armchair). Next the seat ceased to be a chest with the disappearance of its four "walls." The back became lower, but it was still solid; later in the century it was also "opened," when we find chairs with a splat back. The legs are simply square or columnar, the latter having a molding suggesting a base and capital, and are joined close to the floor with substantial stretchers.

Considerable time elapsed before the legs were freed from these low stretchers, generally put together in the shape of a rectangular frame. The unevenness of the floor, made in the medieval and Early Renaissance periods of red earthenware pavement tiles and stone pavements, would quickly dislocate the legs continually knocking against the rough points except for these strong reinforcements. Of these "lighter" chairs, all with seats of wood, some were made of square plan. One early type, of which a comfortable number are still extant, is the so-called *caquetoire* (a chair for cackling, hence, a *chaise de femme*), though the application of the name to this particular type of chair is strongly disputed. Later in the century the chair of square plan was made without arms to accommodate the extravagant dimensions of the *vertugadin* (a frame of hoops that lined the women's skirts), a fashion, as the word itself, *verdugado*, of Spanish origin. Soon people spoke of the *chaise à vertugadin*.

The genuine enthusiasm existing in France for the sculptured, elaborate, and architectural furniture being produced in Renaissance Italy gave a kind of family resemblance to French and Italian furniture, especially in the second half of the sixteenth century when French furniture became thoroughly saturated with the spirit of the Italian Renaissance. The engravings of Du Cerceau, who introduced many new models of furniture, examplify this fact. Not only was walnut the fashionable wood in both countries, but the antique ornament—terms, lions' heads, caryatids, dolphins, masks, pilasters, and acanthus, to mention but several—all derive from a common vocabulary. However, although the furniture is now in the new style, the nomadic ways of the great nobles continued in a certain measure much longer than might be imagined. Scarcity of furniture, especially elaborately carved furniture, even in the richest châteaux, and the abundance and richness of woven stuffs which were easily transportable were marked features of this era. Rich and colorful fabrics were thrown over seats, chests, and tables, while the *carreaux*, or flat squab cushions, were perhaps the most frequently used of all seats. Provided with a big tassel by which they could be carried, they were placed on seats, chests, or simply on the floor.

This lack of native luxury furniture is owing, in no small part, to the religious wars between the Catholics and the Huguenots, which prostrated the country from 1562 to 1598 and were detrimental to the cultivation of native craftsmanship. Then, too, the framework of a certain amount of furniture, especially seats, chests, and beds, was covered entirely with fabric. This fashion for upholstered furniture became more pronounced in the succeeding Louis XIII style, when the testered bed, whether it was heavily draped in modest red serge or in sumptuous silks and velvets, edged with braid and fringe, showed not one square inch of wood from its feet to its vase-shaped finials. Perhaps this explains why so little of the furniture used by the well-to-do classes during the reign of Louis XIII remains, since its most important element was of an impermanent character, and when the fabric was worn out, the wood frame was irretrievably lost. French and Flemish pattern books issued in the second half of the sixteenth century illustrate the typical bed of this period. The tester is no longer hung from the ceiling, as in Gothic times, but is carried by four pillars which are replaced at times by terminal figures.

As a rule, the Henri II style furniture is classified in either one of two principal schools, defined by vague geographical boundaries. One great region includes the country of the Loire and Île-de-France, the other Burgundy and its surrounding districts. The furniture of Île-de-France is one of refinement and restraint. The sense of proportion is often most pleasing and the carving, which is usually in very low relief, contained within firm enframing lines, is remarkable for its exquisite delicacy and graceful rhythm. No piece of furniture exemplifies more aptly the style of Île-de-France than the important and fashionable double-bodied walnut cupboard, or *armoire à deux corps,* with the upper part a little less wide and a little less deep than the lower part and with its crowning pediment, triangular or sometimes arched and frequently broken. Decorating the two doors in each section are panels carved in low relief with long fluid nude figures of classical deities mirroring in their subtle refinement the graceful elegance of the stone sculptures by Jean Goujon. Sometimes the *armoire à deux corps* is further enhanced with finely veined plaques

82

ABOVE LEFT: Oak *chaise à bras* (c. 1540–50). The back is carved with a medallion; the front legs are columnar. *Courtesy Musée des Arts Décoratifs, Paris. Photo Mella.* ABOVE RIGHT: *Chaise à bras* of the *caquetoire* type (c. 1575). *Courtesy Kunstindustrimuseet, Oslo.* LEFT: *Chaise à vertugadin* (last quarter of the sixteenth century). *Courtesy Metropolitan Museum of Art. Rogers Fund, 1924.* (See page 81.)

83

Probably *Diane de Poitiers*, attributed to François Clouet (Fontainebleau School, sixteenth century). Toilet mirrors of metal and encrusted with pearls and precious stones, frequently mentioned in Royal inventories, were no doubt similar to the one in this painting. *Courtesy Worcester Art Museum.* OPPOSITE: *The Death of Henri II* (1519–59), woodcut by Jacques Perrisin. A glimpse of the royal bedroom: the curtains have been looped up around the terminal figures supporting the tester; the table is covered with the usual carpet or cloth. *Courtesy Philadelphia Museum of Art.* (*See page 82.*)

of marble inlaid in places most wisely chosen. This *armoire*, the entire shape of which is quite architectural, reflects the influence of Pierre Lescot, Jean Bullant, and Philibert Delorme and embodies the highest qualities of French Renaissance craftsmanship. Also displaying finished workmanship is the walnut *dressoir*, a descendant of the Gothic *dressoir*, characterized by a rectangular horizontal body fitted with hinged doors and resting on an open lower portion.

In Burgundy, a diverse political and geographical area at different periods in its history, there are so many masterpieces of vigorous and exuberant stone sculptures that the carving on furniture, its artistic adjunct, also developed exuberantly. Architectural details almost smothered under its abundance, with its pronounced carved reliefs overflowing the structural forms. It was Burgundy that witnessed the conquest, as supports of fantastic terminal figures twined with a profusion of garlands and incredible monsters, such as griffins, with the wildest physiognomies. Not a square inch of the surface remained free from the carver's chisel; neither a molding nor a turned member was left undecorated. This type of carving cannot be praised for its purity of taste, but its bold delineations express a dramatic vigor that silences any reproach. The forceful energy animating the figures makes them full of life and feeling, and the eye is charmed by

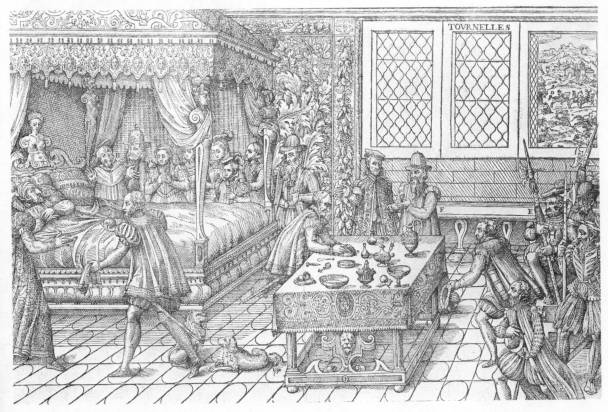

85

their free and unbridled spirits. This ornamental style, in which fanciful compositions of muscular caryatids, lions' heads, swags of fruit and flowers, and grotesque masks play a dominant role, is in the manner of the architect-craftsman of Dijon, Hugues Sambin, d. 1602, whose own designs for furniture were influenced not only by the pattern books of De Vries and Dietterlein emanating from Flanders and Germany but also by the engravings of Du Cerceau. Sambin founded a distinctive school of furniture-making in Burgundy, and, as in the Île-de-France school, his style of work is seen most advantageously in the *armoire à deux corps,* the *dressoir,* and the chest, or *coffre.* In the last quarter of the century, owing to the wide dissemination of pattern books, the best known of which is that of Du Cerceau, the style of French furniture became more unified. Although the art of the Renaissance was to continue a precarious existence through the reign of Louis XIII, 1610–43, it was incontestably impoverished by the end of the sixteenth century.

LOUIS XIII STYLE

The establishment of the Bourbon dynasty in the person of Henri IV, 1589–1610, was an important turning point in France's cultural development, for the Bourbon monarchs regarded art as one of the essential factors contributing to the dignity and prestige of the state. They wished to express through art their personal glorification, and with this in mind they developed a well-conceived plan to organize all branches of art under the control of the central government. This ascendancy of France in the arts, which reached its fulfillment under Louis XIV, had its inception during the reign of Henri IV, who, in 1608, began the practice of providing free workshops and apartments in certain parts of the Louvre for painters, sculptors, goldsmiths, cabinetmakers, engravers, and a host of other craftsmen. Although these artists did not work directly for the Crown, it was a singular mark of royal favor to acquire lodgings in these galleries, and it

OPPOSITE ABOVE LEFT: Île-de-France walnut *armoire à deux corps* (second half of the sixteenth century). It is inlaid with plaques of veined marble. The triangular broken pediment is decorated with a standing female figure. The doors are carved in low relief with oval panels enclosing figure subjects, suggesting the influence of the school of Jean Goujon. *Courtesy Musée des Arts Décoratifs, Paris. Photo Mella.* (See page 82.) ABOVE RIGHT: Walnut armorial *dressoir* bearing the arms of Guyrod d'Annecy (second half of the sixteenth century). It is carved in the style of Hugues Sambin. *Courtesy Victoria and Albert Museum. Photo Librairie Larousse.* BELOW LEFT: Door panel (School of Burgundy, second half of the sixteenth century). The bold yet restrained carving is an excellent example of French craftsmen using the typical ornamental style of Northern Renaissance. *Courtesy Metropolitan Museum of Art. Rogers Fund, 1905.* BELOW RIGHT: Walnut chest (second half of the sixteenth century). The carved strapwork, grotesque masks, and swags of fruit and flowers, showing the influence of Hugues Sambin, are characteristic of the Northern Renaissance style found repeatedly in the later books of De Vries and Dietterlein. *Courtesy Victoria and Albert Museum.*

also gave the workers certain important privileges of freedom from the trade guilds.

The Louis XIII style of 1589–1643 corresponds roughly to the first half of the seventeenth century, spanning that time during which the essence of the Louis XIV style was being developed. Because it is full of contradictions and comprises many incongruous elements, the art of this epoch, with certain exceptions, does not possess a really national character. Spanish, Flemish, and Italian influences were all at work to produce a curious intermingling and exchange of ideas. Gradually the French artist discarded, assimilated, or modified that which he had borrowed. The final result is the emergence of the sumptuous and resplendent baroque Louis XIV style, triumphant in scale and remarkable for the skillfull originality of its planning, which reached its culmination around 1700.

Because of the prevailing foreign influence—Italian, Spanish, and Flemish—French furniture for the first half of the seventeenth century possessed a cosmopolitan character. Like all the French arts of decoration in this period, the furniture is much more Flemish than Italian until about 1645, when the ratio between Italian and Flemish influence was gradually reversed. However, Flemish art had been strongly influenced by Italian art through the work of Rubens, so indirectly Italian influence was a factor throughout the Louis XIII style. Some of the French furniture also displayed evidence of the Henri II style, showing the influence of Du Cerceau, but the articles are encumbered with meaningless details and the carved ornament is in a commonplace fashion, displaying neither invention nor character, the craftsmen confining themselves to copying Renaissance motifs that had become mere stock pieces.

Louis XIII style furniture, essentially rectilinear in form, is rather simple and severe, as may be seen in the typical Louis XIII chair of "square" pattern, with an upholstered seat and back panel secured to the frame with decorative gilt or silvered nails, which the French engraver Abraham Bosse, 1602–72, so often represented in his charming engravings of domestic French interiors. The low backs are either square or of greater width than height. The legs of this low-back chair, which is stiff and

OPPOSITE ABOVE: *Winter,* from *The Four Seasons* (engraving by Abraham Bosse, c. 1630), showing chairs of square plan and a stool with columnar supports. The tester bed is an integral part of the furnishings of the room. *Courtesy Cooper Union Museum.* BELOW: *Sight,* from *The Five Senses* (engraving by Abraham Bosse, c. 1630). The young lady contemplates herself in an adjustable mirror supported by a hinged strut, a relatively new creation. The draped toilet table is provided with an extra cloth that was easily changed. Chairs of square plan and a tester bed surmounted with vases of feathers at each corner are part of the furnishings. *Courtesy Metropolitan Museum of Art. Dick Fund, 1926.* (See page 90.)

Jcy viennent à la haste   La Cuisine les attire,   Monsieur, dict vne Maistresse,   Mais cette picotterie
Les Enfans de Mardy gras   Soit par coustume, ou par ieu,   Si vous touchez mon tein,   Se termine incontinent,
Mettre la main à la paste.   Et les bignets les font rire,   Ie repandray de la graisse   Et toute leur raillerie
S'éscrimant à tour de bras.   Tandis qu'ils sont pres du feu. Sur vostre habit de Satin.   Est de Caresme-prenant.

L'HYVER

Quod mens est animo quod Sol clarissimus orbe,   Il n'est rien de pareil sur la terre ou sur l'onde
Est mea cerui ei cara pupilla tua,   Aux charmes que la Veue a dans sa famille,
Qui rapit humana similicem cernere menti   Puis que c'est par les yeux qu'on voit tout le beauté,
Veriatum, oculi me belvamque ducem   Et que l'Astre du iour est iesu de tout le monde

VISVS.
LA VEVE.

square at all points, are sometimes columnar in form, standing on a box frame resting on small bun feet. Occasionally the entire framework is upholstered or covered in fabric. The great majority of extant examples have, however, knobbed, baluster, or spirally turned legs joined with an *H*-form stretcher, with an extra stretcher joining the front legs above, which both strengthens and decorates at the same time. Chairs with spirally turned members enjoyed a great vogue and are typical of the era. The arms of the armchair rest upon armposts that are a continuation of the front legs. They commonly terminate in a plain turned button, occasionally a female bust serves as the upper part of the armpost, and the end of the arm is joined into the back of the head. This class of chair, when characterized by a high upholstered back that generally extends to the seat, dates from the following Louis XIV period.

Foreign luxury furniture, such as Italian *pietra dura* cabinets and Florentine *pietra commessa* or stone mosaic tables, is a feature of this period. Of interest are the fashionable ebony cabinets distinguished by their simple, square, and massive structure, necessitated by the contemporary technique of handling ebony, which is halfway between solid wood and veneering. Sheets of ebony of sufficient thickness—about one third of an inch—to permit carving in shallow bas-relief are glued to the carcase and are contained within framed geometric compartments. Incised foliage and

Walnut armchair of square plan, spirally turned (first quarter of the seventeenth century). The back is shorter than its width. *Courtesy Musée des Arts Décoratifs, Paris. Photo Mella.* OPPOSITE: Ebony cabinet carved in very shallow bas-relief (c. 1650). The heavy exuberance of the carvings is in the Flemish manner. The interior is provided with cabinet drawers. *Courtesy Palais de Fontainebleau. Photo Caisse Nationale-Mella.*

floral scrolls were often engraved on the surface not enriched with the very flat carvings, which chiefly depicted religious or mythological themes. The heavy exuberance of the decoration proclaimed it to be of Flemish origin, or at least a slavish reproduction made in France. Other cabinets richly inlaid with ivory or bone were of German provenance, but they were also made in Antwerp, France, and Spain. From Holland and Flanders, tables, cupboards, and writing cabinets were exported, richly decorated with floral polychrome marquetry. There were also ebony cabinets and bureaux displaying a marquetry of tortoise shell and brass. Their artistic use is inseparably associated with the name of André Charles Boulle, although the method was not invented by him. In brief, during the seventeenth century princely cabinets were either two doors or a drop-front panel, serving as a writing board, fitted with an interior of small doors and drawers, frequently displaying a tabernacle in the center, were the final word in elegant furniture. It was through assimilation of the forms and technique

of this furniture by French craftsmen that the characteristic luxury furniture of the Louis XIV period was gradually developed.

Unhappily these luxury pieces display nothing or hardly anything that is French. At this time, French tradition is best expressed in less costly pieces having turned members. The use of turning, especially spiral turning, is the most constant and best-known characteristic of the Louis XIII style. Never was this method more widely employed, nor was the best work of this period ever surpassed. Not only popular subjects for the turner's lathe were the entire framework of chairs, the legs and stretchers of tables and their decorative finials, such as vases or *toupies* on the cross-piece of an *H*-form stretcher or the intersection of an *X*-form stretcher, but also the ornamental columns flanking and dividing the doors in the tall single or double-bodied cupboard, which in the seventeenth century had become the most important piece of middle-class furniture, with the two-part variety often also serving as a buffet. Favorite forms of turning are knobbed or *en chapelet*, the most rudimentary; baluster or *en balustre*, the most artistic; and spiral or *piliers tors*, the most frequent. Occasionally in spiral turning a narrow fillet or band was arranged in the bottom of the groove, so that the deeper depressions were not too dark. Although spiral turning almost always turned from left to right, sometimes it was done in opposite directions, when it was employed for symmetrical perfection on pieces of the finest workmanship.

Moldings, which have a kinship with turnery, were also a marked feature of Louis XIII-style cabinetwork. Some of the most handsome seventeenth-century pieces of furniture have moldings as their sole decoration. No piece illustrates more effectively the use of moldings for decoration than the tall single or double-bodied cupboard distinguished by its heavily molded projecting horizontal cornice, matched below with a conforming base that projects almost as strongly. Other moldings mark the general divisions of the entire piece and the subdivisions of its parts and in large quantities strongly enframe the doors. The division of the long doors into molded panels was by no means a decorative conceit, but a necessity if the heavy doors were to be practical and retain their shape. The enhancing of the surface within the enframing—the best of which was precise, geometrical, and severe—was accomplished in a number of ways, such as with bevels and moldings or by subdividing the surface into a geometrical outline, such as a cross or lozenge. By far the favorite and choice is the faceted ornament, the whole being cut into a slab of thick wood. In this method, suppose a lozenge is cut into the solid wood, accompanied by four small triangles; as the bevels are increased indefinitely, the projecting table ground proportionately disappears until it is finally reduced to a point. In its simplest form, this faceted ornament, properly called a diamond point, comprises a lozenge pyramid flanked by four small triangular

Walnut *armoire à deux corps* with spirally turned pillars and diamond-point ornament on the doors. *Courtesy Musée de Cluny.* BELOW: Walnut drawtop table (sixteenth century). The columnar legs are carried on a molded stretcher supported by flattened ball feet. When the two leaves are extended, an arrangement of slanting grooves slides them up to the level of the fixed top. The finest extension tables of the period were of this kind. *Courtesy Parke-Bernet, from the collection of Brummer.* (*See page 94.*)

pyramids. Serving as a starting point, this faceted diamond motif became diverse and complicated. One of the most common and pleasing is a kind of star, called *pointes de gâteau,* on a square panel comprising eight elongated pyramids, the four center ones being triangular and the four corner ones being quadrangular, with their sharp apexes converging toward the center, marked by a boss. Diamond-point ornament was worked with conspicuous success in Gascony and Guienne, where it was noted for its purity and firmness and where it remained in fashion indefinitely for the decoration of cupboards crowned with their horizontal, overflowing molded cornices.

When the medieval table made of boards laid on trestles went out of fashion, but not out of use, around the middle of the sixteenth century, tables became noticeably Italian in aspect. Typical was the massive refectory table with an oblong top and elaborate trestle-end supports, the table having a round, square, or octagonal top mounted on a heavy central support. To be able to increase or diminish the size of the table at pleasure, there were tables with draw tops and folding tops, the latter foreshadowing the seventeenth-century tables of gate-leg construction. Apart from the more ambitious tables were the simpler ones, almost always with rectangular tops set on four legs in the shape of plain turned columns joined together at the bottom by a stout rectangular frame. In the seventeenth century this typical table became the proper sphere of the turner; legs turned as plain pillars, knobbed, spiral, or baluster-shaped, reveal all the resources of the turner's art. For these tables the *H*-shaped stretcher is most frequent.

Lighter, more graceful, as well as later and almost always belonging to the Louis XIV period, are tables with *X*-shaped stretchers. The ends of these stretchers are not mortised into the legs, but are supported by four flattened ball feet, which in their turn support the legs. Occasionally a fifth foot is placed at the intersection, which prevents the stretcher from sagging and protects it from all kinds of hazards. (This type of curving *X*-shaped stretcher cut from a plank of wood is familiar to all of us, as seen in the English Late Jacobean tables, especially when the legs are in the form of S-scrolls.) Affiliated with the category of tables is the Louis XIII bureau, deriving its name from a kind of fabric, *bure.* First the bureau was the table cover made of *bure,* next a table covered with such a cloth, and finally a table made to write at conveniently. One type of bureau of table form displayed a recessed superstructure of numerous small drawers, a cabinet; the front part of the table served as a writing surface. Another type, without any superstructure, is of kneehole form, which was destined in the next two centuries to acquire a number of different names —the bureau *semainier,* bureau *à caissons lateraux,* and bureau *ministre.*

Louis XIV

The sumptuous, baroque Louis XIV style with its solemn and heroic classicism was the style of the king—a king who knew wonderfully well how to make his palace at Versailles a painted Olympus, a veritable theater in which he could play the part of god rather than king. Under gifted French artists, baroque art was skillfully planned; they imbued it with an air of triumphant and stately elegance, of lofty and majestic grandeur. Three phases or periods can be distinguished in the Louis XIV style. Indeed, the style is so closely related to the monarch that it was inevitable that there should be three phases of development in the arts in general, just as there were three phases in the life of the monarch. The early phase under Cardinal Mazarin, 1642–61, was dominated by Italian influence. In the second phase, when Louis XIV, though only twenty-two years old at Mazarin's death, began his personal rule, the arts were under the aegis of Charles Le Brun, 1619–90, *premier peintre du roi*. The foreign elements were eliminated, modified, or assimilated; the style was unified, reaching its resplendent maturity around 1685–90. These were the triumphal years of Louis XIV's life, when he believed himself to be a god upon earth. In the final phase, after 1690, come decline and decay for the aging king. The Louis XIV style rapidly crumbled away in the closing years of the century as a new style, seen in the work of such ornamentists as Jean Bérain, under the influence of the nascent rococo, began to evolve considerably before the death of the grand monarch in 1715.

In the decorative arts, the preceding period of Louis XIII witnessed the introduction into France of foreign luxury furniture, resulting in a more elegant mode of living and the retreat of French taste before this onslaught of foreign influence from the Low Countries, Germany, and Spain. This was followed by an invasion of Italian taste, due to a considerable extent to the Italian-born Cardinal Mazarin, who surrounded himself with luxury to a degree unprecedented in France. An inventory of his collection, drawn up in 1653, exemplifies his incredible accumulation of luxury objects. Apart from his furniture acquired abroad, Mazarin brought foreign craftsmen to Paris, whom he lodged in the Louvre. Such were the distinguished Dutch cabinetmaker, Pierre Golle, d. 1684; the Italians Domenico Cucci, d. c. 1705, Philippe Caffiéri, 1634–1716, the latter being the first of that celebrated family of bronze workers; and the mosaicists Megliorini, Branchi, and Grachetti. Soon they were joined by French craftsmen, including Jean Macé of Blois, who after studying in the Low Countries worked for the Crown from 1641 until his death in 1672. He was the most celebrated among the creators of the French school of marquetry, in which André Charles Boulle was to achieve enduring fame. Craftsmen such as these formed the nucleus around which the Gobelins manufactory, purchased by Colbert in 1662 for the Crown, was definitely organized in 1667 under the title of *Manufacture Royale des Meubles de la Couronne,* and where most of the magnificent furniture and furnishings were made that decorated the grandiose interiors of the royal houses— Versailles, Trianon, Marly, Saint-Cloud, and others.

The work of André Charles Boulle, 1642–1732, opens with a blaze of glory the period of marquetry in French furniture, where the technique was to reign triumphant and supreme until the end of the Ancien Régime. Boulle's great work, which reflects the mature taste of Louis XIV, adopted the ideal and style of Le Brun—a style of stately and ponderous solemnity saturated with reminiscences of classical Rome. His furniture, severe in its black, reddish-brown, and golden harmony, possessed the monumental and noble qualities that made it worthy to play a leading role in Le Brun's conception of grandeur.

Only in Boulle's later work, with its swelling forms presaging the style of the Régence, does this quality of sober splendor occasionally desert him. Cabinets, *armoires,* bureaux *plats, coffres de mariage* mounted on stands, and from which the *serre-bijoux* with a drop-front panel was derived, commodes, pendulum clocks, pedestals, and mirrors were favorite subjects for Boulle marquetry—as it were, *créations d'apparat.* His art was continued by his four sons until 1754, when death brought to an end the work of this distinguished family of *marqueteurs.* From around 1775 onward the taste for Boulle work flourished with considerable vitality. Such well-known *ébénistes* as Levasseur, Delorme and Montigny provided fine reproductions. An observation made around 1780 that "fashion had not exercised its caprice on his works" was still valued almost a century later since the vogue for Boulle work continued through a greater part of the nineteenth century resulting in both good and bad imitations.

Boulle work has always been and is still regarded as the supreme expression of the Louis XIV style. Sometimes during the early part of his career he used exotic woods for his marquetry, a technique originating in

Armoire veneered with ebony and a marquetry of various colored woods, chased and gilt bronze mounts (from the atelier of André Charles Boulle, seventeenth century). The two doors are veneered with a vase of flowers realistically treated in the style of the painter Jean Baptiste Monnoyer, the pre-eminent *fleuriste* of the seventeenth century. *Courtesy Musée du Louvre. Photo Giraudon-Mella.*

Marriage coffer (probably from the atelier of André Charles Boulle about the end of the seventeenth century). One of a pair, it is veneered with ebony and a marquetry of engraved brass on a tortoise-shell ground worked in a design of scrolling foliage; it has chased and gilt bronze mounts. The stand, which is similarly veneered, centers a bronze mask in the frieze drawer; an *X*-form stretcher is inserted between the legs, which are in the form of two superimposed C-scrolls, and the bun feet. OPPOSITE: *Armoire* (attributed to André Charles Boulle, seventeenth century). One of a pair, it is veneered with ebony and marquetry; part of the design is in engraved brass on a tortoise-shell ground, and part is in the reverse combination; it has chased and gilt bronze mounts. Each door is decorated with a classical subject: on the left, Apollo and Daphne, on the right, the Flaying of Marsyas. *Armoires* of this type are portable; this example is dismountable in nine sections. *Courtesy Wallace Collection, London.*

Italy. However, in his most characteristic work the surfaces are decorated only with tortoise shell, metal, and ebony—a style of marquetry bearing his name. In this work a sheet of brass and a sheet of tortoise shell were lightly glued together with a sheet of paper on which were traced symmetrical compositions of sinuous and stylized foliage. These designs were cut out with a saw and, when unfastened, produced a ground in duplicate, both of tortoise shell and brass, and also the ornament in duplicate. The tortoise-shell ground and brass ornament, which is described as *de première partie*, or of the first part, as distinct from *de contre-partie*, or of the counter part or reverse combination, was considered to be the more ar-

tistic and thus more desired. Boulle also developed the skill of combining both kinds of marquetry on a matched pair of *armoires* or the like with superb success.

Boulle harmoniously combined this marquetry with chased and gilded bronze mounts, which emphasized the essential architectural structure of the severe, rectilinear forms and contributed to the solidity by serving either as a reinforcement or a protection. Gilded bronze figures of gods and goddesses in low relief were favored for the earlier panels, while elsewhere in high or completely round relief were caryatids, grimacing fauns, and masks. Because mythological allegory was one of the most deep-

rooted habits of mind among men of the seventeenth century, Louis XIV, who had chosen the sun as his emblem, may often be seen in the guise of Apollo, with Marie Thérèse as Diana. The admirable unity existing between the bronze mounts and the marquetry, which has never been surpassed, was undoubtedly due to the fact that Boulle was a draftsman and sculptor as well as an *ébéniste*. At the end of the seventeenth and early eighteenth century the compositions of Boulle marquetry were often in the style of Jean Bérain, 1637–1711, who, together with Pierre Lepautre, c. 1648–1716, infused a new vivacity into their decorative designs, which "released" French art from Le Brun's solemn classicism and put it on the way to the Régence. Typically Bérain are his gossamer and playful grotesques, impregnated with fantasy, in which he introduced the simian tribe and their frolics (*singeries*) and perched his figures on airy pedestals under a web of lambrequin, the arrangement resembling the stage of a theater with the figures in the foreground.

Like Boulle marquetry, other practices employed in furniture making—gilding, marquetry of various colored woods (*en bois de rapport*), veneering, and upholstery—which until about 1650 were relatively rare, became quite usual in the second half of the seventeenth century. In a period

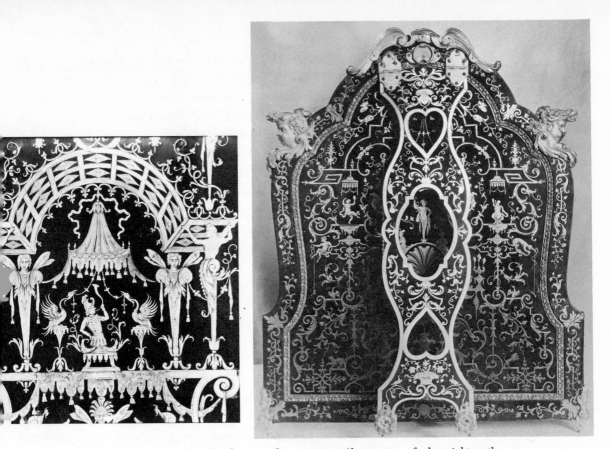

OPPOSITE: Low cabinet veneered with ebony and marquetry (beginning of the eighteenth century). The two doors decorated with Bérainesque grotesques of engraved brass on a tortoise-shell ground probably come from the workshop of Boulle; the frame of elbow height appears to be later. In the center of each door is a fanciful arch supported by caryatid terminal figures; monkeys, squirrels, dogs, masks, and scrolls are introduced into the rest of the composition. ABOVE LEFT: Detail of cabinet door opposite. ABOVE RIGHT: Back of a toilet mirror veneered with ebony and marquetry of engraved brass on a tortoise-shell ground, in the style of Bérain (attributed to André Charles Boulle, early eighteenth century). It is mounted on chased and gilt bronze. In the center is a terminal figure of Love beneath a canopy (partly obscured by the hinged strut that supports the mirror). Monkeys, birds, animals, and figures of dancing girls are intermingled among the foliage scrolls of this fanciful grotesque. *Courtesy Wallace Collection, London.*

that preferred richness, real or apparent, above everything else, it is only to be expected that carved and gilt wood furniture should play an important role in court furnishings. Of course Louis XIV would have preferred to have his furniture made of solid gold; but failing that, he accepted the next best: furniture made of silver, which after his vainglorious wars was melted down in an attempt to avert national bankruptcy. The *Mercure Galant* in December 1682 gives a full account of the furnishings at Versailles, where the court had been installed earlier that year, and it is no surprise to read that a great deal of the furniture in the state rooms is of silver. The best artists and craftsmen worked for the king, who continually needed new furniture for his royal houses of the Louvre, Saint-Germain, and Fontainebleau; they also worked for the royal princes and the ministers of state. This engaged all, or nearly all, of their time. Other

101

families of wealth, the great nobles, imitated the court according to their finances; their furniture was in the same style, but the craftsmen were not the greatest and the materials were less precious. The well-to-do bourgeoisie continued to use plain undisguised Louis XIII furniture.

Louis XIV and his court delighted in everything that came from China. All the gorgeous stuffs that China wove, embroidered, and painted were used in the upholstery work of court furniture. Because of the prevailing fashion for oriental lacquer wares, such as cabinets and screens, workshops were allocated in the Gobelins to improve this medium of decoration, which in the ensuing century achieved a remarkable standard of excellence, especially in the exquisitely executed *Vernis Martin* work. There was a veritable craze for pagodas, or *magots* as they were later called, those little Chinese figures which were made of every kind of material and chosen for their exoticism—Pu-Tai Ho-Shang, laughing and obese, with an unclothed belly, reclining against bags of money, Buddha meditating on a lotus blossom, and Shou Lao, an old man with a large protuberance on his bald head, sometimes sitting on a buffalo—to mention but several out of an almost countless number. The taste for oriental porcelain, which led to its subsequent imitation in Europe, was carried to the extreme, as may be seen in the designs of Daniel Marot, who illustrated not only lavish designs of tiered shelves arranged in pyramid fashion above the doors and chimney pieces for the reception of porcelain but also brackets, particularly small ones arranged in rows to hold cups and saucers. The ultimate, however, are the porcelain cabinets or small rooms especially designed for the reception of porcelain. This invasion of oriental art offered a surprising contrast to the Olympian splendor pervading the great parade rooms, with their ceilings filled with Apollos and Hercules and the walls resplendent in marble and gold. As a result of this genuine enthusiasm for Chinese art, a great interest in everything pertaining to the Orient developed, to which can be partially attributed that remarkable phenomenon of European *chinoiseries,* which were found mingled in rich baroque compositions late in the seventeenth century in the work of such ornamentists as Marot and Bérain.

The spirit of the French baroque, with its boastful and triumphant air, was captured with remarkable success in the Louis XIV furniture blazing with magnificence. Perhaps the most striking as well as most usual feature of this epoch is greatness. Everyone was enamored with greatness and everywhere its presence was felt, from the *grands appartements* at Versailles to the towering headdresses—the lofty feminine creations of lace and ribbon known as *fontanges* and the huge *perruques* with curls arranged in stages worn by the men. No piece of furniture embodies the characteristics of the style and of the period itself more than the stately upholstered armchair with its air of imposing strength and immobility.

Deſſein du Cabinet de Porcelaine à Charlottenbourg du côté de l'entrée vis a vis les trois Fenestres qui donnent sur le petit jardin d'orangers.

ABOVE: Porcelain room at Charlottenburg, royal palace just outside of Berlin (early eighteenth century). The room was designed by the Swede Eosander van Goethe to house the Chinese porcelain collection of Prince Frederick III of Brandenburg (1701–6). The room has survived intact, at least until 1937. *Courtesy Metropolitan Museum of Art. Gift of Harry Friedman, 1956.* LEFT: Armchair of carved and gilt wood (c. 1680–95). The arms have a free sweeping curve and at the extremities expand into a wide volute. It has an *H*-form stretcher composed of six S-scrolls, and flattened ball feet. *Courtesy Metropolitan Museum of Art. Fletcher Fund, 1929.*

103

Contributing to its greatness is the raked, rectangular upholstered back showing no wood and of excessive height to frame the lofty headdresses, the seat almost big enough for two, the great wooden down-curving arms invariably terminating into a wide volute and the legs solidly joined with a heavy *H*- or *X*-form stretcher. The legs are tapering baluster-shaped, sometimes pedestal-shaped, and very often scroll-shaped.

Stretchers, an absolute necessity because the chairs are so heavy, are inserted between the base of the leg and the foot, which is very often in the form of a flattened ball. In some instances, however, when the legs are scroll-shaped the tip of the leg rests directly on the ground instead of on the stretcher. Elaborately scrolled stretchers are a distinguishing feature. The *X*-shaped stretcher, which is more elegant than the stretcher of *H*-form and can be of immense importance decoratively, enjoyed a great vogue. Because scrolls are in high favor and are found almost everywhere, either as a support or motif, the supports for the arms are preferably scroll shape, that is, curved to console shape. Besides the richly carved and molded gilt wood chairs, other chairs, generally of walnut, are often enriched solely with carefully designed moldings, which like all Louis XIV moldings are strongly emphatic, perhaps at times heavy but never flabby.

For those of moderate means, simpler armchairs were made, copying the general lines of the Louis XIV chair just described, but they are without carvings or moldings and have all their members simply rounded. Because the shape of the end of their arms, which approximates a copy of a volute, resembles a crow's beak, they are known in certain parts of France as a *chaise à bec de corbin.* Around the end of the seventeenth century the cabriole leg, terminating in a *pied de bêche* (cloven-hoof foot), was introduced in fashionable chair design and was to dominate French furniture design for more than sixty years, when it yielded to the rectilinear neo-classic vogue.

Upholstered-seat furniture—"confessional" *bergères* winged chairs with solid sides, *canapés,* or sofas which at this time are also generally winged, *banquettes* (benches) useful to seat a number of persons in a small space, *placets,* or *tabourets* (stools)—had the same legs, same stretchers as the Louis XIV armchair. An important creation of the upholsterers under Louis XIV was the *canapé,* whose "parent," the *lit de repos,* or rest bed, made its debut about 1625. Shortly after the introduction of the *canapé,* armchairs were made to match, comprising the classical suite of seat furniture that has become permanently associated with the idea of a drawing-room. There was also the *chauffeuse,* a small upholstered chair with short legs, a very high narrow back, and no arms, easy to move about, to bring close to the hearth, and with a seat low enough to enjoy its warmth, enabling the occupant to "gossip" at ease by the fireside. Much in evidence were *car-*

RIGHT: Carved walnut armchair (late seventeenth century). It has scroll-shaped legs and a curving X-form stretcher. *Courtesy Metropolitan Museum of Art. Bequest of Benjamin Altman, 1913.* BELOW: Walnut armchair (c. 1700). Carved and gilded, its cabriole legs are set obliquely and end in cloven-hoof feet. *Courtesy Metropolitan Museum of Art. Gift of J. Pierpont Morgan, 1907.* BELOW RIGHT: *Basket of Flowers* by Jean Baptiste Monnoyer, the leading *fleuriste* of the seventeenth century. His great bouquets of flowers were a principal source of inspiration for needlework on canvas used in upholstery. *Courtesy Philadelphia Museum of Art.*

ABOVE: *Le Bénédicité* after Jean Baptiste Siméon Chardin, engraving by Lépicie (1744). *Courtesy Philadelphia Museum of Art.* RIGHT: Turned *chaise à capucine* painted green (c. 1710). Each slat is composed of two S-scrolls of simplified form set end to end. Toward the end of the reign of Louis XIV little chairs without arms and with straw seats had become everybody's chairs because of their convenience. *Courtesy Mrs. James B. Mabon. Photo Taylor and Dull.*

106

reaux (more or less flat cushions); placed on the floor they served as seats "in the Spanish manner." Caned chairs, generally provided with cushions tied to the chair with cords, were first made in France late in the seventeenth century.

At this time, when there was no dining-room, *ployants*, or *pliants* (folding stools) and *perroquets* (folding chairs) were most useful, since they were easy to bring to the table and put away after the meal was finished. It appears that they were also used in carriages when additional seats were needed. Finally we come to the *chaise à capucine*, a charming small chair with turned members and a straw seat. Their marked simplicity did not prevent them from winning a place in the richest houses, even at court where cushions of silk were tied to the straw seat. Even a cursory examination of eighteenth-century French paintings will reveal that they became everybody's seat, rich or poor. We find them in the genre pictures of popular interiors painted by Greuze, Jeaurat, and Chardin. No doubt when our thoughts turn to straw chairs we see the little girl seated on one in the celebrated *Bénédicité*, a domestic scene which Chardin translated into poetry.

Equally characteristic of the Louis XIV period are the monumental beds having four tall posts (*lit à colonnes*), their wood frames covered with fabric and their several sets of hangings that served as a guarantee against drafts. Since beds were regarded as perhaps the most convincing of all signs of wealth, the selection of stuffs bordered on extravagance for all classes, from princely beds hung with silk brocades and velvets to the simplest beds draped with wool serge—red, green, or rose—belonging to people of modest estate. The last word in overwhelming magnificence was the *lit de parade*, or state bed adorned with fringes, cords, braids, tassels and above all the four *bouquets de plumes* composed of different-colored feathers, as many as 100 ostrich feathers arranged around aigrettes of heron feathers, which surmounted the tester. Occasionally flowers of gold or silver were substituted for feathers in these bouquets.

It should be mentioned here that beds of such splendor were never intended for daily use, but were the decoration of the *chambre de parade*, as it was called, the reception room in which all the luxury of the house was concentrated, the room for receiving distinguished visitors and for the social side of family life. The *lit de parade* goes back to medieval times when the great chamber was provided with the most magnificent bed and was used as a private supper room by the lord and lady of the house, as well as an audience or reception chamber. The custom of having a state bedroom was so firmly entrenched that even in the engravings of Abraham Bosse representing French life in the reign of Louis XIII, as we have seen in the preceding chapter, the fashionable apartments in which suppers and

Face de L'Alcove pour la Chambre a coucher de S. A. R.

other social events are held invariably contain a bed. In houses of wealth the *chambre de parade* was never used as a sleeping chamber except by visitors of distinction, but in houses of modest means the lady slept in the room, which served as her boudoir and drawing-room.

Returning to the panaches of feathers, the fashion for which dates back to the sixteenth century, Evelyn comments on this taste during his sojourn in Paris in 1652. He writes that in the palace of the Duchess of Chaulmes "the pennaches or tufts of plumes belonging to one of her beds only are estimated worth fourteen thousand livres, which amount to near a thousand pounds sterling in our money." Late in the seventeenth century, beds were provided with a breadth of stuff attached to the tester and hanging flat against the wall. In front of this fabric was a headboard (*dossier*) either covered in fabric or finished in carved and gilt wood, distinguished by a profile cut in pronounced baroque scrolls, from which it received its name, *chantourné*, and the bed, *chantourné de lit*. Marot gave several designs for *chantournés*, over which, like all Louis XIV art, the spirit of symmetry presided. About the same time cleverly draped hangings, cunningly disarrayed with much assistance from cords and tassels, came into vogue and were aptly referred to in contemporary writings as "hyperboles in velvet."

Carved and gilt wood console and side tables with marble tops became the pieces under the Bourbon monarchs in which decorative richness displayed itself with the greatest abundance and at times even extravagant excess. These tables permanently placed against the wall were an integral part of the decoration of a room and were adopted by their forms and proportions to a special place. The richly carved gilt wood console table served as a *cul-de-lampe* or pendant to the *trumeau*, perhaps three times its height, beneath which it was placed, and its decoration made a unit with that above the mirror. The frieze of the table displays a fancifully shaped pierced and carved apron. When the molded legs are not in the form of a scroll or double scroll, they are pedestal or baluster-shaped. Of the approximately fifteen kinds of balusters used by architects, the cabinetmakers chose those of tapering form, such as urn or vase balusters, square or circular. Stretchers were made of S-scrolls arranged in different combinations; those of X-form composed of four raised scrolls meeting in a central block were very fashionable. Unfortunately their lines were too

OPPOSITE ABOVE: *Louis XIV bestowing the Cordon Bleu on the Duc de Bourgogne,* after Antoine Watteau, engraving by Nicolas de Larmessin (first quarter of the eighteenth century). The event takes place in the *chambre de parade;* in the background is the *lit de parade* enriched with panaches of plumes, the balustrade and fluted columns. (*See page 107.*) BELOW: Drawing by Gilles Marie Oppenord (1716). This was made for the bedroom of the Regent and illustrates the architectural treatment of the balustrade and columns for the *lit de parade.* The profile of the headboard is cut in baroque scrolls, a fashion that came into vogue around the turn of the century. *Courtesy Cooper Union Museum.*

frequently lost under an excess of decorative carving. Other side tables less ornate but still quite rich were made in natural or painted wood.

The specialization of tables according to their use, for writing, gaming, toilet, and "tea," continued to evolve under Louis XIV. Undoubtedly one of Boulle's happiest creations was the bureau *plat*, which Cressent, working in the style of the Régence, was to imbue with remarkable gracefulness and nobility. This flat-top writing table, provided with a row of frieze drawers, was very often accompanied by the *serre-papiers,* an elegant auxilary piece with either open compartments or drawers or a combination of both, placed at one end of the table. Shortly afterward the *serre-papiers* was frequently mounted on a stand, or *armoire* of the same height as the table, which stood on the floor beside the writing table. The tiered writing table, or bureau *à gradin,* distinguished by its low, long, and shallow superstructure (a rectangular shelf comprising pigeonholes flanked by sets of drawers), was a fashionable form of writing furniture around the beginning of the eighteenth century. No doubt the most celebrated of these was made by Boulle in 1715 for the Elector of Bavaria. There was also the bureau *semainier,* of kneehole form with each tier of drawers supported on four tapering baluster or scroll-shaped legs generally resting on X-shaped stretchers. Boulle and his immediate followers made a great number of these bureaux, the majority of which have seven (*semainier*) drawers.

Serving as a table *à café* or *à chocolat* was the *cabaret à café,* a light table with two trays used to carry and pass around china, especially coffee

OPPOSITE: Side table (c. 1680–90). Made of carved and gilt wood, it has an ornately shaped and pierced apron depending from the frieze, tapering baluster-shaped legs with gadrooned capitals, and an X-form scrolled stretcher meeting on a central block. *Courtesy Metropolitan Museum of Art. Gift of J. Pierpont Morgan, 1906. (See page 109.)* ABOVE: Bureau *à gradin* (c. 1715). Veneered with ebony and a marquetry of engraved brass on tortoise shell in a Bérainesque design, it is richly mounted in chased and gilt bronze. Made in the workshop of André Charles Boulle for Maximilian Emanuel, Elector of Bavaria, the table with its six cabriole legs reveals marked deviations from the classical severity of form of Boulle's earlier work. *Courtesy Musée du Louvre. Photo Bulloz-Mella.*

cups. (The fashion for *thé à l'anglaise* came much later, in the 1780s.) From around the mid-eighteenth century onward, a variety of light tables, usually for practical reasons provided with a marble top and very frequently furnished with gilt bronze handles to facilitate the moving of them, were introduced as tables *à café*.

Toilet tables came into general use and, according to representations in pictures and engravings, practically all of them were completely enveloped in fringed draperies and richly worked covers. In medieval times the *toilette,* diminutive of the French *toile,* or cloth, was a modest square piece of linen on which were placed the cosmetics; after the beauty treatment was finished, the paints, powders, and salves were gathered together in the *toilette* and put away in the chest. Soon the square of linen was discarded for a gay and costly *toilette* of silk or velvet with gold lace trimming. As time passed, the *toilette* gave its name to the articles—the mirror, powder boxes, brushes, and combs—arranged on it; then to the operation for which they were used; to the box in which they were kept; and finally to the table especially designed to hold them.

Since the cloth, or *toilette* was permanent on the early tables and made of costly material, it was covered by one of muslin with rows of ruffles, which was easily changed. Under Louis XIV, elaborate toilet sets made of silver were in high fashion; they comprised a mirror supported by a hinged strut, boxes for powder, rouge, and patches, scent bottles, covered unguent jars, brushes, combs, and other beauty requisites, not to mention caskets for jewels, candlesticks, ewers, and rose-water basins that were very often a part of these sets. So great was the consumption of silver for this purpose that Louis XIV, in 1672 and again in 1678, banned the sale of silver mirrors under a heavy fine.

Owing to the passion for gaming, particularly at court where a war was constantly being waged against boredom, the need existed for a variety of gaming tables (tables *à jeu*), each planned for its particular game according to the number of players. Thus there were triangular tables for *tri,* or three-handed *ombre;* for *quadrille* there were square tables often inset with circular wood trays at each corner for candlesticks, while for five-handed *reversi* and *brelan* pentagonal tables were designed, not to mention tables for basset and loo played by any number of persons. In the succeeding Louis XV period, when *piquet* played by two persons was all the rage, an ingenious table with a folding top mounted on a pivot made its debut and became the classic French card table. All tables were mounted with cloth, usually green cloth and occasionally velvet. The *Mercure de France* (1682), in describing the Salon de Jeu at Versailles, mentions that at each corner of the tables *à jeu* was placed a small *guéridon,* or candlestand.

In addition to these small *guéridons* of table height, there were the tall

Cavalier and Lady Drinking Chocolate, engraving by one of the Bonnart brothers. The lady wears the high headdress known as a *fontange.* The Moorish servant or *guéridon* holding the tray became the model for figures carved in wood to be used as candlestands. Through association, these were also called *guéridons. Courtesy Metropolitan Museum of Art. Elisha Whittelsey Collection, 1954.*

and elaborately carved gilt wood *guéridons,* which were often designed en suite with gilded console tables and mirrors. No wonder there were 455 of them listed in the Crown inventories under Louis XIV. When the *torchère* developed at the beginning of the eighteenth century, the *guéridon* became the very small occasional table (table *ambulante*) that served every sort of purpose. Perhaps we should mention here that the *guéridon* became general in France around 1650; the original model had a small round top, a central standard, and three or occasionally four splayed feet to make it firm and steady. Essentially they were like the ancient candelabra, the stands on which the people of antiquity placed their lamps. Why were they called *guéridons,* the name given by the French to young Moors brought from Africa to serve as pages at the court? Because very often under Louis XIV the candlestand was in the form of a *guéridon,* or little black servant, dressed in brilliant attire and holding up a circular tray for reception of the candlestick.

113

ABOVE: Commode *en tombeau* (purchased by Louis XIV from André Charles Boulle in 1708–9 for use at the Trianon). It is veneered with ebony and a marquetry of engraved brass on tortoise shell in a scrolling foliage design and has chased and gilt bronze mounts. It is one of a pair known as the Mazarine Commodes, from the Bibliothèque Mazarine (now at Versailles); they are the only extant pieces identifiable from contemporary records as works by Boulle himself. *Courtesy Château de Versailles. Photo Caisse Nationale-Mella.* BELOW: *Bibliothèque basse* (c. 1775–85). Veneered with coromandel wood and a Boulle-foliated marquetry of tortoise shell on brass, it has chased and gilt bronze mounts. The center door is enhanced with an oval medallion chased with a design of the Rape of Helen. Stamped E. Levasseur (Maître 1767). *Courtesy Wallace Collection, London.*

Of all the new furniture introduced at this time, the commode, or chest of drawers was destined to have the most brilliant career. Making its debut around 1690, the commode, properly placed under a *trumeau,* or pier mirror, was generally designed with either two or three rows of drawers.

Boulle made some famous ones known as commodes *en tombeau*, because the curved profile of their two rows of drawers is in the form of a sarcophagus used in Italy in the eighteenth century in funerary monuments; the same shape also appears in Italian Renaissance *cassoni* and French *coffres*. The first pair of sarcophagus form, whose definite date of construction has survived, are the celebrated Mazarine commodes made for the chamber of Louis XIV at the Palais de Trianon and for which Boulle received payment in 1708 and 1709. Though the marquetry of metal and tortoise shell combined with handsome gilded bronze mounts that decorates these commodes merits our wholehearted admiration, it must be confessed that the design of the commode with its eight legs is highly irrational. In striking contrast to the commode *en tombeau* is the Louis XIV commode of rectangular plan with its three rows of drawers extending almost to the ground.

Also of rectangular plan are the great and handsome Louis XIV *armoires*, now commonly in one piece, with two long paneled doors, characterized by a projecting cornice which is almost always horizontal and displays a complicated style of moldings. The mistress of every provincial château was proud to own and display one of these *armoires*, their decorative value in a large room or the hall of a château being unrivaled. Many served as dowry pieces and were solidly filled with linens, both inherited and spun by the bride-to-be from childhood. There were also *bas d'armoires* and double-bodied buffets. On the other hand, *coffres*, except for marriage *coffres*, were banished or stored in garrets by the wealthy; they were only made now for country people and in most instances were mounted on stands generally provided with frieze drawers.

The cabinet of cube-like form, having been the pre-eminent piece of sumptuous furniture for almost a century, began to go out of fashion around 1690. French designs for cabinets with their elaborate stands, frequently having front supports in the form of caryatid terminal figures, may be seen in the designs of Jean Lepautre. Later in the eighteenth century, owing to the high fashion for *meubles d'appui*, many cabinets, especially those by Boulle and his imitators, were dismounted from their stands and cut down to *armoires* of elbow height and mounted on *toupie* feet.

The bookcase as a special piece of furniture was introduced around 1700, and Boulle more than once has been credited with its invention. Bookcases did not come into common use until the fashion of a small format for books became general. Especially favored was the low bookcase (*bibliothèque basse*), no more than breast high and properly with a marble top. It was about five to six feet wide, and the doors were fitted with a trellis of wire, behind which were silk curtains. Sometimes the doors were glazed.

Louis XV— including Régence and French Provincial

RÉGENCE

The Régence style, in an exact sense, has no more valid existence than the Directoire style, but it is a convenient classification for furniture still retaining certain features of the Louis XIV style and already displaying some that belong to the Louis XV style. Historically the Régence covers that period of time from 1715 to 1723 when Philippe II, Duc d'Orléans, was appointed regent for Louis XV. In cabinetwork, however, the Régence roughly extends from about 1700 to 1720. It seems scarcely necessary to say that styles neither began nor ended with the reigns of kings. The traditional names of styles rarely coincide with their incidence, for it would be strange indeed if the death of a king should change the manner in which furniture is made. Régence cabinetwork possessed the nobility and symmetry proper to the Louis XIV style, but those singular qualities of greatness and formal grandeur were gone, and in their place were signs of the supple gracefulness so typical of the Louis XV style. Out of the Régence there was to develop the most imaginative style of all, known as *rocaille,* or rococo, which differs essentially from baroque in its lightness and avoidance of symmetry. In the perfected or pure Louis XV style, dating from about 1750, the *rocaille* was subdued and simplified, as the early harshness and agitation of its sinuous curves yielded to a more ample and tranquil rhythm.

At this time one great figure soars high above all his contemporaries, one who was to dominate French art until the advent of the painter David —the celebrated painter Antoine Watteau, 1684–1721, whose serene idyllic art conjured up a dream world where poetic imagination loved to wander, as represented in his painting *Embarkation for Cythera.* Our interest in Watteau, however, is not primarily in Watteau the painter, but in Watteau the decorative artist, for he was a great creator of ornamental compositions. Much of his knowledge of decorative designing was acquired in the

116

atelier of the talented painter and ornamental designer Claude Gillot, 1673–1722, who in 1711 succeeded Bérain as Dessinateur de la Chambre et du Cabinet du Roi. (In this capacity he was commissioned to make designs for the royal festivities, theatrical performances and ceremonies of different kinds.) Watteau's *fêtes galantes* owe something to Gillot, but their poetry, their exquisite sensibility is all his own. Both Watteau and Gillot profited from the ornamental compositions of Bérain, but they imparted far more vivacity to their work. Especially fashionable were their *chinoiseries, singeries,* and decorative compositions inspired by the Italian *commedia dell'arte.* Their use of numerous curves anticipated the rococo style of ornament, a style delighting in sinuous, undulating lines that are its graphic formula.

During the Régence a new spirit, which was to be the spirit of the eighteenth century, the century of gallant amenities, began to transform the arts from the stately and heroic to the amiable and gallant. In mural decoration the Apollos and Hercules, devoted in a large measure to the glorification of Louis XIV, were dethroned in favor of Venus and Adonis, Cupid and Psyche, subjects of a romantic nature. But mythological themes were no longer entirely sufficient. In the search for something more amusing and stimulating, a completely new world of fabulous figures made their debut in ornamental compositions inspired by oriental art. This part of the world was becoming slightly better known, thanks to the writings of such travelers as Tavernier and Charden, to commercial relations—the Compagnie des Indes—and to diplomatic relations—the embassy from Siam in 1686, from Persia in 1714, and from Turkey in 1721. Orientalism began to be all the fashion in the theater and in literature. Starting from these sources of inspiration, decorative artists began to elaborate on this absorbing theme of exoticism. They created fantastic doll-like figures of pseudo-Turks, Hindus, Persians, and above all Chinese, resembling masqueraders at a fancy-dress ball. The Chinese brought with them the suitable accessories, dragons sometimes playing with pearls, pagodas, peacock feathers, parasols, bells, gnarled trees, and arched bridges. To this imaginary world full of delightful surprises, Gillot and Watteau mingled reminiscences of the theater. From the *commedia dell'arte* they created a repertory of gay, exquisite, fairy-like figures—Harlequin, Scaramouche, Columbine, Isabella, Mezzetin, and Pierrot (Gilles). In the work of Watteau these enchanting figures were given immortality and at the same time French nationality. *Singeries* became more whimsical and lively, with audacious monkeys clambering onto colonnades to hang their swings from them.

These themes, which were to inspire the new decoration, were found on almost everything from wall paneling to snuff boxes. They were mingled with the classical Louis XIV motifs, such as shells and acanthus foliage, which, during the Régence, were slowly being softened and

117

LEFT: A decorative composition after Watteau (engraving by Louis Crépy, 1680–1750). Charles Cressent often drew inspiration for his bronze *espagnolettes* from the charming young women Watteau introduced into his ornamental compositions. *Courtesy Cooper Union Museum.* (*See page 117.*) RIGHT: Detail of the top of a cabriole leg made by Charles Cressent (early eighteenth century). A charming bronze *espagnolette* ornaments the top of this leg from the bureau *plat* on which the Treaty of Versailles was signed. *Courtesy Palais de Versailles. Photo Caisse Nationale-Mella.* BELOW: Bureau *plat* made by Charles Cressent (early eighteenth century). It is veneered with amaranth and palissander, embellished with handsome chased and gilt bronze mounts; the tops of the cabriole legs have the fashionable *espagnolettes*. *Courtesy Musée du Louvre. Photo Caisse Nationale-Mella.*

modified. For example, the firm and concise Louis XIV curve with its short radius began to show evidence of "loosening," foreshadowing the long and languid Louis XV curve. The upright shell with two long acanthus foliations starting from its base may be regarded as the "stock" motif of the Régence; it was often carved in the center of the valance beneath the chair seat or in the center of the frieze of tables. The taste for attributes increased; they became less heroic and more familiar. Trophies of pastoral life, of gardening, the hunt, and music, and, of course, symbols of love, like bows and arrows, were to be highly favored as the eighteenth century advanced.

If Boulle is the representative par excellence of the Louis XIV style, Charles Cressent, 1685–1768, is equally so for the Régence. Naturally during his long life his style changed in accordance with the prevailing fashion. Cressent, who was also a sculptor, modeled his own bronzes and supervised their execution. He often drew the inspiration for his bronze ornament from Robert de Cotte and for his figures from Gillot and Watteau, such as their frolicsome *singeries* with monkey acrobats dancing on ropes or balancing on swings and with monkey musicians. From Watteau he borrowed those charming busts of smiling young women, called *espagnolettes*, with which he liked to ornament the top of the cabriole legs of his bureaux *plats*. Cressent, who is credited with selecting the woods employed in his veneers, favored amaranth, palissander and violet wood. Their warm tones, which cover the entire range of purples from reddish wine-tone mahogany to a violet brown inclining to black, afforded a superb background for his gilded bronze mounts, which played the leading role in his furniture. His bureau *plat,* his most perfected work, exemplified the spirit of the Régence, when nobility and gracefulness, symbolic of the Louis XIV and Louis XV styles respectively, were harmoniously combined.

At this time the study of chairs gives us the most complete picture of the evolution or transition from the Louis XIV style to the Louis XV. At one end is the great and stately upholstered armchair of rectilinear form with stretchered legs, immovable or nearly so, and at the other end is the smaller, lighter, and above all more comfortable chair, without stretchers, displaying not a single straight line, and which can be moved about easily with one hand. The principal difference between a late Louis XIV chair and one obviously belonging to the Régence is the armposts, which in the latter set back on the upholstered seat, a new feature of design resulting from the fashion of panniers. Typical Régence features include *manchettes,* or armpads; a shaped wood apron beneath the upholstered seat, joining the cabriole legs in an unbroken molding; the gradual disappearance of stretchers as the chair became less heavy; and the upholstered chair back displaying a carved wood frame. The cabriole leg, instead of terminating in a cloven-hoof foot, began to end in a small volute with an acanthus leaf starting up from it. The rectilinear uprights of the chair back and the quadrangular plan of the seat persisted the longest of all Louis XIV characteristics. When the transition was complete, the chair no longer possessed a single straight line; it was Louis XV.

Tables, with the exception of consoles, followed the development of chairs; the valanced or shaped frieze beneath the table top curved in an unbroken line into the cabriole legs, and stretchers were discarded. The ponderous Régence commode, provided with three rows of drawers extending almost to the floor, acquired a new form already seen in the commode *en tombeau*. Under its marble top, the first stage of the façade was concave, the middle strongly convex, and the lower part curved back. In brief, a vertical curved line which gives the whole a cabriole outline was applied to the body. This massive commode *à la Régence* remained in favor during the first half of the eighteenth century. In contrast is the lighter Louis XV commode, also with a serpentine front, but having long curving legs and only two rows of drawers. It is also *bombé*, but a perfected *bombé*; the difference between the two types of commodes can be recognized at first glance. *Bombé*-shaped commodes continued in fashion until the Louis XVI style, when the pre-eminence of the straight line was once more established.

Carved oak *fauteuil* (early eighteenth century). This displays typical Régence features. *Courtesy Metropolitan Museum of Art. Gift of J. Pierpont Morgan, 1906.* OPPOSITE: Commode *à la Régence*. It is veneered with kingwood and palissander, enriched with chased and gilt bronze, and has a serpentine front and a *bombé* case. *Courtesy Parke-Bernet, from the collection of Baron Maurice de Vaux.*

LOUIS XV

Rocaille, or rococo, with its indulgence in caprice and fancy, evolved from the baroque during the Régence and was extensively employed by French craftsmen from around 1720 to 1755–60. When the Louis XV style was in vogue, however, the term *rocaille,* meaning rockwork, was not used to describe this singular form of asymmetrical ornament, but rather it was given to the elaborate artificial grottoes, works of architecture in imitation of marine grottoes, which were in fashion in Italian and French gardens since the Renaissance. The most famous of these *rocailles* in France were constructed by the *rocailleur* Bernard Palissy for Catherine de' Medici in the gardens of the Tuileries. These *rocailles* were decorated with natural rocks incrusted with pebbles and shells, shaped to represent waterfalls, the fringe of waves, stalactites, madrepores, and other ornament. Gradually these motifs in a modified form spread into the decorative arts, with the ornamentists Nicolas Pineau, 1684–1754, and Claude Audran III, 1658–1734, a disciple of Bérain, being among the chief pioneers to develop these new ideas. The use of the French word *rocaille* to indicate this fashion in decoration dates from around the end of the eighteenth century, while the French word rococo is of even later usage.

Imagination is the basis of this new decorative style, in which rocks and shells, with flowers and foliage, provide the dominant theme. Contrast and asymmetry are its essential features. In architecture its influence is seen only in interiors, where pilasters and columns disappear and are replaced by capricious sprays and tendrils, shells and a profusion of sinuous lines, entwining and interlacing. From around 1730 the movement was expanded and accelerated by the work of such ornamentists as Gilles Marie Oppenord, 1672–1742, and Juste Aurèle Meissonier, 1693–1750, who were among the principal designers of these more extravagant forms; this phase was marked by a more deliberate and organic use of asymmetry. In fact Meissonier's name has become practically synonymous with *rocaille*. Born in Turin, Meissonier, a disciple of Borromini, possessed the Italian facility for creating novel forms. Unfortunately his work was marred very often by his fondness for complicated curves and swirling lines, which imbue his designs with restlessness and endless movement. The names of Pineau and Jacques de Lajoue, 1686–1761, a disciple of Watteau, are sometimes linked with Meissonier as being the three principal creators of this more intensified phase. The work of François de Cuvilliés, 1695–1768, was chiefly inspired by the designs of these three men. There are also the different members of the Slodtz family, of whom René-Michel, 1705–64, called Michel-Ange, was a great inventor of *rocaille* ornament. Fervent in their devotion to the *rocaille* are such *ébénistes* as Cressent and Antoine-Robert Gaudreau, c. 1680–1751, who was one of the leading *ébénistes* in the employ of the Crown at this period. Gaudreau's best-known work is the medal cabinet, made in 1738 for one of Louis XV's private apartments at Versailles. Among his most important identified works is a commode made for the king's bedchamber at Versailles in 1739. The design was probably adapted from a drawing attributed to one of the Slodtz brothers.

Freed from the exaggerations of the *rocaille*, the perfected Louis XV style featured a more moderate use of curved lines and less fanciful ornament. In a word, it is *rocaille* subdued and simplified. The pure Louis XV style, the most completely French of all styles, possesses a light and inventive elegance and a spontaneous gaiety that are in accordance with the true traditions of French art. The most notable quality of *rocaille* that the French artists assimilated was asymmetry, which reigned triumphantly until the classical revival. *Ébénistes* working in the pure Louis XV style have given us perfect examples of French furniture at its finest. The king of French *ébénistes*, from about 1750 till his death in 1763, was Jean François Oeben, a German by birth. In 1760 Oeben, who was holder of the title *ébéniste du roi*, began the celebrated *Bureau du Roi*, a cylinder-top desk for Louis XV, which was completed in 1769 by his former apprentice, Jean Henri Riesener, perhaps the greatest *ébéniste* working in the Louis

Commode (1739). Veneered with kingwood and mahogany, it has a serpentine and *bombé* front. It was made by Antoine-Robert Gaudreau for the bedchamber of Louis XV at Versailles. The lavish mounts of rococo scrolls, shells, floral sprays, and foliage are by Jacques Caffiéri. The center of the façade is enriched with a handsome bronze cartouche. *Courtesy Wallace Collection, London.* BELOW: Commode veneered with ebony (c. 1750–55). The serpentine front and sides are decorated with panels of black and gold lacquer depicting a fantastic Chinese landscape; the panels are enclosed in handsome rococo frames of leaf scrolls and flowers. It was made by Joseph Baumhauer, called Joseph (d. 1772). *Courtesy Victoria and Albert Museum.* (*See page 124.*)

XVI style. In addition to Oeben, there were many other Parisian *ébénistes* whose work was most representative of the Louis XV style. Such were Joseph Baumhauer, called Joseph, d. 1772; Roger Vandercruse, called Lacroix, m. 1755; Jacques Dubois, m. 1742; members of the Migeon family, Claude Charles Saunier, m. 1752; Jean-François Leleu, m. 1764; B.V.R.B. or Bernard van Ryssen Burghe, fl. before 1767, to mention but a few out of hundreds. There were also the *menuisiers en sièges* among whom shone two members of a famous family, Quimbert and François Foliot.

Oeben's principal customer, according to the entries in the extant day-book of Lazare-Duvaux, Parisian dealer in furniture and curios, was Madame de Pompadour, who from her "accession" in 1745 until her death in 1764 had innumerable houses to furnish. There were the rustic one-storied pavilions or hermitages at Versailles, Compiègne, Fontainebleau, and else-where; châteaux built or altered by her, such as Crécy, Champs, Bellevue, and Ménars; the Hôtel de Réservoirs at Versailles, the magnificent Hôtel d'Evreux in Paris, in addition to suites of apartments at Versailles, Fontainebleau, Marly, Compiègne, and other royal palaces. All the artists were constantly receiving commissions from her. At Bellevue the paneling was by Verberckt and the painted decorations by Vanloo and Boucher, the two most successful exponents of the rococo style in French painting. Much has been written concerning the role she played, if any, in the creation of the new classical style that was to rout the rococo. Suffice it say that she protected, supported, and advised the great artists of her time. Her contemporaries were aware of this and were duly grateful. This is seen in the *Mémoires Secrets* of Louis Petit de Bachaumont, who writes about her death: "This evening [April 15] Madame de Pompadour died; the distinguished protection she afforded to men of letters, and her taste for the arts, make it impossible to pass over this sad event in silence."

From the beginning of *rocaille* there was an undercurrent of protest in certain circles against asymmetry and the lavish use of sinuous curves, for it was felt they did not express the finer artistic instincts of the French, which were always inclined to moderation and restraint. The celebrated architect Jean François Blondel, 1681–1756, who has left an interesting work entitled *De La Distribution des Maisons de Plaisance* (1737), apologizes for the examples he gives of asymmetrical ornament from the drawings of Pineau and derides "the absurd jumbles of shells, dragons, reeds, palms and plants." But the strongest attack came in 1754 from Charles Nicolas Cochin, the engraver. In the *Mercure de France* appeared his well-known and often quoted supplication to "goldsmiths, chasers and woodcarvers . . . that when a thing may be square without offense, they will refrain from torturing it; and that when a pediment may legitimately be semicircular, they will not corrupt it by those S-shape contours which they seem to have borrowed from a writing-master." Finally owing to the

Veneered tulipwood writing table of kneehole form (bureau *à caissons lateraux*) (late 1760s). The eight inset Sèvres plaques are decorated with a polychrome painting of flowers enclosed in bright green borders. It was made by Joseph Baumhauer, called Joseph, and belongs to the transitional period. *Courtesy Metropolitan Museum of Art. Gift of the Samuel H. Kress Foundation, 1958.*

discoveries at Herculaneum and Pompeii, which resulted in an overwhelming enthusiasm for the antique, an evolution began around 1755–60, leading from the Louis XV style to the neo-classical Louis XVI style, which was established before the accession of that king in 1774. Furniture belonging to this era, displaying a compromise between *rocaille* and classicism in a French guise, is regarded by many as the finest of all.

The eighteenth century was the age of the celebrated French *ébénistes*. From the middle of the seventeenth century or earlier until 1743 they had been members of the *menuisiers'* guild, but in that year this guild was officially renamed the corporation of *menuisiers-ébénistes*, and, at the same time, cabinetmaking was divided into two groups: the *menuisiers d'assemblage*, or joiners of solid wood furniture, such as chairs and beds, and the *menuisiers de placage et de marqueterie*, or the veneerers and *marqueteurs*. This latter group adopted the name *ébéniste*, deriving from *menuisier en ébène*. There were more than 1000 *maîtres* in the eighteenth century in Paris who stamped their work. The first guild statutes of 1467 ordered the members of the corporation to stamp their work, but the ruling was not strictly enforced and relatively few *maîtres* placed marks on their work. The order was given again in 1741, and new guild statutes issued between 1744 and 1751 compelled each *maître* to possess an iron stamp, having his name or occasionally his initials with which he must stamp every piece of his furniture made for sale. As a rule, the *maître* stamped his furniture under the marble tops of commodes, on the underframing of chairs and tables or some similar place which would not mar the appearance. After the guilds were dissolved in 1790, the stamp was no longer necessary. In addition there were two groups of craftsmen who were free from guild restrictions. One group known as *artisans privilégiés* made most of their furniture for the Crown; the other, *artisans libres,* managed to work in places still protected by medieval rights of refuge.

Aside from the *menuisiers-ébénistes,* two other guilds were especially well represented in furniture making, namely the *foundeurs* and the *ciseleurs-doreurs,* who jointly made the bronzes *d'ameublement,* as well as the chased and gilt bronze mounts which were applied to so much of the furniture. In fact, the eighteenth century is the golden age for furniture mounted in chased and gilded bronze. As in the earlier seventeenth century, mounts continued to perform a utilitarian function, but their decorative role was considerably expanded, as may be seen in paneled pieces, such as commodes and *encoignures,* and in elaborate tables. The most beautiful bronzes were cast, chased, and gilded. The process of gilding, or *à l'or moulu* was generally by the mercury process, that is to say, gold with a mixture of mercury. After the heat had vaporized the mercury, the gold adhering to the bronze was either burnished or given a matte finish. It is reputed that the matte finish, so often found on the gilt bronze of the late Louis XVI and Empire periods, was the invention of Pierre Gouthière, 1732–1813/14, the outstanding *foundeur-ciseleur* of the Louis XVI style. Under Louis XV, two members of a famous dynasty were pre-eminent, Jacques Caffiéri, 1678–1755, and his elder son Philippe II, 1714–74. The former, a prolific inventor of *rocaille* bronzes, which he conceived with admirable taste, is regarded as the greatest of all. Gilding was not employed as freely on bronze furniture mounts as is generally believed. The daybook of Lazare-Duvaux shows that Madame de Pompadour was constantly sending bronze mounts to be cleaned in acid and re-lacquered.

The art of lodging people comfortably and privately, heretofore unknown, became of primary importance in the eighteenth century. This desire for material comfort and an intimate social life brought about a great transformation in the house, which increasingly affected the development of furniture. Everything had to be *agréable* and *joli.* The rooms were reduced to a more reasonable size, while the furniture became smaller, perfectly adapted to the human needs and, above all, more comfortable. The many small rooms, each with its special purpose—for conversation, music, games—are characteristic of this period and may be seen in the large hôtels in Paris that were being built by a rich and increasingly powerful bourgeoisie. In addition to a large drawing-room was a smaller reception room, the *salon de compagnie,* a less imposing retreat where

Le Déjeuner, after François Boucher, engraving by Lépicie. Scenes such as these are interesting for their portrayal of objects in daily use. The *trumeau* fitted with rococo candlebranches, the bronze *cartel* of asymmetrical form, and the table with its slender cabriole legs give harmony and distinction to this fashionable interior belonging to well-to-do members of the Parisian bourgeoisie. *Courtesy Metropolitan Museum of Art. Whittelsey Fund, 1960.*

intimate friends were received. There were the little rooms or cabinets, such as the *cabinet de café,* where persons retired after meals, *cabinet de lecture,* and still others.

The fondness for comfort and intimacy was fully shared by the king, who preferred the more intimate life of the salon and boudoir to the formal existence of the grand parade rooms of the time of Louis XIV. At Versailles he arranged for his personal use a suite of rooms, the *petits appartements,* comprising fifty rooms and seven bathrooms. All these small rooms which the architects were increasingly called upon to build de-

127

manded not only smaller but also fewer pieces of furniture. Thanks to the improvement in mechanical devices in which certain *ébénistes*, especially those from across the Rhine, excelled, combination pieces came more and more into use from around 1750 onward. Compact, elaborately fitted, multiple-function furniture, such as tables that could be transformed by complicated locking devices into toilet, writing, reading, and sewing tables, is a notable feature and attained its apogee under Louis XVI.

Louis XV furniture, of which an enormous amount was made, delightfully adapted itself to meet the needs of all classes of society. Simple pieces made for the citizen have often as much or even more beauty than the ambitious examples, which are sometimes marred by their overwhelming richness. The sense of harmony and proportion and, above all, the sense of graceful curves can be fully appreciated in this less costly furniture, because the real beauty of Louis XV furniture is not in its rich decoration but in the graceful suppleness of its lines, in its delicate moldings that affirm the structural lines and in its harmony of silhouette. A piece of Louis XV furniture, for example, a chair or table, may be almost always recognized at a glance by the curving character of all its lines, and notably legs of cabriole form, which are invariably used. Straight lines are only employed when necessary, such as for the vertical members of an *armoire*. A love for harmonious and undulating lines, especially long, S-shaped curves, distinguishes the style. An abhorrence of rectangles is a marked feature, and everything that can be rounded is rounded.

Gilt *fauteuil en cabriolet* with a cartouche-shaped back (c. 1760). It is notable for the curving character of all its lines. Stamped I. Lebas (Jean Baptiste Lebas, Maître 1756). *Courtesy Metropolitan Museum of Art. Rogers Fund, 1926.*

Continuity of form is another principle; this may readily be seen in chair design in which each member seems to flow or melt into one another without any feeling of separation. Delicate, flexible moldings treated with consummate skill affirm the continuity. These beautiful moldings with their richly swelling curves are an outstanding characteristic and play an important role in Louis XV furniture made of solid wood; many chairs have no other decoration. The principle of asymmetry, although not an invariable rule, characterizes the Louis XV style of decoration. Fortunately the French craftsmen possessed the technical ability to achieve asymmetry without loss of balance. For example, in the case of a molded panel, one has to look very closely to realize that the opposite sides of the axis do not exactly repeat one another. To achieve this exact equilibrium is a delicate feat, but when it is solved the rewards are great, for the eye is charmed by the unexpectedness of the detail and the mind is satisfied by the balance of its parts.

From the time the Dutch East India Company was founded in 1602, the taste in France for Chinese and Japanese objects, in particular porcelain, lacquer, and silk stuffs, steadily increased. By 1674 the fashion for collecting oriental porcelain was sufficiently great to have inspired the creation of the Trianon de Porcelaine, a building at Versailles completely decorated on the exterior with painted faïence in what was considered to be an oriental manner. Before the end of the seventeenth century, the Compagnie des Indes was importing large quantities of wares from the Orient. All the arts were deeply affected by *le goût de la Chine*. Mention has been made of the *chinoiseries*, as European works in the oriental taste were called, in rich baroque compositions by Bérain and Marot. In 1708 *chinoiseries*, believed to be the work of Watteau, were painted in the Château de la Muette on the walls of a small room, one of those miniature retreats designed for the relaxation of the mind, where everything was done to make the decoration playful and gallant. From that time onward, *chinoiseries*, which are so closely related to rococo ornament, were propagated by such decorative designers as Gillot, Watteau, Pillement, whose work was greatly admired in England, where he spent several years in the 1750s, and Boucher, one of the most prolific inventors of all kinds of rococo decoration. *Chinoiseries*, which attained their apogee around 1750, reigned supreme in the domain of exoticism until the end of the Ancien Régime. Other digressions in the exotic, a taste so dear to the eighteenth century, are seen in the *turqueries*, with their stars and censers, crescents and scimitars which played a subordinate role from around 1730.

The enthusiasm for oriental lacquer inspired the *ébéniste* to adapt it to the decoration of furniture. In the beginning it was the practice either to incorporate imported lacquered panels into a Western framework or to

Title page from *A New Book of Chinese Ornaments*, invented and engraved by Jean Pillement. Designed in the form of a cartouche, bells, flowers, and pagodas have been introduced into the composition with great inventive charm. *Courtesy Cooper Union Museum.* OPPOSITE: Detail from one of a set of six *chinoiseries* panels in oil on canvas, painted by Jean Pillement (c. 1780). Into this fanciful design, replete with birds, bells, pagodas, and scrolls, the painter, especially noted for his ingenious flower compositions, has introduced a delightful floral treatment beneath which are two small Chinese figures. *Courtesy Duveen Brothers, New York.* (*See page 129.*)

send the panels to the Orient to be lacquered. Owing to the expense and delay, it is only natural that an attempt was made to imitate it. From around 1660, painter-varnishers were quite active in France, and they were constantly trying to improve this medium of decoration. But it was not until the following century that European lacquer, which is done in an essentially different method from that practiced in the Orient, reached its acme of perfection in the work of the Martin brothers. Their famous lacquers, known as *Vernis Martin,* became the symbol of the most refined luxury and the final word in magnificence. Every imaginable object, from *frivolités* to sedan chairs, from carriages to entire suites of rooms, was an appropriate subject for this beautiful decoration, which remained in high fashion until the end of the Ancien Régime.

A great deal of furniture of solid wood was still produced; in the provinces, practically nothing else was made. Oak, walnut, wild cherry, beech, elm, and chestnut were all favorite native woods. Next was the large family of fruit trees, such as cherry, plum, apricot, and pear, the latter being generally stained black because of its poor grain. Furniture made of fruit wood was not always of provincial origin. Lazare-Duvaux furnished plumwood and cherrywood tables for his Parisian customers, as well as furniture of rosewood and mahogany. It is generally believed that *acajou*, or mahogany was imported into France from the time of the Régence. The first mention of it occurs around 1740 in a French inventory, and from around 1755–60 onward it enjoyed a great vogue. On one occasion Lazare-Duvaux delivered to Madame de Pompadour six commodes and twelve writing tables in mahogany with gilded bronze mounts. Under Louis XVI, mahogany became the customary wood for fine furniture for the third estate. Ebony was almost entirely discarded, except for furniture either in the manner of Boulle or decorated with lacquered panels; the latter, however, often had a green, red, yellow, or even white ground. There was also satinwood, amaranth, and palissander; the popularity of the last two is credited to Cressent. By the middle of the eighteenth century a greatly increased variety of native and exotic woods, almost 100, were available to *ébénistes*. The number was increased still further in selection by the practice of staining some woods a variety of colors—greens, yellows, blues, and reds. Because of the wide range of woods, together with an influx of German craftsmen into France who enjoyed a fine reputation as *marqueteurs*, pictorial marquetry began to flourish. It was most often in the form of floral decoration, but sometimes trophies, landscapes, figures in the taste of Boucher, realistic representations of domestic utensils like cups and saucers or teapots, and later architectural compositions in the antique taste were used. Unfortunately, owing to the passage of time, the brilliant polychrome appearance of this work has faded. Veneering and marquetry flourished in Paris, where a sufficient concentration of wealth assured the purchase of these deluxe pieces. Because of the character of the surfaces of the Louis XV style, which undulated in every direction, more technical skill was required to execute the veneering and marquetry than in the subsequent Louis XVI period.

Painted furniture, by no means a novelty, became much more popular. Console tables, toilet tables, screens, and notably seats were appropriate pieces to be painted, which was generally *réchampi* or "picked out"; the ground was in a neutral tint, while the moldings and carvings were in a strong color or gilt. Under Louis XV, no one was afraid of strong and vivid colors; it was in the following Louis XVI style when there was a mania for light, delicate colors. The *Livre Journal* of Lazare-Duvaux lists

LEFT: Table *ambulante* provided with bronze lifting handles to facilitate moving it about from place to place. The green lacquer is enriched with bronze mounts and two Sèvres plaques, one of which bears the date letter K for 1763; it is attributed to Bernard van Ryssen Burghe, who flourished before 1767. *Courtesy Metropolitan Museum of Art. Gift of the Samuel H. Kress Foundation, 1958. (See page 131.)* BELOW LEFT: Veneered *bonheur du jour* (c. 1770). Handsomely inlaid with a pictorial marquetry of cups and saucers, jugs, coupes, inkwells, a quill pen, a letter, a book, and other utensils, its novel feature is the oval shape. A *haricot* or kidney-bean-shaped undershelf connects the four slender cabriole legs. *Courtesy Parke-Bernet, from the collection of Georges Lurcy.* BELOW RIGHT: Painted *chaise voyeuse*. The occupant sits in a reverse position using the crest rail as an armrest. The chair is made unusually long between the front and back to provide space for this fashionable sitting position. *Courtesy Parke-Bernet, from the collection of Baron de Vaux.*

133

many red toilet tables and corner shelves of red or green and gold. When Madame de Pompadour moved to her new suite of rooms at Versailles in 1751, which once belonged to Madame de Montespan, one room was paneled in red lacquer by the Martins. Caned seat furniture, the forms of which were the same as the upholstery pieces, was extremely fashionable; the frames were often painted and occasionally gilded. Though gilt wood furniture was less popular than in the time of Louis XIV, gilt seat furniture and console tables, to harmonize with the carved and gilt wood decoration of the mirrors above them, were still frequent in elegant houses. The leading role played by gilt bronze mounts on paneled furniture has already been mentioned. Marbles, which were almost as varied as the woods, were also an important decorative accessory. They provided a superb touch of color for the tops of commodes (only the simplest kind were without them), consoles, different kinds of tables, *bas d'encoignures,* and the like. As an embellishment for furniture, the *ébéniste* introduced the practice of applying porcelain plaques, which came in with the fully developed Louis XVI style, enjoying a great vogue from about 1766 to 1786.

The upholstery was the last word in comfort. Silk, satin, velvet, damask, and pekin (a silk painted with flowers reputed to be Madame de Pompadour's favorite fabric) were the most usual materials employed. For seats in constant use there was moquette, a velvet-like woolen material generally woven in bands, while for the caned *chaise à poudreuse* or *chaise à bureau,* morocco leather was preferred. Chintz and painted linens were popular summer stuffs; somewhat later, *toile de jouy* was extensively employed. For costly seat furniture, tapestry, principally woven at Beauvais, was highly favored. Tapestry coverings with either flowers or figure or animal subjects were the most fashionable. Floral designs were popular because they were adaptable to any kind of wall decoration or wall hangings. It is surprising how often seats ornamented with animals are combined with backs adorned with figure subjects. Two great animal painters, François Desportes, 1661–1743, and Jean Baptiste Oudry, 1686–1755, helped establish the fashion for animal furniture tapestries. Oudry's celebrated tapestries of the royal hunt, *Chasses de Louis XV,* and his sets of humble animals of the countryside, chickens, sheep, etc., honoring La Fontaine's *Fables,* are notable. Pastoral scenes with lovely girls dressed as shepherdesses and pretty peasants engaged in pleasurable pursuits or pretending to work in holiday clothes against a hazy and enchanting landscape found their master in the celebrated rococo painter François Boucher, who was the great tapestry designer of the eighteenth century. His *Noble Pastorale* series woven at Beauvais exemplifies this Arcadian taste stripped of its last vestige of realism, a taste so greatly admired in the eighteenth century.

The validity of Michelet's phrase, "a return to the sense of life and humanity," which he used to describe the Louis XV style, is clearly conveyed when one compares the rigid form of the Louis XIV *fauteuil* with a Louis XV *bergère*. The latter is delightfully adapted to human needs and to a size proportionate to human stature, and conceived in every detail to accord with an easier, less formal mode of living. Louis XV chairs can be recognized at a glance by the curving character of all their lines. If the back is slightly concave to fit the body, the chair is described as *en cabriolet*. The molded chair frames are often enhanced with rich floral, foliage, and shell carvings. Even the most modest chair is seldom without a flower carved in the center of the top rail, on the knees of the cabriole legs, and in the center of the valanced seat rail. *Fauteuils* with so-called cartouche-shaped backs were in high fashion. Medallion, or oval backs are a later development and are principally identified with the Louis XVI style. As a concession to the feminine fashion for panniers, the armposts are set back and joined to the side seat rail. In other *fauteuils* where the armposts are not set back, but are above the front legs, they curve backward and outward at the same time, and the twisting and expansion of the moldings is agreeably effective. With a few exceptions the *manchette*, or padded elbow rest is mandatory.

The most typical Louis XV chair is the *bergère*, a wide, low, and deep armchair, that made its debut around 1720. Characterized by solid sides, that is, without any opening between the arms and seat, and by a loose seat cushion, *bergères* were made in a variety of forms, of which three are especially well known. One type is closely related to the *fauteuil*, but has closed sides. A second type, which is most familiar, has a more rounded appearance; it is more or less gondola-shaped and is described as *en gondole*. The third is a winged type of "confessional" shape having wings or ears (*à oreilles*) serving to support the head. Madame Campan records in her *Mémoires* that when Madame Victoire, a daughter of Louis XV, was asked if she was planning to become a nun like her sister, Madame Louise, she replied that she was too fond of the comforts of life, and, pointing to her *bergère*, said, "Here is an armchair that will be my ruin."

Canapés developed into a variety of types. One form, often called a *marquise*, is merely an enlarged armchair that corresponds to the English courting chair or love seat. Perhaps it was made to accommodate the wide panniered skirts. A small . *canapé* intended for two persons only was generally known as a *confident*, *tête-à-tête*, or *causeuse*. The majority of *canapés* were made to accommodate three persons. In high fashion was the basket-shaped *canapé*, one of the most sought-after types at the present time. Known as an *ottomane* or *canapé à corbeille*, it is designed with a gracefully arched back, the ends of which continue to curve around the front, forming semi-circular ends. Properly, pillows are placed at each end, and it is provided with a long, loose seat cushion.

ABOVE LEFT: Carved and painted *fauteuil* with a medallion-shaped back (c. 1765). Stamped Bara (Charles Vincent Bara, Maître 1754). *Courtesy Metropolitan Museum of Art. Rogers Fund, 1932.* ABOVE RIGHT: Carved beechwood *bergère* (1760s). Resembling a *fauteuil*, the chair has upholstered sides, and the seat has a movable cushion. Stamped Claude Chevigny (Maître 1768). *Courtesy Parke-Bernet, from the collection of Thelma Chrysler Foy.* BELOW: Gilt wood *canapé à corbeille* (transitional, c. 1765–70). The Louis XV curvilinear frame is richly carved with bowknotted ribbons and other neo-classical motifs. *Courtesy Parke-Bernet, from the collection of Countess Sala.* (*See page 135.*)

It is well to mention here that the terminology of the Louis XV and Louis XVI periods was so loose that the meanings of many of the names in current use are frequently confusing and not always exact. At least the names, which are often most seductive, convey a delightful impression of perfect adaptability to human needs, of intimacy, as well as an element of fantasy—typical Louis XV ingredients.

At the time, when ladies of fashion were fond of receiving *en déshabillé*, the daybed was given a variety of novel forms and a bewildering assortment of names, such as *veilleuse, sultane, turquoise, duchesse*. Of these, the *duchesse*, distinguished by its gondola-shaped back, is most typical and enjoyed a great vogue from around 1740 to 1780. The *duchesse* became a *duchesse brisée* when it was designed in two or three parts, the latter having a low gondola-shaped foot end (*bout de pied*). The *turquoise*, whose name reflects the period's delight in anything supposedly Turkish, like the *sultane,* is characterized by two ends of equal height; while a *veilleuse* is a variation of an *ottomane* and distinguished by its sloping back, which is noticeably higher at the end where the head is to rest. There was also the *chaise-longue,* whose chair end frequently had deep upholstered wings, the same as the confessional *bergère*.

As for the beds belonging to this era, the *lit à colonnes* gradually disappeared, but was revived again in the Louis XVI style. The shapes in high fashion were the *lit à la duchesse, lit d'ange,* and *lit à la polonaise,* which no doubt received its name in honor of the queen of France, Marie Leszczynska. Both the duchess bed and the angel bed have a flat, oblong tester, but in the case of the former it extends the length of the bed. The tester is supported from the wall at the back or from the ceiling, thus eliminating the necessity of posts. The Polish bed has two ends of equal height; each of the four corners supports an iron rod that curves inward and, at a certain height, holds a dome or crown from which curtains are hung and gracefully fastened back at each rod with bows. Of particular interest are the so-called Turkish beds (*lit à la Turque*), in vogue from around 1755 to 1785, which can be converted into sofas in the daytime. This form of bed was placed lengthways against a wall and correctly has a small narrow canopy from the wall. It has a backpiece and two side or end pieces of equal height; although it is actually a bed, it differs essentially from the sofa only in its dimensions. When the bed is dressed, each end is fitted with a rolled cushion.

Tables, which became simpler and lighter, with the exception of certain large types, have one characteristic in common, that is, cabriole legs. When the legs are not fitted with small shoes of gilt bronze (*sabots*), they generally end in a small volute resting on a plain small square of wood or occasionally are finished in a graceful projection that somewhat resembles a cloven-hoof foot. The dining table (table *de salle à manger*) began to

come into use, and then very seldom, only at the end of Louis XV's reign. Tables of the extension type especially designed for dining were apparently inspired by English influence. They did not come into any considerable use until Louis XVI's reign, when they were frequently known as tables *à l'anglaise* as far as we can learn from the baffling terminology. The dining-room in France was a creation of the eighteenth century, but even under Louis XVI it was generally found only in great palaces and houses of the aristocracy. Until the Revolution, even rich bourgeoisie served their meals in the ante-chamber, as the kings had formerly done. Consequently simple trestle tables set up for that purpose and completely concealed with a white cloth were still often used. Before leaving the dining-room there is one piece that is most characteristic, the *rafraîchissoir*, a kind of dumb-waiter or *servante* in the form of a small table with shelves. The upper part was provided with a metal-lined recess or well in which wine bottles could be chilled. (At the present time the wells are

138

OPPOSITE ABOVE: Carved walnut *duchesse brisée* comprising a *bergère en gondole* and an extended lounge rest (c. 1750–60). *Courtesy Musée des Arts Décoratifs. Photo Mella.* OPPOSITE BELOW: Gilt wood *veilleuse* carved with rococo scrolls, shells, floral sprays, and foliage (c. 1755). Stamped J. B. Tilliard (Maître 1752). *Courtesy Victoria and Albert Museum.* ABOVE: *Madame Boucher,* by François Boucher. This delightful painting of dainty femininity shows the artist's wife lolling upon her *chaise-longue;* the chair end is designed in the form of a "confessional" *bergère. Courtesy Frick Collection, New York. (See page 137.)* LEFT: *Le Souper Fin,* engraving after Moreau the Younger (1783). This shows the tables, *rafraîchissoirs,* which have recesses for cooling bottles of wine and shelves for plates and cutlery that were used at intimate supper parties; it also illustrates how happily Louis XV tables blend in a Louis XVI interior. *Photo Bulloz-Mella.*

139

often used to contain plants, a pitiful plight for a *rafraîchissoir*.) They were used for intimate supper parties, one being placed next to each guest, so he could serve himself without the presence of servants. In the pursuit of privacy, the ultimate, however, is the table *volante,* a "flying" table, the first of which Louis XV installed in the *petits appartements* at Trianon. The *Mercure de France* writes about these "magic" tables: "When the company passes into the dining room . . . all that is seen is a very smooth floor. . . . At a given signal the leaves disappear beneath the floor, and a table spread with a meal rises from the ground." The use of tables *volantes* was by no means confined to France, for we find Frederick the Great had one installed in the Stadtschloss at Potsdam. Continuing on the subject of mechanical and "flying" furniture for personal convenience, mention may be made of the *chaise volante,* or lift which Louis XV installed at Versailles for the use of Madame de Châteauroux in 1743.

Medium-sized and small tables, the aristocracy of eighteenth-century French furniture, reveal all those brilliant and versatile qualities which marked the achievements of Parisian *ébénistes* of the golden age, the period of Louis XV and Louis XVI. Of infinite variety and with a legion

140

of names, these elegant tables began to multiply from around 1750 onward, when they were designed in an ever increasing number to serve more than one purpose. An advertisement in 1789 mentions *"une toilette à six fins."* This great family of French furniture, made for every imaginable purpose, suitable for the drawing-room, salon, boudoir, bedroom, and study, derived from the fastidious demand for comfort and convenience and the multiplication of small rooms. Above all, they testify to the improvement in mechanical devices for transforming furniture. First there were the graceful and delicate very small occasional tables (tables *ambulantes*) with their *haricot*, round, oval, cartouche, or serpentine-shaped tops, looking as if a flick of the finger would upset them. For the bedroom there were other little tables, such as the *vide-poche* (pocket-emptier) with a raised edge, the *serre-bijoux* (jewel-box table), and tables designed so that the upper part with its four short legs can be lifted off and placed on the bed, very convenient for meals in bed. A wide range of bedside tables are known as tables *de chevet;* many of these were equally suitable for use in other rooms. Tables *de nuit*, opened or closed, generally provided with lifting handles, were placed by the bed during the night and stowed away in the morning. To the variety of card tables mentioned in the preceding chapter we may add the gaming table designed for *tric-trac*. Before leaving the subject of cards, we must not forget to mention *bouillotte*, a card game that became very fashionable at the time of the Revolution. Under Louis XVI, the *bouillotte* table, distinguished by its circular marble top, a frieze of conforming shape, and a pierced metal gallery, made its debut, and like all Louis XVI furniture its four legs were straight and tapering.

Because in the social gatherings of the time women still observed the custom of sewing while seated in the boudoir or salon where intimate friends were received, there were the small tables *à ouvrage*, or work tables. Of these and especially well known are the *tricoteuse*, characterized by its high gallery to contain spools or balls of wool, and the *chiffonnière* with its two or three superimposed drawers, used by the ladies "to keep their needle-work or trifles (*chiffon*) in"; the latter is not to be confused with the *chiffonnier* (a tall chest of drawers, sometimes called a *semainier*, since the majority were designed with a drawer for each day of the week), which is also a feminine piece. Work tables having an adjustable easel so that the top could be raised to form a reading stand (*pupitre*), or perhaps on which to write a small note in this epistolary age, were fashionable and choice articles of furniture.

As we all know from the literature of the period, to say nothing of representations in pictures and engravings, it became the custom for ladies of fashion to receive their close friends, of both sexes, seated at their toilet tables, while the maid arranged their coiffure and they themselves applied the rouge with a hare's foot or carefully considered the most effective spot on which to place a patch. The classical eighteenth-century toilet table, now called a *poudreuse*, which was to remain in fashion until the end of the Ancien Régime, is one of those rare pieces whose graceful form was not achieved at the expense of utility. Characteristic features include a rising framed mirror and two sides fixed on hinges that opened from right and left to form two horizontal shelves on which the toilet articles contained in the compartments and drawers could be arranged. In addition to the popular *poudreuse*, there were smaller fashionable toilet tables, often pear-shaped or some other curious rococo shape, frequently fitted with casters, when casters were still quite rare. Since toilet tables were intended not only for women, there are those designed for masculine use.

Occasionally toilet equipage was incorporated into other articles of furniture, such as commodes or different forms of writing tables or desks. Both men and women, however, still liked the decorative setting of elaborately draped toilet tables, for they are frequently represented in pictures of fashionable interiors, as may be seen in paintings by Lancret and Drouais, with the mirror on the table being partly concealed by heavy folds of fabric. Finally there are the toilet chairs, mounted with cane and generally

ABOVE: *L'Après-Diner*, after Nicolas Lancret, engraving by Nicolas de Larmessin. A couple is shown playing *tric-trac*. The carved traverses in the slat-back chair, each one consisting of two figures resembling question marks set one against the other lengthwise, are extremely pleasing. This motif was popular in America for a class of slat-back chairs, the so-called "salamander" type. *Courtesy Metropolitan Museum of Art. Bequest of Annie C. Kane, 1926.* CENTER: Veneered *poudreuse* (c. 1750–65). It is decorated with a marquetry of flowers and musical trophies in tinted fruitwoods, and enriched with gilt bronze. In the more carefully finished models the compartments had covers that opened backward. *Courtesy Duveen Brothers, New York.* LEFT: Pear-shaped toilet table called table *de papillon*. The hinged top lifts vertically and is fitted on the reverse side with a mirror. Small toilet tables of this type probably served as accessory pieces; properly they were provided with casters when casters were rare, showing that they were intended to be moved about. The small size of the top can be increased by the two hinged frieze drawers in the shape of butterfly wings that open out at each side; hence the name. *Courtesy Parke-Bernet, from the collection of Charles E. F. McCann.*

LEFT: Carved walnut *chaise à toilette* or *chaise à bureau* (c. 1750). This charming type of Louis XV chair has a low and rounded back, mounted with cane and usually cushioned with leather. In this example, the seat is semi-circular at the back and serpentine-shaped in front. *Courtesy Metropolitan Museum of Art. Gift of J. Pierpont Morgan, 1908.* OPPOSITE ABOVE: *Le Bureau du Roi Louis XV.* Begun by Oeben in 1760 and finished by Riesener in 1769, this is probably the most celebrated piece of furniture in the world. BELOW: *Le Bureau du Roi Louis XV,* rear view. *Courtesy Musée du Louvre. Photo Caisse Nationale-Mella.* (*See page 146.*)

having a leather cushion, characterized by their low and rounded "gondola-shaped" backs. In some models the seat is circular in plan, while in others it is semi-circular in the back and serpentine-shaped in the front; this latter type, by far the favorite, has three legs across the front and one centered in the back. The caned toilet chair is also the typical chair for the writing table, which brings us to that elegant class of *secrétaires* and bureaux, either one of which was *de rigueur* in every study.

In writing furniture the *ébénistes* embodied with extraordinary felicity the temper and taste of France. The simplest kind of Louis XV writing table is the large bureau *plat* supplemented by the *serre-papiers*, the most popular piece of writing furniture during the first half of the eighteenth century. But the crowning glory was the bureau *à cylindre* introduced around the middle of the century and probably created by Oeben. The cylinder top was a happy invention: at a touch it covered the writing table and concealed from view the clutter of writing paper, notes, and writing equipage.

However, before we continue, a word about the roll-top desk known as *Le Bureau du Roi Louis XV*, perhaps the most beautiful piece of furniture in the world. The lavish marquetry decorating its ample surface illustrates the fashionable taste for attributes and flowers. The lower part, the kneehole part, is entirely veneered on all four sides with floral sprays and mounted with heavy swags of laurel. The cylinder top is ornamented with two circular compartments; the left are symbols of dramatic poetry, the

right of lyric poetry. The panel in the center of the cylinder was originally filled in with emblems of royalty, which were removed in 1794 after the downfall of Louis XVI. A marquetry depicting attributes of learning (books), flowers, and other motifs was substituted. The upper part on the right side is veneered with emblems of war, the left with seafaring symbols. The lower portion on each side centers an oval plaque of the Three Graces in white biscuit on a blue ground; these also were new additions after

1794, supplanting the cipher of Louis XV. The back no less handsomely decorated centers a bronze plaque in relief chased with cupids, two of them supporting a medallion of Minerva. The marquetry panel on the left of the plaque represents the attributes of mathematics, to the right those of astronomy. Apart from the pictorial marquetry, the elegant proportions, and the rich bronzes that protect all its edges, we must not forget the intricate mechanism, a miracle of ingenious devices to facilitate its use. This masterpiece was created by Oeben and was completed by Riesener; the bronzes were by Duplessis, Winant, and Hervieux. It is signed on the marquetry at the back: *Riesener H. 1769 à l'arsenal de Paris.*

Side by side with these large masculine bureaux, the *ébénistes* produced a variety of bureaux of the utmost refinement, with delicate marquetry and bronzes, for feminine use. Such were the bureau *à pente* (slant front) and the *bonheur du jour.* The former, designed with a frieze drawer, is characterized by its slant front, which when let down served as a writing board and revealed an interior fitted with pigeonholes and small drawers. Occasionally at the back was a rising screen of silk or India paper that protected the writer from any glaring light. The *bonheur du jour,* taking its name from the speed with which it achieved success, is in the form of a table, with a frieze drawer. Its distinguishing feature is a small recessed superstructure or low *gradin* (the table *à gradins* or bureau *à gradins* is essentially the same as the *bonheur du jour*). There is also the writing table with lateral compartments (*caissons*) and a space for the knees, essentially a simplified version of the bureau *semainier,* but at this time it has less drawers and only four legs. This form of kneehole table was an especially popular model for the *poudreuse.* (When additional drawer space is required for any article of furniture used with a chair, the advantages of the kneehole are obvious.)

The tall and upright *secrétaire* with a drop front (*abattant*) and interior fitted with drawers was introduced around 1750. It was destined to have a great career under Louis XVI, when its ample surface was sometimes decorated with superb marquetry. The lower portion of the typical *secrétaire à abattant* was fitted with two cupboard doors; when it was designed in the Louis XV style, it rested on a valanced base that curved into feet of cabriole form. This imposing *secrétaire en armoire,* which occasionally matched either the commode or *encoignure,* and in some instances both, remained in fashion until the time of Louis Philippe.

Honor to whom honor is due; the commode holds the first place as much by reason of its superb workmanship as by its importance as a piece of drawing-room furniture, of which it is the undisputed queen. The typical Louis XV commode, created around 1725, with its undulating and convex surfaces embodies an essential difference from the Régence commode inasmuch as its drawers are made as invisible as possible. The marquetry or

Pen and wash drawing for a *rocaille* cartouche of pronounced asymmetrical design, by Pierre E. Babel. With the advent of *rocaille*, the cartouche became a favorite ornamental device and assumed a distinctive form. *Courtesy Metropolitan Museum of Art. Anne and Carl Stern Fund, 1957.* BELOW: Veneered commode (c. 1750–55). It is richly mounted in chased and gilt bronze. The marquetry of floral sprays, surrounded by beautiful cartouche-shaped borders from which spring handles of graceful foliage scrolls, makes a delightfully rococo façade. Made by Joseph Baumhauer, called Joseph. *Courtesy National Gallery of Art, from the Widener Collection.* (*See pages 148–149.*)

LEFT: *Bas d'encoignure* or low corner cupboard (1743). Made for Madame de Mailly, the favorite of Louis XV, for her rooms in the Château de Choisy. In blue and white lacquer and enriched with silvered bronze mounts, it bears the stamp of M. Criaerd (Maître 1738). *Courtesy Musée du Louvre. Photo Bulloz-Mella.* BELOW: Mahogany commode (c. 1770). Inlaid with a tulipwood and satinwood veneer, mounted in chased and gilt bronze. It belongs to the transitional period; the bronze borders are no longer sinuous and undulating, but rectangular. In this example the angles of the borders are squared off, and the space is filled in with rosettes. Made by P. Dupré (Maître 1766). *Courtesy Frick Collection, New York.* OPPOSITE: *Le Thé à l'anglaise chez le Prince de Conti,* by Michel Ollivier (1766). The scene, one part of four paintings, depicts an "English" tea given by the Prince de Conti at his palace in honor of the young Mozart who is seated at the harpsichord. *Courtesy Musée du Louvre. Photo Giraudon-Mella.*

lacquer panels and bronzes are distributed over the surface without consideration for their existence; in brief, to efface them. This idea is predicated on the principle of unity, for the commode played an important part in the architectural decoration of a room. Properly placed beneath a *trumeau,* the commode served as a *cul-de-lampe,* or pendant and echoed the decoration above it.

At this period, the cartouche, originally a partly unrolled scroll, became an ornament with a peculiar swelling and undulating outline, which is often more or less pear-shaped. This cartouche, in the form of a decorative frame which evaded the traditional symmetry, spread itself profusely in the wall paneling and repeated itself in the form of a capricious bronze border on the façade of the commode. In order to conceal the handles as much as possible, floral sprays gracefully freed themselves from the rococo border to form the bronze handles, while the escutcheons nestled, if possible, in a branch of the spray.

Of remarkable elegance are the commodes with two rows of drawers,

148

providing the curves are carefully studied, decorated with a marquetry of capricious sprays of flowers and leaves wandering lightly over the entire surface. In the characteristic transitional commode, that is, from rococo to classicism, the only rococo features remaining are supports slightly tending to cabriole under chamfered angles and the effacement of the drawers; the latter was to remain in favor into the Louis XVI style. The surfaces are no longer undulating; they are now flat, while the bronze borders, in order to harmonize with the new wall paneling, became rectangular, often sloped off at the angles, either rounded off or squared off, the slope being adorned with a small bronze rosette.

Closely akin to the commode because they belong to that family of furniture known as *meubles d'appui* are the *bas d'encoignure, bas d'armoire,* and commode *à vantaux,* their height being determined by the dado of the paneling. These pieces responded to the aesthetics of the time when furniture that could be incorporated into the architecture of a room enjoyed a great vogue. Under Louis XV, when angles were the common enemy, corner furniture was in high fashion. Around 1750 no room was considered complete without low corner cupboards, made with either a serpentine or bow-shaped façade and a valanced base. Madame de Pompadour placed an order one day with Lazare-Duvaux for thirty *encoignures* in mahogany for her Château Crêcy. Both the commode *à vantaux* and the *bas d'armoire,* though known under Louis XV, achieved their popularity under Louis XVI. Their characteristic feature is a façade with doors; however, the doors of the commode *à vantaux* conceal a chest of drawers.

PROVINCIAL

The Louis XV style has always been the favorite of the French people living in the provinces. Provincial furniture is a more modest or simple interpretation of the prevailing French styles, generally made in solid native woods, such as oak, walnut, beech, and fruit woods, by the local cabinetmaker. The similarity of all provincial furniture is far more pronounced than its differences. The diversity is chiefly found in its decorative detail, for the needs of most people in all the provinces were much the same. In brief, they entertained, ate, slept, and stored their possessions in a like manner. Because of this existing similarity in demands, the same shapes, which were generally the simplest and most practical, are essentially found in all the provinces. Naturally the person whose house as well as purse could accommodate the fashionable pieces being created in Paris, such as toilet tables with rising framed mirrors and all kinds of small occasional tables, had such pieces, but in a simplified version and not in the deluxe Parisian models adorned with marquetry and elaborate bronzes. The difference between the two reminds one of a Dior original and a copy of it made by a local, but capable, dressmaker.

The great century for provincial furniture, as for all French cabinetwork, was the eighteenth, when comfort became an important consideration in the provincial homes of both the upper and lower middle classes. Much better off financially, they could afford to indulge in a few luxuries that would make their homes more enjoyable. All the characteristic articles of provincial furniture necessary for pleasant country living were introduced, the amount and variety of which, as well as its quality, dependent on the social standards of the people who were to use it. *Chaises à capucine, canapés* fitted with loose cushions covered in gay and colorful chintz, comfortable *bergères* with turned supports, *armoires,* buffets, *dressoirs,* kneading troughs (*pétrin*), hanging bread cupboards (*panetière*), oblong tables with frieze drawers frequently serving as writing tables, hanging wall shelves (*étagères*) for pewter, brass, and earthenware, hanging glazed cabinets in which were kept the more costly glass pieces, salt boxes (*boîte à sel*), flour boxes (*boîte à farine*) used to flour fish before frying, slant-front desks (bureau *à pente*), commodes, secretary commodes, tester beds, and tall case clocks were made by the local cabinetmaker. At last provincial furniture began to flourish.

When one looks at the cupboard doors and examines the gay and piquant molded panels with their animated and graceful curves, so en-

Turned *chaise à capucine,* distinguished from its Louis XV predecessors with their scrolled slat backs by the so-called "hat" design of the slats, identifiable only with Louis XVI. The pleasing proportions and pure lines give this chair artistic value. *Courtesy Mrs. James B. Mabon. Photo Taylor and Dull.*

tirely beguiling in their avoidance of symmetry, one is hardly surprised that in the provinces the Louis XV style endeared itself to everyone. At the time the Louis XVI style became fashionable the majority of provincial cabinetmakers never advanced beyond the transitional stage. These pieces retained their valanced base and cabriole legs, but their carved decoration was in the neo-classical taste, such as vases flanked by a symmetrical arrangement of flowers or, later, revolutionary emblems. Although the straight lines of the Louis XVI style were easier to execute than the sinuous Louis XV curves, the former, devoid of carved decoration to soften the angular aspect of its lines, is rather poverty-stricken, while the real charm of the Louis XV style is in its graceful curves. Even the village joiner sometimes made a crude but courageous attempt to make a peasant kitchen table with cabriole legs, reminding one of a country girl trying to make a court courtesy. Naturally in some of the provinces, particularly in cities near Paris, the Louis XVI style was adopted in form as well as in ornament. This may be seen in the commode of semi-circular plan, a form much favored in the Louis XVI style. In the ensuing nineteenth century some provincial furniture showed to a certain degree the influence of the French Empire; early Biedermeier, flourishing in Germany, inspired much of this work.

Undoubtedly one of the most unique pieces of provincial furniture is the *lit clos,* resembling a huge cupboard with its solid paneled sides and paneled doors made with shutters, spindles, or pierced ornament. This distinctive bed, found in all the colder regions, assured the occupants of privacy, since many of the cottages consisted of only one room, and, of equal importance, it served as a protection against the cold climate. For the same reasons, the *lit à colonnes* with its four tall posts was the favorite tester bed. The *lit clos,* which was very often provided with an upper berth, was also made without doors, when it became a *lit demi-clos;* this type was furnished with curtains.

The tall and imposing single-bodied *armoire,* all in one piece, with its two long cupboard doors, introduced in the previous century, is, together with the bed, the most important article of provincial furniture. Very soon, no home, no matter how humble, was without one of these roomy and decorative *armoires,* which were part of a bride's dowry. Throughout her life, the good housewife polished it, as if her one goal in life was to give the walnut, oak, or cherry wood a lovely patina that would win the respectful admiration of all her friends. Each long cupboard door of the Louis XV *armoire* is divided into either two or three gracefully curving molded panels. When there are three panels, the middle one is smaller. The base is valanced and curves into feet of cabriole form, terminating in a volute, which often rests on a plain small cube. By these characteristic features, that is, the asymmetrically shaped panels, the valanced base, and cabriole feet, one can recognize at a glance not only a Louis XV *armoire* but any piece of Louis XV paneled furniture. There were, of course, other types of *armoires,* such as the *bonnetière,* which was much in demand because of its slender proportions, being usually fitted with a long single door. Sometimes the top panel of the single door was decorated with turned spindles; this type is closely related to the *garde-manger,* or food cupboard, which requires some form of openwork for ventilation. Because the Louis XV style has an aversion to angles, the popularity of the corner cupboard (*armoire d'encoignure* or simply *encoignure*) was assured. Some are low (*bas d'encoignure*) when they are usually surmounted with a tier of shelves arranged in pyramid fashion, while others are tall, being either single or double-bodied.

Then there were all those cupboards that served as buffets and *dressoirs.* Such were the buffet *bas,* a low cupboard (*bas d'armoire*), usually with two and sometimes three or more cupboard doors that resembled, when it was composed of two cupboard doors, the lower part of the no-longer fashionable *armoire à deux corps;* the buffet *à deux corps* with the upper part sometimes so tall that it looked like a tall single-bodied *armoire,* mounted on a slightly wider low *armoire,* having two doors in each section, and the tall buffet *vaisselier,* a kind of *dressoir* in the form of a low cupboard surmounted with a deeply recessed superstructure, fitted with several rows of narrow open shelves, which always has a back

ABOVE LEFT: Provençal carved walnut *armoire* (eighteenth century). The asymmetrically shaped panels and a valanced base curving into cabriole feet are typical Louis XV features. The long steel buttress hinges and fret-pierced keyplates extending the entire length of the cupboard doors are especially identified with Provençal cabinetwork. CENTER: Provençal carved walnut *panetière* (eighteenth century). *Courtesy Musée Arlaten.* LEFT: Carved walnut commode with a serpentine front (eighteenth century). *Courtesy Parke-Bernet, from the collection of Gertrude Hill Gavin.* (*See page 154.*)

of solid wood. There was also the *vaisselier horloge,* which is the same as the buffet *vaisselier,* except for a tall case clock centered in its open recessed shelves. This unique article of furniture is identified with the regional work of Bresse. These *dressoirs* are always charming pieces in a country dining-room, with their ample shelf space for the display of colorful earthenware, brass, and pewter. Some of the much wider models often combine the purpose of a commode; in these examples the lower section centers a tier of drawers, flanked by cupboard doors.

Last, but choice, is the buffet *crédence,* an original Provençal creation, whose "parent," like the buffet *vaisselier,* was the low cupboard. The majority were made at Arles, the great center for Provençal furniture. This delightful piece of Louis XV provincial furniture is also known as a buffet *à glissant* because of the sliding end panels in its very low, deeply recessed paneled superstructure, which is its distinguishing feature and is mounted on a low cupboard. In accordance with traditional custom, a set of open shelves for pewter vessels must hang above the buffet *crédence.* Like all Provençal paneled pieces, the moldings enframing the panels are firm, clear-cut, and rich, while the shapes of the panels are gay, animated, and almost frivolous; at least they are never sedate. Long steel buttress hinges and fret-pierced keyplates often extend the entire length of the cupboard doors, and, although this curious size of the pins and escutcheons is by no means limited to Provence, they are a feature of the work. The *pétrin,* or kneading trough and the *panetière,* a small hanging cupboard for bread, with its decorative turned spindles, are also delightful pieces of Provençal furniture, the latter often being credited as an Arlesian invention.

The Louis XV commode with its *bombé* and serpentine contours was also a fashionable provincial piece and in most cases was made with three rows of drawers. Some with a pronounced *bombé* contour are poorly proportioned and obviously proclaim themselves as "villagers." No doubt some of the most pleasing commodes omitted the *bombé* form, relying entirely on gracefully swept serpentine lines and gay asymmetrical panels. The commode, allying itself with the bureau *à pente* or slant-front desk, became the secretary commode with a slant front which opened to an interior fitted with pigeonholes and small drawers. Some models became even more complicated by having a tall upper portion fitted with two doors.

One final word, before leaving French provincial, about the wall fountain with a basin (*lavabo*), a decorative but necessary accessory generally made of pewter, copper, faïence, and somewhat later of *tôle.* Usually found in a niche, its use was by no means restricted to the provinces, for it was customary for the servants to rinse the glasses and cutlery in full view of the guests.

Louis XVI

The interest in classical archaeology in Europe in the eighteenth century provided a focal point for the reaction against rococo. In particular, the rediscovery of the buried classical cities of Herculaneum and Pompeii and their systematic excavations in the middle of the eighteenth century excited civilized society with a lively curiosity about antique art, which until that time had been confined chiefly to a small group of archaeologists. As these cities emerged from their sheets of ashes and lava, all the decorative arts of the Romans came to light, their houses and furnishings, their seats, couches, tripods, and candelabra. Thus, for the first time, men living in the eighteenth century were able to learn firsthand how the ancients lived.

The taste for the antique was propagated by a continuous stream of publications, a whole series of works on ancient Greece and Italy, accounts of travelers who went to Italy to see the ruins, collections of documents and archaeological studies. The learned Comte de Caylus, a notable amateur in art and patron of artists, widened the field of interest through the publication of his own collections of classical antiquities in a series of volumes issued between 1752 and 1767, entitled *Recueil d'antiquités égyptiennes, étrusques, grecques, romaines et gauloises.* The *Recueil* made available to designers an immense repertory of completely new motifs. On the theoretical side, the movement reached its climax with the publication in 1764 of Johann Winckelmann's *Geschichte der Kunst des Altertums,* in which he extolled the virtues of antiquity and exhorted artists to take their models from it. But nothing inflamed the thinking and imagination of the times as much as the collection of engravings first appearing around the mid-eighteenth century by the noted Venetian etcher Giovanni Battista Piranesi, 1720–78. In these splendid plates lauding the beauties of Imperial Rome, the play of *chiaroscuro* and *contre-jour* emphasized the ruins of mighty arches and colonnades

155

and deepened their mystery, conjuring, as it were, a romantic vision of the past that awakened an elegiac or sentimental melancholy in the minds of all who saw them. In the course of time, the graceful and indefatigable needle and burin of the Piranesis (father and son) furnished decorative artists and architects with almost countless reproductions of Roman monuments, vases, tripods, candelabra, and bas-reliefs. It is interesting to note here the appearance of Egypt on the scene with its sphinxes and winged solar disks, both in the works of Comte de Caylus and Piranesi; the latter showed most individual projects in the Egyptian taste in his *Diverse*

OPPOSITE: *A Ruin Fantasy,* attributed to J. L. Clérisseau (1722–1820; flourished in Italy 1750–70). The taste for fanciful architectural ruins in the Italian manner as typified by this pen and water-color drawing was a result of the neo-classicism of the times. Antique ruins became a fashionable subject for pictorial marquetry under Louis XVI. *Courtesy Cooper Union Museum.* ABOVE: A detail of the drop front of a *secrétaire* (c. 1750–70). It is veneered with a pictorial marquetry which represents classical ruins and architecture enclosed in a rectangular bronze frame. Also of bronze is the ribbon and armorial trophy consisting of two suits of armor, among other things. It bears the incised signature Foulet (either Antoine, Maître 1749, or his son Pierre-Antoine, Maître 1765). *Courtesy Wallace Collection, London.*

Manière, 1769. Then, too, the Sir William Hamilton collection of Greek and Etruscan vases described and reproduced in the work of d'Hancarville supplied inspiration to the artists.

It was inevitable that the charming rococo style had to succumb to such an onslaught. In 1770 when Madame du Barry gave a reception for the opening of her new Château de Louveciennes, that vanished marvel, the most exquisite masterpiece of the Louis XVI style, it was apparent that the Louis XV style had become quite out of fashion, at any rate in Paris, before the death of the king whose name had been given to it. Once again antiquity triumphed, and, as the flamboyant Gothic art of the Middle Ages yielded to the Italian Renaissance, so now the rococo, an art that was also purely French and modern, surrendered to a second Renaissance of interest in antiquity. Architecture was the first to submit. As early as 1753, the neo-classic taste manifested itself in the new wings of the Château de Compiègne designed by the architect Jacques-Ange Gabriel, who also between the years 1762–64 constructed for Louis XV the Petit Trianon, a building exactly in the style of Louis XVI. Furniture as always, but more slowly, followed architecture. In 1763, Grimm, the good friend of Madame d'Épinay and Diderot, writes about the style *à la grecque,* as it was then called: "For some years past, antique forms

157

LEFT: Veneered tulipwood *guéridon* table (c. 1770–75) having a gilt bronze candelabrum with two movable candle arms, perhaps by Martin Carlin (Maître 1766). The circular top and undershelf are inset with marble painted in colors with a garland of flowers and bowknots. *Courtesy Parke-Bernet, from the collection of Thelma Chrysler Foy.* RIGHT: Veneered *serre-bijoux* (c. 1775) attributed to Martin Carlin. It is inset with plaques of Sèvres porcelain painted with flowers and mounted in chased and gilt bronze. *Courtesy Metropolitan Museum of Art. Gift of the Samuel H. Kress Foundation, 1958.*

and ornaments have been in request. . . . The internal and external decoration of buildings, furniture, stuffs and jewels of every kind, all things in Paris, are Greek. . . ." We may assume from Grimm's remarks, as well as records describing articles of furniture delivered to customers (there is no mention of antique in Lazare-Duvaux's daybook, which is available for the years 1748–59), that the Louis XVI style came into existence about 1760.

Of course furniture did not all in a year and *en bloc* assume the new classical decoration and form; as happens in all styles, there is a time of transition, in this case about a decade, when the new principles are being perfected. As always the ornament is first to respond, then the lines and structure. When the transition to Louis XVI was completed, the structural lines were based chiefly on the rectilinear and the curves of the circle and ellipse supplanted the sinuous curves of the rococo. Straight tapering legs superseded cabriole legs. However, even under Louis XVI some belated pieces had not yet resigned themselves entirely to abandoning their cabriole legs, as may be seen most frequently in small occasional tables and other delicate tables designed for feminine use. The last of all the arts to respond to the neo-classical movement was painting, which, under the vigorous impetus of David, bore once more the yoke of antiquity. The "reign" of the Greeks and Romans began in 1784 when David's *Oath of the Horatii* was received with ecstatic admiration.

Although the furniture of the First Empire differs widely from that of the Louis XVI style, both styles are founded on the same principle, that is, the imitation of antiquity. However, since society from 1760 to the Revolution was as epicurean and worldly as in the first half of the eighteenth century, the original creators of the Louis XVI style applied this principle with considerable discretion and respect for the national taste. The general enthusiasm of the French for classical antiquity, which affected taste so profoundly in the second half of the eighteenth century, did not alter the essential unity of the period; the manners and customs were the same after 1760 as before and were to remain the same until 1789. Antiquity under Louis XVI was only a fashion, even among many very learned people; it was to be made French, and if the adherence to classical precedent interfered with comfort and convenience, the former had to yield. For this reason, even though the least educated eye can recognize at first glance a Louis XV from a Louis XVI piece, a peculiar affinity exists between the two styles.

Owing to the double character of society under Louis XVI (they loved the simplicity of the ancient days and the worldly comforts of the eighteenth century), the task of the cabinetmaker up to the end of the Ancien Régime was to harmonize the noble and simple beauty of antiquity with the graceful and the amiable of the eighteenth century. Refined simplicity, subdued elegance, and precision softened by an abundance of graceful and delicate ornament are the ideals and essence of Louis XVI furniture. Much of the grace and beauty were achieved through the perfection of proportions, the faultless balance of all parts, and the harmonious division of the surface into panels and the accuracy of their framing. Never in the history of French furniture did the *ébéniste* display more assuredness in his technique. He displayed this same sureness of taste in his selection of ornament that was sufficiently rich to alleviate the bareness, but within the boundary of deliberate moderation.

In spite of all the excavations and progress in archaeology, what was best understood in ancient art around 1760 was Roman architecture, and accordingly it paced the new style. Of course ancient architecture immediately brought back symmetry in ornament and in form. Straight lines and semi-circular arches—Roman architectural bequests—mark the style. Semi-circular or elliptical arches and ellipses or ovals are much in evidence. For example, the tops of chair backs, mirrors, and panels of

OPPOSITE ABOVE: Commode *à vantaux* (delivered April 1785), bearing the stamp of Martin Carlin and the mark BV of the Château de Bellevue. It is veneered with ebony and the façade, divided into three parts that open as doors, is decorated with panels of black and gold Oriental lacquer. It was made for the use of the King's aunts at Bellevue. *Courtesy Musée du Louvre. Photo Caisse Nationale-Mella.* (*See page 159.*) OPPOSITE BELOW: Commode *à étagères* (c. 1780–85). It is veneered with tulipwood and ebony, richly mounted in chased and gilt bronze. The circular Sèvres plaque is painted in polychrome with a basket of flowers. The mirror-backed shelves are intended to hold choice pieces of porcelain and the like. Stamped A. Weisweiler (Maître 1778). *Courtesy H. M. The Queen.* ABOVE: Veneered mahogany *desserte* by J. H. Riesener (Maître 1768). It has rounded ends and is richly mounted in chased and gilt bronze. Louis XVI presented it to the Grand Duke Paul Petrovich of Russia in 1782. *Courtesy Duveen Brothers, New York.*

woodwork are often in the shape of a semi-circular arch; chairs are given medallion-shaped backs, tables with oval tops, frames of panels and mirrors in the shape of ovals; commodes, *armoires,* and all kinds of side tables, large and small, are frequently of semi-circular plan. The rectilinear, or box-like appearance of paneled furniture, especially commodes and the like, is considerably softened at times by incorporating at each end either shelves (*étagères*) shaped to quarter circles, full or re-entrant, or two little quarter-cylindrical cupboards. Commodes of this form with rounded ends were much favored under Louis XVI. Such pieces with shelves either open or closed are sometimes called commodes *à encoignures;* however, when the shelves are visible, the name commode *à étagères* is also used. Full or re-entrant quarter circles also frequently link the façade of oblong side tables with the wall against which they are placed. The curves introduced into the furniture, however, never detract from the directness of the horizontal and vertical structural lines. Numerous Louis XVI pieces adhere to the straight line to the very end,

ABOVE: Commode *à vantaux* (c. 1785). It is veneered with mahogany and thuja wood and mounted in chased and gilt bronze. Stamped A. Weisweiler. *Courtesy Metropolitan Museum of Art. Fletcher Fund, 1925.* RIGHT: *Serre-bijoux* (c. 1785). This jewel cabinet fitted with a series of drawers was made by J. H. Riesener for the Comtesse de Provence, Louis XVI's sister-in-law. The bronze mounts have a jewel-like quality. Bronze female caryatids supplant the columns in the cabinet portion; arrow feathers at the top of each leg are clearly visible, hence the name "quiver leg." *Courtesy H. M. The Queen.*

162

possessing not a single curve. All this geometry in design—the impersonal traced with ruler, square, and compass, which supplants the sinuous, freehand lines that the Louis XV style had placed everywhere—would be extremely arid if it were not almost always softened by graceful ornament, the amount and kind due primarily to the taste of either the *ébéniste* or the customer.

Another distinguishing feature having its provenance in architecture is the treatment of a plain surface by a border or several parallel borders in place of ornamentation. Undecorated mahogany surfaces were extremely fashionable under Louis XVI. Many pieces of furniture rely entirely for their decoration upon framed panels. As a rule, the borders are moldings of either gilt bronze or wood covered with brass, while others toward the end of the period are in the form of narrow bands of brass inlaid in the wood, or simply bands of wood of a contrasting color. As for the moldings under Louis XVI, their use is less pronounced than in the previous period; they are flatter, neater, and more uniform, and they are combined according to ancient architectural rules.

A marked characteristic of the Louis XVI style is the small scale on which practically all ornament was treated by the woodcarver and especially by the bronze worker. The jewel-like quality of the bronze mounts resembles more the work of the goldsmith than that of the *fondeur-ciseleur*, and is in marked contrast to the splendid amplitude of Louis XV mounts. For the untrained eye, bronzes by Caffiéri will far outshine those by Gouthière. Then, too, a basic difference exists between the kind of ornament used in the two styles. Louis XVI ornamentation most often makes use of a repetition of like elements arranged in a line or joined in a running motif, as may be seen on the friezes of tables or commodes. Among the many favorite running motifs, which also happen to be an architectural bequest of antiquity, are dentils, leaf bands such as acanthus, bay, or oak, bead chains, *entrelacs* or two interlaced ribbons, guilloches, imbricated coin bands, and, above all, short rows of fluting. Also borrowed from antiquity and incorporated once again into furniture design are such architectural legacies as pilasters, consoles, and balusters. By far the most important are columns, either detached or more frequently engaged, having a capital, fluted shaft, and turned base, and found at the corners of commodes and other pieces. Toward the end of the epoch the capital was supplanted frequently by a circular molding covered with brass. The caryatid also makes its appearance at this time as a substitute for the column.

Apart from the decorative elements belonging to classical architecture, a countless number of motifs, both ancient and modern, drawn from a great variety of sources—from mythology, the vegetable world, the animal kingdom, domestic objects made by man, Roman and Renaissance art—

were used in the Louis XVI style. They were interpreted, as were the architectural details, in the lighter form of the eighteenth century and were artfully blended in charming compositions by such ornamentists as Jean Charles Delafosse, Jean François de Neufforge, François Boucher, son of the famous painter, and Richard Lalonde. As the *ébéniste* looked through the collections of engraved ornament, he saw much to tempt him. Such were the delightful pastoral scenes by Jean-Baptiste Huet, whose work was largely inspired by Boucher and Oudry, light and elegant interlacings of foliage arranged as running motifs by Salembier, and by Ranson the trophies and bouquets hung by bows and ribbons (those bowknots and streamers so much used and abused during this epoch). There were sometimes architectural compositions of antique ruins, a perfect solution for the marquetry on the *secrétaire à abattant*. The master of these was the painter Hubert Robert. His elaborate landscapes, depicting the eternity of Nature combined with Roman ruins, evoked a dream of antiquity that excited the romantic imagination of the French and flattered their sentimental philosophy.

By a conjunction somewhat difficult to explain, the neo-classical movement is accompanied in its early phase, this era of light manners, by a sentimental mode exemplified in the paintings of Greuze and encouraged by such writers as Diderot. This love for simplicity, domestic virtue, and sensibility, which anticipates the romanticism of the nineteenth century, seems to have been dictated by a sentimental idealization of the ancient world. In furniture the taste for sentimental art may be seen in the rise of such pedestrian objects as cups and saucers, bowls, and pitchers employed as motifs in marquetry. (The *bonheur du jour* illustrated in the preceding chapter represents this taste.)

Evidences of these tendencies are apparent in the realistic modern motifs recruited in the latter part of the Louis XV style as a reaction against the fantasy of *rocaille*. Such are the profusions of flowers, roses, lilies, and cornflowers gathered from a French garden, and pastoral attributes, the large straw hat of the shepherdess, her wicker basket for gathering strawberries in the woods, the crook and reed flute of the shepherd—symbols of the simple pleasures of the countryside. But, as these motifs helped banish the *rocaille,* they in turn were to be crushed under an accumulation of new antique motifs copied from Egyptian, Grecian, and above all Pompeian art, with its delicate grotesques, palmettes, tripods, lamps, perfume, and incense burners, forecasting the Directoire style, which logically evolved into the style of the First Empire.

All those brilliant and versatile qualities which marked the achievements of Parisian *ébénistes* under Louis XV were continued under his successor. Little of any importance remained to be discovered in this domain, as we shall see when we consider briefly the work of several

Elevation of a bedroom wall, a project by the French ornamentist Pierre Ranson (c. 1780). The trophies, garlands of flowers, and bowknotted ribbons are typically Ranson's style. The canopied dome of the *lit à la polonaise* is surmounted with a panache of feathers. *Courtesy Cooper Union Museum.*

great *ébénistes*. The same woods were used, native and exotic; above all, mahogany enjoyed remarkable favor. The taste for mahogany received considerable impetus both from the more plentiful supply of West Indian mahogany after the ending of the American War of Independence and from the wave of Anglomania that swept over France in the last ten years or more before the Revolution. Simple mahogany veneers were widely adopted for commodes and the like mounted in gilt bronze. Ebony recovered some of the popularity it enjoyed under Louis XIV. Marble tops continued in fashion and were carefully chosen for color.

A gallery of pierced brass is a novelty of the Louis XVI epoch met with again and again around the tops of tables and on the three sides of marble tops of such pieces as *bonheurs du jour, chiffonnières* with five or more drawers, one upon another, and *vitrines* (glazed cabinets for the display of curios). The return to straight lines made possible the use of much more turning; round tapering legs, *toupie* (top-shaped) feet, balusters, and columns are typical for the turner's lathe.

Toward the end of the reign, in the search for something new, some *ébénistes* experimented with brass. For instance, they inlaid the grooves of flutings with brass; they used brass plaques in the squares above the legs, and we have mentioned already moldings covered with brass and the narrow bands of brass inlaid in the wood. At the same time, other

LEFT: Veneered mahogany *bonheur du jour* (c. 1780). The recessed superstructure is provided with doors of tambour construction. The pierced brass gallery, the rectangular framed panels, and the tapering cylindrical fluted legs are typical of the Louis XVI period. Stamped Jean-François Leleu (Maître 1764). *Courtesy Services du Conseiller Culturel, Ambassade de France, New York. Photo Adant. (See page 165.)* RIGHT: Mahogany *bouillotte* table mounted in brass (late eighteenth century). The frieze drawer moldings are covered with brass, while brass plaques are inset in the squares above the tapered quadrangular legs. The *bouillotte* lamp, one of the most sought-after types today, with its metal shade, was introduced during the first French Empire. *Courtesy Parke-Bernet, from the collection of Baron Maurice de Vaux. (See page 165.)* OPPOSITE: Veneered mahogany commode (c. 1780–85), stamped J. H. Riesener. It is enriched with chased and gilt bronze mounts in the manner of Pierre Gouthière (1732–1813/14), and has the trapezoidal panels that are a feature of Riesener's later work. *Courtesy Wallace Collection, London.*

ébénistes painted decoration in oils on a ground of natural wood. As for textiles, the general tendency toward more delicate tones in interior decoration was carried out in fabrics, which were also of lighter weight. Otherwise there was little change in the choice of fashionable textiles employed in upholstery.

A celebrated galaxy of *ébénistes*, from Riesener to Weisweiler, distinguishes the Louis XVI style. Many, like Saunier, Leleu, and Riesener, began their careers under Louis XV. Riesener, 1734–1806, the uncrowned king of *ébénistes* under Louis XVI, was one of many German craftsmen

who went to Paris in the eighteenth century to seek their fortune. After the accession of Louis XVI, they came in even greater numbers, hoping for the favor of the queen. The patronage extended to such *ébénistes* as Beneman, Weisweiler, Schwerdfeger, and Riesener reveals that they were not disappointed. We have already mentioned that Riesener completed the famous *Bureau du Roi* and that his name alone appears on it. Riesener embodies all the qualities that are the essence of the Louis XVI style when it was most pure. His commodes and *secrétaires à abattant* mounted in chased and gilt bronze, whether they are decorated with marquetry, lacquer, or simply veneers, generally of plain mahogany, are notable for their faultless proportions and sober elegance softened by abundant grace. For these two pieces he frequently favored a panel in the shape of a trapezoid, the oblique sides of which are concave.

In his later work, Riesener preferred a marquetry comprising a network of lozenges, each lozenge centering a flower, usually a rose, narcissus, or cornflower, said to have been the queen's favorite flowers. Because this kind of marquetry appears on pieces he made for Marie Antoinette, it is popularly known as *à la reine*. Riesener liked to decorate the center panel of his commodes and the drop fronts of his *secrétaires* with a medallion of either wood, usually adorned with floral marquetry, or gilt bronze, chased with such themes as a Sacrifice to Love. The

ABOVE: Veneered *secrétaire à abattant* stamped J. H. Riesener and delivered for the use of Marie Antoinette at Versailles on February 12, 1783. The bronze mounts are in the style of Pierre Gouthière. The center of the drop front is enriched with an oval gilt bronze plaque chased with a scene of a Sacrifice to Love, in the manner of Claude Michel, called Clodion (1738–1814). *Courtesy Wallace Collection, London.* (*See page 167.*) RIGHT: Gilt bronze plaque similar to the one inset above. *Courtesy Cooper Union Museum.* OPPOSITE LEFT: Combined music stand and writing table (c. 1780) stamped Martin Carlin. It is inset with a Sèvres plaque painted with a musical trophy. The gilt bronze swags of fringed drapery with bowknotted ribbons are a favorite device of Carlin. *Courtesy Victoria and Albert Museum.* OPPOSITE RIGHT: Combined work, writing, and reading table (c. 1783) stamped M. Carlin. It is mounted with plaques of Sèvres porcelain painted with baskets and vases of flowers. The plaque at the front of the table is hinged at its lower edge; two drawers are concealed beneath its drop front. The entire top, which may be raised or lowered on a vertical ratchet, may also be turned into a revolving reading desk by pressing on a knob at the back. The Sèvres plaque at the top is hinged at the front and is raised on a ratchet to form a book rest. Writing slides directly under the top may be pulled out from each side. *Courtesy Wallace Collection, London.*

168

medallion is framed in a gilt bronze molding, and above it, also in gilt bronze, are sprays of flowers tied with the traditional bowknot and ribbon streamers. Riesener, like most *ébénistes* from the Rhineland, excelled in complicated locking devices for transforming furniture, which attained their peak of complexity under Louis XVI. His combination pieces and pieces with secret compartments are a miracle of accuracy and attest to his German heritage. Much of Riesener's work, like that of Oeben, bears no stamp, because furniture made for the Crown was free from guild regulations.

Martin Carlin (d. 1785) is also a perfect exponent of this charming Louis XVI manner with its refined and graceful elegance. His exquisite bronze mounts range from very small stylized motifs, such as ropes of beads, to garlands of realistic flowers. Bronze swags or festoons of tasseled drapery are typical of Carlin's style. He was adept in producing small combination pieces, such as combined sewing, writing, and reading tables, which were so common under Louis XVI. Elaborate combinations of rich materials are characteristic of the Louis XVI style, and Carlin, like most of his contemporaries, possessed the technical brilliance to work in the most varied materials—panels of marble mosaics, lacquer or mar-

quetry, and plaques of Sèvres porcelain. Carlin liked to use Sèvres plaques, generally painted with bouquets of flowers reserved in a white ground, for his very refined pieces especially designed for feminine use, whether small work tables or *secrétaires*.

It is interesting to note here that the taste for porcelain plaques, which continued up to the Revolution and later, is a distinguishing feature of the Louis XVI style. Madame du Barry, an important customer of Carlin's, possessed a considerable number of pieces decorated with porcelain at the Château de Louveciennes, which no doubt encouraged the fashion. The logic and propriety of using porcelain for the decoration of furniture are perhaps open for discussion. Suffice it to say that all that looks like an error in taste to outrage need not have actually been so then. It is necessary to envisage it in its proper setting. The same remark might apply to Florentine *pietra commessa* or *pietra dura*, which, in the form of panels, German *ébénistes* working in Paris, such as Weisweiler, used for the decoration of furniture during the latter part of Louis XVI's reign.

David Roentgen, 1743–1807, was a German, like Riesener, but his work was less French in spirit and in execution than that of Riesener. Though Roentgen became a maître of the Paris guild in 1780, he was not in a strict sense a French *ébéniste,* but a German cabinetmaker. His chief workshop was at Neuwied on the Rhine, where he had many assistant craftsmen. He was perhaps the most successful cabinetmaker in Europe. Though the forms of his furniture are rather heavy, he was, however, the undisputed master of the art of pictorial marquetry. Flowers accompanied by ribbons, themes inspired by mythology or the Comédie Italienne are typical of his repertory. His great contemporary reputation was owing to a large extent to his mechanical genius. He was expert in designing harlequin pieces of furniture equipped with complex mechanisms, which, when set in motion, controlled their transformation and secret hiding places. In 1779 Marie Antoinette conferred on him a specially created appointment, *ébéniste-mécanicien du Roi et de la Reine.*

Toward the end of the reign, around 1785, many pieces of furniture depart from the pure Louis XVI style. On the one hand, and this is particularly true of the deluxe pieces such as console tables and commodes made for the royal apartments, a remarkable resemblance can be found in their grandeur and heavy forms to that of the Louis XIV style. Until very recent times the leader of this style was incontestably the *ébéniste* Guillaume Beneman (d. after 1811), who produced a number of works for the Crown. Typical of his style, which is reminiscent of the grandeur of Boulle, are his four monumental mahogany commodes lavishly mounted in gilt bronze made for Fontainebleau and Compiègne in 1786 and 1787. Well known to all of us because of its countless copies is the one designed with a large center panel in the form of a great elliptical arch, shaped like

ABOVE: Commode *à vantaux* (c. 1780) stamped A. Weisweiler. It is veneered with ebony and inlaid with rectangular plaques of *pietra dura*. The façade is divided into three sections, each opening as a cupboard door. Some of the *pietra dura* panels, possibly all of them, date from the reign of Louis XIV. *Courtesy H. M. The Queen.* BELOW: Commode *à vantaux* (c. 1780–90) by David Roentgen. It is inlaid in various woods with a pictorial marquetry of scenes from the *commedia dell'arte. Courtesy Victoria and Albert Museum.*

ABOVE: Commode *à vantaux* by J. Stöckel (Maître 1775) and reconstructed by G. Beneman (Maître 1785) in 1786. It is veneered with mahogany and purple wood. The two doors open to five drawers in the interior. At each of the four corners is a bundle of mahogany fasces bound with gilt bronze ribbons, to harmonize with the handsome bronze military trophy. *Courtesy Musée Nationale de Fontainebleau. Photo Caisse Nationale-Mella.* LEFT: Detail of a bronze caryatid (c. 1785–90). From a *guéridon* table of tripod form made of bronze

a basket handle, centering a medallion in blue and white biscuit modeled with classical figure subjects. At the four corners are heavy fluted columns of mahogany supported on *toupie* feet. Almost as familiar is the commode having the same center panel in the form of an elliptical arch but centering bronze trophies emblematic of war—Roman plumed helmets and shields (the treatment recalling the heroic grandeur of similar Roman body armor under Louis XIV). To harmonize with the military trophies, at each of the four corners is a bundle of arrows bound with intercrossed bronze ribbons resting on a lion's paw of gilded bronze. Though bearing Beneman's stamp, it appears that these commodes were essentially alterations of other slightly earlier commodes made by Joseph Stöckel (d. 1802), who merits the credit for their basic design.

Apart from this work, certain *ébénistes*, unabashed, made copies of Louis XIV pieces. Such are the imitations of the sumptuous pieces of Boulle, with their marquetry of metal and tortoise shell, produced by Montigny, Levasseur, Séverin, and other *ébénistes*. The favor accorded Boulle furniture in the latter part of the eighteenth century is an important aspect of the Louis XVI taste.

Other pieces belonging to this period instead of recalling the style of "*le Roi Soleil*" forecast that of the Directoire and Empire. Certain pieces, such as *guéridon*-tables, whose forms and materials followed Pompeian tripods very closely, may even be said to belong to it already. There can be little or no doubt that the original creators of the Louis XVI style had no desire to adhere too closely to antique models. Nevertheless, the so-called Etruscan or Pompeian style, the latest and most austere development of the Louis XVI style, was the logical outcome of the teachings of such men as Caylus. This style, which became more and more the fashion for interior decoration from the late 1770s onward, generally derives its decorative motifs and often its actual forms from classical objects found at Pompeii and Herculaneum. It is more self-consciously archaeological than the pure Louis XVI style, but until the end of the Ancien Régime the grace of sentiment continued to temper the austerity of archaeology.

The *ébéniste* whose compositions and mounts are most representative of the Pompeian style is Adam Weisweiler, flourishing between 1778 and 1809, one of the most appreciated *ébénistes* at this time, who worked for Marie Antoinette at Saint-Cloud. Weisweiler, who was trained in the

and lapis lazuli and attributed to Weisweiler. *Courtesy Frick Collection, New York. (See page 174.)* RIGHT: Bureau *de dame* (1780s) stamped A. Weisweiler. This combined writing and reading table is veneered with ebony, the book rest decorated with black and gold Japanese lacquer enclosed in a border of aventurine. Frieze panels of polished steel form the background for the bronze mounts. The bronze caryatids and interlaced stretcher centering a basket recalling the shepherdess' basket is typical of Weisweiler. The bronze mounts are attributed to Pierre Gouthière. This extremely rich table was in Marie Antoinette's *cabinet-intérieur* at the Château de Saint-Cloud in 1789 and is characteristic of the miracles of cabinet-work that were at the Château toward the end of Louis XVI's reign. *Courtesy Musée du Louvre. Photo Caisse Nationale-Mella.*

workshop of Roentgen at Neuwied, used a wide range of materials—lacquers, marquetry, veneering, tortoise shell, metal, porcelain, Wedgwood plaques, and Florentine *pietra commessa*. As a rule, his work is notable for its delicacy of design and the refined finish of its mounts. Nothing is more typical of Weisweiler than his slender and elegant bronze caryatids in the form of a half figure of a laughing young woman, sometimes carrying a basket of flowers on her head. Her hair is parted in the middle and plaited, the two long braids resting on her breast. Beneath her waist is a fringed drapery; the figure is mounted on a slender elongated leg. Weisweiler used these caryatids in place of columns on such pieces as *secrétaires* with a drop-front panel, and as decorative supports for various types of tables. Though Weisweiler heralded the new, he also made pieces recalling Louis XIV, as may be seen in the commode inlaid with *pietra dura*.

Chairs of the Louis XVI period are in general more angular than those of the preceding style, and in that respect less comfortable, or at least they appear to be so. On the other hand they are more varied in form and ornament. The basic difference between a Louis XV and a Louis XVI chair is that the former has not a single straight line, while the latter always has at least straight legs. Because of the architectural influence, another major difference is that all the members or parts of a Louis XVI chair are at the same time joined and separated by well-defined joints,

OPPOSITE: Painted *bergère* (c. 1785) with baluster-shaped arm supports. *Courtesy Parke-Bernet.* ABOVE: *Qui en dit l'Abbé* by Nicolas Lavreince; engraving by N. de Launay. Chairs with medallion-shaped backs are shown here; it is interesting to note the continued popularity of the draped toilet table and the classical treatment of the wall paneling. *Courtesy Metropolitan Museum of Art. Dick Fund, 1954.* (*See pages 176–177.*)

175

while a Louis XV chair is composed of continuous curves that flow into one another without any visible separation. This marked feature of the Louis XVI chair often detracts from the beauty, as may be seen in chairs with baluster-shaped arm supports; the joining of the base of the baluster with the top of the leg is often very awkward. The Louis XVI chair frame is simply molded or carved with running motifs derived from classical sources; flutes, wave bands, bead chains, and Greek key designs supplant the freer flowers, foliage, and shells of the rococo epoch, while the quality of the carving reveals a greater delicacy and refinement. Sometimes carved at the center of the chair back, particularly chairs with oval medallion

backs, is a ribbon bow or, but much less frequently, a tiny floral wreath flanked with two sprays bound with ribbon.

The back of the upholstered *fauteuil* may have a variety of shapes. However, irregardless of its shape, if the back is slightly hollowed out, it is said to be *en cabriolet.* Medallion backs and rectangular backs are especially characteristic; the latter in turn is treated in a number of forms. Many are square or almost square. Others have uprights vertical or slanting slightly outward, and the crest rail is arched like a basket handle (they are then called *anse de panier*); or the crest rail is rectangular or very slightly arched, sloped off at the angles in a concave curve (these are referred to as *en chapeau,* or hat-shaped). The uprights of these last-mentioned backs, which are occasionally slender columns detached from the framework of the back, are surmounted with carved finials often in the form of a pine cone or plume of feathers. The arm, which is always provided with a *manchette,* is joined to the back by a more or less graceful curve that sometimes starts at the very top of the uprights of the back. As a rule, the arm terminates in a rather modest volute, under which the armpost joins it. The armpost is almost always joined to the top of the straight leg; rarely is it set back on the side rail of the seat, as in the Louis XV style. But since panniers were still fashionable, the armpost curves inward. Later, when panniers were no longer in vogue, baluster-shaped armposts reappeared. A molded vertical leg tapering off toward the foot is the neo-classic type. Some are square in section when they often terminate in a projecting dice-shaped foot. Other legs are round, turned slightly conic with a gorge molding at the top and another projecting molding at the foot; they are fluted vertically, with or without cabling, sometimes spirally. Above the leg is a square or die, a necessary reinforcement, which is joined to the seat rail and decorated on two sides generally with a square rosette. The round fluted leg, which is much more characteristic for chairs than the square leg, is often called a quiver leg (*pied en carquois*), even when there is no representation of arrow feathers at the top. Toward the end of the style, in pursuit of the antique, the legs and armposts are sometimes, though not often, designed as one unit, in the form of a terminal figure.

Bergères, the most comfortable of all seats, continued in high fashion. Many *bergères* differ very little from the *fauteuil* except for their closed sides; others have gondola-shaped backs and display a continuous line from the end of one arm to that of the other; still others, but much less common, are the winged type or "confessional" shape.

Chair design under Louis XVI achieved a very high degree of technical excellence. Such *menuisiers* as Boulard, Foliot, Lelarge, Delanois, Sené, and others brought to their work notable skill as wood carvers. Georges Jacob, 1739–1814, one of the great wood carvers of the eighteenth century, created and executed a wide range of chairs. His work shows the evolution in taste from Louis XVI to Empire. Typical of Jacob's work is the lyre motif, and, although it had been used for a number of years for lyre-shaped candelabra and clocks, Jacob is credited with introducing it into furniture making. He used it chiefly for the backs of chairs, which brings us to a new family of expensive chairs, namely, those with backs all of wood and open-worked, in contrast to those with upholstered or caned backs. They were painted, gilded, or made of mahogany; the use of this wood in chair-making is an innovation introduced in this period. The majority of these chairs are decorated with pierced splats in the English style; thus they are called *chaise à l'anglaise.* The most popular design is a lyre-shaped splat. Even the modest *chaise à la capucine* with its straw seat is sometimes provided with a splat of lyre form. Almost as well known as the lyre back is the "sheaf" back with its graceful bundle of rods spreading out in fan shape (*chaise en gerbe* or *chaise en éventail*). There are even *chaises en montgolfière* with a splat shaped like an early fire balloon, celebrating the

RIGHT: *Chaise à l'anglaise* (c. 1785). It is painted gray and has a pierced splat of lyre form. *Courtesy Metropolitan Museum of Art. Gift of J. Pierpont Morgan, 1906.* BELOW: *Pliant,* one of an order of forty *pliants* and twelve *tabourets;* frames made by J.B.C. Sené (Maître 1769), carved by Vallois, gilded by Chatard, and delivered in 1786–87 for use in the Queen's game room (*salon de jeu*) at Compiègne. *Courtesy Cleveland Museum of Art, John L. Severance Fund.*

first balloon flight in 1783 by the brothers Montgolfière. We must not forget to mention stools (*pliants* or *tabourets*), which continued to be much in demand. As we have already read, originally *pliants* could be folded and put away.

Since fashionable ladies before the Revolution were accustomed to spending their time in languorous ease, *canapés*, sofas, and daybeds were much in demand. As in the Louis XV style, *canapés* were designed with solid or open sides. Those with solid sides are very often provided with a long seat cushion and seem more like a sofa or daybed, since they served to rest or loll upon. Some *canapés* retained the graceful lines of the round basket-shaped model or *ottomane* of the Louis XV period. The curves, however, are no longer sinuous; they are controlled. There is one quite

179

new shape, the very large *canapé* called a *confident,* which at both ends is flanked by two additional quadrant-shaped pieces outside the arms. *Confidents* enjoyed a great vogue in the 1770s.

Beds at this period almost invariably had a canopy to protect the occupant from dirt and flakes of paint falling from the ceiling. There was a revival of interest in the *lit à colonnes* with its four tall posts. However, the beds most frequently seen are the *lit à la polonaise* with a domed canopy and the *lit à la duchesse,* having a rectangular canopy supported from the ceiling. The reappearance of a plume of feathers (shades of Louis XIV!) surmounting the different types of testers illustrates so well the often repeated statement that it is to the Louis XIV style that we must look for the origin and first signs of the Louis XVI style. The *dossiers* of the beds, in most instances, assume the same shapes as those of the *fauteuils;* they are square, arched as a "basket handle," or "hat-shaped." The uprights are fluted, or in the form of detached columns or balusters, and surmounted with finials—perhaps a pine cone or very often a plume of feathers. Beds with two ends were one of the types most frequently encountered from the 1780s. Probably they were often intended to have a canopy supported on a light metal frame rising from the four corners. Frequently they were placed lengthways, often in an alcove, with a canopy and draperies suspended from the wall above, and since domed canopies with a crown of feathers were in high fashion, as may be seen in the contemporary engravings, the canopies were treated in this manner.

Whatever has been said about chair legs applies also to the legs of tables. As we have already had occasion to mention, cabriole legs were retained sufficiently long for small delicate tables under Louis XVI that it

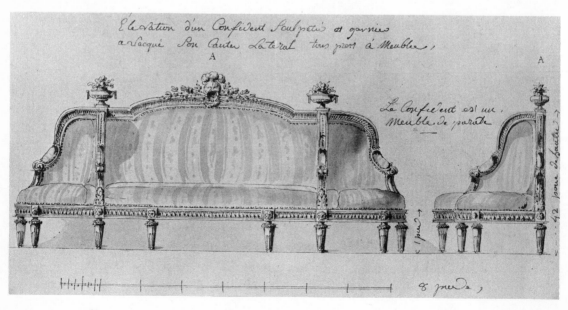

OPPOSITE: Design for a *confident* (1770) by Richard de Lalonde (flourished 1770–96). Front and side elevation. ABOVE: *Lit à la polonaise* (c. 1785), bearing the stamp of Georges Jacob. It is carved with Roman helmets, fasces, shields. The bars, which rise in a curve from the tall uprights to support the domed canopy, should be entirely concealed by the draperies; the dome should be surmounted with a panache of feathers. *Courtesy H. M. The Queen.*

181

La nuit de mariage by Jean Démosthène Dugourc; engraving by Moreau the Younger and J. B. Simonet. This gives a good idea of a fashionable domed canopy with an elaborate crown of feathers. In the background is a *paravent* and to the extreme right a small table (*chiffonnière*). *Courtesy Parke-Bernet, from the collection of Thelma Chrysler Foy.* (*See page 180.*) OPPOSITE: Table *à ouvrage* (c. 1785–90) of the *tricoteuse* type, attributed to Georges Jacob. It is veneered with tulipwood, inset with a Sèvres plaque, and has chased and gilt bronze mounts. *Courtesy Frick Collection, New York.*

182

is necessary to note their use. Toward the end of the period new shapes of legs for lighter tables were introduced, such as curving legs of ancient curule or X-form and lyre-shaped supports. Stretchers, generally discarded under Louis XV, are reintroduced, but their use, except for console tables, is far from general. They are horizontal and often more complicated than is required for strength. Weisweiler's stretchers of interlaced design are typical of this taste. As a rule they center an antique urn or the like frequently festooned with flowers, but gilt bronze baskets, recalling the shepherdess' wicker basket, occasionally are used. A square or cube of wood, such as that above the leg, joins with mortise and tenon the stretcher to the leg. An undershelf, needed for solidity and generally conforming to the shape of the top, is common to both the Louis XV and Louis XVI styles for many of the lighter tables. The top of the table is no longer serpentine or undulating. As a rule it is elliptical, a most fashionable shape, round, square or oblong; the last two mentioned often have outset corners, rounded or square, depending on the shape of the leg. For dining, extension tables with leaves, *à l'anglaise* as they were called, are the most frequent, though no kind of dining table is plentiful.

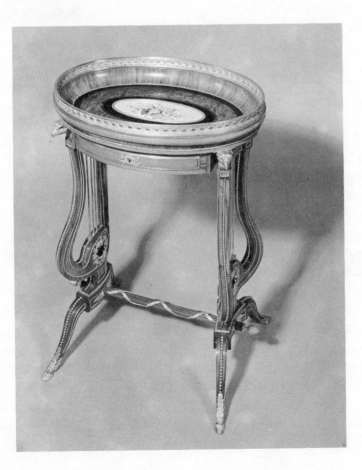

ABOVE: Console table of carved and gilt wood (c. 1770). Lavish swags hang from the frieze in the manner of J. C. Delafosse, a prolific designer in the Louis XVI style. *Courtesy Metropolitan Museum of Art. Gift of Mrs. Herbert N. Straus, 1941.* RIGHT: *Brûle-parfum* or perfume burner, made by Pierre Gouthière. The perfume pastille is held in a container within the neck of the fluted red jasper bowl which is supported by a chased and gilt bronze tripod. Marie Antoinette acquired this choice object in 1782 when she instructed her agent to purchase it for her at the sale of the Duc d'Aumont's collection. *Courtesy Wallace Collection, London.*

Since console tables are designed to be a part of the decorative scheme of a room and are adopted by their form and proportions to a particular place, they reveal a great diversity of aspect. They range in size from small designed with one leg to large with four legs. Console tables of semicircular plan mounted either on legs or consoles, the latter being more architectural in style, were much in fashion. Markedly neo-classical in character are the heavy swags, very often of laurel, depending from the frieze in the style popularized by Delafosse. Perhaps, after bows of ribbons, rich swags, or festoons of flowers and foliage are most traditional of the Louis XVI style. Also much in evidence are drapery swags on the backs and beneath the seat rails of *canapés* and on the testers of beds, as may be seen in the furniture designs of Lalonde. We have mentioned already that bronze drapery swags are characteristic of Carlin's work.

Nearly everything that can be said has already been said about tables. There was scarcely any novelty to be introduced. To that remarkable family of small movable tables (tables *ambulantes*) of indefinite uses, in which the delicacy of the Louis XVI style is triumphantly represented, is added the table *à déjeuner* and table *à fleurs,* later called a *jardinière.* Toward the end of the reign, many *guéridon* tables in pursuit of the antique show a change of form away from the original *guéridon* with its

184

ABOVE: Commode *desserte* (c. 1780–85) attributed to J. H. Riesener. It is veneered with mahogany and mounted in gilt bronze. BELOW: Veneered mahogany *desserte* (c. 1780–85) stamped J. H. Riesener. It has rounded ends and is mounted in chased and gilt bronze. *Courtesy Frick Collection, New York.* (*See page 186.*)

central standard and tripod base toward antique tripods with three slender supports. As under Louis XV, some are fitted at one side of the top with a gilt bronze candelabrum of two lights supported on movable arms. Inspired by classical tripods and introduced in the 1770s is the *athénienne*, with three slender incurvate bronze supports often mounted at the top with rams' heads and terminating in goats' feet, and supporting an urn or bowl of jasper or similar material. It seems to have served several purposes, even as a vase or bowl for flowers; its use as an incense burner or *cassolette* is especially typical, as may be seen in the painting *La Vertueuse*

185

Athénienne by J. B. Vien, which shows a young priestess burning incense at such a tripod. The profusion of *athéniennes, cassolettes, brûle-parfums, guéridons,* and *jardinières* born at this time, and which continues until the end of the Empire, is an important feature of the Louis XVI period.

The elegant class of *secrétaires* and bureaux introduced under Louis XV remain in high fashion. Cabinets also furnish a notable category of luxury pieces. Since furniture planned to harmonize with the wall decoration continues as a dominating idea under Louis XVI, such pieces as commodes, commodes *à vantaux, bas d'armoires,* and *encoignures* flourished. The façade of many fine Louis XVI commodes is still decorated as one unit; the division of the drawers is disguised as much as possible. As for the handles, the most frequent form is that of a ring, perhaps a wreath, framing a circular back plate often in the form of a rosette; sometimes the back plate is oval and the handle is merely a half ring; while other handles of marked simplicity and severity are rectangular, accentuating the angular aspect of design. Louis XVI commodes have a diversity of shapes; those of graceful demilune form were much favored and seem to have come into existence about 1780. Before mentioning the commode with shelves, now sometimes called a commode *desserte,* it is interesting to note here that sets of corner shelves (*étagères*) were occasionally introduced not only in commodes but also in other pieces, as *secrétaires* and cabinets to lighten the silhouette. The commode *desserte* or commode *à étagères,* whose use is generally interpreted as a buffet, is flanked to the left and right by quadrant-shaped shelves, full or re-entrant. To lighten the piece further still, the partitions are often covered with mirrors.

Deriving from the commode with corner shelves is a new piece of furniture, often known now as a *desserte,* which retains only the frieze drawers. The number of shelves and their arrangement vary considerably; in some models the rear panel is covered with a mirror, while in others the rear panel is omitted entirely. It seems that this general class of commodes *ouvertes,* as they were called by the ornamentist Aubert, was intended for the dining-room, since some are referred to in French furniture literature as *servantes à étagères.* Like the commode with corner shelves, they are generally veneered in mahogany and mounted in gilt bronze and are one of the *chefs-d'oeuvre* of Louis XVI.

Directoire

The Directoire style, which takes its name from the Directory, the government of the Directors that lasted four years, 1795–99, is not a finished and independent style in itself, but a transitional style, if it even exists at all, which formed a connecting link between the Louis XVI and Empire styles. In a word, it is the Louis XVI ending and the Empire beginning. The double character of the furniture produced during this time of transition, which extends roughly from around 1790 to 1804, recalls the Régence, when the Louis XV style was being evolved. The movement toward a closer imitation of the antique, which ultimately triumphed in the style of the First Empire, had its inception under Louis XVI. In the domain of furniture the collections of such designers as Dugourc, Lalonde, and Aubert display quite a few purely antique models before 1789. Chairs with rolled-over and concave backs of Grecian inspiration, tables decorated with daisies, lozenges, and stars, beds having *dossiers* with triangular pediments were all being produced from about 1790. Thus the Revolution of 1789 did not effect any rapid change in furniture fashion, but it helped and hurried the movement in every way, because it was going exactly in the direction required to satisfy the tastes of the revolutionary current, which ardently admired the ancient republics.

Many pieces identified with the Directoire style carry on the direct tradition of Louis XVI classicism treated with greater severity. Stripped of the sober elegance of their decoration and carved very often in weak relief, they may have the appearance of poor relations, but nevertheless still relations, for the basic forms are little altered. Other pieces, having the antique as their avowed source of inspiration, show more often than not an excess in novelties. From the time of the National Assembly, 1789–91, a wave of new ideas swept over every branch of art. Patriotic subjects, by which we may understand subjects inspired by the events of the Revolution or Plutarch, were dominant. Everyone was either making

Greek pieces more Greek or decorating pieces that were entirely Louis XVI with revolutionary emblems. An advertisement in 1790 makes mention of "patriotic beds with the symbols of liberty." It states that bonnets (caps of liberty) are used in place of a plume of feathers for the finials which surmount the uprights in the form of a bundle of lances or pikes, a decorative element we have seen already at the corners of Louis XVI commodes. At this time, when the taste for allegories was rampant, revolutionary emblems are met with again and again not only on furniture but also on mural decorations and textiles. These include Phrygian caps (liberty), spirit levels (equality), clasped hands (fraternity), pikes (freedom of man), triangles with an eye in the middle (reason), the three orders of the nation or the cross (clergy), sword (nobility), and spade topped by the Phrygian cap (third estate), etc. By the time of the Directory the fashion for revolutionary emblems began to wane. Of course the capture of the Bastille was a favorite theme for wood carvers.

In the frenzied epoch of the Revolution, the French politicians, by the processes of reason, drafted laws for liberty, equality, and fraternity, based on a study of the ancients. Following the revolutionary current of the time, antiquity became sacred to the artists; they arrived at the tenet that the beautiful had been realized for all time by the ancients and no one could do anything better than copy it. In support of this doctrine there appeared, as if by predestination, the painter, politician, and antiquarian Jacques Louis David, 1748–1825, who, under the Republic and Empire, became the dictator of art. "We must go back to raw antiquity," he declared. Furniture decorated with antique ornament was no longer sanctioned by fashion; it had to be copied exactly from pieces that the excavations of Pompeii had disclosed or from representations on antique vase paintings or bas-reliefs. This was the official style of the Republic and to adopt it was a sign of patriotism.

David, an important political figure, did more than anyone else to establish this new taste. He designed a group of pieces, more or less exact copies of Greco-Roman models, and gave the order to Jacob to make them in 1789 or 1790. He introduced these pieces in his paintings and they were quickly copied by everyone, painters and designers. Among these well-known pieces are mahogany chairs with wood backs as "round as a tower" and decorated with gilt bronze, chairs of ancient curule form with X-shaped supports, chairs inspired by the Grecian klismos, the graceful daybed with its pure lines on which he depicted Madame Récamier, and also appearing in the same painting the footstool and candelabrum. The fashion for imitating the ancients also brought simplicity in hair styles and clothes for both sexes. Madame Récamier's costume, which David designed as appropriate for his furniture, is arranged in the classical folds of Greek statuary. She is posed and clothed as to remain, in the artist's own words, "untouched by the changes of fashion." It was David who gave the order for the furniture for the new Salle de la Convention at the Tuileries to Jacob and two young architects and designers, then relatively unknown and for whom the commission was the start to fame and fortune, Percier and Fontaine. Shortly after the completion of this commission, Jacob, an ardent disciple of antiquity, gave his huge workshop on the Rue Meslée in 1796 to his two oldest sons, Georges and François-Honoré. The latter, under the name of Jacob-Desmalter, became the outstanding *ébéniste* in the Imperial epoch.

As we know, the Revolution brought in its wake the suppression of the craft guilds, which were dissolved in 1791. This meant that the rules and regulations by which the trade guilds had governed the thorough training of the craftsmen, their long apprenticeship and *compagnonnage*, were abolished and that complete freedom of production was permitted in all of the crafts. Luxury arts, such as furniture making, began to decline starting with this reform, except for the deluxe furniture made under the First Empire, and in any case produced by craftsmen trained in the great traditions built up with such care by Louis XIV and his two successors under the craft guild system. Later the standards of craftsmanship were further depressed, as we shall see, by the introduction of industrialization and mass-production methods. The Reign of Terror, the uprising in the West, and the foreign war brought to an almost complete standstill the making of furniture from 1792 to 1795. Napoleon, from his days as First Consul, made an effort to encourage the luxury arts which he had inherited from the Bourbons. But society, impoverished by social upheavals at home (nearly all the old fortunes had been swept away by the Revolution, and later by the Napoleonic wars), was no longer able to spend vast sums on the luxury arts that the eighteenth century had supported in such a grand manner. The France that had made luxury furniture for the royalty and aristocracy of all Europe had vanished with the Ancien Régime.

As soon as the Reign of Terror was over, the country, still bleeding from wounds inflicted by divisions of the past years, attempted a comeback in industry. Workshops were reopened, and most of the furniture grouped under the Directoire was made after 1795. The imitation of the antique was more than ever the absolute law, animated by a deliberate archaeological spirit. The aim was to copy the exact forms of antiquity where classical precedents existed, such as couches, chairs, tripods, and candelabrum, and for pieces unknown to the ancients, the great majority, to furnish designs that were fully consistent in character. The most famous interior of the last years of the Republic belonged to Madame Récamier, the designs for its furnishings having been chiefly under the guidance of Percier and Fontaine. Made of mahogany, the chairs and daybeds, with

Designs for antique chairs, artist unknown (c. 1800). *Courtesy Cooper Union Museum.*
OPPOSITE: *Portrait of Madame Récamier* by Jacques Louis David. *Courtesy Musée du Louvre.*
Photo Mella. (*See pages 188–189.*)

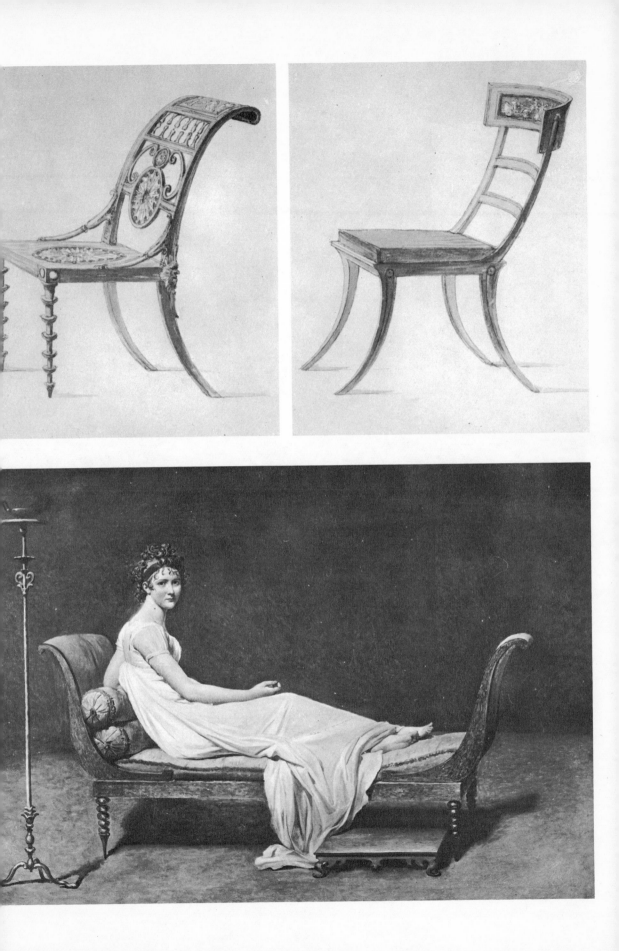

their sweeping curves approximating very closely their Grecian prototypes, are remarkable for their refined and archaeological approach. Other furniture of this epoch was extravagant with ornament half archaeological and half symbolic, including Roman glaives, the fulmen of Jupiter, hocked animal legs and lions' heads, reputed to be drawn from the best antique examples of three civilizations—Roman, Greek, and Egyptian. The excessive use of symbolism and allegorical furniture, such as stools in the form of drums and beds in the shape of camp beds, so appropriate for a warrior, is a prominent feature of this decade and shows the insatiable demand for novelties at any cost. By the time the Imperial era arrived, these exaggerations were discarded and only their essence retained; the designs were more restrained and were given uniformity, in other words, style.

The fashion for Egyptian ornament was inevitable after Napoleon's Egyptian campaign, in which accompanying the military staff was a staff of writers, scientists, and archaeologists. In this group was the architect and archaeologist Dominique Vivant de Denon, 1747–1825, who, while in Egypt, gathered material for his book, *Le Voyage dans la basse et la haute Égypte,* published in 1802. This important work, notable for its descriptive writing and its detailed visual record of sphinxes and pylons,

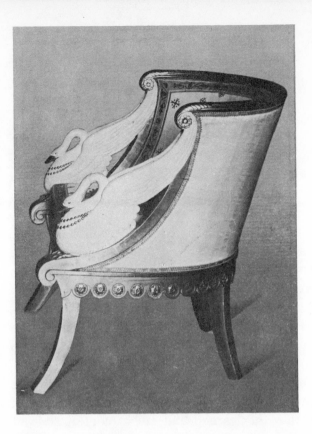

OPPOSITE: Carved mahogany *fauteuil, lit de repos,* and table belonging to Madame Récamier (end of the eighteenth century). *Courtesy Caisse Nationale des Monuments Historiques. Photo Mella.* (*See page 189.*) LEFT: *Fauteuil* with swans from the Château de Malmaison (beginning of the nineteenth century). The back is hollowed out to about one half of a cylinder; it has saber legs. BELOW: Bedchamber of the Empress Josephine, Château de Malmaison (beginning of the nineteenth century). The bed is ornamented with swans, and the head- and foot-ends with cornucopiae. *Courtesy Extrait du Style Empire de P. Francastel. Photo Librairie Larousse.* (*See page 194.*)

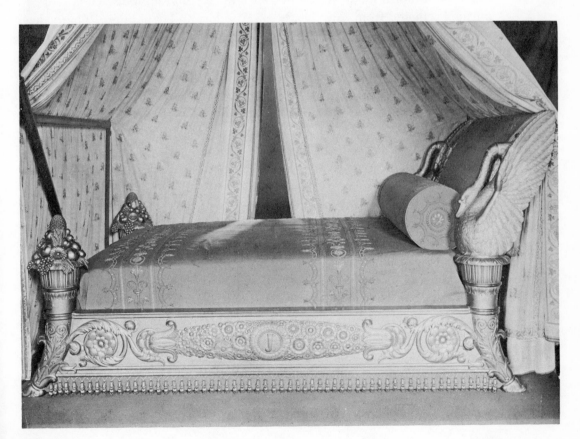

was most influential in propagating Egyptian ornament. Shortly after its publication, numerous Egyptian pieces appeared in collections of designs by Percier and Fontaine.

By the coup d'etat of November 9, 1799, Napoleon established the Consulate and became First Consul. In the realm of art it inaugurated the reign of Napoleon, even though he did not see fit to make himself Emperor Napoleon until 1804. Dreaming of peace and prosperity and French luxury in its glorious traditions, he said: "We must lay aside our jack-boots and think of commerce, encourage the arts, give prosperity to our country." One of his first interests was gradually to remake a court, and he wanted to have palaces, if not built for him, at least furnished for him in a manner consonant with his achievements and his régime. For this purpose he employed Percier and Fontaine, ardent devotees of antiquity who were to do all of Napoleon's work, to redecorate Malmaison, which Josephine had purchased in 1798. These two men, like David, who had presented them to Napoleon, were wonderfully adapted to fit in with Napoleon. After completing Malmaison, they redecorated Saint-Cloud, the Tuileries, the Louvre, and other palace apartments in a style expressive of this epoch imposed on France by Napoleon and his conquests. So it is under the Consulate that the learned and archaeological style of the First Empire made its debut, sprung, it almost seems, complete and finished chiefly from the heads of Percier and Fontaine. There were symbols of war and victory, figures of victory with widespread wings and flowing gowns; later, Imperial emblems, such as the eagle, made their appearance. Obviously Greek art with its quiet simplicity could not adequately express the spirit of Napoleon with his lofty idea of power. He required the solid and grandiose luxury found in Roman art. Fortunately Percier and Fontaine possessed the genius, and it is to their lasting credit that they captured the spirit of the antique and the spirit of national pride and conquest in their style of decoration, in which simplicity and grandeur are harmoniously combined.

Articles of furniture given new forms before the Empire are relatively few. In chair design two types are most frequent, and like all chairs in the Directoire style their rear legs, square of section, curve outward. Their line is directly continued by the uprights of the back; this is the first sign to appear in imitation of the Greek *klismos* and presents a very elegant line. Of the two typical Directoire chairs, one form is still close to the Louis XVI chair. The uprights of the slightly concave back flare outward and backward toward the top, making more or less pronounced corners. The other characteristic chair has a rolled-over back, like a form of Greek *klismos*. The refined simplicity and pure lines of the best of these chairs with their slender and severe elegance make them favored above all French chairs by certain connoisseurs. Both forms of chair have front legs

194

ABOVE LEFT: Carved and painted *bergère* (end of the eighteenth century). *Courtesy Parke-Bernet, from the collection of Mrs. H. Batterson Boger.* ABOVE RIGHT: Carved and painted *fauteuil* (end of the eighteenth century). *Courtesy Musée des Arts Décoratifs.* LEFT: Carved and painted *chaise* (end of the eighteenth century). *Courtesy Extrait du Style Empire de P. Francastel. Photo Librairie Larousse.* (See page 197.)

Portrait of Madame Récamier, by Gérard (1802). Probably owing to the elongated seat of the chair it is a part of a daybed having also an extended lounge rest. *Courtesy Petit-Palais, Paris. Photo Bulloz-Mella.* OPPOSITE: Mahogany *lit en bateau*, stamped Jacob Frères; from the Château de Fontainebleau (beginning of the nineteenth century). It is mounted in chased and gilt bronze and has medallions of bronze on a light blue enamel ground. The center medallion is Apollo and is flanked on each side by a lamp, a lyre, two heads of women, an amphora, and a butterfly. *Courtesy Musée National de Fontainebleau. Photo Mella.*

turned round and tapering; the arms terminate in small round knobs, volutes, or are cut off square and decorated with a carved daisy on the top. Especially typical is the small palm leaf or shell carved at the point of the arm where it joins the upright. The armposts are baluster or columnar in shape; sometimes, as one of Madame Récamier's *fauteuils*, the armposts are in the form of winged sphinxes or a similiar motif. At this time the great majority of chairs designed with open backs have backs that roll over. The top rail in some models is baluster turned. The carved ornament, which is very sedate, comprises daisies, stars, *soupières,* a kind of antique vase, fillets in relief, while the lozenge, either complete or with the corners cut off, is one of the most frequently repeated of all these typical Directoire motifs.

Perhaps the most celebrated piece of Directoire furniture is the daybed, inspired by the Grecian couch. Its most distinguishing features are the rolled-over ends either of equal height, like the one made famous by the portrait of Madame Récamier, or of unequal height, while the feet are *toupie* or top-shaped or curve outward like the rear legs of the *fauteuil,* presenting a gracefully swept line. Under the Empire the daybed is occasionally given a back. In this type, called a *méridienne,* the end at the head is always higher. The *lit en bateau,* the typical Empire bed, also made its debut before the First Empire came into being. Many pieces, such as commodes and writing furniture, are essentially a continuation of the Louis XVI style treated with greater severity. As for tables, the great

197

majority are round because no doubt nearly all the Greek and Roman tables are round. The top, as often as it is possible, is of marble, supported in many examples by a central standard mounted on a tripod base, in short, a large *guéridon;* but now its refined and archaeological design proclaims the new style.

Empire and Nineteenth Century
Including Biedermeier

The Empire style, which survived about ten or fifteen years after the period of the First Empire, 1804–14, like the preceding Louis XVI style, has the antique as its avowed source of inspiration, but in this case it is the strict application of the principles by which the Louis XVI style purported to be governed. The style is simple, severe, not very intimate, cordial, nor comfortable, yet withal and in spite of its continued anachronisms it has its own beauty. More than any of the preceding styles, it can less permit mediocrity. The materials and workmanship must be supremely fine; thus it is only in the most costly pieces that those qualities of imposing grandeur and simplicity have been successfully captured, which are the attributes of the style at its best. The figure of the wood must be superb because it is displayed in large masses with little decoration, while the bronzes, isolated as they generally are in the center of large panels of plain wood, and because they often are responsible for the entire decorative effect, assume great importance and must be excellent in composition, sculpturing, and chasing.

It may be said that Percier and Fontaine are the creators of the official Empire style; they understood this epoch when national pride and war-like enthusiasm filled the air. The style of furniture which they conceived, with its broad austere surfaces defined by straight lines and sharp edges and on which they displayed golden Greek palm leaves and wreaths of laurel to crown the victor's brow, or figures of victory with outspread wings and flowing robes, was admirably suited to Imperial France. Other styles have been more truly French, but this learned style, so abstract and arbitrary, imposed on French taste in the same manner that Napoleon's régime was imposed on the nation, was in exact harmony with these legend-like years of French history. Later, in 1814, when this period of exaltation had subsided and the Bourbons were restored to the throne, royalty stripped of its former splendor and the peaceful bourgeoisie mostly

ABOVE: Mahogany commode (1804–14). It is mounted in chased and gilt bronze, and the pilasters are enriched with antique female heads of bronze. *Courtesy Musée des Arts Décoratifs. Photo Adant.* LEFT: Detail of a silver gilt cradle (1811) designed by Prud'hon for the King of Rome, Napoleon I's son. A winged Victory kneels on the hood of the cradle and holds in her outstretched hands a laurel wreath from which the curtains hung. *Courtesy Kunsthistorisches Museum, Vienna.* (*See page 199.*)

parvenus without taste, the style no longer befitted the times. It continued to exist in a desultory fashion, for lack of any compensating originality to replace it and became heavy and dull like the period itself.

Both Fontaine and Percier, who were architects, were fervent disciples of antiquity, and their devotion to Greek and Roman ideals dominates the Empire style. They collaborated on a number of books, and, since they exercised great influence on the entire art of furnishing during the Imperial epoch, it is fortunate that in one of their works, entitled *Recueil de décorations intérieures,* published in 1812, they presented their ideas in the form of a doctrine. First and above all they expressed their bitter contempt for past French art. Only to the art of the sixteenth century are they inclined to be lenient; the eighteenth century received the full brunt of their scorn. They admired everything in antiquity; it is antique, therefore it is beautiful. They reasoned that true beauty is untouched by changes of fashions and since it had been realized for all time by the Greeks and the Romans no one could do better than copy it. "It would be vain to seek for shapes preferable to those handed down to us by the ancients, whether in the arts of engineering or in those of decoration or industry. . . ." In brief, nothing should be in our houses but furniture copied from the Greek and Roman.

Unfortunately there are several excellent reasons to prevent the fulfillment of this ideal. The ancients, who spent their lives in the open air, going to bed in the early hours of darkness and rising as soon as it was light, required but little furniture. Chairs, couches for dining, chests, tables, beds, and tripods were virtually the entire furniture of early peoples. What Frenchman would be content with so little, and so uncomfortable, meant for a way of life entirely different from that of the eighteenth century. The scarcity of surviving examples, partly by reason of the perishable materials of which they were usually made, presented another problem. Greek and Roman furniture made of wood had disappeared; all that remained were articles of bronze, such as tripods, candelabra, legs of tables, frames of couches and folding stools, and such articles of marble as ceremonial throne seats. Most of the knowledge of ancient furniture had to be acquired by studying classical prototypes represented on bas-reliefs, vase paintings, and mural decorations. Fontaine and Percier realized that the strict imitation of antiquity was impossible, since it was necessary to create almost everything and adapt the remainder. Appreciating the need for compromise, they wrote, "We have followed the models of antiquity, not blindly but with discrimination entailed by the manners, customs, and materials of the moderns. We have striven to imitate the antique in its spirit, its principles, and its maxims, which are of all times."

The natural tendency of the times was to turn in prejudice to the opposite in everything, from politics to furniture making, that went before

1789. All the qualities that were the essence of eighteenth-century furniture—comfort, intimacy, charming gracefulness, and refined elegance—were shunned by the creators of the Empire style. They set to work to create a style of austere grandeur, one that conformed to the fixed ideas they held of the ancients and of Imperial France. To achieve the effect of grandiose severity, they made the lines more simple and rigid, bounding large level surfaces with sharp exactness. The Louis XVI style had already eliminated many curved elements, but the Empire style almost waged a war against them. Round supports are very often replaced by members rectangular in plan, such as pilasters and legs of square section. Columns may still be found on certain pieces, but they are generally detached so that the sharp corners are easily seen. The columns are smooth, cylindrical or slightly conical, with the capital and base covered in metal. The use of moldings, which gives interest to even the simplest furniture, was almost abandoned; when they do occur, they are diminutive, as a fillet in low relief.

The most distinguishing feature of the style is its clear-cut silhouette. The corners are sharp and exact, and any attempt to soften them, such as by chamfering, is discarded. In the preceding Louis XVI period, sharp angles also existed, but they are invariably softened by moldings, flutings, or engaged columns extending around the corners. The eye is not drawn to the sharp edge formed by the meeting of two surfaces, while in the Empire style it is the exact opposite; the arris is always emphasized as much as possible. The manner in which the panels are framed was instrumental in achieving the much coveted block-like appearance. Under Louis XVI the uprights and traverses into which the panels are fitted are in relief, framing the panels distinctly. But under the Empire the panels are level with their frames, and a uniform veneer, that much-used veneer of mahogany, covers the entire surface, concealing the structure and joining and giving the piece the desired massive block-like aspect, which no form of decoration could alleviate. The use of heavy bases was introduced to accentuate further still the massive, monumental look. The taste of the time for "pure and correct contours" is also seen at first glance in the principle of symmetry which was observed with uncompromising rigor. In no other style is symmetry so closely followed. In brief, all this—a sharp silhouette, symmetry, and so forth—is what Fontaine and Percier had in mind when they wrote, "Simple lines, pure contours, correct shapes replace the miscelinear, the curving, and the irregular."

OPPOSITE ABOVE: Mahogany *bonheur du jour* (1804–14). It is decorated with chased and gilt bronze mounts. *Courtesy Musée des Arts Décoratifs. Photo Adant.* BELOW: Mahogany bureau *plat* from the Château de Fontainebleau (beginning of the nineteenth century). It is richly mounted in gilt bronze and supported by winged lion heads continuing to chimera legs and paws with claws. Stamped Jacob Frères. *Courtesy Musée National de Fontainebleau. Photo Mella.* (See page 204.)

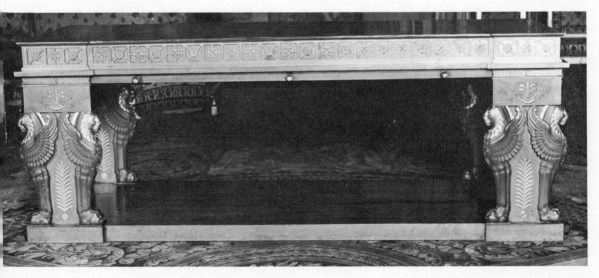

203

Mahogany console with glass, from the Château de Fontainebleau (1804–14). It is ornamented with chased and gilt bronze; the two square tapering pillars are mounted with winged female busts and human feet of bronze. *Courtesy Extrait du Style Empire de P. Francastel. Photo Librairie Larousse.*

Undoubtedly Empire furniture, with its simple lines, no marquetry or lacquer, few or no moldings, little or no carved decoration, except seats perhaps, would be impossibly arid and austere, were it not for the gilt bronze mounts that decorate its polished mahogany surfaces and the race of strange creatures, made of bronze, wood, or a combination of both, acting as supports. These fabulous creatures, frequently borrowed from antiquity, are a distinguishing feature of the new style. Everywhere are found winged sphinxes, winged lions and chimeras of every kind, often with heads of eagles, employed as table legs and chair armposts. Then there are the really incredulous monsters, such as the lion monopodium comprising the head and chest of a lion that has been hopping around since antiquity on a single leg and enormous paw. At least as popular as the sphinx is an odd creature half human and half geometrical, composed of an elongated plain and quadrangular tapering pillar at the top of which is a bust of a woman and below two human feet; sometimes the head and feet are made of gilt bronze. Swans employed as armposts or as entire arms of chairs and sofas are seen in great numbers; they are even seen in certain chairs forming the legs with their bodies and the arms with their wings. It seems scarcely necessary to say that these decorative supports have to be superbly designed and executed to keep within the realm of good taste. Otherwise, they become ridiculous extravagances.

The French *ébéniste* recognized the necessity for decorating the large even surfaces of dark shining mahogany with gilt bronze mounts. An interesting characteristic of Empire bronzes is that their use is more often for decoration only than in any of the previous styles when so many of the bronzes have some use or at least pretend to usefulness and are thus generally found in the same position. Under Louis XVI, mounts as pure ornament multiplied, such as the running motifs decorating the friezes of tables and commodes. However, under the Empire the great majority are simply flat decorations made for no specific use or particular piece or place; identical mounts might be found on a commode or clock and their position is essentially arbitrary. Another feature of these mounts is that each is isolated in its own place and meant to be interesting in itself, to be considered individually. Apart from these special features, the bronzes are often notable for the ingenious symmetry of their composition, the clarity of their lines, the effectiveness of their light silhouette against a dark ground, and above all for their chasing and gilding, which in the fine pieces, such as some of the bronzes by Thomire, are superb. Bronze mounts appear on almost every article of furniture, even on chairs and sofas, where their use is always of doubtful taste. Unhappily on some massive pieces the mounts seem too delicate and meager for the amount of mahogany surface they are required to decorate, but no one can deny their beauty. The French *ébéniste,* in achieving his goal of flat uninterrupted surfaces, frequently omitted the handles on drawers, and it was necessary to pull out the drawers by means of a key placed in the keyhole, which was often almost invisible. If the drawers have handles they are either in the form of loose rings framing a back plate in the form of a rosette, as under Louis XVI, or *patères,* flat knobs or disks, miniatures of those holding back the curtains, which from a short distance resemble a rosette.

Practically all the motifs that are found in these bronze mounts are borrowed from antique Greco-Roman or Egyptian art. Stiff and flattened acanthus, Greek palm leaves, tightly woven wreaths, quivers of arrows, rosettes, and stars are typical of the new style. Winged Victories in flowing gowns presenting laurel crowns and blowing trumpets, Olympian gods and goddesses, Greek and Roman heroes and sacrificial scenes are popular subjects. Everything is good, provided it is Greek and Roman. There is a multitude of objects of every kind, gleaned from altars, tombs, Pompeian mural decoration, and even Roman goldsmith work. Such are antique heads, cornucopias, the winged thunderbolt of Jupiter, Neptune's trident, Mercury's caduceus, Bacchus' thyrsus, casques, lamps, tripods, kraters, amphorae, winged torches, and musical instruments—lyres, tubas, and sistrums. Then there are emblems of victory, war-like emblems and Imperial emblems, motifs from the animal world and floral motifs, of which poppies are much favored. From the art of Egypt appear winged globes, uraei, lotus plants, sphinxes, to mention but a few.

The taste for furniture adorned with Sèvres plaques persisted in a peculiar manner, as may be seen in five extant large *guéridon*-tables made at the Sèvres manufactory under the Empire. Properly they are objects of ceramic art rather than of cabinetmaking, made as they are of porcelain and bronze, but because tables of this kind were made in the nineteenth century and are frequently met with, it is interesting to note their origin. The taste for the monumental which so often characterizes the creations of the Empire epoch is clearly expressed in these tables, three of which have circular tops resting on a massive pedestal or column mounted on a block-like base, triangular or square. In one model, the *Table des Maréchaux*, the circular top made of a single piece of porcelain has been taken from a design by Percier, but made much more attractive. It centers Napoleon surrounded by thirteen golden rays, each having the name of one of his famous victories. Between the rays are thirteen medallions with bust portraits of eleven marshals of the Empire and two great dignitaries. The top rests on a porcelain column depicting allegorical figures. Another table, the *Table des Grands Capitaines de l'Antiquité*, centers an imposing profile of Alexander the Great, which is surrounded by twelve portrait medallions of Caesar, Pompey, Hannibal, and other celebrated men of

OPPOSITE: Design for a woven fabric (1804–14). The composition has typical Empire ingredients. *Courtesy Cooper Union Museum. (See page 205.)* ABOVE: Detail of the *Table des Maréchaux* (Table of the Marshals; dated 1810). The circular top is made of Sèvres porcelain and bronze; the work was commissioned by Napoleon I. *Courtesy Musée National de Malmaison. Photo Caisse Nationale des Monuments Historiques-Mella.* BELOW: Detail of the top of the *Table des Grands Capitaines de l'Antiquité* (Table of the Great Leaders of Antiquity; 1812). *Courtesy H. M. The Queen.*

207

arms. The bronze column on which it rests is in the form of a bundle of lances tied with crossed ribbon. The temper and taste of Napoleonic France is strikingly revealed in these designs.

Since many new combinations of lines for chairs were attempted, the variety of Empire chairs is much greater than might be expected. As a rule, the forms are stiffer and heavier than those of the Louis XVI period. The lines are broad and simple but by no means always straight, as may be seen in rolled-over chair backs whose profile resembles the line of an elongated S; in gondola-shaped chair backs hollowed to a half cyclinder and joined to the front legs by a concave curve; in arms without armposts that terminate in a large open volute resting directly on the tops of the legs (a form which remained in vogue until around the middle of the century), and in concave rear legs, square and tapering, which are typical of the style. Concave front legs, square and tapering, the so-called saber legs were not employed to any appreciable extent until after 1815. Then of course there are chairs and stools of ancient curule form with gracefully curving X-form supports.

The back of the Empire *fauteuil* is always upholstered. Rolled-over backs and straight rectangular backs are the two types most frequently seen. While on the subject of chair backs, let us not forget a very typical ornament appearing for the first time on the Directoire chair, namely, the little palm leaf or shell that surmounts the point where the arm of the arm-chair is joined to the upright. The perpendicular armposts are a direct

OPPOSITE ABOVE: *Table des Grands Capitaines de l'Antiquité. Courtesy H. M. The Queen.* OPPOSITE LEFT: Mahogany *fauteuil* (1804–14). It is enriched with gilt bronze, and the armposts and legs, in the form of terms, are mounted with antique female heads and paw feet of bronze. *Courtesy Philadelphia Museum of Art.* OPPOSITE RIGHT: Mahogany *fauteuil* (1804–14), stamped Jacob D. (Desmalter), Rue Meslée. The terminal figures are mounted with winged Egyptian heads and paw feet of bronze. *Courtesy Musée des Arts Décoratifs.* RIGHT: Carved and painted *fauteuil,* from the Château de Compiègne (1804–14). The armposts are a direct continuation of the line of the front legs. *Courtesy Extrait du Style Empire de P. Francastel. Photo Librairie Larousse.*

continuation of the legs; frequently these two members form one motif, as an elongated terminal figure. By far the majority of chairs are made of mahogany. Ambitious examples may be mounted in bronze; in other chairs the carved enrichments in emulation of the bronze mounts may be gilded.

There is little to say of sofas; most of them resembled very large armchairs. One shape, the sofa *à la Pommier*, is characterized by a very low straight back that continues at right angles to form the sides or arms. Daybeds are imitated from antique rest beds. For hours of languorous ease, the type made famous by David's portrait of Madame Récamier and the *méridienne* are preferred. The latter always has a back panel which joins both ends, and since the end at the head is always higher than the end at the foot, the top of the back panel is either a straight slanting line or, much more graceful, an undulating line. At this period, daybeds are more or less related to the "boat" bed, and their ends forming a graceful elongated S assume the lines of the lyre-form sofa, so familiar to us in the work of Duncan Phyfe.

Under the Empire, beds are given an entirely new shape derived from the antique; properly they are seen from the side and frequently placed in a richly draped alcove. They are called *lit en bateau*, or boat beds and with a fertile imagination one can see a slight resemblance. The head and foot ends, which are of equal height, with a small roll or volute at the top, widen toward the lower part; frequently the top line of the side piece or rail is concave, continuing the curve of the head and foot ends in an unbroken line. Some models have low vertical ends surmounted with antique fulcra. Made of mahogany and adorned with gilt bronze, boat beds are not without elegance. Apart from them, other beds were also intended to be seen from the side, having vertical ends and columns surmounted with finials, in the form of antique heads or globes sprinkled with stars. Small dome-shaped canopies extending from the wall are typical for this general class of bed.

OPPOSITE: Carved and painted *méridienne,* from the Château de Compiègne (1804–14). *Courtesy Extrait du Style Empire de P. Francastel. Photo Librairie Larousse.* ABOVE: Mahogany *lit en bateau* (1804–14). It is mounted in gilt bronze; the antique fulcra end in bronze winged sphinxes. *Courtesy Musée des Arts Décoratifs. Photo Mella.* BELOW: Project for a *lit à dome* by La Mesangère (1804). Beds of couch form, dome-shaped canopies attached to the wall, and hangings enriched with borders trimmed with fringe were in high fashion. *Courtesy Extrait du Style Empire de P. Francastel. Photo Librairie Larousse.*

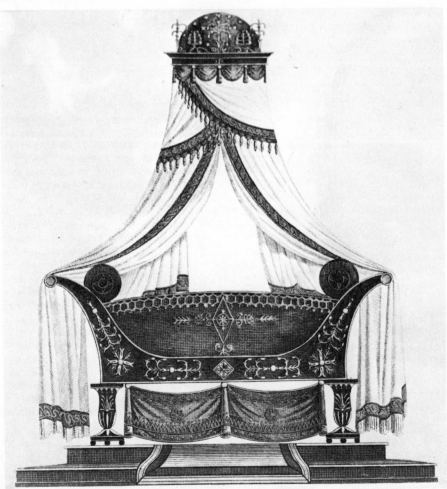

ABOVE LEFT: Table of tripod form from the Grand Trianon at Versailles (1804–14). It is supported by winged sphinx-heads continuing into animalistic legs and paws. *Courtesy Extrait du Style Empire de P. Francastel. Photo Librairie Larousse.* ABOVE RIGHT: Mahogany toilet table designed by Prud'hon, bronzes by Odiot and Thomire (1810). It was a gift from the city of Paris to the Empress Marie-Louise. *Courtesy Extrait du Style Empire de P. Francastel. Photo Viollet-Librairie Larousse.* (*See page 214.*) LEFT: Mahogany *psyché*, from the Château de Compiègne (1804–14). It has gilt bronze mounts; winged female sphinxes of bronze support the slender uprights in the form of quivers. The candle arms, which slip into the bronze ornament under the middle band of each quiver, are missing. *Courtesy Extrait du Style Empire de P. Francastel. Photo Viollet-Librairie Larousse.* (*See page 214.*) OPPOSITE: *Lavabo,* based on a design by Charles Percier and made by Martin Guillaume Biennais, goldsmith to Napoleon I (1804–14). It is made of amboyna wood mounted in chased and gilt bronze. Detail of *Lavabo* showing the circular top supported on swans' necks and wings. *Courtesy Metropolitan Museum of Art. Bequest of James Alexander Scrymser, 1926.* (*See page 214.*)

As for tables, from massive dining tables to small *guéridon* tables, the great majority are round, no doubt because almost all of the Greek and Roman tables were round. Table tops, as often as it is possible, are of heavy marble. Some tables with circular tops are supported by a central column, while others are designed with three legs and occasionally four. When the legs are not in the form of columns with a capital and base of bronze, a most incredible assortment of strange figures may be seen supporting the tops. The legs or supports rest on heavy block-like bases which vary in design according to the number of supports and the shape of the top. For instance, tables with round tops and three supports generally rest on a triangular plinth; tables with a rectangular top may have an *H*-form plinth. Console tables are nearly always rectangular, the back between the rear legs frequently fitted with a mirror, while the heavy base is recessed between the two front supports. They are chiefly made of mahogany with gilt bronze mounts; others are painted, the ground generally a light-colored gray, white, or straw and the flat carvings in a much darker color or gilded.

At this period the charming eighteenth-century toilet table fitted with a rising framed mirror and two hinged ends that opened outward was supplanted by a new distinct type. The Empire toilet table has a rectangular top, in most instances of marble, a frieze drawer containing the necessary toilet equipage, and usually lyre-form or curving *X*-shaped supports.

213

Secured to the top are two slender uprights provided with candle arms, to which is attached by swivel screws a framed mirror. Accompanying the toilet table is a *lavabo,* a small circular basin stand copied from an antique tripod. Properly at the rear rising above the basin are one or two slender uprights that support a small mirror and a towel rail.

It was possible to transform almost any table into the Empire toilet table by simply placing on the flat top a movable toilet mirror of the same kind; in brief, a miniature cheval glass, or *psyché* as it was called in France. The tall cheval toilet mirror sufficiently large to reflect the whole person was a most fashionable piece of Empire furniture, so it is understandable that a miniature *psyché* was an exciting toilet accessory.

Writing furniture does not require any special description. *Secrétaires* with drop fronts, bureaux with cylinder tops, the massive bureau *ministre* of kneehole form, and the *bonheur du jour* are in high fashion. Then there are the block-like commodes, low cupboards, and *bibliothèques;* on the stiles of these and similar mahogany pieces flourished that austere clan of bronze antique heads. Important to an Empire drawing-room are two musical instruments, the harp, so typically Empire, and the pianoforte, a rare and costly novelty with its pedals often of lyre form. Finally there is the new table lamp, the *flambeau-bouillotte,* with its dish-like base and shaft fitted with candle arms made of bronze and its painted tin shade—a lamp of great elegance and refinement and one still highly esteemed.

The Empire style, which embraced practically all of Europe, being especially well developed in Italy and Germany, is the last great classical style and marks the end of the golden age of French cabinetwork. Even under the Empire, ordinary furniture is inferior to that of the eighteenth century because cabinetmakers were less conscientious since the guilds had been dissolved. On the other hand, there is nothing to surpass the cabinetmaker's art displayed in the fine work of Desmalter, who was Napoleon's favorite *ébéniste;* the careful selection of materials, the exactness of joining, the execution of the veneering, the finish of the bronzes are superb. Apart from the abolition of the guilds, the introduction around 1814 of the factory system, even in a very simple form, further depressed the standards of craftsmanship. As the nineteenth century progressed, industrialism with its mass-production methods opened the gates to the great rush of imitative styles that eventually overwhelmed the art of cabinetmaking.

Under the restored Bourbons, Louis XVIII, 1814–24, and Charles X, 1824–30, the Empire style, for lack of any new decorative movement, was continued in an aimless manner and kept growing more and more impoverished and heavy. Late in the second decade a revival of the Gothic style was essayed, but this neo-Gothic furniture with its shapeless forms and gingerbread Gothic arches is without artistic merit. Some of the best

Music room of the Empress Josephine. *Courtesy Extrait du Style Empire de P. Francastel.*
Photo Librairie Larousse.

Boudoir in the Gothic style. Water color. *Courtesy Musée des Arts Décoratifs. Photo Giraudon-Mella.*

work of this so-called Restauration style is in chair and table design. Chairs with gondola-shaped backs, rolled-over or concave backs, arms that scroll over and under to form armposts, and saber legs are typical. Lighter tables with either lyre or curving X-shaped supports are, as a rule, of pleasing design. The block-like forms of Empire commodes and similar pieces continued. Naturally the ambitious cabinetwork enriched with the superb gilt bronzes of the Napoleonic era is seldom found. In addition to mahogany, light-colored woods, such as maple and lemon wood, were quite popular. As we have seen, marquetry was no longer used. But inlay work in a contrasting color, such as amaranth inlaid on a light-colored wood or vice versa, which was employed to some extent under the Empire, became more and more fashionable under the Restauration, when it very often took the place of metal mounts. The majority of inlaid designs resemble a simplified version of Empire bronzes. Stiff acanthus leaves, palmettes, rosettes, and the like are favored for this precise and delicate inlay work, the great part of which is found in the same places on a piece of furniture formerly adorned with bronze mounts. As under the Empire, the practice of inlaying stringing lines and narrow bands continued, but unlike the Empire, when commonly metals, brass, steel, and even silver were employed, they are now generally in contrasting woods.

The so-called Charles X style outlived the reign of that monarch, who was deposed in the July Revolution in Paris, to be succeeded by Louis Philippe, 1830–48, another member of the house of Bourbon. Much of the furniture belonging to this era is a potpourri of Empire, Gothic, Renaissance, and baroque Louis XIV, with a predilection for the marquetry of Boulle. About 1840 or earlier, the rococo Louis XV was revived, and it is with this style that the Louis Philippe pieces are closely associated. Ill proportioned and with lines at the same time both beggarly and too generous, revived rococo furniture is characterized by exaggerated cabriole legs, coarse carvings, and excessive decoration often in the form of Sèvres plaques. The good sense to copy was also lost. The furniture under the Second Empire, 1852–70, like all nineteenth-century cabinetwork coming after the style of the First Empire, displayed no fresh source of inspiration nor a unified style, but only a pattern of imitation drawn from the exclusive cult of past French traditional styles. The best of the furniture revealed fine craftsmanship, such as that by Fourdinois, who worked for Napoleon III and the elite of society. Unfortunately the flaunting and ostentatious character pervading art and society under the Second Empire is mirrored in the furniture, which was often extremely showy and ornate, to the point where it destroyed most, if not all, of its value. The desire for lavish display was apparent in the richly tufted and fringed upholstery work. Sofas, chairs, and the like were masterpieces of the upholsterer's art, with no trace of wood visible. Late in the nineteenth century a movement to emancipate furniture from the traditional styles of the past and to create a new style of design crystallized in Art Nouveau, a new "realistic" approach in the arts, seeking inspiration from nature. In furniture the style had but a brief career, which brings us to the Modern movement.

Classicism, as we have seen, reached its peak under the Empire, and it ends in the bourgeois Biedermeier, a style chiefly confined to Germany

218

OPPOSITE ABOVE: Bedroom of the Empress Eugénie in the Château de Saint-Cloud. Water color by F. de Fournier (1860). BELOW: Drawing room of the Empress Eugénie at the Château de Saint-Cloud. Water color by F. de Fournier (1860). *Courtesy Extrait du Louis Philippe, Napoleon III, de H. Clouzot. Photo Librairie Larousse. (See page 217.)* ABOVE LEFT: Table veneered in various woods and painted in India ink, Vienna (c. 1820). RIGHT: Mahogany table, Vienna (c. 1820). *Courtesy Österreichisches Museum für Angewandte Kunst, Vienna.*

and Austria, which flourished from about 1820 to 1850. The term Biedermeier, first used in 1853, was given to a political caricature appearing in the *Fliegende Blätter,* who typified a well-to-do middle-class man without culture. Biedermeier furniture, marked by its commonplace forms, is a potpourri of early nineteenth-century classicism—Sheraton, Regency, Directoire, and especially French Empire—with certain traits of its own. The best of this furniture belongs to the early period when it frequently displays an honest simplicity in form and decorative detail, especially in chair and table design, which gives the work a simple dignity. The furniture is characterized by a preference for curving lines, such as chairs with concave or saber legs, backs forming an elongated S profile, and table legs of lyre form. The curves are usually precise and neat, plain but agreeable. From around 1830, turned supports, especially spirally turned, are much in evidence. Chairs and sofas are occasionally enriched with decorative supports in the form of swans, dolphins, and griffins with the carved detail picked out in gilt, reflecting Empire influence. Cupboards, chests of drawers, and the like are extremely plain, often displaying the block-like

219

aspect of Empire working. In later cabinetwork, curves become more pronounced and exaggerated, while the ornament is richer and more freely used. Carved rococo scrollwork began to appear and by 1840 much of the furniture was in the revived rococo taste, which remained the principal inspiration until after the middle of the nineteenth century.

Elizabethan and
Early Jacobean

In England, Gothic art was of a surety neither dying nor even in its decline toward the year 1500, and it took a new lease on life in its final and transitional phase under the name of the Tudor style, 1485–1558, when such charming masterpieces of domestic architecture as Hampton Court Palace were built. Owing to the vitality of her Gothic style, England was the last European country to be influenced by the Italian Renaissance, which made its belated and initial appearance practically 100 years after its birth in Florence, in the famous tomb of Henry VII in Westminster Abbey. This beautiful monument, in a pure Italian Renaissance manner, was executed between the years 1512 and 1518–19 by the Florentine sculptor Pietro Torrigiano, who was one of a considerable group of artificers working for Henry VIII, 1509–47, and his courtiers.

There were also the Italian artists Toto del Nunziata, who was employed on the celebrated palace "Nonsuch," near Cheam in Surrey, built by Henry VIII and torn down in 1670, and Giovanni da Maiano, who made the terra-cotta portrait medallions of Roman emperors at Hampton Court Palace. But because a good defense was made by real native art against this foreign invasion, Henry VIII's attempts to naturalize the Italian style in England failed, though he used Italian craftsmen whenever he could. In fact so slow was the assimilation of the Italian Renaissance style that 200 years later, in the early Georgian era, it was still the goal of such architects as Kent and Lord Burlington, the most famous of the aristocratic amateurs, to reform the style of building in England according to principles established by Palladio, who was much studied by English architects from the time of Inigo Jones onward.

The influence of these Italian craftsmen scarcely affected form and structure, which essentially remained Gothic, but was confined to Italian ornament which took its place side by side with linen-fold panels, tracery, and the like. For instance, in chair design the chair retained its Gothic box-like form and linen-fold panels, but frequently let into the back was a delightful panel of "antick work" or grotesques, so called because the ornament was imitated more or less from antique wall paintings and stucco decoration in the underground tombs or "grottoes" of Rome. Portrait medallions of Italian origin, the Italian prototypes no doubt deriving from ancient coins, were also much favored. Frequently these "Romayne" medallions, as they were known in England, were carved on the paneled backs of Gothic chairs and on the deep underframing of joint stools of trestle construction. These hybrid pieces are often very pleasing, since the two styles are brought together with a fancy and ingenuous ease that amuses the eye without shocking it by a lack of harmony.

A little later under Elizabeth I, 1558–1603, the Italian influence yielded to German and Flemish, which was only to be expected, especially in the case of the Netherlands who received the bulk of English foreign trade. Even before the persecution of the Protestants, when many craftsmen sought refuge in England, there had been a tendency for German and Flemish skilled workers to seek their living in a country where their superior training afforded them an advantage over the natives. We have already seen that in the sixteenth century Italian Renaissance ornament was adopted and transformed by artists and designers of Northern Europe, especially in Germany and the Netherlands, who created an independent style of decoration in which strapwork, cartouches, and grotesque masks figured prominently. This ornamental style of Northern European Renaissance is found repeatedly in the pattern books of such German and Flemish ornamentists as Dietterlein and Vredman de Vries. In their designs, features borrowed from classical architecture, such as columns, pilasters, and arches, were unharmoniously crowded together with scant consideration for structural purpose; surfaces were seldom left undecorated. These books of ornament propagated the style in England. However, irrespective of foreign influences, a highly individual native style emerged, displaying a degree of exuberance and fantasy that the popular idea of the period by no means exaggerates. With a whole alphabet of Renaissance motifs introduced by either foreign craftsmen domiciled in London or pattern books, design in the Elizabethan period blossomed out into a rich panoply of display, largely composed of classical units extravagantly misapplied. A better understanding of Renaissance details used with knowledge and appreciation of their effect was soon to be intelligently translated by Inigo Jones.

The art of furniture followed in the movement, and we might carry to considerable lengths the parallel between the Elizabethan great house, with its exuberant exterior and colorful interior, literally a pageant in woodwork, plaster, and stone, and the furniture belonging to this period. In furniture perhaps the most typical feature of this love of rich ornament

Oak chair (c. 1525). It has linen-fold panels, the top panel carved with Renaissance ornament. BELOW: Oak hall and dining table (c. 1590–1600). It has a draw-top, carved and bulbous legs, and a molded stretcher. The frieze is inlaid with checker patterns. *Courtesy Victoria and Albert Museum.* (*See page 224.*)

was the bulbous excrescence or excess, the so-called cup and cover, that occurs on the legs of long hall and dining tables, the supports of court cupboards and hall and parlor cupboards, and the foot posts of tester beds. In the majority of cases the shape resembles that of a thick, squat vase with a well-defined cover, which is occasionally surmounted by a crude Ionic capital; as a rule, the surface of the vase is richly carved with foliage, generally acanthus, while the cover is most frequently decorated with bold gadrooning. Bulbous supports were of Flemish and German origin. In Elizabethan examples the girth is greatly exaggerated, while in the ensuing seventeenth century, under the first two Stuarts, the bulbous support gradually changed in character, becoming much less pronounced and often baluster turned.

The Elizabethan age witnessed a considerable advance in domestic comfort and in refinement of taste, but nothing like a revolution in taste is found, as was the case after the restoration of the monarchy in 1660. Although, under Elizabeth I, types of furniture that had been scarce became more plentiful and new forms were introduced, the amount of furniture was still very limited and rooms generally contained very few pieces. The general character of Elizabethan furniture was still of a rather primitive nature. Essentially the English cabinetmaker developed a style of furniture along native English lines, characterized by simplicity of construction and extreme solidity. It was massive and for the most part made of oak, though walnut was used to some extent in the furniture destined for royal palaces and a few great houses.

The decorative effect was obtained both by carving and inlay; the latter, a new and favorite method of the Elizabethan cabinetmaker, was done with woods of native trees of light and dark contrasting color, such as holly and bog oak respectively. Inlay work, perfected in Renaissance Italy, came to England through Germany and Flanders. English inlay was coarse and lagged far behind the technical accomplishments produced on the continent. Favorite subjects for the English inlayer were stylized flowers and foliage and simple geometrical patterns, such as the familiar checker pattern. Fantastic domed buildings with towers or turrets were sometimes represented in inlay work. Although they show a broad resemblance to a contemporary representation of Henry VIII's palace of Nonsuch, they more probably have their provenance in similar German prototypes. The so-called Nonsuch chests may have been made in England by members of the German colony, but there can scarcely be any doubt concerning their foreign origin. As for Elizabethan carving, it was always vigorous and robust, possessing a striking quality of barbaric richness. The display of heraldry, so common in that age and denounced by Philip Stubbes in his *Anatomie of Abuses* (1583), was a favorite subject for the wood carver, which he used in combination with the whole family of Renaissance

Nonsuch chest (late sixteenth century). Made of oak, it is inlaid with bog oak and holly.
Courtesy Victoria and Albert Museum.

ornament—caryatids, grotesque masks, arcadings, miniature classical orders, strapwork—to mention but a few.

The chair, which in medieval times had been an object of great rarity, intended for the master of the house or guests of honor, now began to take its place as a normal article of furniture. However, even though several varieties were in use in the second half of the sixteenth century, contemporary inventories show that chairs were still few and greatly outnumbered by joined stools even in great houses. On ceremonial occasions chairs retained their ancient significance; at court their use was reserved exclusively for the king. The principal joined chair was a development of the medieval chair of box-like form and still had a paneled back, but it was made with open arms supported on turned armposts and with turned legs joined with a stretcher close to the floor. In later Elizabethan examples there is a tendency to florid enrichment in a manner akin to opulent Flanders. To mitigate the discomfort of the plain wood seats of these wainscot chairs, as well as other kinds of wood seat furniture, such as settles, benches, or forms and stools, loose cushions often enriched with embroidery were much in evidence.

Toward the end of Elizabeth I's reign, upholstered chairs, first introduced from Italy into England about the middle of the sixteenth century, were becoming more plentiful in royal palaces and a few great houses. Under the early Stuarts, upholstery work was given serious consideration, owing, no doubt, to the new forms of upholstered furniture introduced from the French court of Louis XIII. As in France, some of the more luxurious furniture made in England in the early seventeenth century

LEFT: Oak armchair (c. 1600). It is elaborately carved and inlaid with checker patterns; the back panel is carved with "antick work." *Courtesy Duveen Brothers, New York. (See page 222.)* RIGHT: Walnut "farthingale" chair with plain columnar front legs (c. 1610). *Courtesy Victoria and Albert Museum.*

relied for effect on the rich elaboration of the upholstery. Chairs of traditional *X*-form were made in a more sumptuous manner; they were entirely covered in costly fabrics and lavishly trimmed with a fringe of straight silk-of-gold threads secured by gilt-headed nails. The craftsmen responsible for the most elaborate models were members of the Guild of Coffermakers, who also covered coffers and traveling trunks, not only with leather but also with rich silks and velvets. Especially typical of the period is the chair of "square" plan with a padded back panel stretched between the two uprights and an upholstered seat. In general design they resemble contemporary French and Flemish examples and those depicted in the engravings of domestic interiors by Abraham Bosse. Many of these low-back chairs were made without arms and were intended to accommodate the farthingale, or hooped skirt which by then was of incredible amplitude; in brief, the farthingale chair was the counterpart of the French *chaise à vertugadin*. Frequently the wood frame, when it was not painted, was completely covered with fabric to match the upholstery and was rudimentary in structure. Stools and benches were gen-

Oak bed (c. 1600). The head of the bed is richly decorated with carved and painted coats of arms. *Courtesy Victoria and Albert Museum.*

erally upholstered en suite; the benches were often of extreme length and supported on several pairs of plain columnar legs joined with low stretchers.

A perfect symbol of the period are the Elizabethan beds lavishly enriched with carving and inlay and occasionally painting and gilding. In medieval times the hangings were supported on a light undecorated framework. But in the first half of the 16th century the joined wooden bed was gradually developed, resulting in the Elizabethan type, with massive turned and carved foot posts, a headboard and tester of wainscot, with the bedstock or frame for the bedding standing free from the foot posts—an arrangement fairly common under Elizabeth I. Rich hangings of velvets, silks, tapestry, or embroidered linens contributed to their splendor. Although wainscot beds continued to be used by those who owned them, from around 1610-20 fashionable society began to prefer beds every part of which was covered with the most magnificent stuffs—like those in vogue in France. Tester beds when upholstered with the utmost elaboration were very costly, but most important houses possessed at least

LEFT: Oak "joyned" stool with turned baluster legs (c. 1625). *Courtesy Metropolitan Museum of Art. Gift of Russell Sage, 1900.* RIGHT: Walnut court cupboard (c. 1590). It is richly carved and inlaid and has finely modeled bulbous supports. Both friezes open as drawers. OPPOSITE: Oak hall and parlor cupboard dated 1610, with carved and inlaid decoration. *Courtesy Victoria and Albert Museum.* (*See page 230.*)

one example, and, as in France, they were not intended for ordinary domestic purposes but for state occasions. After the Restoration these draped, fringed, and plumed beds became triumphs of the upholsterer's skill; they remained in fashion until about the time of Chippendale when mahogany came into vogue. In most instances their almost incredible height was accentuated by four gorgeous bouquets of plumes which surmounted the tester, one at each corner—a fashion originating in Elizabethan times and a very expensive one.

By the time of Elizabeth I, long trestle tables for dining had been discarded to a great extent in favor of tables with fixed or joined frames often equipped with leaves that could be drawn out from underneath. There is an entry of a new "joyned drawing table" in an inventory of 1558, which is about the time of their introduction in England. The seats used at these tables were ordinary joint stools and benches with plain wood tops and turned legs generally splayed to ensure greater stability, and of course the legs were joined with low stretchers. The immovable character of these long hall and dining tables, which continued to be made throughout the seventeenth century, prompted John Evelyn to observe that they "were as fixed as the freehold." Trestle tables continued to be used because they were so easily disposed of

when a room had to be cleared for a masque and other revels. Thus, in *Romeo and Juliet*, after the banquet Capulet orders the servants to clear the hall and "turn the tables up."

Especially notable and characteristic are the richly carved oak cupboards, sometimes further enriched with inlay, for the display or storage of plate. A specialized variety known as a court cupboard (probably from the French *court* is a simple open superstructure of three shelves upheld in the front on bulbous-shaped supports, or occasionally on grotesque animals or birds, one above the other, the uppermost shelf thickened by a little cornice, the middle one by a row of drawers, the lower forming the base. A reference to such a cupboard, which served only for the display of plate, occurs in *Romeo and Juliet* when the servants are clearing the hall of the Capulets' house for revels, "Away with the joint stools, remove the court cupboard, look to the plate." Another variety, the so-called hall and parlor cupboards, show a greater diversity

in design, but the space between the two upper stages is always enclosed by doors, and sometimes the lower portion is treated in a similar manner, making the piece entirely closed for storage. Those with only the upper portion enclosed are structurally closely related to the contemporary court cupboard. There were, of course, other types of cupboards, such as food and livery cupboards with doors pierced or spindled for ventilation, and presses enclosed by solid doors fitted with shelves for linen or pegs for clothes. Finally there are the chests, which were still the commonest and most useful piece of furniture.

During the reign of the first two Stuarts, James I, 1603–25, and his ill-fated son, Charles I, 1625–49, the essence of classical design itself, rather than merely the repertory of Renaissance ornament as was the case heretofore, was brought to England. The banqueting house at White-hall and the Queen's House at Greenwich designed by Inigo Jones, 1573–1652, were built in the pure Palladian manner. In his capacity as surveyor-general to the king, Inigo Jones designed scenery for court masques in the Italian style, which played an important part in fa-miliarizing the fashionable world with the new style. But his influence during his lifetime was not widespread and hardly affected the design of domestic furniture.

Essentially Early Jacobean furniture is a continuation of the Elizabethan style which continued to dominate furniture design as long as the fashion for oak prevailed. After the Restoration in 1660, when walnut became the fashionable wood, the massive oak furniture of earlier generations was gradually banished from the homes of the richer classes. Carving often in low relief, inlay, a more frequent use as well as a greater variety of turning, faceted ornament, split balusters, pendants and spindles sometimes stained black and applied to the surface of furniture for ornamentation are typical features of Early Jacobean furniture. Elaborate strapwork as developed in Flemish ornament literally ran riot in England from around the end of the sixteenth century for the next three decades. As for new forms, the familiar gate-leg table with a pivoted gate leg on either side to support the two drop leaves made its debut under the early Stuarts, although late Elizabethan tables with a folding top and single gate foreshadowed their arrival. Another newcomer was the upholstered settee evolved from the settle and coinciding with the introduction of upholstered furniture into richly appointed houses. An extant example dating from around 1610–20 is winged, and the four legs turned as plain columns or pillars and joined with a low stretcher resemble those found on contemporary farthingale chairs. At this time several distinct varieties of furniture were in the process of evolution, of which the chest of drawers is by far the most important.

The establishment of the Protectorate in 1649 ushered in an era of simplicity and austerity; the production of luxury furniture was practically at a standstill, since the Puritans preferred plain substantial furniture in which the quality of usefulness was dominant. Especially favored were pieces that could serve a dual purpose, such as the ordinary combination chair-table and settle-table. The so-called Cromwellian chair with its knobbed legs, stretchers, a padded back panel, and seat of leather secured by brass-headed nails is typical of the times. Decorative furniture was occasionally made, as may be seen in a curious class of oak chests and "transitional" chests of drawers dating from about 1650 to 1665. Inlaid with ivory or bone sometimes combined with mother-of-pearl, they have a most elaborate molded façade, often highly tormented in its composition, decorated with geometrical beveled panels with centers frequently boldly projected in a style akin to Flemish and German woodwork of an earlier date, while the inlay reveals Moorish inspiration. The Protectorate was brought to an end with the restoration of the monarchy in 1660, which was to witness an era of splendor and prodigious spending unknown in England up to that time.

Oak chest of drawers dated 1653. It is inlaid with ivory and mother-of-pearl; the cupboard doors in both sections enclose drawers. *Courtesy Victoria and Albert Museum.*

Late Jacobean

The revolution in the whole standard of English social life after the restoration of the monarchy and the return of Charles II in 1660 was reflected in architecture, decoration, and furniture. There was a strong flavor of continental tastes in the love of luxury and refinement that attended "the politer way of living" brought into being by Charles II, which the Royalists had freely imbibed during their time of exile. As for furniture, the taste for new fashions revealed itself not only in the introduction of new types but also in the kind of wood employed in construction and the methods of decoration used in their enrichment. Heretofore the types of furniture in use in England had been few in number; simple chairs, stools, benches, tables, chests, and cupboards made of native oak served all the requirements of domestic life.

The more advanced civilization of the continent having inspired the Royalists with a desire for increased comfort in their homes called into being many new forms of furniture from the time of Charles II, 1660–85, onward. In many instances they have changed but little up to the present time. Thus we find for the first time chests of drawers, writing cabinets, bureaux or desks, toilet tables, candlestands, bookcases, bracket clocks and tall case clocks representing some of the more familiar varieties of furniture. At first found only in the houses of the wealthier classes, these new forms soon began to be adopted in simpler and less costly pieces, quite plainly made of walnut and in some instances of oak, by the middle classes of moderate wealth. Walnut superseded oak as the fashionable wood. The richer classes no longer patronizing the massive oak furniture of Tudor and Early Stuart times, its quality gradually became inferior and its traditional forms of construction obsolete; in remote country districts, however, traditional oak pieces continued to be used for many years.

Under Charles II, the baroque, a style of Italian origin, made its debut in English furniture design, but it never really triumphed in England if only for the reason that it flourished best in Catholic countries. Examples of baroque exuberance can be found in Late Jacobean caned chairs and gilt wood stands for the reception of lacquer cabinets, lavishly carved with amorini, scrollwork, and intricate wreaths; in the florid festoons of fruit and flowers that surround the chimneypiece, a popular theme on which wood carvers such as the versatile Grinling Gibbons practiced their virtuosity. The baroque predilection for curved forms manifested itself in riotous C-scrolls and S-scrolls, serving both ornamental and structural purposes. For instance, in the case of the latter, armposts, legs, and stretchers were often shaped in the form of scrolls.

From the time of the Restoration, the fashions for English furniture were almost completely dictated by foreign influence. The history of furniture design reveals that continental Europe has consistently taken the lead in introducing new ornament, forms, and techniques and that England has always followed, if at times slowly, continental innovations. During the Late Jacobean period, which also spans the brief reign of Charles II's brother, James II, 1685–88, French and Dutch cabinetwork exerted the greatest influence, with the latter prevailing, owing no doubt to the close commercial and social ties existing between the two countries. Indeed, as long as walnut remained the fashionable wood, Dutch influence persisted, but it was less pronounced after 1700 when the cabinetwork gradually became more Anglicized. The ascendancy of France in all branches of art under the Bourbon monarchs began to affect English work and became much more apparent in the succeeding baroque style under William III, 1689–1702.

The era witnessed a notable advance in cabinetmaking. Funds provided by the expansion of trade and the interest of a prosperous aristocracy encouraged English cabinetmakers to develop their skill in using new continental forms and methods of decoration. Though under the tutelage of Dutch immigrants, English cabinetmakers were not only quick to assimilate the new techniques, but in the majority of cases evolved a distinctive idiom of their own. In short, they were not long in proving themselves to be craftsmen of superior ability. Thus we find John Evelyn writing: "Joiners and cabinetmakers and the like from very vulgar and pitiful artists, are now come to produce works as curious for their fitting and admirable for their contriving as any we meet with abroad."

English cabinetmakers were quick to appraise the possibilities of producing surfaces of great richness through the technique of veneering. In the more ambitious pieces the veneers displaying the greatest variety and richness of figure were selected. Then, too, by an ingenious and artistic use of the figure of the woods, elaborate patterns were obtained; in

ABOVE: Cabinet japanned in black and gold (c. 1675). It is mounted on a gilt stand. The supports in the form of terminal figures are joined by a deep apron carved with acanthus foliage, festoons of flowers, and amorini, in the florid manner of the times. *Courtesy Parke-Bernet.* LEFT: Cabinet (c. 1670). It is decorated with floral marquetry on ebony panels, surrounded by walnut "oyster" pieces and bandings of holly. Originally, the spirally turned legs were supported on a shaped, flat stretcher and flattened ball feet. *Courtesy Victoria and Albert Museum.* (*See page 236.*)

235

brief, a kind of mosaic of woods or parquetry—a form of veneering often used in the early walnut period in combination with marquetry. A distinctive type of parquetry frequently used until the close of the seventeenth century is formed of "oyster shells" of wood cut traversely from branches about two to three inches in diameter of certain trees to produce circular or oval figures made of the annual ring markings; thus the name oystering for this technique. Parquetry was sometimes inlaid; a table top, for instance, might be veneered with parquetry; then lines of holly or boxwood and sometimes ivory in the form of stars, circles, and similar designs were laid into the ground—a style of inlay inspired by contemporary Dutch work. English cabinetmakers also learned for the first time the technique of veneering with marquetry decoration in various colored woods; the immediate inspiration for Late Stuart marquetry also came from Holland. At first under Charles II the marquetry designs were of flowers and birds realistically treated in the Dutch manner. Many of the woods were stained to obtain the desired colors. Portions of the design, such as petals of flowers, were shaded by dipping the pieces into hot sand, while the use of ivory, like leaves stained green, frequently interspersed in the design attested to the survival of Dutch influence.

The taste for brilliant colors and lavish display so typical of the years following the Restoration found a suitable expression not only in polychrome marquetry but also in the imitation of oriental lacquer, or japanning as it was called in England. From the time of Elizabeth I's reign, Chinese and other Eastern wares, particularly Chinese and Japanese lacquer panels, silks, and porcelain, had been imported into England, but the taste for oriental wares did not become widespread until Charles II's reign. The admiration lavished on the lacquers of the Far East and the desire to copy them or imitate them ended in the discovery of the process of lacquering, but the method employed was quite different from that used in the Orient. In England, as a result of a technical treatise by John Stalker and George Parker entitled *A Treatise of Japanning and Varnishing* (1688), the art of japanning became a fashionable hobby. Screens, cabinets mounted on carved gilt wood stands, and tall case clocks were much favored for this kind of decoration, most of which was the work of amateurs. Though the finished work possessed a singular naïve charm, it cannot be compared in technique or artistic merit with the perfected lacquer wares made in the East.

In addition to veneering, parquetry, marquetry, and japanning, such other practices as carving, upholstering, gesso gilding, and silvering enriched the technique of furniture making, to say nothing of such royal and princely caprices as furniture entirely covered in embossed silver, for example a hanging mirror with a side table and pair of stands made en suite. Wood carving achieved a notable standard of excellence under

Top of a walnut table (1660–1685). It is veneered with a marquetry decoration in various colored woods of tulips, carnations, and other flowers realistically treated. *Courtesy Victoria and Albert Museum.*

the aegis of Grinling Gibbons, 1648–1721. He first attracted the attention of John Evelyn, who, in an entry of his diary dated January 18, 1671, describes how he found the young man in a "poor solitary thatched house" busy at work on a carving so beautiful that "there being nothing in nature so tender and delicate as the flowers and festoons about it, and yet the work was very strong. . . ." These qualities earned for Gibbons a great reputation as a wood carver. His style of highly naturalistic ornament was imbued with an airy lightness but retained the strength Evelyn was quick to perceive. In the last quarter of the seventeenth century carvings such as on mirror frames are often a characteristic product of a school of carvers influenced by Grinling Gibbons.

Since there was a tendency among fashionable society to prefer a more brilliant surface decoration in furniture, wood carving had serious rivals not only in marquetry and japanning but also in gesso gilding. Italy, that motherland of every kind of magnificence, was the first to originate the art of gesso gilding in the Middle Ages, and this taste did not fail to find its way into France, from whence it probably came to England. Though gilding became more common in England after the Restoration,

237

its finest period spans the years from about 1700 to 1745 when the great Palladian houses were being built. Of course nothing is more familiar to us than the ornately carved gilt wood stands with a deep apron luxuriant with winged amorini, foliage scrolls, fruit and flowers, and frequently with caryatid supports, on which were placed the lacquer cabinets resplendent in reds, greens, and gold. Parcel gilding (part gilding) was also used as a medium of enrichment on certain deluxe walnut and painted pieces, such as chairs and decorative tables. A set of armchairs with painted and gilt frames upholstered in crimson velvet with gold braid borders mentioned in the 1679 inventory of Ham House furnishes a striking example of this taste.

Finally, before leaving the methods of decoration that are a notable feature of this period which above all preferred richness, whether real or apparent, mention must be made of Ham House, a synonym for prodigality in its day. Time has erased some of the splendor of Ham, but sufficient furniture has been preserved, together with inventories of the furnishings drawn up in 1679 and 1683, to substantiate Evelyn's observation that the house was "furnished like a great Prince's," and to show that it was rich in upholstery and magnificent hangings—tapestries,

OPPOSITE: Detail showing acanthus leaves, flowers, and seed pods carved in ash from the balcony of a staircase by Grinling Gibbons. *Courtesy Metropolitan Museum of Art.* (*See page 237.*) ABOVE: The north drawing room, Ham House. RIGHT: Gilt and painted armchair, carved with dolphins, one of a set of six from Ham House, Surrey (c. 1675). It has always been a favorite model for costly reproductions of Charles II chairs. *Courtesy Victoria and Albert Museum.*

brocaded damasks and velvets often of bright colors—which people loved to surround themselves with at this time, a fashion stemming from the court of Louis XIV. Among the items listed in the inventories, many of which are extant and attest to the luxuriousness of the Lauderdales' taste, are chairs "carv'd and guilt, 2 scriptors (writing cabinets with fall fronts) garnished with silver, a tea table carv'd and guilt, 2 blackamore stands [candlestands or *guéridons*], 2 Japan cabinets and frames, 1 table, stand and looking glasse frame of ebony flowered, 12 back stooles with cane bottoms japaned, 1 ebony table garnished with silver, 2 sleeping chayres [provided with a ratchet to adjust the back] with carv'd and guilt frames covered with crimson and gould stuff with gould fringe." Such costly appointments as silver-mounted chimney furniture—andirons, tongs, bellows, and hearth brushes—vividly portray how the "politer way of living" soon passed to luxury and intolerable expense. No doubt it was an allusion to Ham that prompted Evelyn or his daughter Mary, in a satire on the extravagances of the times, to write, "The chimney-furniture of plate, for irons now quite out of date."

Soon after the return of Charles II, a new type of chair was introduced, originating in the Netherlands, later imported and finally imitated in France. Walnut was combined with caning for the first time, the chair being given a caned-back panel and seat. In early English examples the

uprights, armposts, legs and *H*-form stretcher and a supplementary front stretcher above were spirally turned (a kind of turning much favored under Louis XIII); these members at the points of junction were mortised and tenoned into rectangular blocks. This "turned all over" chair, essentially of square plan, stiff and poor in line, was transformed by the craftsman's exuberant fancy into the typical tall-back Charles II chair. Like its continental prototype, it was given a cresting, a wide frame around the narrow caned-back panel and a broad front stretcher, one of its most distinguishing features; these were developed as decorative areas, being pierced and lavishly carved with baroque ornament. A crown supported by amorini (suitable to the restored monarchy and thus the name restoration chair) is among the most popular motifs, which also include grape-laden branches, flowers, birds, and foliated scrollwork. Under Charles II the armposts, legs, and stretchers are spirally turned or scroll-shaped; to such examples as the latter the description "cutt with scrowles all over," which appears in contemporary accounts, obviously applies. From around 1685–90 turned supports of baluster form became fashionable for the uprights and armposts; and though scroll-shaped front legs

OPPOSITE: Ebony table enriched with silver mounts, Ham House (c. 1670). The supports are in the form of female terminal figures. BELOW LEFT: One of two carved and gilt "sleeping chayres," Ham House (c. 1675). BELOW RIGHT: Walnut armchair, spirally turned, with a caned back and seat (c. 1665). *Courtesy Victoria and Albert Museum.*

were made after 1690, legs of vertical form became the fashion, as we shall see in the next chapter.

The upholstered chair with its tasseled or tufted fringe followed the evolution of the carved and caned restoration chair. The tall rectangular back was entirely upholstered, and the arms which often turned outward and ended in volutes, a typical feature of Louis XIV chairs, were open, closed sides being a later development. Large upholstered winged chairs, described as "easie" chairs in contemporary inventories, made their debut about the middle of Charles II's reign. Benches and stools, either caned or upholstered, also took on an ornamental character and were made to match the Charles II chair. This brings us to the daybed, which resembles a bench in character, only wider, and is provided with a hinged, adjustable backrest at one or occasionally both ends. These carved and caned daybeds were made comfortable with squabs and cushions. Upholstered daybeds with a back no longer movable and covered like contemporary winged chairs and settees date from the end of Charles II's reign.

OPPOSITE LEFT: Walnut armchair, carved and turned, with a caned-back panel (c. 1675–80). *Courtesy Victoria and Albert Museum.* (*See page 241.*) OPPOSITE RIGHT: Walnut armchair with removable cresting (c. 1680). It has scrolled front legs and arm supports, and a front stretcher carved with scrolls. *Courtesy Metropolitan Museum of Art. Collection of Irwin Untermyer.* RIGHT: Table decorated with "bantam work," the contemporary English name for incised lacquer. It is mounted on S-scrolled legs, which were in vogue in the 1680s. Ham House. *Courtesy Victoria and Albert Museum.*

At this time rooms set apart for dining came into general use among the upper classes, and oak joined tables with oblong tops were superseded by tables with round or oval tops, generally of the gate-leg variety. It was the fashion to serve meals at several small tables instead of a large one; thus the marble dining-room at Ham had three oval tables, while the great dining-room had eight tables. In those days when social customs kept the centers of rooms clear of furniture for the assemblage of guests standing or walking, the advantages of smaller tables with drop leaves placed against the wall when not in use are readily seen. For the dining-room there were also long side tables employed as sideboards for the serving of meals or holding plate (in this sense "long sytte bordes" are recorded as early as 1553). Small walnut tables of lighter aspect used for different purposes—cards, gaming, or tea, the latter a fashionable but expensive luxury—were made in large numbers; "a little table with a drawer" was a common entry in the inventories of this time. A feature of these tables, as well as oblong stands for veneered cabinets and chests of drawers, is the flat, shaped stretcher, very often X-shaped, cut out of

243

ABOVE: "Scriptor" or writing cabinet with a fall front, from Ham House (c. 1675). It is veneered with burr walnut, on a spirally turned and carved stand, and enriched with silver mounts. *Courtesy Victoria and Albert Museum.* RIGHT: Walnut chest of drawers on a stand (c. 1680). It is decorated with a marquetry of birds and flowers in various colored woods on an ebonized ground. *Courtesy Parke-Bernet.*

244

a plank. Their ends are not mortised into the legs; they are carried by four flattened balls and support the legs in their turn. As for the legs, they are spirally turned, while from around 1680 S-scrolled supports were adopted, in most instances for the more ambitious models.

Cabinets opening with two doors, one of the foreign luxury novelties introduced into England under the early Tudors, came into general use as a decorative variety of furniture after 1660. Mounted on a stand and occasionally on a chest of drawers, cabinets besides being veneered with figured walnut were frequently decorated with floral marquetry or parquetry, very often of "oyster-pieces" or a combination of both—the last word in elegant Carolean furniture. Perfectly attuned to the love for brilliant color are the japanned cabinets with their metal mounts of double lock plates, corner and angle plates copied from Chinese examples and placed on gilt wood stands opulent with baroque carvings. No doubt owing to the increased use of glass, a distinguishing feature of this period, and to the fashion for oriental porcelains, cabinets were designed with glazed doors having small rectangular panes of glass framed in plain molded bars.

Before leaving the subject of cabinets, a word is necessary about writing cabinets, which brings us to the kind of writing furniture in use at this time. We already know that cabinets characterized by an interior composed of small drawers originated in Italy, and that there were two kinds, opening either with two doors or a single flap, which when let down is held on the level by slides that pull out and serves as a writing board. Small portable writing cabinets appear to have been made in England, but it was not until after 1660 that the writing cabinet with a fall front mounted on a stand became one of the more elaborate varieties of furniture. The other principal piece of writing furniture at this time was the small portable desk fitted with drawers and a slant-front top hinged so that it opened backward. Both types were among the small objects of luxury covered with leather or velvet and "garnyshed with gilt nails" listed in the well-known inventory of Henry VIII's possessions, which rescues from oblivion the splendor of his palaces.

After 1660 the chest of drawers dethroned the chest and took its place as the essential piece of domestic furniture. The evolution of the chest of drawers from the chest with drawers was most natural and practicable. The greater convenience of drawers must have been obvious from the time the chest was first provided with a draw. For luxuriously appointed bedrooms, chests of drawers were veneered with walnut and decorated with floral marquetry. Contemporary with the veneered examples are the oak chests of drawers decorated with elaborately molded geometrical panels and applied split spindles, typical Early Jacobean features, but no doubt made after the Restoration, perhaps in the provinces. Chests of drawers

Silver mirror frame, from a toilet set bearing the London hallmark of 1683–84. Chased and embossed with acanthus foliage and amorini, the cresting centers a classical medallion. *Courtesy Victoria and Albert Museum.*

mounted on stands also made their first appearance toward the close of Charles II's reign. As for the metal mounts, brass supplanted the earlier wrought iron; handles in the form of a bulbous drop suspended from a circular back plate are typical.

Though not an absolute innovation, toilet mirrors did not come into regular use until around 1660. Up to this time, small hand mirrors of metal or crystal were generally used for dressing, since mirrors of glass do not appear to have been made in England until early in the seventeenth century and their manufacture was discontinued or at least very limited under the Protectorate. Hence it is not surprising that the toilet mirror supported on a hinged strut introduced from France after the Restoration was enthusiastically received. The costly and elaborate silver toilet sets in vogue in France under Louis XIV became the rage among fashionable society. Many of the fine English sets were made by Huguenot refugees. As for the kind of table used to display such sets, representations in pictures and engravings of this time show that many toilet tables were completely covered in fringed draperies. For those of moderate means who could not afford silver plate, the great majority by far, japanned toilet accessories were a popular substitute and were arranged perhaps on a japanned table. Stalker and Parker in their *Treatise of Japanning* offer various suggestions and designs for toilet articles of Japan work, such as for "combe boxes, a pincushion trunk for jewels, powder and patch-boxes. . . ." that were to be spread upon a cloth termed a toilet.

William and Mary

In the late seventeenth century the forms of English furniture developed as a result of royal alliances with Holland and the influx of Protestant refugees who came to England from France after the revocation of the Edict of Nantes in 1685. English art was immeasurably enriched by the work of the Huguenots, who were skilled in the arts of cabinetmaking, silversmithing, tapestry, and silk weaving. One name stands out among all Huguenot craftsmen, that of Daniel Marot, c. 1662–c. 1722, the celebrated architect, furniture designer, and engraver of ornament who came over to England from Holland and spent several years in the service of his Dutch patron, William III. Through his personal influence and engraved designs, Marot undoubtedly played a more important role than any other artist in introducing into England the baroque style which flourished in France under Louis XIV. His designs, whether for interior decoration or for such pieces of furniture as magnificent state beds surmounted with bouquets of plumes, pier mirrors, and tables, are opulent with shells and masks, heavy scrolls of C- and S-form, festoons and pendants of fruit and flowers, caryatids for supports and C-scrolls intertwined with foliage, but fortunately were tempered by a fine artistic sense.

It must be confessed that the assigning of a piece of furniture to a particular style is very arbitrary, but every classification, whether with regard to furniture or any subject from art to science, calls for simplification, the elimination of many exceptions and hybrids, and insists that only what remains shall be counted. With this in mind, the most identifying feature of the William and Mary style, 1689–1702, is the shape of the legs found on chairs, tables, and stands. We have seen that straight legs, spirally turned, began the reign of Charles II, but it ended with the frequent use of scroll-shaped legs, either single or double scroll. Under William III, these legs were in great measure superseded by a form of straight leg of baluster shape, turned but also often square or octagonal,

247

beginning from a cap and tapering as it lowered to the stretcher, which was inserted between the base of the leg and a spherical foot or sometimes a molded square or octagonal foot. Of course this most familiar leg reproduces in turning the typical Louis XIV richly carved and tapered pillar leg with its bold capital.

At this time caned-back chairs become lighter and, though still embellished with florid ornament, there was a noticeable tendency toward more disciplined design. The back became narrower and increased in height, producing a feeling of instability accentuated by an elaborate pierced and carved cresting, in most instances arched, composed of scrolls symmetrically arranged. Chairs ornamented with half-hoop crestings are often popularly referred to as periwig chairs, because the backs rose well above the occupants and effectively set off the tall headdresses and periwigs. The cresting rested on the uprights now of baluster form. The broad front stretcher is also often arched and composed of a bold arrangement of scrolls; it is now lower and frequently sets back; finally it disappears. With the disappearance of the broad front stretcher, flat serpentine X-form stretchers decorated at the point of intersection with a carved or turned finial of vase form are typical, replacing the earlier H-form stretcher. As an alternative to the round or square foot, the so-called Spanish foot, which scrolls under, is sometimes used. The arms turn outward and terminate in volutes; an entry of 1697 mentions chairs with "the elboes [arms] to turne on the corner." The canework, in the final phase of this

OPPOSITE LEFT: Walnut table (c. 1690). It is decorated with seaweed marquetry. The fashionable S-scrolled supports of the 1680s continued to be used throughout the 1690s. *Courtesy Metropolitan Museum of Art. Collection of Irwin Untermyer. (See page 247.)* OPPOSITE RIGHT: Oak table (c. 1690). It has a tray top, probably intended for needlework or tea, a valanced apron, turned baluster legs, and curved X-form stretcher. *Courtesy Metropolitan Museum of Art. Leonard A. Cohen, 1951.* LEFT: Curio table, carved, painted, and partly gilded (c. 1690). The pillar legs and stretcher display French influence. *Courtesy Metropolitan Museum of Art. Rogers Fund, 1911.* BELOW LEFT: Chair of carved and painted beechwood with caned seat and back panel (c. 1690–95). BELOW RIGHT: Carved walnut chair with caned-back panel (c. 1690). The legs terminate in the so-called Spanish feet. *Courtesy Victoria and Albert Museum.*

249

LEFT: Walnut chair (c. 1690). The cartouche-shaped back filled in with pierced foliage and scrollwork recalls designs by Daniel Marot. *Courtesy Metropolitan Museum of Art. Collection of Irwin Untermyer.* RIGHT: Carved walnut chair (early eighteenth century). This new type, introduced from Holland, became "naturalized" in Queen Anne's reign. *Courtesy Victoria and Albert Museum.*

type of chair, became extremely fine. Some chairs with opulent carvings dating from William III's reign recall the designs of Daniel Marot, having the space between the uprights filled in with pierced foliage and scrollwork, hence the name Marotesque chair.

Of course upholstered chairs followed the development of caned-back chairs; their tall narrow rectangular backs, and sometimes toward the close of the century arched backs, were entirely upholstered and had a pronounced rake, so characteristic of the Late Stuart upholstered type. Benches and stools were often designed en suite with chairs, while upholstered settees with projecting wings and padded arms often took the form of a double-back chair. They displayed the typical tapering legs (generally six or eight of them) and "mushroom" cappings united by gracefully scrolled stretchers.

An important milestone in chair design occurred around 1700 when a new type of walnut chair of a more reticent style, based upon the principle of contrasted curves, was introduced from Holland. The English cabinetmaker was quick to appreciate the features of design embodied in these early imported models. He freely adapted them and in the process largely transformed them into the very popular Queen Anne splat-back chair, in which curved lines dominate the design and cabriole legs, hoop backs, and vase-shaped splats figure prominently. The cabriole leg, which from a distance suggests the line of a stag's hind leg with the hock eliminated, was to dominate English furniture design for about a half century, when it yielded to the rectilinear neo-classic vogue. The leg was no doubt originally derived from a form of animal leg much employed by the Romans as a support for tables and was revived in Italy in the curved profile on Renaissance sarcophagi and *cassoni*. At the end of the seventeenth century, as we have already seen, French designers such as Boulle adopted this curved profile and applied it to chairs, tables, and commodes. In the early models the cabriole leg terminated in the cloven hoof of a ruminant and was joined with stretchers.

We have already seen in France to what extent Louis XIV and his court delighted in everything that came from China—Chinese stuffs full of figures embodying the whole religion of that country or full of plants from which sprang branches of flowers with birds and butterflies; lacquer boxes, cabinets, and screens on which hares scamper over waves or sparrows are perched on swaying bamboo. Everywhere, on tables, shelves, and cabinets, were porcelains with Chinese motifs. In England these exotic objects were not imported in sufficient quantities to have any considerable effect until after the Restoration; sometime later, under William III, collecting porcelain, either Chinese or its imitation, Delft faïence, enjoyed an unheard-of vogue. No doubt Queen Mary's porcelain collection kindled the craze in England. After the queen's death in 1694, an inventory of the possessions at Kensington Palace drawn up in 1696 gave a detailed list of Queen Mary's porcelain; in the Garden Room alone were "143 pieces of fine china" arranged on tiered shelves above the chimneypiece and the lintels of the doors. This manner of displaying porcelain appears in Marot's designs, and one must see these to appreciate to what extremes the porcelain craze could be carried. Then, too, recruited for the display of porcelain were brackets, cabinets with glazed doors, and hanging corner cupboards; the latter with their solid doors came into general use during the reign of William and Mary.

The Kensington Palace inventory, besides the entries of porcelain, also listed furniture of "India Japan," with nearly all the furniture in the queen's New Bedchamber being decorated in this medium. We have already mentioned that lacquer imported from the East was soon imitated in England, the raised variety being much more frequent than the incised or cut variety known as "bantam work" in the seventeenth century. Oriental lacquer or English Japan cabinets placed upon carved gilt wood stands occupied a conspicuous position in luxuriously appointed houses, while in bedrooms chests of drawers and toilet sets, very often the work of amateurs, were much in evidence. Japanning by amateurs did not become a fashionable hobby until after 1690 when a description of the process, directed rather to the amateur than to the craftsman and presented in a manner readily comprehensible, appeared in the *Treatise of Japanning* (1688). Thus, either by experienced craftsmen or by amateurs, that vast amount of Late Stuart japanned furniture was obtained, which expresses so eloquently the taste of the age that delighted in bright and vivid colors.

Tea may well figure here, for it has probably exercised as pronounced an influence upon the customs of the Western world as any of the curios that began to be imported into Europe from the Far East in the seventeenth century. Probably the earliest mention of tea by an Englishman occurs in a letter of 1615 from Mr. Wickham, an agent of the East India Company in Japan, asking a fellow agent in China to send him "a pot of the best sort of chaw." At first tea was regarded as chiefly medicinal, being recommended by physicians for curing various ailments; it was also approved as a cure for excessive drinking, "tea being friendly to the stomach and head." In spite of the high prices and heavy import duty, tea gradually became a much sought-after beverage. In 1679, when tea was a fashionable but very expensive luxury, the inventory of the possessions at Ham House lists "one Indian furnace for tea garnished with silver, a tea table carv'd and guilt, a Japan box for sweetmeats and tea." Around the end of the seventeenth century tea tables primarily designed for holding the tea equipage came into general use. Early tea tables were made with either oblong or round tray-shaped tops, mounted, respectively, on four legs or on a central standard and tripod base. With the advent of tea tables, stands for the silver teakettle and its spirit burner, the earliest of which is believed to date from the time of Queen Anne, were introduced. Teakettles were an important tea accessory, since it was customary to infuse tea at the tea table. Apparently early tea stands were in the form of small tripods having a round top, central standard and tripod base; they were similar to the plain walnut tripod candlestands, which no doubt served other purposes including that of a stand for the teakettle. (See illustration *An English Family at Tea* in the following chapter.)

In the carved and gilt wood side tables and stands, made under William III, French influence is clearly apparent. The tapering pillar legs with boldly gadrooned capitals and elaborately scrolled stretchers, the frieze decorated with foliated strapwork pendants, have their provenance in the designs of Bérain and Marot. Also having their counterparts in Louis XIV designs are the tall, richly carved gilt wood candlestands of tripod form, generally with a vase-shaped top, tapering standard, and base composed of three baroque scrolls, the latter being a marked feature. Pieces

ABOVE: Four designs for japanning the drawers of a cabinet. From *A Treatise of Japanning*, 1688, plate 19. LEFT: Cabinet japanned in black and gold with carved and gilt wood stand and cresting (c. 1690). The cresting and finely designed stand show unmistakable French influence and are reminiscent of Daniel Marot's designs. *Courtesy Victoria and Albert Museum.*

253

BELOW: Oak side table (c. 1695). It has tapered baluster-turned supports with inverted cup-like cappings. *Courtesy Metropolitan Museum of Art. Collection of Irwin Untermyer.* RIGHT: Toilet mirror japanned in blue and gold (c. 1700). The stand is fitted as a desk, and the long drawer is furnished with toilet equipage. *Courtesy Victoria and Albert Museum.*

such as these attest to the presence of the numerous French craftsmen in England, which is also confirmed by the furnishing accounts of the royal palaces. But there was little really English in all this. Fortunately it was in the princely furniture that the tradition was lost; it was different with less costly pieces, which simply copy the general lines.

To the large family of plain, well-proportioned, useful furniture generally made of veneered and solid walnut and in some instances of oak belongs the toilet table, a kind of oblong side table known as a lowboy in America. Tapering legs supported on flat, shaped stretchers generally of X-form, spherical feet, an arcaded underframing, sometimes ornamented with small turned pendants (reproducing in fanciful outline the elaborate pendanted frieze of Louis XIV tables), and fitted with a row of drawers to hold the toilet articles, are its distinguishing features. This type of toilet table and the familiar small kneehole table retained their popularity throughout the first half of the eighteenth century, even after toilet tables provided with toilet mirrors and compartments for cosmetics had become fashionable. The advent of toilet tables with a row of frieze drawers coincided with the introduction of the swinging toilet mirror mounted on

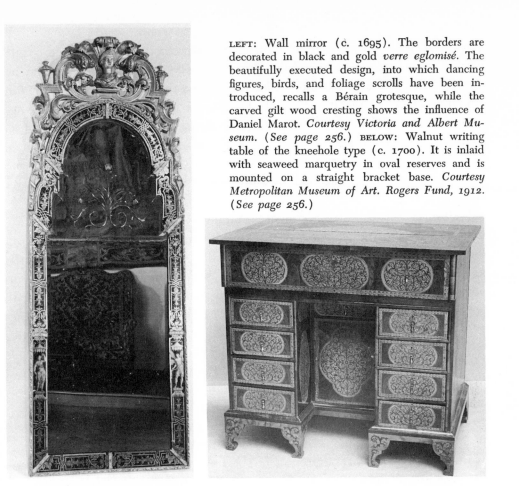

LEFT: Wall mirror (c. 1695). The borders are decorated in black and gold *verre eglomisé*. The beautifully executed design, into which dancing figures, birds, and foliage scrolls have been introduced, recalls a Bérain grotesque, while the carved gilt wood cresting shows the influence of Daniel Marot. *Courtesy Victoria and Albert Museum.* (See page 256.) BELOW: Walnut writing table of the kneehole type (c. 1700). It is inlaid with seaweed marquetry in oval reserves and is mounted on a straight bracket base. *Courtesy Metropolitan Museum of Art. Rogers Fund, 1912.* (See page 256.)

a box stand, the mirror being supported on uprights by swivel screws. In the early examples the stand was frequently a miniature version of a desk with a slant front; the long drawer in the stand was fitted with small compartments to hold the toilet requisites. In most instances they were veneered with walnut, others were japanned; later of course, since they continued to be made throughout the eighteenth century, they were chiefly of mahogany. In addition to the toilet mirror on a box stand, there were the silver toilet mirrors placed on elegantly draped toilet tables. Under William III the mirror belonging to the elaborate silver toilet sets discarded its square shape and solid cresting; now the frame was arched at the top, recalling the style of the contemporary hanging mirrors.

Though wall mirrors began to play a part in decorative schemes from early in the seventeenth century, it was not until late in the reign of Charles II that they occupied a prominent position in elegantly appointed rooms, where they were generally placed between windows with a table and a pair of candlestands below them, very often made en suite. Under William III the taste for elaborately carved and gilt wood wall mirrors became more pronounced, while mirrors with glass borders, frequently decorated with *verre eglomisé,* an art introduced into England from France, also became fashionable. The royal accounts for 1695 mention in the queen's New Bedchamber "a lookinge glass the frame all covered with lookinge glass." The character of the design for wall mirrors was considerably changed in the closing years of the seventeenth century. Square shapes were abandoned, while the height was noticeably increased, which necessitated the use of two or sometimes even three plates of glass to form the mirror; above the arched heading was an elaborate cresting with a fancifully shaped outline.

Writing furniture was augmented under William III by several very important types: the slant-front bureau with drawers down to the ground, the writing table of kneehole form with a deeply recessed center compartment and drawers to the right and left down to the ground, and the tall bureau cabinet or secretary cabinet with a slant front. Up to this time the portable desk and oblong writing cabinet with a fall front had been the only forms of furniture especially designed for writing. With the general introduction of bureaux toward the close of the seventeenth century, small portable desks did not disappear but continued to be made throughout the eighteenth century; their slant front opened to an interior of small drawers and pigeonholes that reproduced the arrangement adopted in the larger bureaux. Frequently these small desks were mounted on stands. Walnut writing cabinets, found in considerable numbers around the close of the century and the beginning of the next, are now generally mounted on a chest of drawers and, like walnut cabinets with two doors, are designed with a pulvinated or cushion frieze, a distinguishing feature.

The tall secretary cabinet, from its double-hooded cornice to its globular feet, is a notable piece of William and Mary furniture; particularly colorful and picturesque are the japanned examples. Designed in two sections, the upper structure, fitted with two doors, is placed on the narrow shelf at the top of the slant-front bureau, which is occasionally of kneehole form. The double-arched or double-hooded top outlined by a boldly molded cornice and adopted around 1690 is a notable feature of these pieces; the two paneled doors are conformingly arched, recalling the style of contemporary wall mirrors. In some examples of secretary cabinets, mirrors beveled and engraved frequently take the place of molded panels in the doors of the upper portion.

Finally, before we leave this second of the picturesque baroque styles belonging to the seventeenth century, mention must be made of chests of drawers and the seaweed marquetry employed to decorate ambitious examples of veneered walnut furniture such as cabinets, tall case clocks, side tables, and chests of drawers. Seaweed or arabesque marquetry composed of a fine symmetrical foliated scrollwork became fashionable in William III's reign, superseding the polychrome floral marquetry of the

LEFT: Walnut secretary cabinet. It has a double-hooded cornice surmounted by a carved and pierced silvered cresting, and is mounted on globular feet. The moldings, handle plates, and other details point to a date in the early years of Queen Anne's reign. *Courtesy Victoria and Albert Museum.* RIGHT: Detail showing the top of a table inlaid with seaweed marquetry (c. 1690). *Courtesy Metropolitan Museum of Art. Collection of Irwin Untermyer.*

Carolean period. Only two woods were employed—box or holly for the over-all design of delicate scrolls and walnut for the ground. Naturally it was not as colorful as floral marquetry, but the technical skill demanded of the marquetry cutter cannot be denied. The cabinetmaker to the Crown, Gerreit Jensen, c. 1680–1715, of Dutch or Flemish origin, whose work extended over four reigns from Charles II to Queen Anne, achieved notable success in this medium. It can be learned from royal household accounts that Jensen's furniture was also decorated with japanning and in a few instances with a marquetry of metal; apparently he was the only craftsman in England at this time employing the Boulle technique. Jensen had two houses and a warehouse on St. Martin's Lane, a famous street in the annals of English furniture, where such eminent cabinetmakers as Hallett, Chippendale, Vile, and Cobb took premises.

Among the contemporary novelties, the tallboy or chest on chest introduced around 1700, with its additional storage space, received a warm
welcome. In spite of a large increase in clothespresses and wardrobes in
the second half of the eighteenth century, tallboys continued to be made
in considerable numbers. Chests of drawers mounted on stands provided
with drawers never enjoyed the popularity in England accorded to them
in America, where they are known as highboys. Under William III, chests
of drawers were frequently mounted on arcaded stands with drawers in
the frieze and turned tapering baluster supports with inverted cup-like
cappings, united by shaped, flat stretchers and mounted on ball feet,
recalling the style of contemporary plain walnut toilet tables. As in the
Carolean period, deluxe chests of drawers were veneered with walnut
and embellished with marquetry, but of course it was now seaweed
marquetry arranged in cartouche-shaped panels. Flattened ball feet or
straight bracket feet are characteristic for chests of drawers. All these
types of chests of drawers were favorite subjects for the amateur japanner,
expressing so eloquently the fashion for colorful decoration, a distinguishing feature of the Late Stuart period.

Queen Anne and Early Georgian

QUEEN ANNE

In the early years of the eighteenth century under Queen Anne, 1702–14, the last regnant Stuart, English furniture design showed a gradual development in mobility and comfort without introducing striking innovations. Sound construction, utility, and elegant simplicity are united in the best furniture of this time. Baroque exuberance was developed a stage further by Sir John Vanbrugh, an architect of genius. But in furniture and most of the decorative arts there was a noticeable relaxation, a period of relative calm and reserve. The period was marked by a newly awakened appreciation of form and proportion, strikingly revealed in the Queen Anne splatback chair with its upholstered seat. New standards of comfort were achieved in the co-ordinated curves of its structural lines. Throughout the eighteenth century, regarded as the golden age of English cabinetwork when foreign techniques were skillfully mastered and assimilated with the native tradition, chairmakers never surpassed their accomplishments in the opening years.

The era witnessed the abandonment of lavish surface ornament. Beauty of surface was still of primary importance, but now an effective decorative use was made of carefully selected veneers of walnut and other woods, while delicate carving in low relief replaced the florid carving of the two preceding picturesque baroque styles. The shell motif was by far the favorite carved ornament; sometimes combined with a small husk pendant or acanthus pendant, it frequently appeared on the knee of the cabriole leg. The taste for japanned furniture reached its peak; amateurs as well as more practiced hands were still roused to enthusiasm by its beauty and decorative value. The fashion for curved forms and extravagant baroque S- and C-scrolls, which had come in with the Restoration, was carried into the new century. But the curves are more controlled and as a rule serve a

259

Walnut chair with a vase-shaped splat (c. 1710–15). The two front legs are carved with a splay of honeysuckle and terminate in club feet *Courtesy Parke-Bernet, from the collection of Mrs. Theodore A. Havemyer.*

structural purpose. For instance, the structural members of the graceful Queen Anne splat-back chair are based upon the principle of curvilinear design—the undulating uprights, the hoop back, the curving seat rail, the solid vase- or fiddle-shaped splat that conforms to the shape of the sitter's back, and the two front cabriole legs.

The most persistent of these curved forms is the cabriole leg, which swept aside every form of leg and dominated English furniture design for almost half a century. With the introduction of Gothic and Chinese tastes about 1750–60, the straight leg reappeared, but the cabriole leg continued to be employed on furniture designed in the French rococo manner. The influence of the classical revival, with which the name of Robert Adam will always be associated, caused the cabriole leg to be generally discarded about 1770 in favor of a slender tapering molded straight leg, square or round, based upon Louis XVI models. However, it was still employed in an attenuated form by Hepplewhite on a few fashionable chairs and tables designed in the Louis XV taste. Cabriole legs follow a broad structural evolution; at first relatively narrow, they gradually assume greater width. In chair design the narrow cabriole legs are joined with *H*-form stretchers which were rendered superfluous as the legs became bolder, and, of course, they seldom harmonize with the continuous curved line of the cabriole leg.

Soon after 1710, when in a general sense stretchers were discarded, the ball-and-claw foot, a form of foot derived from the oriental design of a dragon's claw holding a pearl, a motif of great antiquity, was adopted as a terminal for the cabriole leg. It succeeded the club foot, though the latter continued to be used until around the mid-eighteenth century. Eagles' claws were at times substituted for dragons' claws. As an alternative to the ball-and-claw, a whorl foot, a form of terminal borrowed from France, was employed from about 1740 to 1765, particularly for chairs and tables designed in the French rococo taste.

We have already mentioned in the preceding chapter that certain features of the Queen Anne splat-back chair, adopted from Dutch models, were gradually developed and naturalized in Queen Anne's reign. There is some reason to suppose that the form of the back derived ultimately from oriental models; a royal furnishing account in 1717 mentions a set of chairs having "India backs." Of course the description is not sufficient to determine their character. But we know, however, that Ming chairs have a solid splat which is shaped to the occupant's back and joins the seat rail, and have at times a hoop back—distinguishing features of the Queen Anne splat-back chair.

Before leaving Queen Anne seat furniture, we must not forget to mention settees and wing chairs; by now the designs of the latter tended toward uniformity, the wings finishing in padded armrests with an outward scroll. The arms and wings appearing as one continuous piece present a more graceful and pleasing line than that found in late eighteenth-century models when the arms extend to the back of the chair and the wide wings rest upon them. Indeed the Queen Anne wing chair is a choice piece of eighteenth-century upholstered furniture. Also notable for the graceful simplicity of its lines is the upholstered Queen Anne chair with open arms continuing to looped terminals on incurvate supports; the height of the back of these chairs was considerably reduced from the tall backs of the William and Mary epoch. Besides settees with either open arms or closed sides, chair-back settees usually designed with two or three chair backs, made in England as early as 1660, were reintroduced toward the close of Queen Anne's reign and continued in vogue throughout the eighteenth century.

Perhaps, after the splat-back chair, the best-known piece of Queen Anne furniture is the card table having an oblong folding top, outset round

ABOVE LEFT: Wing chair (c. 1715). The wings are prolonged in padded armrests; the graceful cabriole legs end in club feet. ABOVE RIGHT: Walnut armchair (c. 1720). The cabriole legs are enhanced with a "bracelet" and end in club feet. *Courtesy Parke-Bernet, from the collection of Mrs. Harrison Williams. (See page 261.)* RIGHT: Walnut card table (c. 1725). The top is covered with needlework, and the cabriole legs, which are carved on the knees with shells, finish in ball-and-claw feet. *Courtesy Parke-Bernet, from the collection of Mabel Brady Garvan.* OPPOSITE: *Breakfast Scene,* after William Hogarth's *Marriage à la Mode* series (1744). Queen Anne card tables with their folding tops extended are represented in the room beyond the arched entrance. *Courtesy Philadelphia Museum of Art.*

corners dished to hold four candlesticks and four sunken wells for money or counters. The top is covered with cloth, the conventional green cloth often being replaced by needlework or velvet. Benjamin Goodison, an eminent Georgian cabinetmaker, supplied in the 1730s to George II "two walnut-tree card tables covered with green velvet, one trimmed with gold lace, the other plain." The passion for card playing and gambling, which became little short of a mania during the early eighteenth century, continued unabated throughout the century, making card tables indispensable. As the century progressed, changes in design in accordance with the prevailing fashions were made in the card table with the folding top, which remained the classical form during the Georgian period. Attempts by George III to discourage gambling by excluding it for a time at the royal palaces and also legislation at the end of the century to curb it probably explain the small attention card tables were given by contemporary designers. Sheraton in his *Cabinet Dictionary* (1803) grudgingly notices them with the remark that they are "oftener used than to good purpose."

Gaming tables are of early origin. No doubt the earliest was in the form of a gaming board marked out with lines. Chessboards are frequently mentioned in medieval inventories, and contemporary illuminations show

263

The Toilette of the Countess, after William Hogarth's *Marriage à la Mode* series (1744). *Courtesy Cooper Union Museum.* OPPOSITE: *An English Family at Tea* (British School, eighteenth century). *Courtesy Tate Gallery, London.*

ladies and gentlemen engaged in the game. Before the fifteenth century, when card playing was introduced into England, backgammon (known as "tables") and dice as well as chess are frequently mentioned by contemporary writers. Chess and backgammon retained their popularity, and though entries of gaming tables often appear in Stuart inventories, their character cannot be recognized from the description. It seems reasonable to suppose that English gaming tables were more or less similar to extant Dutch models dating from the second half of the seventeenth century, which were often made for both games; the reversible top is inlaid on one side for chess and opens to a well inlaid for backgammon. The practicability of this design was not overlooked, as may be seen in extant examples of French *tric-trac* tables and English gaming tables made in the eighteenth century.

While on the subject of tables, a few words about tea tables and toilet tables. Though many toilet mirrors on box stands, now frequently without

the desk portion, were made under Queen Anne, in pictures of fashionable interiors draped toilet mirrors are frequently represented, as in Hogarth's *Marriage à la Mode* depicting the toilet of the countess. Indeed the arrangement of elegantly draped mirrors and tables often draped to match the mirror continued in vogue for at least the greater part of the eighteenth century. Thus we find Chippendale, in the third edition of the *Director*, 1762, illustrates "Draped Toylet Tables." Of one of these he writes that the frame of the toilet glass and table should be gilded or japanned, the draperies should be of silk damask with gold fringe. These elegantly draped pieces provided a flattering background for the lovely Georgian women who received their admirers and friends seated at their toilet tables in a coquettish déshabillé while the hairdresser arranged their curls.

We have already mentioned in the preceding chapter while writing about the introduction of tea tables that it was customary to infuse the tea at the tea table. In the painting *An English Family at Tea* this is

Double chest of drawers, or tallboy, veneered with walnut (early eighteenth century). The inlaid stellate in box and holly is a motif borrowed from Holland and is often found on walnut tallboys of this time. BELOW: Secretary cabinet japanned in red and gold with a slant front (c. 1705–10). The broken-arched, boldly molded pediment is a characteristic feature for this class of furniture under Queen Anne; it is mounted on straight bracket feet. *Courtesy Victoria and Albert Museum.*

clearly represented. In the left foreground is the open tea caddy case, and the hostess is measuring the costly commodity into the lid from one of the caddies. Behind the maid is the kettle stand for the reception of the tea-kettle and spirit burner. The maid has removed the teakettle filled with hot water from the burner and is ready to infuse the tea. The tea table with a rectangular top and four cabriole legs and the kettle stand with a circular top, central standard and tripod base are the favorite forms for these two pieces under Queen Anne.

Finally a few words about the metal mounts and the chests of drawers and like pieces on which they are found. The beginning of the eighteenth century witnessed the creation of a new type of drawer mount, which was, with certain modifications, to become the principal form until about the mid-eighteenth century. This is the loop, or bail handle attached to a flat, shaped back plate, at first solid and later elaborated in openworked designs. As for the chests of drawers and all other pieces with drawers down to the ground, straight bracket feet are typical of the time. Writing furniture, which was augmented at this time by the secretary tallboy, book-cases, and chests of drawers, is marked by extreme simplicity, relying for effect on excellent proportions and finely figured walnut veneers. Secretary cabinets surmounted by a double-hooded cornice or broken-arched pediment, enriched with japanned decoration prepared from formulas popularized by Stalker and Parker, were in high fashion.

EARLY GEORGIAN

The century between the death of Queen Anne and the accession of George IV witnessed the rise and decline of several distinct styles. Baroque extravagance yielded to rococo caprice and that to refined classicism, which at the close of the century was supplanted by an archaeological revival founded on a study of the remains of ancient civilizations. The dominating influence of this intensely aristocratic age was not, as in France, a royal court but the aristocracy and gentry themselves, who from Lord Burlington down to Horace Walpole were actively engaged in advancing the arts. This accounts for the far greater individualism asserted in English designs.

The Early Georgian style, placed between the simple and dignified furniture associated with the reign of Queen Anne and the rococo period with its indulgence in caprice and fantasy covers a period of about three decades, 1720–50 and has certain distinguishing features. One word, Palladian, is indelibly stamped on this era when cultured and traveled amateurs regarded a knowledge of architecture as essential to every educated man. An endeavor to purify English architecture from the style associated with the later Renaissance and Sir Christopher Wren and to revive the style of Palladio and Inigo Jones was inaugurated in the 1720s by Lord Burlington,

the best known of the aristocratic amateurs. Through his ability and the pronounced enthusiasm of the fashionable world for Italian architecture, the Palladian style was soon successfully established. Palatial Palladian houses—Holkham, Houghton, and Rousham, to mention but several—having state rooms of great size and height, lavish with decorative paintings, stucco, and marble, were built by the great landowners, to be followed in the course of time by many smaller Palladian houses as the style became better known.

The grandiose interiors of the great Palladian houses demanded suitable furniture. Thus a new style, baroque in conception and based upon Italian and French models, was made in England essentially for this purpose. The principal leader of this new manner of furnishing was William Kent, 1684–1748, who, after a sojourn in Italy, was introduced to English society by Lord Burlington and soon earned the reputation as an arbiter of taste. Kent was the first English architect to design his furniture in direct relation to its architectural setting. Like Robert Adam in the second half of the century, his furniture formed an integral part of the general scheme. But before considering certain features of this furniture, a few words about

mahogany are relevant. From around 1720, after the repeal of the heavy import duties, mahogany from the West Indies was imported in ever increasing quantities and gradually replaced walnut as the fashionable wood. The influence of mahogany, hard and close-grained and wonderfully suitable for carving, became noticeable in the design and decoration of furniture. The demand for lavish enrichment consonant with the grandeur of the great Palladian houses found an appropriate outlet in this new material. Thus it came to pass that the second phase of the English baroque style was launched by the Palladian arbiters of taste.

The furniture by Kent and other members of his school was designed as far as possible on architectural lines and lavishly enriched with large-scale carved decoration essentially plastic in conception. For instance, in wall furniture, in which the architectural treatment is noticeably pronounced, mahogany cabinets and bookcases of massive construction are framed between columns or pilasters and surmounted with entablatures and pediments, the latter generally broken and often centering an acroter. Enormously heavy library or writing tables of pedestal form, designed to occupy a position in the middle of the room and well suited

269

OPPOSITE ABOVE: Mahogany library table in the manner of William Kent (c. 1730–35). It is probably one of a pair which originally stood back to back forming a writing table in the center of the room. The stiles are carved with pendants of bellflowers and are crested with lion masks bearing gilt bronze handles in their mouths. *Courtesy Parke-Bernet, from the collection of Walter P. Chrysler.* OPPOSITE LEFT: Carved and gilt side table, one of a pair (c. 1730). Having scroll-shaped supports, it was designed by William Kent to stand below a mirror in the salon at Houghton Hall. The baroque design is of Venetian inspiration. *Courtesy Lady Cholmondeley. Photo Country Life.* OPPOSITE RIGHT: Project for a baroque side table and mirror frame (Italian, c. 1700–25). The top of the table is supported by cornucopiae; a cartouche is centered between the two putti who are seated on C-scrolls. *Courtesy Cooper Union Museum.* ABOVE: Side table, carved and gilt, designed by Henry Flitcroft (1726). The scroll-shaped legs are crested with eagle heads; swags of fruit are centered in a shell pendant. *Courtesy Victoria and Albert Museum.*

to architectual treatment, were in high fashion for the libraries so characteristic of great Palladian houses. Indeed they remained so much in demand that Chippendale gave no less than eleven designs for pedestal library tables in the third edition of his *Director* (1762). The salient carved ornament on a great deal of the finest mahogany furniture made from around 1725 to 1740 was gilded.

The opulence of Palladian furniture is perhaps most extravagantly expressed in mirrors, side tables, and consoles made of pine wood overlaid with gesso gilding and lavish with scallop shells single or double, masks, and broadly handled acanthus leaves—favorite Palladian decorative ingredients. The carving for such baroque side tables with marble or scagliola tops equaled the lively grace of their Venetian prototypes. Marked features of these tables are the supports generally of scroll shape, like the architectural consoles in fashion, and sometimes headed with lion or satyr masks or eagle heads, the frieze decorated with such classical detail as wave or Greek fret patterns, and, depending from the frieze, the apron of heavily carved ornament—swags of fruit, flowers and foliage centering a female mask, scallop shell, or like motif.

271

ABOVE: Gilt console table (c. 1730). The frieze is carved with the fashionable wave pattern. The plinth supports an eagle displayed, seated on a rock. *Courtesy Philadelphia Museum of Art.* BELOW: Carved and gilt console table (c. 1730). Interlaced dolphins support the table top on their tails. *Courtesy Frank Partridge, Inc., New York. Photo Albert Waks.* OPPOSITE LEFT: Gilt X-form armchair (c. 1730) showing Venetian influence, in the manner of William Kent. The frame is carved with heavy foliated scrolls, shells, and scales, and the arms terminate in serpents' heads. *Courtesy Wallace Collection, London.* OPPOSITE RIGHT: Gilt X-form stool, one of a large set by Henry Williams (1737). The scaled frame is carved with acanthus scrolls and shells. *Courtesy H. M. The Queen.*

Especially favored by the votaries of Palladianism are the consoles having a marble top supported by two scroll-shaped brackets or consoles, hence the name console tables or, more simply still, consoles. Characteristic examples of the period show the marble top supported by a boldly conceived eagle with wings displayed standing on a rock, or another treatment sometimes adopted shows a pair of interlaced dolphins supporting the marble top on their tails. Architects such as Kent, Campbell, and Gibbs also introduced carved and gilt wood stands both of pedestal and term form; their solid proportions were well adapted for the reception of such coveted objects of art as marble or bronze busts and vases of

porphyry or alabaster. Also in high fashion and destined for the reception of busts and vases were wall brackets; their substantial character was in consonance with their choice burdens. Console brackets having a scroll-shaped profile and eagle brackets were much in vogue.

Of the carved and gilt wood furniture so fashionable for reception rooms, none is more distinctive than the chairs, settees and stools designed by Kent and inspired by Venetian models he saw on his travels, which he adapted to accord with the Palladian architectural setting. The ponderous character of their florid baroque style harmonized with the large gilded side tables. The backs of the chairs and settees are surmounted by a cresting often of heavily scrolled acanthus. Kent liked to fill the space beneath the seat rail with large acanthus scrolls or swags of fruit centering a mask or perhaps a double shell, one of Kent's favorite motifs. The legs, of course, are usually scroll-shaped, frequently headed by masks, probably a female or Indian mask with a feathered headdress or a lion mask. Other chairs and stools show a revival of the traditional X-form. The cumbrous quality of this Venetian-inspired furniture brings to mind Horace Walpole's often quoted censure that the architect's hand was "immeasurably ponderous," and since Kent designed the gilt furniture at Houghton Hall for his father, Sir Robert Walpole, he had, at least, lived with the fashionable architect's style. Of the furniture at Houghton Hall, the state bed, sixteen feet in height, designed for the Green Velvet Bedchamber, is unique. Rising above the pediment surmounting the headboard is an enormous double scallop shell extending almost to the tester and proportionately wide, while two husk chains depending from the shell effectively secure it to the pediment. Naturally this so-called architect's furniture, from mahogany bookcases to gilded side tables, planned to harmonize with Palladian architecture and baroque decoration, is, when removed from its proper setting in a room of proportionate magnitude, overpowering and incongruous, at least in its more extravagant forms, when placed with other styles.

Some of the earliest engraved designs for furniture published in England are chiefly in the style associated with Kent, but illustrate it in a simplified form adapted to the houses of the middle classes. Among the best known are the designs for side tables, bookcases, and cabinets given by William Jones in his *Gentlemen's and Builder's Companion* (1739), and by Batty and Thomas Langley in their *City and Country Workmen's Treasury of Designs* (1740). A number of bookcases illustrated in the latter are described as "true after any of the Five Orders."

The furniture made for the great majority of people during the reign of George I, 1714–27, and most of the reign of George II, 1727–60, followed the traditions of the style of Queen Anne with certain developments. The contour of the furniture remained essentially the same, but it became more massive and solid in character and the ornament was elaborated. For some years after the death of Queen Anne, the simple and dignified furniture associated with her reign continued to be made. Indeed it is generally believed that furniture of this kind in walnut or mahogany was made to some extent until around the middle of the eighteenth century. However, from the accession of George I, the development in fashionable furniture was from the plain to the decorated. It is doubtful if any of the enriched examples, which mark the initial phase of Early Georgian design, were made before 1720. By that time the plain and solid splat of the Queen Anne curvilinear model is frequently decorated with carved acanthus scrolls on either side. The seat becomes wider; the front seat rail is often enriched with a pendant shell or is shaped to resemble one or more pendant shells, and the cabriole legs develop greater width and finish off under the seat rails in wide brackets. In brief, there is an increase in heaviness and solidity, as well as elaboration of ornament that became even more pronounced in the 1730s.

As for ornament, carved mask motifs—lion, female, male, Indian, and satyr—constituted the most conspicuous ornamental feature on chairs and other furniture, while scallop shells and bold acanthus are favorite decorative details. Between 1720 and 1735 furniture enriched with lion masks represented the newest development in fashionable design. At this time the head, thick mane, hocks, and paws of the animal are modeled with re-

State bed at Houghton Hall, designed by William Kent; the bill bears the date 1732. *Courtesy Lady Cholmondeley. Photo* Country Life.

ABOVE LEFT: Walnut chair (c. 1735). The carving has traces of gilding. The splat is carved with acanthus scrolls, while boldly carved foliage decorates the knees of the cabriole legs finishing in ball-and-claw feet. (*See page 274.*) BELOW LEFT: Richly carved mahogany armchair (c. 1740). This illustrates the phase of English cabinetwork dominated by lion motif decoration, including heads, masks, and paws. ABOVE RIGHT: Detail showing the arm finishing in a lion's head. BELOW RIGHT: Detail showing the short cabriole leg which is carved at the knee with a lion mask and terminates in a lion-and-ball foot. *Courtesy Metropolitan Museum of Art. Collection of Irwin Untermyer.*

markable force and realism; the broad head mask almost covers the shoulder of the cabriole leg, which terminates in a lion's paw. No consistency was followed in the use of the lion motif; for example, the arms of chairs may terminate in eagles' heads, while the legs in lions' paws. The eagle motif, one of great antiquity, is as characteristic of the period as the lion ornament and is carved with notable virtuosity. The dolphin motif was revived late in the reign of George I; legs of chairs are sometimes scaled and terminate in dolphins' heads. Many of the finest specimens of chairs are gilded or parcel gilded to match the gilded tables and mirrors in the Palladian drawing-rooms and to enliven their solemn grandeur.

There is ample evidence that much of the furniture, chairs and other pieces in "houses of consequence" was made of walnut at this time, but its use was gradually abandoned. From about 1740, owing to several events—the increased supply of mahogany and a proportionate demand and the encroachment of the French *rocaille* influence—a lighter style of mahogany furniture both in form and ornament began to evolve. At this time in chair

ABOVE LEFT: Carved walnut chair. The back is pierced with a shell design. This particular model enjoyed great popularity in the second quarter of the eighteenth century and in more recent times as well; many reproductions exist. *Courtesy Victoria and Albert Museum.* ABOVE RIGHT: Carved mahogany chair (c. 1740). This interesting example of the transitional phase has a pierced splat and crest rail finishing in bold volutes. *Courtesy Parke-Bernet, from the collection of Anna E. Erickson.* (See page 278.)

design a noticeable change occurs in the treatment of the back of the typical Queen Anne curvilinear model. The solid splat generally retaining its vase shape is now openworked, while the hoop back is, in most instances, discarded and the uprights become almost vertical, flaring slightly outward to meet the bow-shaped top rail. Toward the middle of the century this new style based on an asymmetry alien to Palladian principles swept aside the ponderous baroque of the Early Georgian period.

No doubt as a result of the more luxurious manner of living, a tendency toward specialized varieties of chairs may be seen at this time. Of these, perhaps the most familiar is the so-called corner or roundabout chair, easily recognized by its three legs in front and one in the rear and by its low back consisting of three turned uprights and two solid splats (later the splats were often pierced) supporting a semi-circular top rail. It is generally believed they were used in the library for reading or writing. Equally distinct as a type and particularly designed for use in libraries is the chair generally covered with leather, in which the occupant sits astride and rests his arms on the padded supports, having an adjustable wood board for reading or writing secured to the back. Sheraton some years later in his *Cabinet Dictionary* (1803) described such chairs as "intended to make the exercise of reading easy and for the convenience of taking down a note or quotation from any subject. The reader placed himself with his back to the front of the chair and rests his arms on the top yoke." Representing another distinctive type usually known as a writing chair, though the purpose for which they were intended is not entirely determined, are the chairs with a solid wooden cartouche-shaped back that continues into the arms, which form a continuous curve with their supports.

Besides chairs for libraries, a special variety was made for halls known as hall chairs, having solid wood backs and commonly wood seats; they look as comfortable and inviting as Elizabethan paneled-back wainscot chairs. Sheraton writes in his *Cabinet Dictionary* that they are "for the use of servants and strangers waiting for business." Also a servant's chair is the so-called page and porter chair used by menservants on duty to open the doors in the large houses. Upholstered in a durable fabric, these tall chairs with deep wings which continue to form an arched canopy or hood to exclude drafts have their prototype in the continental *guérite* made of wicker and in general use in the sixteenth century. This chair in wicker was not unknown in England, for a record of 1688 mentions, "Twiggem chaires made of owsiers and withen twigs, haveing round covers over the heads of them like a canapy. . . ." and continues that they were used by invalids as well as by women who have "bine lately brought to bed . . . [hence] child-bed chaires."

No description of early eighteenth-century English chairs would be complete without considering Windsor chairs, distinguished by their all-

ABOVE LEFT: Carved walnut writing chair (c. 1720–25). The arms terminate in eagles' heads, and the cabriole legs are carved with shells and end in club feet. ABOVE RIGHT: Mahogany reading and writing chair (c. 1720). It is provided with an adjustable wooden rest; below the arms are hinged trays with three circular wells. The seat rail is fitted with a drawer. *Courtesy Victoria and Albert Museum.* BELOW: Walnut writing chair (c. 1720). The cabriole legs which finish in ball-and-claw feet are carved on the knees with a splay of honeysuckle. *Courtesy Parke-Bernet, from the collection of Alfred Caspary.* RIGHT: Page and porter's chair. *Courtesy Victoria and Albert Museum.*

Hoop-back Windsor chair with a fret-cut and pierced splat (c. 1790). This type of splat pierced with a wheel or star form was introduced in the late Georgian period and is still being made at the present time. *Courtesy Parke-Bernet, from the collection of Irwin Untermyer.*

wood seats into which are doweled the supporting members of the back and the stretchered legs. Because of their "stick" construction, they are also known as "stick" chairs, a more descriptive but less elegant name. The origin of the name Windsor, which appeared in royal household inventories at least as early as 1729, is not known, but it may have been taken from the town of Windsor located near High Wycombe, where their manufacture has centered for more than 200 years. This Buckinghamshire town is located near the beechwoods of the Chilterns, a wood widely used for inexpensive rustic chairs and all kinds of turnery work. Windsor chairs served as indoor seats in cottages and farmhouses and as outdoors seats in gardens and summerhouses, where they are usually painted as a protection against rain. Green was the most popular color; but red and yellow Windsors were not uncommon.

Since Windsor chairs were inexpensive, light, and durable, they were a favorite seat for tea gardens, inns, and other places of public resort. Even the aristocracy were aware of their practicability, for they are mentioned in eighteenth-century inventories especially as chairs for the library. It is also evident from numerous extant examples provided with a lateral attachment fitted to the arm and serving as a bookrest or desk that they were in general use as writing or reading chairs. In America, Windsor chairs, which were first made at Philadelphia around 1725, enjoyed a great vogue and virtually surpass in every aspect of design their English prototypes. The pierced splat introduced into the spindled back of some English Windsors gives these chairs a peculiar pretentiousness not in character with their marked simplicity. This feature never occurs in American Windsors, which also display a greater variety of designs for the backs. In addition to the two principal English types, comb back and hoop back, American Windsors have four other well-known types—low-back, fan-back, loop-back, and New England armchair. Windsors have never been superseded and those made at this time still retain their traditional patterns.

Finally, before leaving Early Georgian, a few words are necessary about several new pieces of furniture and about certain changes in some not-so-new pieces. Though dining tables of gate-leg form were still used, as soon as mahogany became more plentiful the fashionable dining table was made with an oval or circular top and cabriole legs, one swinging out on either side to support the drop leaves. Some of these mahogany tables could be extended by means of an additional leaf, while others were designed in pairs with square drop leaves so that they could be placed together when necessary. During the first half of the eighteenth century dining-rooms were practically devoid of drawer or cupboard furniture. Even the sideboard tables were without drawer space. The cutlery was kept in knife cases or boxes usually made in pairs and placed at each end of the sideboard table. These sideboard tables, almost always having a marble or scagliola top, were similar to the long side tables found in reception rooms or halls. In addition to the extravagant gilt wood sideboard table, others generally of mahogany and having cabriole legs are less distinctly Palladian in character, though they exhibit the same ornamental details—shells, masks, acanthus, key and wave patterns and openworked aprons.

At this date, both in details and in general lines a fashionable class of secretary cabinet, apart from Palladian examples, derives from Dutch influence. The pattern for this narrow secretary cabinet fitted with a single door, as the pattern for the Queen Anne chair, first appeared in English furniture around 1700. Characteristic features include a scrolled or swan-neck pediment terminating in whorls or floral bosses and centering an escutcheon, fluted pilasters flanking the door, and sometimes a so-called kettle-shaped base. Early Georgian enriched examples of this model are notable.

Around 1740 the bookcase with a broken front was introduced; this type having the entire center portion projecting vertically was destined to

LEFT: Carved and parcel-gilded walnut secretary cabinet (c. 1725). The shaped architectural pediment terminates in floral bosses and centers an escutcheon; it has fluted pilasters with Corinthian capitals. The lower section with kettle base is fitted with a fall-front secretary drawer. It is mounted on massive lion's-paw feet. Traces of Dutch influence first appearing in England around 1700 can be seen. *Courtesy Parke-Bernet, from the collection of Anna E. Erickson. (See page 281.)* ABOVE: Walnut wall mirror, carved and parcel-gilded (c. 1735–40). The broken S-scrolled or swan-neck pediment ends in rosettes and frames a cartouche. *Courtesy Victoria and Albert Museum.*

enjoy long popularity. After the middle of the century the solid glazing bars in bookcases and also in cabinets were gradually replaced by astragals arranged in a great variety of designs, many being very elaborate. In most instances these tall pieces in two sections, the lower section being provided with doors or drawers or both, are mounted on a plinth or bracket base; the latter is also characteristic for the chest of drawers. At this time the bachelor's chest, a smaller chest of drawers with a folding top for writing, was introduced. An architectural character is occasionally conveyed in chests of drawers by decorating the stiles with fluted pilasters.

From about 1725 the design of wall mirrors was directly inspired by their architectural background. The architectural character manifests itself in the pediment and in details of the architrave and frieze.

Chippendale

Toward the middle of the century the ponderous baroque style of furniture associated with the Early Georgian period yielded to one which was its complete antithesis. At no other time did furniture to such an extent emancipate itself from the trammels of architecture. This new style, which derived from the *rocaille* of Meissonier, Pineau, Lajoue, and other contemporary French ornamentists, cast aside the bondage of symmetry, while lighter forms superseded baroque solidity. Interlaced scrolls in countless variety with a medley of naturalistic ornament—rocks and shells, a profusion of light flowers and serrated foliage—provided the dominant theme. The scallop shell lost its regularity and broke away from its axis; it became sharply pointed at the edges or was even pierced. Broadly speaking, it was combined with the bean motif, whose name reveals its origin. Apart from naturalistic ornament, the favorite motif was perhaps the cartouche, composed of an anomalous-looking substance which could be fashioned into any shape the artist's imagination prompted. It often took a peculiar form, becoming rather like a pear standing upright—a shape frequently used for keyhole escutcheons, for the gilded bronze mounts on the façades of serpentine and *bombé*-shaped French commodes, and for the cartouche-shaped backs of Louis XV chairs.

Rococo aimed at a kind of logical disorder; capricious sprays and tendrils escaping from the mass, entwining and interweaving, wandered lightly over the background, while asymmetric curves were deftly and consistently exploited. The style more than any other relied on the curved line, the continuous use of serpentine or undulating lines being a distinguishing feature of rococo, which disliked everything rectilinear. "How inelegant," remarked the artist Hogarth, "would be the shape of all our moveables without it." The curve par excellence, which Hogarth called "the line of beauty," is a continuous double curve, part concave and part convex. In other words it combines two successive and opposite Cs (one of

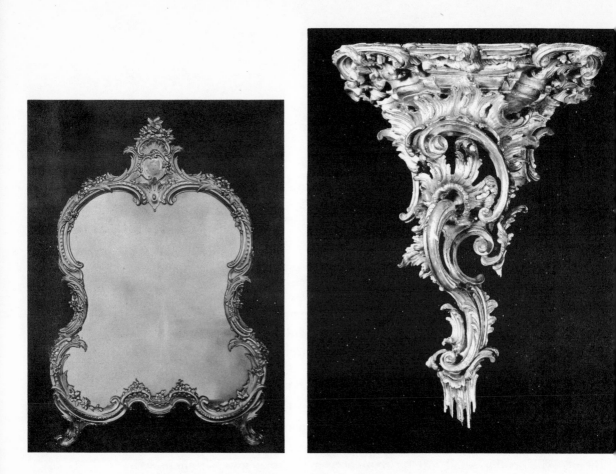

the elementary curves from which all others are derived) in a continuous curve to form an open, elongated S. In his *Analysis of Beauty* (1753), Hogarth discusses and illustrates its application to chair legs; in a word, the cabriole leg—the French rococo leg which by 1750 had become the standard support for all kinds of furniture throughout Europe. In French rococo commodes, with their horizontal and vertical curving surfaces, it may be seen in the profile of the stiles with their undulating outline.

In the hands of the celebrated French ornamentists and cabinetmakers, many triumphs were achieved in the rococo style. The imagination and ingenuity necessary to create its more fanciful forms were not nearly so conspicuous in English designs as in those by the French. Indeed the rococo was never completely assimilated in England, where the designers tended to exaggerate the obvious and were rather oblivious to its more subtle qualities. One of their most frequent errors was to place too much emphasis on rococo motifs of plastic and asymmetrical character. Fortunately many of these extravagant and fanciful designs were never realized or were freely modified in the course of manufacture; as a result, most of the English versions of *rocaille* are characterized by innate good sense and sobriety. The more determined efforts to emulate the French

284

rococo may be seen in such carvers' pieces as pier mirrors, girandoles, brackets, frames for marble slabs and candlestands riotous with rocks and shells, stalactites, dragons, reeds, long-billed stork-like birds, C-scrolls, and tortuous curves. But even in this general class there are many extant examples which represent the style in its more coherent form. Then, too, the bronze mounts which so eloquently interpret the spirit of the style on such French pieces as commodes were sparingly used and relatively simple on similar English pieces. Nevertheless, in spite of these and other differences, the English derivation of *rocaille* may be said to have prevailed in decoration and furniture for almost two decades, while the fine materials and high quality of craftsmanship that distinguish the work make this period one of enduring merit.

The first English designer who succeeded in capturing something of the lively spirit of the French *rocaille* and rendering it with real assurance was a carver and engraver named Matthias Lock, who produced designs for ornament, sconces, and tables as early as the mid-forties. One of his later books, *A New Book of Ornaments* (1752), was published in conjunction with H. Copland. Lock, who was an accomplished draftsman, is now regarded as the pioneer of rococo in England. But it is in the first edition of Chippendale's *Director* (1754) that the rococo is seen fully developed and naturalized, and combined with digressions into the contemporary Gothic and Chinese tastes. According to recent research concerning the origination of this famous trade catalogue, it has become increasingly evident that Chippendale's personal responsibility for the drawings must be largely disregarded. There is sufficient reason to assume that Lock and his collaborator, Copland, were probably employed by Chippendale in the 1750s and were for almost a certainty responsible for the majority of designs. Chippendale no doubt became familiar with rococo through their work. Being an enterprising young businessman cognizant of the value of advertising, he published at the age of thirty-six the first edition of *The Gentleman and Cabinet-Maker's Director* in 1754 from his shop in St. Martin's Lane. A second edition practically a reprint appeared the following year, while a third and enlarged edition in 1762. The first and second editions each had 160 engraved plates, while the third had 200, of which 105 though entirely new still remained thoroughly rococo in character. So great a difference exists in some of the designs in the *Director*, for instance between a design for a rococo girandole and a bookcase with a classical pediment and moldings, that even to an untrained eye it would appear doubtful if the designs could be the invention of one man.

Regardless of who did or did not do the designs in the *Director*, everyone agrees that it is an invaluable record of mid-eighteenth-century English fashions in furniture, and, being widely circulated, it played an important role in establishing the rococo vogue in England. The *Director* also shows the pervasive influence of Chinese and Gothic fashions, which are also found fused together in other contemporary publications. Though the practice of publishing furniture designs dates back on the continent at least from the sixteenth century, nothing had been done before on such scale devoted entirely to furniture designs. Intended largely as a trade publication, the *Director* illustrated a selection of designs for practically every piece of furniture that might be needed in a well-appointed house, from washing stands to organ cases for a music room. Included in the list of 310 subscribers to the first edition were the names of such prominent peers as the Duke of Norfolk and the Earl of Chesterfield, together with 140 joiners, carvers, and cabinetmakers. The almost overnight success of the *Director* led to the publication of other works by rival firms of cabinetmakers, but none were nearly so ambitious in conception. Of these, Ince and Mayhew's *Universal System of Household Furniture* (1759–63) is the most outstanding. Sometime later, Sheraton, comparing the two works,

286

LEFT: Mahogany library table, supplied by Thomas Chippendale for Nostell Priory, Yorkshire (1767). The stiles are crested with lion' heads and end in paw feet. Neo-classic influence is discernible in the ovals, pendants, and festoons of husks. BELOW: Library writing table veneered with rosewood, provided for Harewood House by Chippendale's firm (c. 1770–75). It is mounted in finely chased gilt bronze. The delicate neo-classical style of inlay clearly shows Adam's influence, and he may be regarded as responsible for the ornamental design. *Courtesy* Country Life.

writes that the *Director* was "a real original as well as more extensive and masterly in design."

Undoubtedly Chippendale's great reputation is chiefly founded on the *Director*. His fame overshadows the accomplishments of all his contemporaries to such an extent that cabinetmakers as skilled as Vile and as fashionable as Hallett are comparatively little known. Until relatively recent times Chippendale has been credited with all the finest mahogany furniture of this period; even now his name is still popularly connected with this work. But the discovery of some of Chippendale's accounts and many other records of his activities have in recent years enlarged the truth about his work. These accounts prove that he was, for the greater part of his career, not a practicing cabinetmaker, but the organizing and energetic head of a highly successful business which undertook the entire furnishing and decoration in large town and country houses. Of the extant accounts, the most valuable are those for the contents at Nostell Priory and Hare-

LEFT: Carved mahogany chair (c. 1755). The splat formed of scrolls and interlaced ribbons resembles designs for ribband-back chairs in Chippendale's *Director,* first edition, 1754, plate XVI. *Courtesy Victoria and Albert Museum.* RIGHT: Mahogany secretary cabinet (c. 1760). The broken scroll-shaped or swan-neck pediment is filled with pierced tracery. The lower portion in the form of a commode with a graceful serpentine front is mounted on ogee bracket feet. The top drawer is provided with writing equipage. *Courtesy Parke-Bernet, from the collection of Walter P. Chrysler.*

wood House, where his work is authenticated by receipted bills and the furniture is still in its original place. The furniture in these two houses, which covers a period from about 1766 until near his death in 1779, shows that from about 1770 Chippendale discarded all the styles which he is known to have favored and illustrated in the *Director* and, under the influence of Robert Adam, produced furniture essentially in the neo-classical taste. It may also be said with confidence that fine material, masterly design, and technical brilliance are eminently characteristic of Chippendale's finished work whether in mahogany, japanning, or marquetry mounted in chased and gilded bronze. It is peculiar and perhaps significant that Chippendale's name does not appear in royal household accounts where one finds the names of such prominent contemporary craftsmen working for the Crown as Benjamin Goodison, John Bradburn, and the partners Vile and Cobb.

There can be little doubt that the wide variety of designs and the manner in which they were presented in the *Director* must have attracted many customers to Chippendale's shop. The title page describes the contents as "being a large collection of the most elegant and useful designs of household furniture in the Gothic, Chinese and Modern taste . . . calculated to improve and refine the present taste, and suited to the fancy and circumstances of persons in all degrees of life." Chippendale's thoughts about architecture and its role in furniture can best be ascertained by what he wrote in the *Director*. "Of all the arts which are either improved or ornamented by architecture, that of cabinetmaking is not only the most useful but capable of receiving as great assistance from it as any whatever. I have, therefore, prefixed to the following designs a short explanation of the Five Orders . . . These, therefore, ought to be carefully studied by everyone who would excel in this branch, since they are the very soul and basis of his art."

Having read part of the title page, as well as Chippendale's remarks on architecture, it can be no surprise to learn that the so-called Chippendale or Director style is a highly eclectic style. Essentially it is a remarkable synthesis to which the Palladian, the rococo, the Chinese, and the Gothic each made a contribution. There are a number of designs in which one of these four styles, if they may be so called, is used by itself. For instance, Chippendale's famous ribband-back chair, of which he was especially proud, is in the full rococo taste. But in the major portion of designs two or more of the styles are combined. For example, everything about a china cabinet may be in what Chippendale termed the "best French manner," from its scrolled or swan-neck pediment carved with rococo foliage to the valanced base curving into short cabriole legs, but the glazing bars have a pattern of Gothic tracery; or the projecting center portion of a breakfront bookcase may have a pagoda cresting hung with bells, while the lower portion mounted on a classical plinth base has solid doors paneled with rococo-decorated serpentine moldings; or a secretary cabinet may have a serpentine front and ogee bracket feet, but the swan-neck pediment is filled with pierced tracery. Naturally in certain designs the combination is obviously incongruous, but in the great majority of designs the various fashions are so inextricably interwoven that the discrepancies no longer matter. Hence, a new style is born—the Chippendale style highly individual with a singular character of its own. Essentially it marks no abrupt break with the past; it is the style of the mid-Georgian period, which was for the most part a native version of French rococo, but now it is greatly enriched with rococo motifs and those other new fashions in ornament—Chinese and Gothic.

We learn from the introduction to the *Director,* as well as from bills and accounts, that Chippendale was not such a slave to mahogany as is com-

LEFT: Bed, japanned black and gold in the Chinese taste (c. 1755). *Courtesy Victoria and Albert Museum.* OPPOSITE ABOVE: Veneered commode of Louis XV contour (c. 1770). It is mounted in chased and gilt bronze; the pictorial marquetry represents vases of flowers enclosed in oval panels. *Courtesy Parke-Bernet, from the collection of Lillian S. Whitmarsh.* OPPOSITE BELOW: Commode in the French taste (1764). It has floral marquetry and gilt bronze mounts. It was made to the order of the sixth Earl of Coventry for the Tapestry Room at Croome Court, Worcestershire, by Peter Langlois, a French cabinetmaker working in London. *Courtesy Metropolitan Museum of Art. Fletcher Fund, 1959.*

monly supposed. It appears that mahogany was customary for libraries, dining-rooms, and halls, while a good deal of furniture was made of soft wood, being gilded, japanned, or less often painted and partly gilded. Especially favored for gilding were such carvers' pieces as mirrors, girandoles, and slab frames destined for reception rooms, while japanned pieces were in high fashion for bedrooms. Of this treatment the most famous example is the japanned bedstead from Badminton House, Gloucestershire, in the Chinese taste with its pagoda-shaped tester ornamented at the four corners with gilt dragons on scrolled finials and headboard of latticework. It was originally in a room "finished and furnished very elegantly in the Chinese manner." Though the use of rosewood was rare at this time, Chippendale in the third edition of the *Director* gives a design for a toilet table in the rococo taste with a cartouche-shaped mirror of "pear-like" form and notes that he has made two from this design in rosewood and that "all the ornaments are gilt." After the revival of polychrome marquetry around 1765, commodes of Louis XV contour and later reflecting neo-classic influence destined for drawing-rooms came into fashion. Chippendale, John Cobb, William Gates, and other contemporary cabinetmakers produced marquetry commodes mounted in gilt bronze of consummate craftsmanship that are ranked among the *chefs-d'œuvre* of English cabinetwork.

Closely related to rococo is the Chinese taste, which had already been the delight of two generations. In furniture the taste was expressed in japanned decoration which was still strong in the 1750s and was to continue as a fashionable medium all through the eighteenth century. As English designers became more familiar with Chinese ornament, certain motifs gradually found their way into the designer's repertory, until by the middle of the eighteenth century a medley of Chinese details—pagodas,

Mahogany china cabinet resembling a design for china shelves, in Chippendale's *Director*, first edition, 1754. It is surmounted by triple pagodas and enriched with delicate pierced fretwork. *Courtesy Parke-Bernet, from the collection of Walter P. Chrysler.* BELOW: Design for china shelves from Chippendale's *Director*, first edition, 1754, plate CXLIII. *See above. Courtesy Cooper Union Museum.*

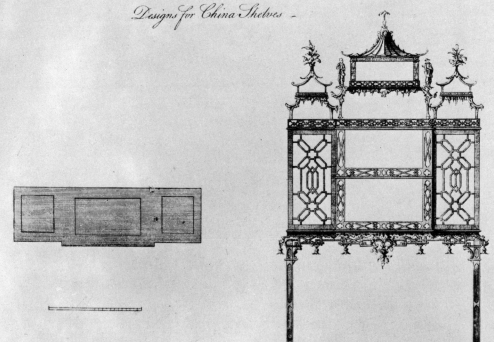

Designs for China Shelves — N.º CXLIII

T. Chippendale inv.t et delin.t   _Publish'd according to Act of Parliam.t 1761_   R. Barly sculp.t

mandarins, dragons, birds, and bells—had become stock motifs. This oriental detail was freely introduced by such fashionable designers as Darly and Edwards, the Halfpennys and Chippendale into their so-called Chinese designs. Of the numerous publications attempting to imitate the Chinese style, one book by Sir William Chambers (1726–96), the first English architect to visit China, stands out as a knowledgeable study. In the preface of his book *Designs of Chinese Buildings, Furniture, Dress, Machines and Utensils* (1757), he expressed a hope that these designs might put a stop to "the extravagant fancies that daily appear under the name of Chinese," but adds that he did not wish to "promote a taste so much inferior to the antique." His drawings for furniture were no doubt from actual pieces and are characteristic of Ming furniture made of rosewood and sometimes bamboo. But these authentic models had little influence on the pseudo-oriental taste that had become a fashionable mode of decoration, and it is doubtful if any reasonable facsimiles were ever actually made.

Of all the motifs recruited to create a Chinese flavor, the pagoda borrowed from Chinese architecture is easiest to recognize. It was much in evidence surmounting the tops of standing or hanging glazed china cabinets and open shelves; it was frequently substituted for pediments on bookcases and secretary cabinets, while in splat-back chairs the pagoda motif was sometimes centered in the crest rail; also it was ingeniously introduced in the openworked splat. In brief, the pagoda was everywhere; it was even introduced as a carved repetitive ornament in a wide molding. Equally prevalent was a form of latticework suggested by Chinese latticework structures and known as "Chinese railing." Designs for different kinds of latticework and illustrations of furniture decorated and constructed with it were freely offered in trade catalogues. Its most successful form may be seen in chairs designed by Chippendale having their backs and arms filled with "Chinese railing." Latticework, or fretwork (since the two terms are practically interchangeable in furniture) was also employed for the glazing bars of china cabinets and similar pieces. Another fashionable way of using "Chinese railing" was to place it as a parapet or railing along the top of cabinets and similar pieces or to fill in the center part of broken pediments. Chippendale gave a design for a small breakfast table of the Pembroke type, having the space between the frieze drawer and a median shelf enclosed with fretwork. Indeed its uses both decoratively and structurally were many. It was also used on a miniature scale as a gallery round the edges of stands, trays, tea and china tables. Probably the tour de force of latticework decoration are the fragile china tables completely decorated with latticework, even to the four straight legs and X-form stretchers; of these, few genuine examples survive because of their extreme delicacy.

A similar motif, which also figured prominently, is, instead of being

OPPOSITE ABOVE LEFT: Mahogany armchair in the Chinese taste (c. 1760). The top rail centers a pagoda cresting. The pagoda motif appears in the back filled with latticework; the legs are turned in imitation of bamboo. *Courtesy Parke-Bernet.* OPPOSITE ABOVE RIGHT: Mahogany armchair (c. 1760). The entire back and sides are filled with "Chinese railing" or interlaced latticework. *Courtesy Metropolitan Museum of Art. Gift of Mrs. Leonard A. Cohn, 1950.* OPPOSITE BELOW LEFT: Mahogany hanging china cabinet (c. 1755). The fretwork doors and sides are in the Chinese taste. (*See page 293.*) OPPOSITE BELOW RIGHT: Mahogany tea or china table (c. 1755). In the Chinese taste, it displays both kinds of latticework decoration, the frieze being carved with a solid fret in low relief. RIGHT: Mahogany tea-kettle stand (c. 1760). It has a pierced gallery and legs of cluster column form ending in guttae feet. *Courtesy Frank Partridge, Inc., New York. Photo Albert Waks.*

openworked as Chinese railing, on a solid ground and carved in low relief. In the form of a flat band it is carved with a countersunk repetitive latticework pattern. This solid fret as it is often called was used on a great variety of objects—china cabinets, chests of drawers, clothespresses, chairs, settees, tables, and similar pieces. Both styles of fret, solid and pierced, are often used on the same piece of furniture. Quadrilateral legs frequently headed with pierced brackets superseded cabriole legs in Chinese designs for chairs and tables; in a few instances they were rounded in imitation of bamboo. Occasionally the supports are of either cluster column form or cut through; these legs sometimes occur in the Gothic taste, which also features straight legs. With the reintroduction of straight legs, stretchers were again employed. The major portion of furniture in the Anglo-Chinese taste was made of mahogany.

The Gothic taste, unlike the Chinese, was at this time a decorative convention peculiar to England. But on the other hand it was like the Chinese inasmuch as it was a pseudo-taste and a fashionable mode of decoration brought into vogue in this case by the votaries of Gothicism. Though Horace Walpole and a group of dilettanti, of whom Richard Bentley and Sanderson Miller were the most prominent, demanded a more organic use of Gothic detail, the taste was not so consistently exploited as the Chinese, and in general a few characteristic Gothic motifs were used only as a variant to the rococo. It soon found its way into pattern books, the first notable examples of this pseudo-medieval style applied to furniture appearing in the first edition of the *Director*. As Strawberry Hill was at this time still unfinished, the novelty of Chippendale's numerous Gothic designs must have taken by the surprise the uninitiated public, who apparently liked them since they were widely imitated in other trade catalogues for at least the next decade. Chippendale, of course, was not interested in copying either medieval forms or material; he seldom did more than enrich contemporary mahogany furniture with cusps, ogees, lancets, and other forms borrowed from tracery work, as well as such details he considered Gothic. His rococo scrollwork often displayed a peculiar affinity to Gothic tracery. Apart from tracery, fretwork or latticework figured prominently; the pattern for this kind of fretwork was suggested by medieval stonework friezes. But an examination of the patterns offered in the *Director* and other catalogues for Gothic fret and "Chinese railing" reveals no fundamental difference between them. Here again, but in this instance owing to a misunderstanding of the character of medieval art, the ornament is rarely used in a pure form. Practically every designer and cabinetmaker including Chippendale regularly confused Chinese and Gothic details. Indeed this fact, together with their rather superficial handling of rococo, explains to a great extent the "ingenious ease" with which they interwove these three fashions into the Chippendale style. But in spite of this imperfect understanding, the eye is amused by these different ingredients which in well-designed pieces possess an undeniable charm.

Before leaving Chippendale, a word or two is necessary about certain new pieces, as well as conspicuous features and changes in some not-so-new ones. We have already noted as distinctive features of splat-back chairs the pierced splat, which, generally retaining its vase-shaped outline, is manipulated in an almost countless number of ingenious designs by Chippendale and his contemporaries; also the crest rail in the form of a cupid's bow terminating in twisted or turned-up extremities or merging with bold curves into the uprights that narrow toward the top and flare slightly outward. In the first edition of the *Director*, chairs of this type when lavishly enriched with rococo scrollwork are designed with cabriole legs. Plainer examples, which are less frankly rococo and also include the ladder-back chair, revived at this time, are designed with straight legs,

LEFT: Carved mahogany cabinet in the Gothic taste (c. 1760–70). Its three ogee arches and glazing bars suggest perpendicular pierced tracery. *Courtesy Victoria and Albert Museum.* ABOVE: Detail of ribband-back chair (c. 1755). It has a bow-shaped crest rail; the arrangement of the interlaced ribbons of the splat with carved tassels is remarkably graceful. Crisply carved tassels enrich the uprights. *Courtesy Metropolitan Museum of Art. Collection of Irwin Untermyer.*

apparently preferred for the dining-room. For these, stretchers were again reintroduced. Chippendale's upholstered "French chairs with elbows," based on Louis XV *fauteuils,* having cartouche-shaped backs, exposed frames carved with rococo foliage, and cabriole legs with French whorl terminals, represent a successful attempt of Anglo-French curvilinear design. At this time the outscrolled arms of upholstered settees became higher and formed a continuation of the undulating back, a fashion borrowed from Louis XV *canapés,* and the most distinguishing feature of Chippendale settees.

After the middle of the eighteenth century a number of accessories came into general use for the service of the dining table—plate and cutlery stands, wood wine coolers lined with lead commonly placed under the sideboard table, cellarettes, plate pails, plate warmers resembling a tall enclosed stand provided with a receptacle for plates and a heater, trays mounted on X-shaped folding stands which, according to Sheraton, are

ABOVE LEFT: Mahogany armchair in the French taste (c. 1765), after a design for a French chair in Chippendale's *Director*, third edition, 1762, plate XXII. The frame is carved with scrolls and rococo ornament and has cabriole legs finishing in French whorl feet. *Courtesy Victoria and Albert Museum.* ABOVE RIGHT: Mahogany tub-shaped armchair in the French taste (c. 1765). The prevailing pattern in its general lines was borrowed from the Louis XV *bergère en gondole. Courtesy Metropolitan Museum of Art. Collection of Irwin Untermyer.* BELOW: Mahogany settee carved with rococo ornament (c. 1760). The cabriole legs finish in French whorl feet. *Courtesy Parke-Bernet, from the collection of Robert J. Dunham.* (*See page 297.*)

used "as a sideboard for the butler who had the care of the liquor at a gentleman's table," and the familiar dumb-waiter described by Sheraton as "a useful piece of furniture to serve in some respects the place of a waiter, whence it is so named." Especially typical is the dumb-waiter with three circular trays increasing in diameter from top to bottom, revolving on a shaft on a tripod base. Furnished with extra plates and cutlery, it enabled guests at a little supper to serve themselves without the bothersome presence of servants, a use aptly expressed in a contemporary passage, "We had dumb-waiters so our conversation was not under any restraint by ye servants being in ye room." At this time sideboard tables with or without a marble top still possessed no drawer space. According to contemporary bills for dining tables, since they were not illustrated in trade catalogues, the fashionable dining table, occasionally having square drop leaves, was designed with semi-circular detachable ends each provided with a drop leaf, "all made to take off with strap hinges, bolt and fork fastenings, the whole or any part to joyn together at pleasure." Thus the firm of Chippendale made for David Garrick in 1771 "a set of mahogany dining tables with circular ends to joyn together complete." This type of extension table with its obvious advantages continued in fashion until the nineteenth century.

Decorative tea and china tables became fashionable in England about the middle of the eighteenth century. Tea tables with a scalloped circular top on a central standard and tripod base, the larger specimens often being made to tilt so they could be placed against the wall when not in use, are frequently described in contemporary inventories as "a mahogany scollop'd tea table on a claw" or "a fine Jamaica mahogany tea table with scoloped corners . . . pilar and claw feet with castors." Occasionally the tops of these tables were divided into compartments, usually eight or ten, when they served to hold the cups and saucers or small plates for an informal meal or supper; hence the name supper table. Smaller tables of tripod form were very plentiful and were no doubt the English counterpart of the French table *ambulante* of many uses. Another variety of tea table illustrated by Chippendale has an oblong top and four legs; of these he writes they are "for holding each a set of china and may be used as tea tables"; hence, china tables.

Because libraries were important rooms in large houses, Chippendale gave no less than fourteen designs for bookcases in the third edition of the *Director*, displaying glazing bars of extremely elaborate patterns, with pilasters and scrollwork being freely introduced. Gothic bookcases figure in all three editions, but it is doubtful if any of the more extravagant designs were executed without considerable modification. Most of the large bookcases were breakfronted, a feature borrowed from classical architecture. Of course the architectural influence is much less pronounced at this

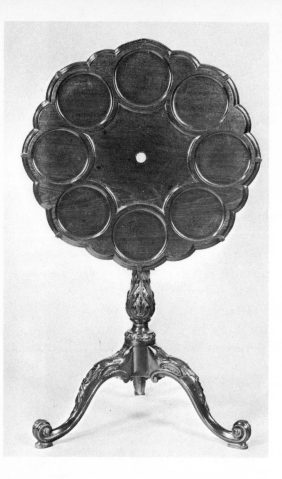

Mahogany supper table (c. 1760). Eight circular compartments are provided for plates; the base of the shaft and scrolled tripod are carved with cabochon and acanthus foliage. *Courtesy Metropolitan Museum of Art. Collection of Irwin Untermyer.* BELOW: Mahogany tea or china table. It has a boldly serpentine-contoured top with a deeply carved and pierced gallery of rococo ornament; the graceful cabriole legs terminate in French whorl feet resting on shaped "shoes" or blocks. Similar feet and shoes appear in a design for a china table in Chippendale's *Director*, first edition, 1754. *Courtesy Parke-Bernet, from the collection of Walter P. Chrysler.* (*See page 299.*)

time than in the Early Georgian period, not only in bookcases but in other pieces of wall furniture, such as secretary cabinets, which lend themselves especially well to architectural treatment. The architectural influence may be seen in classical cornices and straight, broken pediments, but they no longer possess their Early Georgian ponderous character. Broken, scroll-shaped pediments which were also used in the Early Georgian period are a marked feature of the Chippendale period and have acquired a noticeable lightness. Those filled with latticework belong only to Chippendale. Bookcases were augmented by the secretary bookcase having a pull-out writing drawer, a feature which was frequently used in place of a slant front on secretary cabinets since early in the eighteenth century. Indeed there is little if anything except the length to distinguish a secretary cabinet from a secretary bookcase when both are designed with pull-out writing drawers and glazed doors. Generally forming part of the furniture in well-appointed libraries are library steps to reach the volumes on the upper shelves. Apart from examples serving a dual purpose in the form of a chair, stool, or table, other library steps when no combination was attempted are often notable for their elegance and utility.

We have still to examine the bedroom. Mention has already been made of the small breakfast table which was designed to harmonize with the bedroom furniture. Tables designed for dressing came into general use. Toilet tables of kneehole form having the top drawer equipped with a mirror and other toilet accessories are illustrated by Chippendale, who calls them "a buroe dressing table." Destined to remain in vogue throughout the eighteenth century was the toilet table with a hinged box lid which opened to the right and left, forming two horizontal trays on which the toilet articles contained in the compartments could be arranged; it was provided with a rising framed mirror. Smaller and more compact examples having a shaving mirror rising up at the back and compartments for razors and other necessaries were listed as shaving tables in trade catalogues. Enclosed basin or washing stands also frequently adopted a folding box lid top. The tripod basin stand of open structure featuring a molded ring for the reception of the basin, a median trilateral shelf surmounted with a covered urn to hold the soap, and a dished trilateral base for the pitcher is one of Chippendale's most charming accessories, and being light and slender it was easily moved about. As for night tables, or pot cupboards as they were then called, when not combined in enclosed washing stands they tended, with their shallow cupboards, to still look

LEFT: Mahogany library steps (c. 1785), labeled Hervé (Francis Hervé, flourished 1783–89). They are designed to fold into a small table and are enclosed by a hinged flap to which three bracket treads are fastened. *Courtesy Victoria and Albert Museum.* BELOW: Mahogany tripod basin stand (c. 1750). It is elaborately carved and the shelf has drawers and an urn for a soap ball. *Courtesy Metropolitan Museum of Art. Collection of Irwin Untermyer.*

Mahogany clothespress (c. 1750). It has serpentine-paneled doors. The cornice is carved with a classical guilloche pattern, while the apron of the stand is enriched with rococo ornament; it is mounted on cabriole legs terminating in paw feet. *Courtesy Victoria and Albert Museum.*

like them. As a rule a simpler piece of furniture, some were the object of more ambitious work, for at a later date Sheraton in his *Drawing Book* (1791–94) writes that pot cupboards made for "genteel bedrooms are sometimes finished in a style a little elevated above their use." The cupboard part of the night table is not always provided with doors, but has, according to Sheraton, "sometimes a curtain of green silk, fixed on a brass wire at top and bottom"; he, however, preferred a tambour door to the curtains. Sheraton also illustrates two designs for bed steps fitted with a bidet drawer.

Judging by the large number of designs given in contemporary trade catalogues, clothespresses with doors in the upper portion enclosing sliding trays and generally with one or more rows of drawers below were much in fashion, being more favored than wardrobes, which, when made, were relatively plain. Chippendale illustrated designs for a "commode clothespress" with two drawers of *bombé* form, which gives the whole a cabriole leg's outline. Prompted no doubt by the craze for French fashions, Chippendale never overlooked an opportunity to use the name commode for all pieces of furniture fitted with drawers if they were made more or less along French lines.

Adam

Soon after the accession of George III, 1760–1820, rococo with its indulgence in sinuous curves and asymmetry yielded to a newly awakened enthusiasm for ancient art stimulated to a great extent by the discoveries at Pompeii and Herculaneum. The time was ripe for a classical revival, and though Chippendale's third edition of the *Director* was in full rococo, its influence was rapidly coming to an end. Soon it will be banished from interior decoration and furniture to be replaced by classical designs that had fallen for a moment from favor, which the Italians of the Renaissance had already borrowed from the ancients, but now they will be interpreted in the lighter style of the eighteenth century. The serpentine line that everywhere was bending in and out will pull itself together, while the impersonal curve of the compass will constantly take its place, and the pre-eminence of the straight line will once more be established. But this transformation did not take place in a day. The introduction of classical motifs preceded any far-reaching change in form. For example, a chair retains its curvilinear rococo form, but the frame and cabriole legs are carved with sphinxes and other classical motifs. Later when structural changes are introduced, tapered and fluted straight legs, either square in section or turned baluster shape, distinguish at first glance the neo-classic style.

The extent of the transformation from rococo to classicism can be readily appreciated if examples of pure form in both styles are compared; even the least instructed eye can appraise the fundamentally different and conflicting ideals of these two styles, as furniture once more falls under the yoke of architecture. A very important difference is that now in accordance with architectural influence the parts of, for example, a chair are at the same time united and separated by well-marked joints, while in a rococo chair the cabriole legs merge into the body they support without

Demilune commode, designed by Robert Adam for the Drawing Room at Osterley (c. 1775). One of a pair, it is veneered with satinwood and inlaid with medallions of classical figures and mounted in chased and gilt bronze. OPPOSITE: Entrance Hall at Osterley, designed by Adam (c. 1767). It is notable for its strong and broadly handled decoration. *Courtesy Victoria and Albert Museum.*

any distinct joints. Another principle architectural in its origin is that the weight is always placed on rectilinear uprights; in a word, the sides and legs are invariably straight. If curves are necessary for the sake of variety, they are introduced into the plan instead of the elevation, such as semicircular or demilune commodes and side tables. Pilasters, friezes, enriched moldings, and other architectural elements are once again employed to stress the structural framework. But, above all, ancient architecture brings back symmetry in form and ornament.

In England the dominant figure in the neo-classical movement is the great architect Robert Adam, who effected a complete revolution in architecture and the decorative arts. Born at Kinross-shire, Adam came from a family of architects; two of his brothers, James and William, followed the same profession and were at different times his partners. In 1754 Adam went to Italy. There, amid the ruins of ancient Rome and the monuments of the Renaissance, Adam was completely won over to the beauty of classical art and devoted himself to perfecting a contemporary style founded on classical ideals. Returning to England in 1758, he was anxious to reform the prevailing style, which especially in furniture and in-

terior decoration under the influence of rococo had strayed far from classical principles, and to see his new ideas attain definite expression.

In a short time he obtained important commissions from a few persons of great wealth, and into houses such as these he introduced sumptuous furnishings to gratify the taste of elegant society for what he called "the parade of life." Of these, Osterley, belonging to the banker Robert Child, which he undertook in 1761 and finished nineteen years later, is especially notable since the house represents his early as well as mature style. Nowhere did he display to a higher degree the art of interpreting into elegance the elements purveyed by antiquity than at Osterley. Horace Walpole, who made the first of his two visits there in 1773, writes in his letters: "On Friday we went to see—oh, the palace of palaces!—and yet a palace sans crown, sans coronet, but such expense, such taste. . . . There is a hall, library, breakfast-room, eating-room, all chefs-d'oeuvre of Adam, a gallery one hundred and thirty feet long and a drawing-room worthy of Eve before the Fall. . . . Mr. Child's dressing room is full of pictures, gold filigree, china and japan. So is all the house; the chairs are taken from antique lyres, and make charming harmony. . . ." Though other fashion-

able and talented architects, such as Sir William Chambers, John Wyatt, and James Paine, embraced the classical ideals, the ascendancy of Adam was such that within a short period everything—buildings and furniture—was "Adam." Indeed his influence upon interior decoration was profound and prevailed until his death in 1792.

Adam's style in interior decoration was his greatest innovation. It not only routed the rococo but supplanted the earlier type of classicism introduced by Inigo Jones and revived by Kent and the other Palladian architects, who used the same ponderous classical style for exteriors and interiors alike. In their private houses the main rooms were heavy with coffered ceilings, while their favorite treatment for the whole dressing of doors, windows, and chimneypieces was the "tabernacle frame," consisting of columns or pilasters surmounted by an entablature and pediment. Adam regarded these compositions as out of proportion and unsuitable in a private house, calling them "absurd compositions." He contended that the ancients had not used them in decorating the interiors of their private houses, which were "all delicacy, gaiety, grace and beauty."

These aspects of Roman interior decoration employing mural paintings and stucco reliefs, which charmed Adam with their graceful delicacy and

OPPOSITE: Eating Room at Osterley (c. 1767). The decorations, gilt sideboard table and lyre-back chairs are by Robert Adam (the dining table dates from c. 1800). (*See page 305.*)
ABOVE: An ancient Roman ceiling painting of the kind which inspired the grotesques of the Renaissance and the neo-classicism of the eighteenth century. From *Recueil de Peintures Antiques,* by P. S. Bartoli, Paris, 1783. *Courtesy Victoria and Albert Museum.*

refinement, are known to us as grotesques because they were found in the half-buried ruins of Roman tombs, baths, palaces, and villas or "grottoes." Examples of grotesques, whose compositions were small in scale and linear in character and without structural significance, attracted the most attention at the time of the Renaissance. They delighted Raphael, who made use of the same convention in his painted decoration of the Vatican loggias, in this instance inspired by a repertory of such murals found in Nero's Golden House on the Esquiline.

The Romans had employed two types of this decoration—geometrical and fanciful; of the latter the most typical arrangement was a group of small scale pictures framed in tablets or medallions suspended in a gossamer of scrolls and foliage interspersed with a whole medley of fabulous creatures such as winged sphinxes and griffins and all kinds of fanciful devices. It was the fantastic element in these symmetrical compositions which became the hallmark of grotesques and made them a favorite theme for ornamentists from the time of Raphael to the advent of *rocaille*. Though grotesques had played an important role in architecture and the decorative arts on the continent, Adam was the first English architect to use this convention systematically in the decoration of wall surfaces. Moreover, and of

307

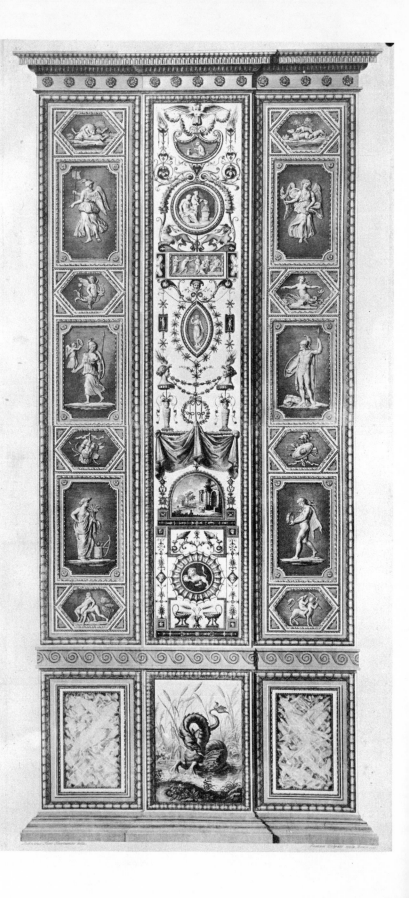

308

OPPOSITE: A panel of grotesque decoration, by or after Raphael in the Vatican loggia. Giovanni Volpato, Rome, 1775. *Courtesy Cooper Union Museum.* (*See page 307.*) ABOVE: Robert Adam's design for the ceiling of the anteroom at Syon House, the seat of the Duke of Northumberland. From *The Works in Architecture of the Late Robert and James Adam,* Volume III, plate VII, London, 1822. *Courtesy Cooper Union Museum.* (*See page 310.*)

great importance, believing that in the frescoes and bas-reliefs of the Romans he had discovered the true classical manner of decorating the interior of a private house, he constantly endeavored to emulate in his own work the salient features of these compositions. Whenever it was appropriate, he used a style of decoration without structural significance, small in scale, flat and linear in form, carried out in very low relief stucco and paint. He discarded large decorative ceiling paintings in favor of small-scale panel pictures in the form of ovals, circles, and squares framed in stucco, which he brought into the closest stylistic harmony with the stucco embellishments.

Adam succinctly expresses his classical ideals which crystallized into the Adam style in the preface to his *Works of Architecture* (1779). He writes: "The massive entablature, the ponderous compartment ceiling, the tabernacle frame, almost the only species of ornament formerly known in this country are now universally exploded, and in their place we have adopted a beautiful variety of light moldings, gracefully formed, delicately enriched and arranged with propriety and style. We have introduced a great diversity of ceilings, friezes, and decorated pilasters, and have added grace and beauty to the whole by a mixture of grotesque stucco, and painted ornaments, together with the flowing rinceau, with its fanciful figures and winding foliage. If we have any claim to approbation we found it on this alone: That we flatter ourselves we have been able to seize, with some degree of success, the beautiful spirit of antiquity, and to transfuse it, with novelty and variety, through all our numerous works."

Adam possessed a passion for completeness and harmony. He believed that the decoration of every fitting and fixture, however slight, was within the province of the architect. In his view an effect of perfect and complete harmony could only be achieved if everything—the design of the ceiling and walls, the furniture, carpets, and hangings—was subordinated to a single style, logically conceived and consistently developed. Indeed so consistently was everything dependent on a ruling style in houses decorated under Adam's supervision that the same classical motifs and patterns are found on wall surfaces, carpets, and furniture. By such repetition he sought to integrate the various parts of his comprehensive decorative schemes.

Since furniture must occupy a conspicuous place in any decorative scheme, it monopolized a considerable share of Adam's attention. He probably made more designs for furniture than any other architect has ever done, and his work in this branch of art makes an impressive monument to his fertile genius as a designer. Included in his repertory of small-scale ornament appropriate for the enrichment of furniture were such favorite motifs as the anthemion, or honeysuckle ornament so frequently used for decorative borders, oval paterae (of all the simple curvilinear

Pedestal, designed by Adam for the Tapestry Room at Osterley (c. 1776). One of a pair, it is carved gilt wood decorated with delicately painted medallions of classical figure subjects and has winged sphinxes on the plinth. The drawing for the pedestals bears the date November 13, 1776. *Courtesy Victoria and Albert Museum.*

forms used by Adam he chiefly preferred the oval or ellipse), festoons of husks, medallions, and tablets of classical figure subjects such as Venus and Cupid or Diana with her hounds. Other decorative ingredients brought into fashion were ram- and female-headed capitals often combined with swags of leaves, vases and urns, winged sphinxes and winged griffins. He generally enriched the surfaces of his furniture with the same kind of chastened classical ornament that he applied to his wall surfaces, that is, an essentially flat and linear kind of decoration which, in the words of Sir John Soane, "was imitated from ancient works in the baths and villas of the Romans."

He invested his ornament with extreme delicacy and the utmost refinement. In fact, in his desire to avoid heaviness, it must be confessed that Adam sometimes went to the opposite extreme, especially in his later phase when his ornament showed a tendency to become so incredibly refined, so purely linear and minute in scale that his decoration at times

RIGHT: Overmantel mirror in a carved gilt wood frame (c. 1775). The classical vase, winged griffins, graceful foliated scrollwork and husk chains are very fashionable motifs in the style propagated by Adam. OPPOSITE: State bed of satinwood at Osterley Park from a design by Robert Adam, which bears the date October 1775. The columns are inlaid with green laureling, mounted with bronze capitals and bases; it is upholstered in green silks and velvets. *Courtesy Victoria and Albert Museum.*

looked too much like lace, possessing a spider-like quality. These characteristics provoked caustic remarks even from his admirers, who preferred a more "virile" antique manner. Sir William Chambers pronounces such extreme delicacy as "filigrane-toy work." At Osterley it is impossible not to notice the striking contrast between the broadly handled decoration in the hall (1767) and the minute and attenuated ornament of the State Bedroom (1775–78). Horace Walpole, after his second visit to Osterley

in 1778, deplores that "from Kent's mahogany, we are dwindled to Adam's filigree, grandeur and simplicity are not in fashion." The bed in the State Bedroom is one of Adam's most ambitious pieces of furniture. Walpole criticized the dome of the bed as "too theatric and too like a modern head-dress." The festoons of artificial flowers surrounding the dome prompted Walpole to query, "What would Vitruvius think of a dome decorated by a milliner?"

ABOVE LEFT: Armchair of carved gilt wood, probably made by Samuel Norman (flourished 1754–64), from a design by Robert Adam, dated 1764, for Sir Laurence Dundas, Bart., of Moor Park, Hertfordshire. From Sir Laurence's London residence at No. 19 Arlington Street. RIGHT: Armchair of carved gilt wood, one of a set of chairs designed by Robert Adam for the State Bedroom at Osterley. The back is supported by winged sphinxes. The original drawing bears the date April 24, 1777. *Courtesy Victoria and Albert Museum.* BELOW: Demi-lune pier table in the style of Adam (c. 1770–80). One of a pair, it is carved and parcel-gilded; the polychrome painted decoration on a cream-white ground is attributed to Cipriani and Pergolesi. *Courtesy Parke-Bernet, from the collection of Walter P. Chrysler.*

From what has been said, it is obvious that Adam's style of furniture underwent considerable modification between the time he returned home in 1758 and his death in 1792. At first he simply grafted his antique ornament, which at this time was bold and "Roman," on rococo curvilinear forms with cabriole legs. By degrees Adam perfected a style which bears some resemblance to that which flourished in France under Louis XVI; yet Adam's rectilinear neo-classic style attained maturity before the French Louis XVI. In his later work the accent is on elegance of form and color. The use of decorative painting in connection with furniture was mainly due to Adam; by this treatment, furniture was brought into still closer relation with the decorative scheme. Pier tables and commodes were especially susceptible to ornamental painting, since they formed an important part of the mural decoration. Indeed some of the more ambitious commodes and pier tables are painted like the ceilings above them, with small-scale panel pictures—rectangular, round, oval, or octagonal—of classical figure subjects and mythological scenes in the style propagated by Angelica Kauffmann, Pergolesi, Cipriani, Zucchi, and other decorative artists. The familiar husk festoons, paterae as well as some details in grotesque composition, were favorite subjects for the painted decoration which is often found on satinwood and harewood (stained sycamore) veneers; in other cases the entire piece is painted in a light color to harmonize with the walls and ceilings of colored stucco. The taste for painted decoration became so fashionable that by the last decade of the eighteenth century it had to a considerable extent supplanted colored decoration by means of marquetry.

At this period during the prevalence of "Adam," that is, the first half of George III's reign, veneering once again enjoyed a great vogue for large and uncarved surfaces which effectively display the variety and richness in figure of carefully selected veneers. Other choice woods apart from mahogany also came into vogue. Veneering in golden-toned satinwood and other exotic woods with marquetry and painted decoration was in high fashion for much fine furniture, with gesso gilding. Applied gilded metal mounts, a favorite form of French decoration for furniture from the time of Boulle, did not really become fashionable in England until the advent of neo-classicism when they were especially found on marquetry commodes and cabinets and other ambitious pieces of veneered furniture. The chief producer of ormolu mounts, as they were known in England, was Matthew Boulton, an engineer of remarkable versatility who produced steam engines in partnership with Watts, while making in his factory near Soho in Birmingham a considerable quantity of fine-quality ormolu mounts in the form of repetitive patterns for friezes, rams' heads, husk festoons, and other classical motifs, as well as such objects of ormolu as candlesticks and cassolettes.

ABOVE: Oval girandole mirror (c. 1775). Made of carved gilt wood and composition, it is one of a pair, festooned and bearing pendants of tiny leaves. *Courtesy Parke-Bernet, from the collection of Anna E. Erickson.* ABOVE RIGHT: Mahogany armchair (c. 1775–80). The framework is carved with fluting; the back is enriched with festooned drapery and the Prince of Wales' feathers; it has turned legs, fluted and tapering. *Courtesy Victoria and Albert Museum.* RIGHT: Mahogany armchair (c. 1780). The framework is carved with beading and the bars are enriched with paterae; quadrangular tapering front legs. *Courtesy Metropolitan Museum of Art. Fletcher Fund, 1929.*

To obtain the extreme lightness that distinguishes Adam's later work, a special composition on metal cores was exploited for the delicate swags, while the diminutive husking was frequently of lead. This imitation of one material by another during the last quarter of the eighteenth century led to a change in the character of some furniture where a similar effect of fragility could never have been achieved with any chance of lasting in wood. Nowhere is the change more apparent than in mirrors enriched with delicate ornament carried out in composition to harmonize with the stucco decoration of the wall. Oval mirrors decorated with perilously fragile festoons of husks or tiny leaves terminating in pendants of the same strikingly illustrate this taste. It is also evident in pier tables, painted or gilded, ornamented with delicate swags of composition flowers and leaves depending from the frieze. Another imitative composition, in this case in imitation of colored marble, is scagliola, which was frequently employed by Adam for columns and floors and for furniture, particularly table tops. Of early Roman origin, the art was revived and perfected in Italy during the Renaissance. In England it was widely introduced into the decorative scheme of many large houses designed by eighteenth-century English architects who brought Italian workmen trained in the method to execute their designs. At this time scagliola tops for tables and commodes were purchased in Italy. Some years later it became available in England, and Adam was instrumental in making it popular.

Around 1770 the influence of the classical revival became evident in mahogany chairs with central openworked splats, which were favored for halls, libraries, and dining-rooms. They are given straight tapering legs, in most instances square in section with fluted or reeded decoration; stretchers are rarely used, the main exception being transitional chairs with the Chippendale type of straight leg. Lyre-shaped splats were much in favor. As the neo-classic style developed, marked changes occur in the construction and shape of the chair back. The back no longer joins the seat rail but is supported by the extension of the rear legs rising above the seat rail; while oval-, heart-, and shield-shaped backs come into vogue. In some of these models the openworked splat is replaced by different filled-in designs as festoons of draperies or radial bars. From about 1770, Adam's chairs for drawing-rooms follow the lines of the contemporary Louis XVI carved and gilt wood *fauteuils* with oval backs and round legs turned slightly conic and fluted. This type became the customary gilt drawing-room chair for the "Adam" period; occasionally it was entirely painted in a light color. Though satinwood was in general use as a veneer at this time, it was seldom used for chairs. In the large drawing-rooms of houses furnished by Adam a formal effect was secured by placing long benches, gilded or painted, against the walls. Adam also liked to place in the deep window recesses benches or stools with sides generally outscrolled.

ABOVE: Gilt chairs and settees, made by Mayhew and Ince for the Tapestry Room at Croome Court, the country seat of the Earls of Coventry (1769). Robert Adam was the architect of the Tapestry Room. Several of Adam's clients used the colors and flowery products of the Gobelins to cover the walls from chair rail to ceiling cornice and also the seat furniture. Tapestry Rooms represented the current fashion in England for interiors "in the French taste." *Courtesy Metropolitan Museum of Art. Gift of the Samuel H. Kress Foundation, 1958.*
BELOW: Carved mahogany window bench, from an original design by Robert Adam for Sir Laurence Dundas, Bart., of Moor Park (c. 1765). The seat rail and round and tapering legs are fluted. *Courtesy Parke-Bernet, from the collection of Walter P. Chrysler. (See page 317.)*

Carved bookcase from a design by Robert Adam, made for General Campbell of Combe Back, Sundridge (1767). It is stained to imitate mahogany and has parcel-gilt decoration. *Courtesy Metropolitan Museum of Art. Calwalader Fund, 1917.*

The designs for bookcases and other similar wall furniture from around 1770 also bear witness to the new classical ideals. They are given architectural pediments and entablatures, but are less ponderous, the moldings more accurate, and the decorative detail more restrained and admirably distributed. The majority of Adam's bookcases were designed to stand in a recess; in some examples the frieze of the bookcase is enriched with the same motif that decorates the frieze round the room, perhaps for example a running pattern of husk festoons or the anthemion. At this time doors filled with a small metal trelliswork backed by silk occasionally replaced doors finished with glass, a practice that was to continue into the nineteenth century. The astragals were of metal and frequently gilded.

319

Torchères and pedestals, gilded or painted to match the decoration of the wall, were extensively used by Adam and his school in drawing-rooms. Pedestals of term form for the reception of antique statues, busts, and vases were very much within the province of the architect and most popular. *Torchères,* for the support of candelabra, with a tripod base and central standard were rapidly transformed by Adam, who gave them the form of a Roman tripod. The type made fashionable by Adam consisted of three long ram-headed uprights supporting a circular top; in most instances the uprights terminate in realistically rendered hoof feet often mounted on a triangular plinth. In some examples swags of leaves or husk festoons depend from the rams' mouths; others with a snake curled round the tripod are reminiscent of the ornament of the classic originals.

In spacious dining-rooms the grouping of the sideboard table, still without drawers of any sort, flanked by urns on pedestals is almost certainly due to Adam and produced a grand effect. The pedestals and urns were generally made of the same material—mahogany, satinwood, rosewood, or painted wood—and harmonized in style with the sideboard table. Sheraton explains in his *Encyclopaedia* (1805) how they were generally used: "One pedestal is used as a plate warmer, and is lined with tin; the other as a pot cupboard and sometimes it contains a cellarette for wine. The vases are used for water for the use of the butler, and sometimes as knife cases." (The practice of rinsing cutlery and glasses in the dining-room during dinner still persisted in the early nineteenth century.) Though in most cases the front of the sideboard table is straight, extant examples belonging to the last quarter of the eighteenth century are also serpentine-fronted, bow- and hollow-fronted. "It is not usual," writes Sheraton, "to make sideboards hollow in front, but in some circumstances it is evident that advantages will arise from it. If a sideboard be required nine or ten feet long as in some noblemen's houses . . ." by this treatment the great length is not so apparent, and "besides if the sideboard be near the entering door of the dining-room, the hollow front will sometimes secure the butler from the jostles of the other servants." This grouping of the sideboard table with urns on pedestals at each end continued in fashion for large dining-rooms till the close of the century.

Mirrors, like pier tables and commodes, were especially receptive to neo-classic influence because they played an important part in the decorative scheme. Immensely tall pier mirrors more than ninety inches in height, formed of a single sheet of glass, became high fashion in the last quarter of the eighteenth century. These long plates had recently become procurable as a result of a new method of casting glass introduced from France in 1773, where it is believed to have been invented about a century earlier. Owing to the high cost of large mirrors, which greatly exceeded that of the frames, old mirrors were often reset, a practice by no means

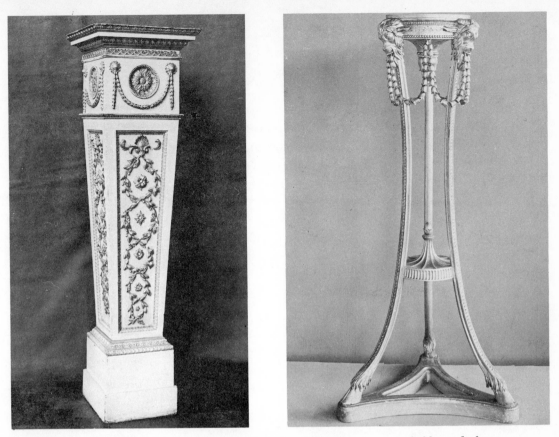

ABOVE LEFT: Pedestal of term form, painted and partly gilded, from a set probably made by Samuel Norman to a design by Adam for Sir Laurence Dundas, Bart., of Moor Park (c. 1765). ABOVE RIGHT: Gilt *torchère* of tripod form carved with rams' heads and festooned with husks (c. 1770). *Courtesy Victoria and Albert Museum.* BELOW: Rosewood sideboard table, made by Chippendale and probably designed by Adam for Harewood House, Yorkshire (early 1770s). It is inlaid and mounted in chased and gilt brass, with matching pedestals, urns, and wine cooler. *Courtesy* Country Life.

new. Benjamin Goodison supplied five new pier mirrors for Kew in 1752 at a small price because he had removed the mirrors from frames no longer fashionable. Mirrors could also be hired for special occasions, but the tradesmen demanded such extravagant prices, no doubt because of the many unavoidable hazards and accidents of handling, that other sources were frequently exploited. According to Horace Walpole, Lord Stanley borrowed mirrors from Lord March to decorate the ballroom for a ball he gave in 1773, because an upholsterer had asked £300 for the use of some.

Hepplewhite

The neo-classic principles embraced by Adam and those who followed in his wake were propagated through trade publications which showed the features of the new style adapted to ordinary household furniture. Of these, the best exposition is George Hepplewhite's book *The Cabinet-maker and Upholsterer's Guide,* in which the neo-classic style associated with Adam is successfully modified and rendered into the vernacular for the use of cabinetmakers. The first edition of the *Guide* was published in 1788, two years after Hepplewhite's death, and contains nearly 300 designs "from drawings by A. Hepplewhite and Co. Cabinet-makers." A second edition appeared in 1789 and a third in 1794. The purpose of the book, as set forth in the preface, is "to unite elegance and utility and blend the useful with the agreeable." Any examination of Hepplewhite's designs, however slight, reveals how well he succeeded, for he imparted to his plain and useful pieces a sensible and simple elegance and refinement that still make them most appropriate for modern houses.

The practical character of the designs made them easy to reproduce, which is most important since Hepplewhite also intended the book to benefit "surrounding nations" who "have in late years much sought" English fashions and workmanship, "our own countrymen and artisans whose distance from the metropolis makes even an imperfect knowledge of its improvements [that is, changes in fashions] acquired with much trouble and expense." He did not profess to any important innovations, but rather "we designedly followed the latest or most prevailing fashion only, purposely omitting such articles, whose recommendation was mere novelty, and perhaps a violation of all established rule." That Hepplewhite was no real originator is apparent in the *Cabinet-makers' London Book of Prices* (1788), where ten designs that bear his name have little to distinguish them from those contributed by other cabinetmakers. The extent of

Hepplewhite's personal responsibility for the designs in the *Guide* cannot be reckoned, since the drawings are not signed. Indeed few facts are known about his life or business, which after his death in 1786 was carried on by his widow, Alice. Since there is no evidence in the form of bills, accounts, or contemporary records to indicate that as a cabinetmaker he conducted a lucrative business catering to fashionable society, it seems reasonable to assume that his shop in Redcross Street, St. Giles, Cripplegate was essentially modest and conservative.

As in Chippendale and later in Sheraton, the popular conception of the Hepplewhite style is also based on a book of designs, in this case the *Guide*, which represents a collective expression of the prevailing fashion rather than the creation of a single individual. The merit of the designs in the *Guide* varies; few if any can be described as fresh and lively exercises in the neo-classic style. The element of sophisticated refinement in Adam's later ornament had begun to pall after so many years of use and slavish imitation, and in the absence of fresh sources of inspiration it was inevitable that the formula began to show signs of growing stale. Hepplewhite's treatment of Adam's neo-classic ornament displayed small imagination, and his repertory was limited to such orthodox classical detail as paterae, anthemion, husk festoons and pendants, drapery swags, urns, and medallions. In accordance with the prevailing taste the designs provided lighter and simpler forms, and the sense of elegance was to be further developed by Sheraton. A considerable quantity of the furniture illustrated in the *Guide* was to be made in satinwood decorated with polychrome marquetry; while for other pieces japanned (that is, painted) decoration was recommended, "a fashion that has arisen within these last few years." Naturalistic ornament—sprays and garlands of flowers—and medallions painted in natural colors or *en grisaille* were favored for the painted decoration. Most of the furniture with painted decoration was made of a soft wood, the ground being painted to harmonize with the delicate-colored walls of contemporary rooms.

Sheraton, in his *Drawing Book* (1791–94), sounded a note of disapproval when referring to the modishness of the designs of some of the furniture represented in the *Guide*. He writes, "Notwithstanding the late date of Hepplewhite's book, if we compare some of the designs, particularly the chairs, with the newest taste, we shall find that this work has already caught the decline, and perhaps in a little time, will suddenly die in disorder." Even to glance through the *Guide* it is impossible not to be struck by the more than seldom occurrence of certain rococo souvenirs such as cabriole legs, for which Hepplewhite recommended a French whorl foot, a terminal favored by Chippendale for his "French" pieces. Long after Adam had renounced the cabriole leg, Hepplewhite, like many of his contemporaries, continued to employ a slender cabriole leg on a few fashionable

ABOVE LEFT: Mahogany armchair in the French taste (c. 1775). It is distinguished by its carved curvilinear frame and concave oval back panel. *Courtesy Metropolitan Museum of Art. Collection of Irwin Untermyer.* ABOVE RIGHT: Lady's writing cabinet or *bonheur du jour* in the French taste (c. 1780–85). It is mounted in gilt bronze; the drawer forming a valanced frieze is fitted with a writing slide having a hinged central section with an easel support. (*See page 326.*) BELOW: Mahogany settee in the French taste (c. 1775). It has a graceful serpentine back, valanced seat rail, and cabriole legs finishing in French whorl feet. A design for a French sofa with cabriole legs is given in Hepplewhite's *Guide,* first edition, plate 25. *Courtesy Parke-Bernet, from the collection of Walter P. Chrysler.*

325

ABOVE: Carved mahogany settee (a type in vogue in the 1780s). It has a serpentine back and a reeded serpentine seat rail, square tapering front legs, brass toe caps and casters. *Courtesy Parke-Bernet, from the collection of Mabel Brady Garvan.* LEFT: Inlaid mahogany toilet mirror (c. 1780). The box stand has a serpentine front containing a single row of drawers; the piece resembles a design in Hepplewhite's *Guide,* first and third editions, plate 70. *Courtesy Metropolitan Museum of Art. Collection of Irwin Untermyer.* OPPOSITE LEFT: Armchair japanned in colors with delicate floral detail on a cream white ground (c. 1785). The oval back enclosing three feathers closely resembles a design in Hepplewhite's *Guide,* first edition, plate 8. *Courtesy Parke-Bernet.* OPPOSITE RIGHT: Carved mahogany armchair with heart-shaped back (c. 1780). The two front square tapered legs finish in spade feet. *Courtesy Metropolitan Museum of Art. Fletcher Fund, 1929. (See page 328.)*

and ambitious chairs, settees, and tables in the French taste. Such costly "French" pieces as tables designed for feminine use, veneered with marquetry, are notable for the light graceful elegance of their curvilinear rococo forms. It is obvious the severity of line imposed by Adam had not yet become universal in the 1780s.

Apparently Sheraton's stricture was not without foundation, for changes were made by Hepplewhite's successors in the third edition of the *Guide,* and all of the changes except one or two were concerned with chairs and sofas. That the section on chairs was freely revised is logical because no class of furniture is more receptive to changes or reveals the character of a period more fully than its chairs. Those with cabriole legs were discarded

in favor of rectilinear designs. About twenty new patterns for chairs with square backs—a shape which had by then come into vogue and is also illustrated in Sheraton's *Drawing Book*—were offered in the new edition to correct the earlier omission of such designs. Several settees with serpentine-shaped backs yielded to a new form with straight horizontal backs, a type also given by Sheraton. Three designs for oval mirrors, a shape much used by Adam, were replaced in favor of others with the more stylish rectangular frame. But oval toilet glasses were still represented. These changes exemplify one of the chief differences between the styles of the 1780s and the 1790s, or between Hepplewhite and Sheraton. In brief the earlier period favored certain curved forms, such as the oval and shield, and had not entirely discarded serpentine curves and cabriole legs, both familiar relics of rococo; while in the last decade of the century rectangular forms were preferred.

Hepplewhite is perhaps best known for his numerous designs for chair backs which offer a representative selection of the types in vogue in the 1780s. Oval-, heart-, and shield-shaped backs are popularly associated with the Hepplewhite style, but credit for their introduction does not belong to him. It may be true, however, that Hepplewhite was the first cabinetmaker

to introduce into his open chair backs the familiar three feathers, which was popular at that period as the emblem of the Prince of Wales' party. He mentions when he illustrates the motif in a chair back that it "has been executed with good effect for the Prince of Wales."

At this time there is countless variety in the treatment of the back for mahogany chairs. Especially popular are interlaced ovals and festoons of drapery forming the heart-shape, and the bar or banister back in the form of a shield filled in with slender curving ribs or bars, three or five of them, converging on a patera at the base of the shield. Occasionally the bars were omitted in favor of wheat ears with rippled blades. Radiating geometrical designs resembling at times the spokes of a wheel were also favored for oval backs. Besides the type of chair backs with filled-in designs, there were those with openworked central splats, which were also made in a great diversity of patterns. Frequently an elongated solid vase was introduced in the center of the splat, while oval paterae, carved or inlaid, were everywhere. Tapered legs, square in section, without stretchers, were especially favored for this general class of chairs; others were tapered and turned round. Indeed, square tapering legs without stretchers were used a great deal by Hepplewhite as supports for his chairs and tables. In most instances they terminated in a projecting die-shaped foot; especially

OPPOSITE LEFT: Armchair japanned in colors on a gray ground (c. 1785). The medallion in the center of the back encloses a musical trophy. OPPOSITE RIGHT: Mahogany chair (c. 1788). The splat is carved with a spray of wheat ears and husk festoons and is inlaid with boxwood paterae. The back closely resembles a design in Hepplewhite's *Guide,* first edition, plate 4. *Courtesy Victoria and Albert Museum.* LEFT: Armchair of the banister-back type, painted black with polychrome decoration (c. 1790). *Courtesy Metropolitan Museum of Art. Rogers Fund, 1931.*

typical is the so-called spade foot of square form that tapers slightly downward.

The new fashion of finishing chairs with painted decoration was much used. According to Hepplewhite, this treatment "allows a framework less massy than is requisite for mahogany, and by assorting the prevailing color to the furniture and light of the room, affords opportunity by the variety of grounds which may be introduced to make the whole accord in harmony, with a pleasing and striking effect to the eye." Thus it satisfied not only the prevailing taste for colored decoration, which brought the furniture into still closer relation with interior decoration, but also the fashionable trend toward lightness and feminine grace; it also explains why the framework of the great majority of these chairs with painted decoration was made of a soft wood and painted rather than of satinwood, which perhaps clashed with the delicate-colored painted walls. The designs for these chairs were based on the fashionable models made of mahogany with open backs. Hepplewhite singles out several of his banister-back chairs as being especially suitable for decorating "with painted or japanned work which gives a rich and splendid appearance to the minuter parts of the ornaments which are generally thrown in by the painter." Related to this taste is a large group of inexpensive chairs having a framework painted black with gilt embellishments; even the designs for these are often virtually identical to the more costly models.

We have already seen that small breakfast tables of the Pembroke type, distinguished by drop leaves on both sides supported on hinged wooden brackets and provided with a frieze drawer, were represented in Chippendale's *Director*. According to Sheraton, they received their name from that "of the lady who first gave orders for one of them, and who probably gave the first idea of such a table to the workmen"—perhaps the Countess of Pembroke (1737–1831). Hepplewhite writes in the *Guide* that Pembroke tables with square or oval tops are the most fashionable; he regards them as the most useful tables of their class and capable of receiving "considerable elegance in the workmanship and ornaments." At this time they were very often made of satinwood, ornamented with rich borders of marquetry or painted decoration round their tops and with decorated drawer fronts, while the four straight tapering legs were generally finished in brass toe caps and casters. "The size of such tables," writes Sheraton, "is from three feet eight inches to four feet wide, that is when open; and from two feet ten inches to three feet long when the flaps are down. The width of the bed should never be less than one foot nine inches; but in general they are from one foot ten inches to two feet one inch, and their height never more than two feet four inches, including casters."

Pembroke table (c. 1780). The drop leaves are edged with ogival contour, and the top is richly inlaid with portrait medallions, oval paterae, and bowknotted leafage sprays; it has square tapering legs, castered. *Courtesy Parke-Bernet, from the collection of Mrs. John E. Rovensky.*

330

Though Pembroke tables were used for diverse purposes, but mainly served for meals. In Jane Austen's *Emma* the heroine replaced a table of this kind with a dining table, "which none but Emma could have had power to place there and persuade her father to use, in place of the small-sized Pembroke, on which two of his daily meals had for forty years been crowded." They also served as tea tables, and even Pembroke worktables are mentioned in contemporary records; the ladies perhaps kept their needlework in the frieze drawer. Toward the end of the century the Harlequin Pembroke was introduced, characterized by a box-like structure equipped with small drawers and open compartments, which was concealed in the body of the table and could be raised to any height until it was entirely out by means of weights. Sheraton writes that this type served "not only as a breakfast, but also as a writing table, very suitable for a lady. It is termed a Harlequin Table, for no other reason but because, in articles of that sort, there is generally a great deal of machinery introduced."

In the last quarter of the eighteenth century notable changes occurred in the treatment of the material as well as the style of such pieces as bookcases, secretary cabinets, clothespresses, and chests of drawers. Carefully selected contrasting veneers now held the field, while inlaid and painted decoration replaced carving. A great deal of the furniture having large surfaces depended entirely for its decorative effect on the rich figure of contrasting veneers, for example, veneered mahogany banded in satinwood. The forms became lighter and very often severely simple. Hepplewhite liked to mount these pieces on a valanced base curving into French bracket feet, a graceful line deriving from French rococo commodes. As an alternative he used a straight molded base and straight bracket feet. Large bookcases, generally called library bookcases in pattern books, having two or four additional wings making their length ten or more feet, were of necessity mounted on plinth bases.

Hepplewhite devoted a plate in the *Guide* to "Doors for Bookcases." In one design the glazing bars are in the form of covered urns with drapery festoons and possess considerable charm. As a rule, Hepplewhite was partial to delicate, straight glazing bars worked in various elongated and polygonal forms. He writes that "the ornamental glazing bars are intended to be of metal, which painted of a lighter color or gilt will produce a lively and pleasing effect." This practice persisted until the end of the century. These designs were of course also used for the two glazed doors of secretary cabinets designed in two stages. Secretary cabinets, which according to Hepplewhite were usually made of good mahogany, were designed with either a slant front or a fitted writing drawer that let down on a quadrant. When bookcases having two glazed doors were given a writing drawer, both pieces looked identical. For the upper portion of bookcases and secretary cabinets Hepplewhite favored a

RIGHT: Design for a desk and bookcase, from Hepplewhite's *Guide*, first edition, plate 41. *Courtesy Cooper Union Museum.* OPPOSITE ABOVE: Mahogany tambour writing table (c. 1785). It resembles with trifling modifications a design from Hepplewhite's *Guide*, first edition, plate 68. *Courtesy Philadelphia Museum of Art.* OPPOSITE BELOW: Semi-circular commode veneered with harewood and satinwood, by William Moore of Dublin (c. 1785). The marquetry of husk festoons, urns, paterae, and tripods are drawn from Adam's neo-classical repertory. The naturalistic treatment of the roses enclosed in an oval panel on the cupboard door is typical of the marquetry in fashion in the last decade of the century. *Courtesy Victoria and Albert Museum.*

straight molded cornice. "On the top when ornamented," he writes, "is placed between a scroll of foliage, a vase bust or other ornament, which may be of mahogany or gilt or of light colored wood."

Writing furniture was augmented by the tambour writing table, which Hepplewhite pronounced "answered all the uses of a desk and had a much lighter appearance"; it was distinguished by a tambour cylinder deriving no doubt from the French desk having a solid cylinder. At this period commodes of semi-circular plan, a form used by Adam, became fashionable. Frequently the front of these commodes opened as a single large door. Since they were used in principal rooms, Hepplewhite notes that they "require considerable elegance. The panels may be of satinwood, plain or inlaid; the top also and border round the front should be inlaid." Hepplewhite illustrates chests of drawers with straight, bow, or serpentine fronts. For the brasses on chests of drawers, as well as for all drawers, a solid back plate was again introduced but it was now ornamented by

LEFT: Inlaid mahogany chest of drawers (c. 1780). Its serpentine front and valanced base continue into French bracket feet; the piece resembles with slight modifications a design for dressing drawers in Hepplewhite's *Guide*, first edition, plate 76. *Courtesy Parke-Bernet.* BELOW: Inlaid mahogany sideboard (c. 1785). It has a gracefully swept concave center section with lateral wine drawers and cupboard door, and square, slightly tapered legs with spade feet. *Courtesy Parke-Bernet, from the collection of Mrs. Harrison Williams.* OPPOSITE: Design for a sideboard published by Thomas Sheraton (1792). From his *Drawing Book*, 1791–94, plate 54. *Courtesy Cooper Union Museum.*

stamping. Ring handles with circular back plates and bail handles with oval back plates are characteristic, although bail handles attached to two small back plates, introduced around the mid-eighteenth century, continued to be used into the following century. From about 1800, small brass-knob handles tended to replace the bail handles.

A practical innovation by the cabinetmakers of the last quarter of the eighteenth century is the sideboard provided with lateral wine drawers and cupboards. This piece of dining-room furniture is still at the present

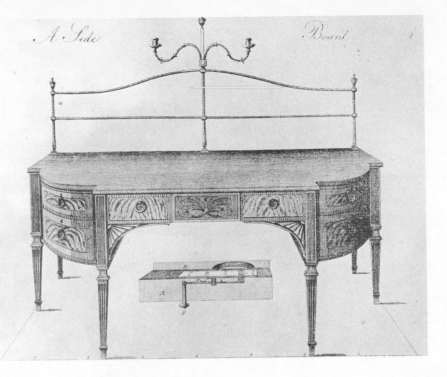

time most popular and familiar. In 1779 the well-known cabinetmaking firm of R. and R. Gillow announced that they were now making "a new sort of sideboard table with drawers etc. in a genteel style to hold bottles." "The great utility of this piece of furniture," we read in the *Guide*, "has procured it a very general reception; and the conveniences it affords renders a dining room incomplete without a sideboard." Sideboards show considerable variation in design, not only in the arrangement and number of drawers and doors but also in the shape of the front, which was straight, bow, serpentine, or hollow-fronted; others were of semi-circular plan or demilune. They varied in length from around five to more than nine feet. Square tapering legs were favored, almost always with four in the front continuing from the stiles and generally two in the rear. The veneered mahogany surfaces of these sideboards were sometimes further enriched with bandings in a contrasting veneer and inlaid stringing lines perhaps of holly. Sheraton's sideboards are similar to the designs of Thomas Shearer and Hepplewhite, but they are characterized by a brass rod at the back extending the entire length. "This rod," writes Sheraton, "is used to set large dishes against, and to support a couple of candle or lamp branches in the middle, which, when lighted give a very brilliant effect to the silver ware."

To a great extent the storage space provided in this new piece of dining-room furniture served the same purposes as those of the pedestals and urns introduced by Adam to flank the sideboard table. According to Sheraton,

Satinwood vase knife case, one of a pair (c. 1780). It is painted with a frieze of "flowing *rinceaux*," medallions enclosing fruit and landscapes, drapery swags, and other fashionable neo-classical motifs. *Courtesy Victoria and Albert Museum.* OPPOSITE: Inlaid mahogany Beau Brummel with a hinged box lid (c. 1780). The mirror is flanked by six compartments for toilet requisites such as soap and razors. *Courtesy Parke-Bernet, from the collection of Mrs. Harrison Williams.* (See page 338.)

"The right hand drawer contains the cellarette, which is often made to draw out separate from the rest. It is partitioned and lined with lead, to hold nine or ten wine bottles. The drawer on the left is generally plain, but sometimes divided into two; the back division being lined with baize, to hold plates, having a cover hinged to enclose the whole. The front division is lined with lead, so that it may hold water to wash glasses; which may be made to take out, or have a plug hole to let off the dirty water. The left-hand drawer is, however, sometimes made very short, to give place to a pot-cupboard behind, which opens by a door at the end of the sideboard. This door is made to hide itself in the end rail as much as possible, both for look and secrecy. For which reason a turn-buckle is not used, but a thumb-spring . . . so by the touch of the finger the door flies open. . . ." Since sideboards are not always of the same shape, all "will not admit of a cupboard of this sort. . . . In large circular sideboards, the left-hand drawer has sometimes been fitted up as a plate-warmer, having a rack in the middle to put the plates in, and lined with strong tin all round. . . . In this case the bottom of the drawer is made partly open, under which is fixed a small narrow drawer to contain a heater, which gives warmth to the plates the same as in the pedestal."

Apart from the new sideboard, sideboard tables made without either drawers or pedestals were in general use in small dining-rooms, "but have generally," Sheraton writes, "a wine cooler to stand under them, hooped with brass, partitioned and lined with lead for wine bottles." In accordance with the neo-classical taste, knife cases, which are placed on sideboard tables, acquired a new form. Besides the customary box knife case with a sloping lid and a serpentine-shaped front, they are now given a form in the shape of a vase. In these vase knife cases the partitions for the knives are arranged concentrically about a central rod.

Finally a word about a kind of table, designed for dressing, that remained popular throughout the second half of the eighteenth century, perhaps the most popular of all toilet tables at that time. The top of the table was designed with a hinged box lid or lifting top that enclosed the mirror rising with a ratchet adjustment and the toilet requirements. It was designed for both feminine and masculine use, the latter often being given the sobriquet Beau Brummel.

Sheraton

The most important trade catalogue published in the second half of the eighteenth century is Thomas Sheraton's *The Cabinet-Maker and Upholsterer's Drawing Book,* a work so comprehensive and well received that it has caused to be classified under his name most of the fine furniture produced in England between 1790 and 1800, especially such as was made of satinwood, and numerous examples have been rashly attributed to him. Yet this association is misleading, for there is no evidence to conclude that Sheraton, who was trained as a "journeyman cabinet-maker," at any time possessed a workshop of his own, or made any considerable amount of furniture or even carried out the designs illustrated in his book. Some light on Sheraton's life can be obtained from *The Gentleman's Magazine* for November 1806, where under the title of "Obituary with Anecdotes of Remarkable Persons" it is stated that in Broad Street, Soho, after a short illness, Sheraton, a native of Stockton-on-Tees in Durham, died at the age of fifty-five. It lists his publications and notes that he was "for many years a journeyman cabinet-maker, but who since the year 1793 has supported himself, a wife and two children, by his exertions as an author. . . . He has left his family it is feared in distressing circumstances."

Sheraton divided the *Drawing Book* into four parts, and it came out in separate numbers between 1791 and 1794. In the first half of the book he gives instructions pertaining to the art of making perspective drawings, and treats of such various geometrical lines as ought to be understood by cabinetmakers. He also gives the Five Orders, as was customary in pattern books of this period; he notes in the preface that he gives many more details concerning the Orders than Chippendale, who gave only a few. Further on, he pronounces that Chippendale's designs are by now "wholly antiquated and laid aside, though possessed of great merit according to the times in which they were executed." The third part of Sheraton's work contains the designs for furniture, while the fourth part comprises moldings and various ornaments. The entire work covers more than 440 pages. In his introduction to the third part he writes that his aim is "to exhibit the present taste of furniture and at the same time to give the workman some assistance in the manufacturing part of it." Later he continues, "I have made it my business to apply to the best workmen in different shops, to obtain their assistance in the explanation of such pieces as they have been most acquainted with." The designs are splendid in draftsmanship and the technical information contained in the descriptive notes is more detailed than that offered in any other book of designs. There can be no doubt that the *Drawing Book* was a powerful formative influence, since more than 600 cabinetmakers, joiners, and upholsterers subscribed to it from every section of England.

Though it is possible to consider the designs in the *Drawing Book* simply as a representative collection of the fashions prevailing in the last decade of the century, if they are compared with the designs in Hepplewhite's *Guide,* it is impossible not to be struck by the strong contrast between the two. It will appear that the neo-classic style in the majority of designs was almost transformed. Yet the evolution in cabinetmaking in the few years that divide these two publications cannot fully account for this change. For this marked difference a large part of the credit must be given to Sheraton, who showed a remarkable sense of style and possessed the talent and technical knowledge to modify and improve upon ideas obtained from different sources. To infuse fresh life into his neo-classical designs, Sheraton, who was a great admirer of French work, drew heavily upon the Louis XVI style, in which the impersonal traced with ruler, square, and compass governed the designs. All this geometry had in it something abstract, something purely rational that pleased Sheraton's mathematical mind, and possessing the skill to use it, he was able to impart to his designs a singular neatness and precision not found in any other pattern book.

One of the designers responsible for bringing about the change in style between the 1780s and the 1790s was the gifted architect Henry Holland, who was responsible for introducing into England the French version of classicism favored by the Prince of Wales and his circle. The grand style of classic severity with its marked predilection for rectangular forms and large bare surfaces defined by borders of simple outline taking the place of ornamentation was employed by Holland at Carlton House, which he began to redecorate for the Prince of Wales in 1783. To impart fresh life into a languishing style, he drastically trimmed the husk festoons and delicate foliage scrolls which under Adam's influence were inclined to invade every vacant space. Horace Walpole, who visited Carlton House in 1785 while it was still incomplete, praised the "august simplicity" in Hol-

Sheraton after Henry Holland, in the Appendix to Sheraton's *Drawing Book*, 1791–94, plate 31, showing a view of the south end of the Prince of Wales' Chinese drawing room in Carlton House. The engraving (1793) is of interest because it reveals the source of some of Sheraton's ideas. *Courtesy Victoria and Albert Museum.*

land's style of interior decoration and continued, "How sick one shall be after this chaste palace of Mr. Adam's gingerbread and sippets of embroidery." (Chastity was to become a much sought-after quality and it was constantly applied to the work of the following Regency style by contemporary writers.)

When Sheraton at a later date had the opportunity to see the completed redecoration of Carlton House, he was so impressed that he included in his *Drawing Book* views and descriptions of the dining-room and Chinese drawing-room. Holland's designs for furniture show that he made good use of the opportunity to study the excellent examples of contemporary French furniture in the Prince of Wales' collection. For example, a feature of the Louis XVI style employed by Holland and in turn by Sheraton was the use of slender columns placed at the angles of commodes and similar pieces, extending the entire height and breaking into the continuity of all the moldings from the base to the architrave. Indeed it was one of Sheraton's favorite devices and it is one of the chief stylistic differences between Sheraton and Hepplewhite, who never employed them. Sheraton at times even used this feature in chairs and tables, extending the legs upward to interrupt the seat rail or the top of the table.

In the *Drawing Book*, Sheraton, following in Holland's wake, employed square or rectangular forms in all his elevations. Even his chair backs and settees, pieces which had given Adam and his school an opportunity to

341

quarter plan

relieve the severity of strictly rectilinear lines with an oval, shield, or other curved shape, were generally rectangular. Essentially his only substantial concession was to introduce shallow elliptical pediments above bookcases and similar kinds of wall furniture, or an occasional dome above a tall case clock, bookcase, or the like. But on the other hand Sheraton liked to enliven the plan of his models with curved recesses and projections, such as commodes with a boldly projecting center portion or library bookcases with convex wings. The technique used by French *ébénistes* to link the façade of objects of rectangular plan such as cabinets with the wall against which they stood by adding to their plans rounded ends shaped to quarter circles, full or re-entrant, fitted with shelves, drawers, or small cupboard doors, was also employed by Sheraton. In his pursuit of variety he designed an elliptic bed and a "kidney" library table of the pedestal type. Of the latter he writes that it is so called "on account of its resemblance to that intestine part of animals." It is the familiar haricot or kidney bean, a favorite French rococo form which was used not only as an ornament but also as a fashionable shape for the tops of small

OPPOSITE LEFT: Satinwood low cupboard (c. 1795). The doors are enriched with oval panels painted in the manner of Angelica Kauffmann, and are surmounted with two tiers of brass shelves. *Courtesy Frank Partridge, Inc., New York. Photo Albert Waks.* OPPOSITE RIGHT: Design for a card table (1793) in the Appendix to Sheraton's *Drawing Book*, 1791–94, plate 11. *Courtesy Victoria and Albert Museum. (See page 341.)* ABOVE: Design for a commode (1794) in the Appendix to Sheraton's *Drawing Book*, second and third editions, plate 15. The oval and diamond-shaped patterns are typically Sheraton. *Courtesy Victoria and Albert Museum.* BELOW: Design for a library bookcase (1794) from Sheraton's *Drawing Book*, second edition, plate 41. *Courtesy Cooper Union Museum.*

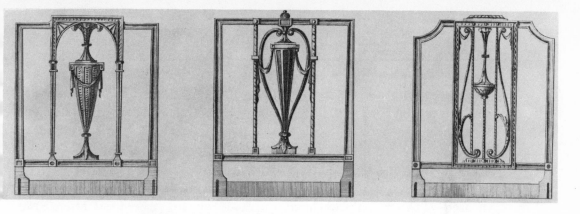

OPPOSITE ABOVE: Design for a lady's writing cabinet with a fall front (1793) in the Appendix to Sheraton's *Drawing Book* 1791–94, plate 16. Sheraton states that "the marble shelves with frets at each end are for tea equipage." *Courtesy Victoria and Albert Museum.* (*See page 342.*) OPPOSITE BELOW: Walnut kidney-shaped writing table (c. 1820). It has a pierced brass gallery and was made by Gillow. *Courtesy Frank Partridge, Inc., New York. Photo Albert Waks.* ABOVE: Design for three chair backs (1792) taken from Sheraton's *Drawing Book,* Part III, plate 36. *Courtesy Victoria and Albert Museum.* LEFT: Mahogany armchair (c. 1790–95). A delicate sobriety of ornament characterizes many of the carved mahogany chairs at this time. *Courtesy Metropolitan Museum of Art. Fletcher Fund, 1929.* (*See page 346.*)

tables; of course being purely rococo it had been abandoned long ago by the French *ébénistes.*

The late eighteenth-century taste toward extreme delicacy, at times bordering on perilous fragility, is seen at its best in the designs for chairs. Sheraton adopted rectilinear forms for his chair backs in preference to the oval and shield shape hitherto in vogue. To the splats, solid or open-worked, he paid great attention, producing a wide variety of graceful patterns often embodying vase, oval, lyre, and diamond forms. Long, delicate, curving lines predominated which enlivened the rectangular form of the back; even the diamond motif was often made of four concave curves.

345

One of Sheraton's favorite devices was to flank the splat by delicate columns often supporting a semi-circular arch. (Quantities of arches, semi-circular or elliptical, were used in the Louis XVI style.) The arms were set high on the back uprights, as in Louis XVI chair design; while tapered legs turned round and often fluted and occasionally spirally turned are typical; others are tapered and square in section. Sheraton always showed a preference for straight, tapered round legs in all his designs.

The fashionable manner of finishing drawing-room chairs is clearly indicated in Sheraton's explanatory notes on his tripod stands. "Sometimes," he writes, "they [candlestands] are finished in white and gold, and sometimes all gold, to suit the other furniture. In inferior drawing-rooms they are japanned [painted] answerable to the furniture." It is also obvious from his notes on drawing-room chairs that the most elaborate and fashionable models were intended for this style of finishing; directions were given for "retrenching" their ornate character, so they might also be rendered in mahogany "without hurt done to the general outline." For example, in a pattern for a painted splat, the drapery festoon under the top rail, a motif much used by Sheraton, may be omitted. In other illustrations that "are meant chiefly to be carved and gilt," he explains that "the mere outlines of any of them will serve as patterns either for painted or mahogany chairs, by leaving out the ornaments for the mahogany, and retaining some of them, or even all of them may be adapted for painting." The framework of the painted chairs of this period was decorated with delicate floral motifs; while figure subjects or floral garlands were introduced on an oval or rectangular panel in the center of the back.

Sheraton, who was no doubt aware of the considerable number of chairs, settees, and commodes imported from France by fashionable society, gave a number of designs for different pieces of furniture whose forms were copied directly from the French; for example, the *voyeuse* in which the occupant places himself with his back to the front and rests his arms on a padded crest rail. Of this chair Sheraton writes, "The manner of conversing lounging on a chair amongst some in the highest circles is copied from the French. Hence we have the term conversation chair. It should be observed that they are made extraordinarily long between back and front, for the purpose of giving space for the fashionable posture; and also that they are narrow in front and back, as an accommodation to this mode of conversing." For daybeds he illustrates the *veilleuse* and the *duchesse*. The latter was also represented by Hepplewhite and they both agree in much the same terms that it comprises "two barjier chairs with a stool in the middle." Apart from slight variations, Sheraton's designs for upholstered settees followed the Louis XVI type. He illustrates them with turned baluster arm supports and fluted cylindrical legs.

The tester bed in general use in the last quarter of the eighteenth cen-

LEFT: Painted satinwood chair (c. 1795). The design of the top rail, which is arched on each side of an oblong panel, was favored for satinwood chairs. The drapery festoon under the top rail is a marked Sheraton feature. *Courtesy Metropolitan Museum of Art. Fletcher Fund, 1929.* BELOW: Satinwood settee (c. 1795). It is carved in part and has painted polychrome decoration. The flat-arched top rail is taken from a Louis XVI type of *canapé.* As in chair design the arms are set high on the back uprights. *Courtesy Frank Partridge, Inc., New York. Photo Albert Waks.*

tury is well represented by Hepplewhite and Sheraton. It is distinguished by tall slender posts, fluted and carved; the molded cornice is sometimes arched, and at the corners of the tester, plumes or vase-shaped finials were often used as in earlier times, but now they are simpler and lighter. Occasionally a scalloped edging of wood heads the valance, which was often formed of swags of rich silk, tasseled and fringed all round of the French kind. In the succeeding century, French Empire boat beds below a canopy attached to the wall that supported the hangings came into fashion, but the taste was relatively short lived. From medieval times various kinds of beds are mentioned in contemporary inventories—trussing beds, field beds, sparver and tent beds, truckle, trundle, or wheelbeds, which when not required were trundled under the large bed and were often occupied by servants in their masters' bedrooms, and dating from Stuart times the press bed. Tent beds, apparently with a tent-shaped or "waggon-tilt" canopy, were still used in the eighteenth century. When George III and Queen Charlotte visited Wilton in 1779, it is recorded in the 10th Earl of Pembroke's letters how at great trouble and expense they borrowed a State bed worthy to accommodate their Majesties, but "When they arrived they brought a snug double tent bed, had it put up in the Colonnade Room where the State bed was already placed. . . ." It appears according to a 1649 record that field beds were often "set in a chamber corner or under a cant roof." A plate in Hepplewhite's *Guide* entitled, "Sweeps for Field Bed Tops," represents five designs with arched testers; the light and plain wood framework, which in several examples was hinged, was to be secured to the tops of the four tall posts.

Press beds designed to fit into a cupboard or wardrobe continued to be made in the eighteenth century. Hepplewhite in the *Guide* draws attention to a wardrobe which resembles a press bed and could be easily adapted by making "the door to turn up all in one piece and form a tester." A description of such a bed occurs in an account of 1710; it notes that the legs fold up under the bed and "the mattress is tied down in several places, so as not to fall off when the bed is being put up; but the pillows and bolsters are first laid behind it. . . . The curtain is attached to the door and rises with it when the door is raised. . . ." Nor does the account overlook its advantages: "It takes up no space in a room, is no inconvenience, and yet does duty as well as the finest bedstead and can moreover be very simply made." Chairs and settees that could be converted into daybeds and beds respectively were also made. An extant example of this kind of dual-purpose furniture was made for Nostell Priory probably by Chippendale's firm in the 1750s. Designed as a chair-back settee, the back comprises two chair backs, the width being four feet. When the leather seat cushion is removed, a double-fold wood framework can be extended outward from its position inside the seat of the settee

348

and is supported by trestle legs that fold up under it. The extending length is more than six feet.

Before leaving the subject of beds, a word about cradles, which are of early origin. The earliest type represented in pre-Conquest illuminated manuscripts was made on the same primitive principle as contemporary chests—a log split transversely and hollowed out; the natural roundness of the wood rendered the use of rockers unnecessary. Cradles, in most instances hooded, provided with turned rocking posts and mounted on rockers and cradles suspended on posts, that is, the swinging type, are represented in medieval manuscripts and have always been the two principal forms. The children of royalty and great noblemen were often provided with two cradles, one a Cradle of Estate reproducing in miniature the magnificence of State beds, the other a cradle for ordinary use. Sheraton in his *Cabinet Dictionary* represents the swinging type hung between two posts and describes it as a "Swinging Crib Bed." The cradle is swung by means of a clock spring; the device was to be improved in the near future so that the cradle would swing by itself an hour and a half.

As far as the types of furniture are concerned, the neo-classic designers had nothing much to add to the wide selection of models which Chippendale and his contemporaries had introduced to the public. Sheraton gave considerable prominence to his designs for work tables, which were introduced as a specialized variety in the second half of the eighteenth century and had not been represented by Chippendale. They are like the French models, generally small, delicate, and more elegant than useful, and in the majority of cases serve more than one purpose. Sheraton illustrated one model with a screen that pulls up at the back; it was "intended for a lady to write or work at near the fire, the screen part behind securing her face from its injuries." Another model is of particular interest because of its lyre-form end supports, a structural feature borrowed no doubt from France, where lyre-shaped supports frequently with brass wire let in to form the strings were favored by the *ébéniste* Georges Jacob, especially for work tables. Sheraton also mounts each lyre support on two splayed feet and joins the two end supports with a shaped shelf which, he writes, "may be used in place of a stretcher." In the early nineteenth century, lyre-form supports were in high fashion for various kinds of tables, not only in France and England but also in America, where they are closely associated with the work of Duncan Phyfe. As a variation of lyre-form supports, Sheraton introduces in his design for a "French Work Table" shaped end supports on splayed feet. Especially favored as a work table was the pouch variety distinguished by a work bag that is suspended to a frame which draws forward; the ladies kept their needlework in the bag, which eliminated the problem of trying to remember where they had put it. In the early nineteenth century the pouch variety was frequently pro-

349

ABOVE LEFT: Inlaid satinwood work table of the *tricoteuse* type, (c. 1795), based on a design for a French work table in Sheraton's *Drawing Book*, 1791–94. It has shaped end supports on splayed feet. *Courtesy Frank Partridge, Inc., New York. Photo Albert Waks.* (*See page 349.*) ABOVE RIGHT: Satinwood work table with mahogany stringing lines (c. 1790). It is fitted with a rising screen, writing drawer, and pouch bag; the top is hinged in front to rise up in order to afford convenience for writing. *Courtesy Victoria and Albert Museum.* (*See page 349.*) LEFT: Inlaid game table with a sliding and reversible top (c. 1795). The top reversed and open shows chess and backgammon boards. The frieze is designed with two mock drawers and one transverse working drawer. There are splayed trestle supports. *Courtesy Parke-Bernet, from the collection of Mrs. Harrison Williams.* OPPOSITE: Satinwood commode with bandings of rosewood and polychrome painted decoration (c. 1790). Garlands of flowers and ovals filled with flowers enjoyed a great vogue at this time. *Courtesy Victoria and Albert Museum.*

vided with a chess board; both illustrations of the pouch type given by Sheraton in his *Cabinet Dictionary* are so equipped.

Sheraton's designs for pier tables are exceedingly fragile, since they are, he writes, "merely for ornament under glass, they are generally made very light." The tops are occasionally of marble, but most commonly veneered in satinwood richly japanned, while the frames are gold or white and burnished gold. Delicate stretchers very often in the shape of horizontal concave curves adorned in the middle with a motif which is most frequently an antique urn are a feature of these tables. Sheraton heartily recommended the stretchers, for "they take off the long appearance of the legs, and make the under part appear more furnished; besides they afford an opportunity of fixing a vase or a basket of flowers, which, with their reflection, when there is a looking glass behind, produces a brilliant effect." Sheraton disclaims any useful purpose for commodes, observing that they are as pier tables merely for ornament. He represents a commode having in the center of the frieze a tablet which he writes is "made of an exquisite composition in imitation of statuary marble. These are to be had, of any figure, or on any subject at Mr. Wedgwood's, near Soho Square. They are let in the wood and project a little forward." However, far more characteristic were commodes ornamented with painted decoration, chiefly flowers—flowers in baskets, in vases, arranged in garlands, etc.

Sheraton regarded mahogany as the most suitable wood for his large library tables of the pedestal type. He writes, "The ornaments should be carved or inlaid what little there is; japanned ornaments are not suitable as these tables frequently meet with somewhat harsh usage." Sheraton gave the subject of writing furniture designed for feminine use considerable attention. "The style of finishing them," he writes, "is neat, and rather elegant. They are frequently made of satinwood, cross-banded, japanned and the top lined with green leather." Of the several new forms of writing tables that were introduced about this time, probably the best known is the Carlton House type, distinguished by a low recessed superstructure, fitted with small drawers, which returns with curved ramps at each end of the table. Sheraton describes it as a "Lady's Drawing and Writing

OPPOSITE ABOVE: Satinwood lady's drawing table with painted decoration in polychrome (c. 1795). The top centers a lift-up reading stand with two hinged flaps, painted with two oval medallions of bouquets of garden flowers. The central section rises on an easel support and opens to disclose a painted flower-filled basket hung from emerald green drapery swags. *Courtesy Parke-Bernet, from the collection of Walter P. Chrysler Jr.* BELOW LEFT: Detail of lady's drawing table. ABOVE: Satinwood Carlton House writing table, decorated with marquetry (c. 1795). It has square tapered legs, brass toe caps. It closely resembles a design (1793) in the Appendix to Sheraton's *Drawing Book*, 1791–94, which also has inlaid decoration. *Courtesy Parke-Bernet, from the collection of Emily Coddington Williams.*

Table." His explanatory notes state that it "is finished neatly, either in mahogany or satinwood, with a brass rim [gallery] round the top part [which is constructed separately]. The rising desk in the middle may be made to slide forward, which will serve to draw upon; and the small drawers before the coves at each end will be found convenient for colors. The drawer in the middle of the front [center frieze drawer] serves to put the drawings in."

The sense of elegance in the designs for bookcases, secretary bookcases, and like pieces was carried still further by Sheraton in his *Drawing Book*. Of a secretary and bookcase having two glazed doors in the upper part and a writing drawer above two cupboard doors enclosing clothespress shelves in the lower part (Plate 28), he writes that "the design is intended to be executed in satinwood and the ornaments japanned. It may, however, be done in mahogany and in place of the ornaments in the friezes, flutes may be substituted. The pediment is simply a segment of a circle and it may be cut in the form of a fan with leaves in the center. The vase (above the pediment) may be omitted to reduce the work." The explanatory note continues that the tops of the pilasters on the bookcase doors are made to imitate Ionic capitals. It is mounted on straight tapered feet; while the veneered surface of the two cupboard doors is broken up into framed oval panels devoid of ornamentation. All the features noted

353

LEFT: Design for a secretary and bookcase (1791) from Sheraton's *Drawing Book*, plate 28. *Courtesy Cooper Union Museum.* (*See page 353.*) RIGHT: Mahogany and satinwood bookcase (c. 1795), corresponding with a design in the Appendix to Sheraton's *Drawing Book*, plate 39. Surmounting the pediment carved with a festooned urn is a delicate spray of acanthus foliage. The oblongs in the center of the glazing bars were intended for mirrors or painted decoration. *Courtesy Yale Gallery of Fine Arts, Mabel Brady Garvan Collection.*

in this piece are typical of the period. Like Hepplewhite, Sheraton paid special attention to his glazing bars, but unlike Hepplewhite he favored long and slender curved lines; elongated ovals, interlaced ovals, and segments of ovals were much used. He also liked an elongated diamond with straight or concave curving lines. In one model Sheraton notes that the doors may be glazed or finished without glass, by green silk curtains only, headed with festoons of drapery. The oval-shaped glazing bars in each door center an elongated diamond intended "to have glass inserted which has a pretty effect," apparently an innovation by Sheraton. The graceful patterns of the slender glazing bars from the time of Adam gave great beauty to this general class of furniture.

Besides the singular excellence of line and proportion that distinguishes so much of the late eighteenth-century furniture, practical cabinetmaking in such matters as carcase construction, dovetailing, and the elaboration of fitting reached its highest standard. Dressing tables, sideboards, library steps, washstands, and the like were often designed as combination pieces and so excellent as a rule was the finish of the cabinetwork that the most intricate mechanism still works perfectly. Late eighteenth-century designers, such as Hepplewhite, Shearer, and Sheraton, gave the general class of basin stands and washing stands considerable attention. In most cases they are skillfully constructed to disguise their real purpose; when closed they look like a chest of drawers or a table with a shallow cupboard portion. The advantage of this kind, writes Sheraton, "is that they may stand in a genteel room without giving offense to the eye." As a rule, those with doors or drawers down to the ground were mounted on bracket feet, either straight or the curving French bracket type. Corner washing stands both open and closed were much favored, while all kinds were very often designed as combination pieces. Sheraton illustrates and describes one of this type as a "Cylinder Wash Hand Table," Plate 53, having five rows of drawers below the cylinder top. "These are," writes Sheraton, "always made of mahogany, and have a cylinder to rise up to hide the washing apparatus, they look neat in any dressing room." The two top drawers are sham and contain the cylinder; the two bottom drawers are also sham and contain, Sheraton continues, "a bidet on the right near the front and a water drawer on the left near the back, so that when the two are pushed home they pass by each other. The drawer in the front, which appears partly out, runs above the bidet and the water-drawer. . . . The bidet drawer is sometimes made to take quite out, having four legs to rest on—— The end of the piece of work is cut out so that the feet can go in without being folded up. . . ." The basin has a plug hole at the bottom by which the water is conveyed off into the water drawer that is lined with lead. The cistern provided with a spigot is of course directly behind the wash basin and the top is hinged so that it can be easily filled with fresh water. There is also a mirror that rises up behind in the same manner as that of a shaving stand.

We have already mentioned that by the last quarter of the eighteenth century it was possible to cast a single piece of plate glass more than ninety inches high. Because of this improvement, toilet mirrors tall enough to reflect the entire person were introduced; they were called cheval, or horse dressing glasses, the name derived from the frame or horse on which they were suspended. The glass of these tall standing mirrors was supported by swivel screws which permitted the glass to "be turned back or forward to suit the person who dressed at them," or was raised and lowered by means of leaden weights "in the manner of a sash window" enclosed in the uprights or standards mounted on two splayed feet. Candle branches were often fitted to the standards. As for wall mirrors, the fa-

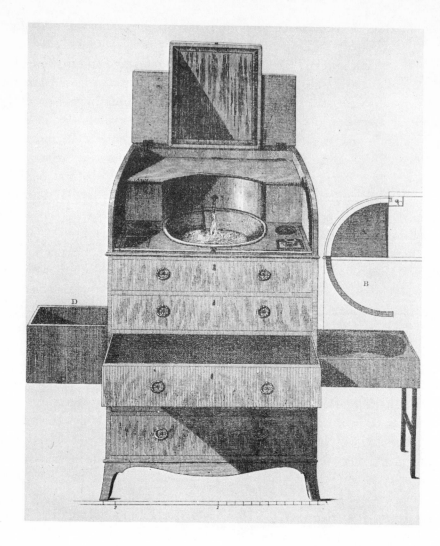

miliar Empire type of circular convex form was introduced from France around the close of the century. In most instances the cresting of these mirrors was in the form of an eagle displayed; while the deep concave border generally enclosed small gilt balls and an ebonized fillet was next to the glass. These convex wall mirrors were in such high favor that they were the only variety mentioned by Sheraton in the *Cabinet Dictionary*, where he writes that "the properties of such mirrors consist in their collecting the reflected rays into a point by which the perspective of the room in which they are suspended presents itself on the surface of the mirror and produces an agreeable effect." Sheraton continues that because of this feature and their adaptability as light holders they have become "universally fashionable."

Sheraton's later style may be seen in his second book, *The Cabinet Dictionary*, published in 1803. Of his last work, which he did not live to finish, entitled *The Cabinet-Maker, Upholsterer, and General Artist's Ency-*

OPPOSITE: Design for a cylinder wash hand table (1792) from Sheraton's *Drawing Book*, 1791–94, plate 53. *Courtesy Cooper Union Museum* (*See page 355.*) ABOVE LEFT: Satinwood cheval toilet mirror with polychrome painted decoration (c. 1790). (*See page 355.*) ABOVE RIGHT: Convex wall mirror of carved and gilt wood (c. 1800). *Courtesy Victoria and Albert Museum.*

clopaedia, one volume was published in 1805, the year before his death. Some of his later designs show a marked deviation from the severe rectangular forms represented in his first work, the *Drawing Book.* The change was by no means confined to Sheraton or to furniture designers, but covered the whole range of decoration and was in consequence of a widespread movement in which the imitation of the antique became more exacting. This change in taste, the so-called Regency style, which became current in England around 1800, is the subject of the following chapter, and since Sheraton in his *Cabinet Dictionary* introduced designs showing its influence, his later work will be considered as part of the Regency taste.

Regency

We have already witnessed in France that as the reign of Louis XVI drew near its catastrophic end the taste for the antique became more exacting. Many pieces belonging to the last years of Louis XVI's reign heralded the styles of the Directory and Empire. In England soon after the opening of the war with France in 1793, a revolution in taste based upon a closer and more intense classical revival also began to take place, in which the imitation of the antique was more than ever the supreme law. The attenuated linear designs by Adam and the severe rectangular forms represented in Sheraton's first book now yielded to a new and widespread attempt to imitate more accurately the exact forms of ancient art. Pieces no longer decorated with antique ornament, but copied from those the excavations of Pompeii had brought to light or disclosed from ancient vase paintings and bas-reliefs were sanctioned by fashion. In this manner the more ardent exponents of the new style believed that they had captured not only the beautiful spirit of antiquity, as Robert Adam had claimed, but the letter.

These new ideas that became current in England at the end of the century, sweeping over the whole field of decoration and furniture, belong to the so-called Regency style, which derived its name from the period when George, Prince of Wales, acted as Regent, 1811–20. In the beginning the style owed something to the French Directoire, as interpreted by Henry Holland, 1746–1806, whose designs for domestic decoration around the turn of the century are a remarkably impressive blend of Directoire and Greco-Roman details. From the early years of the nineteenth century, as a result of the researches into Greek antiquities by contemporary scholars, everyone was making pieces more and more Greek. Sheraton, capable of better things, was compelled by sheer force of circumstances to fall in line in his second book, *The Cabinet Dictionary* (1803), in which he repre-

Design for a Grecian dining table (1803) from Sheraton's *Cabinet Dictionary*, plate 47. *Courtesy Victoria and Albert Museum.*

sented designs for Grecian couches and sofas and even Grecian dining tables.

About the time of Holland's death in 1806, the style acquired an archaeological bias and a marked eclectic character, its principles being drawn from three ancient civilizations—Egyptian, Greek, and Roman; an effect of "Grecian severity" became the rule. Inspired by the ideal set before them by Percier and Fontaine in their *Recueil de décorations intérieures,* it became the avowed aim of the new school of designers to reproduce the exact forms of antiquity where precedents existed, such as for chairs, couches, tripods, and candelabra; and for pieces unknown to the ancients, by far the great majority, to furnish designs which should be fully congruous in character. Indeed, designers tended to become students of archaeology. Thomas Hope, the author of *Household Furniture and Interior Decoration* (1807), even felt obliged to vindicate some of his designs by indicating the classical prototypes on which they were based; of a table he writes, "It is supported by chimeras in bronze, similar to some limbs of ideal animals which have been found among the remains of Pompeii. . . ." Hope's influence consisted in the reproduction of Roman types of furniture and the adaptation of Roman motifs, and for making every form of contemporary furniture consonant with Roman tradition. Some of Hope's designs, carried out for his country house, Deepdene, Surrey, and which are illustrated in his *Household Furniture,* represent

359

ABOVE LEFT: Carved mahogany work table (c. 1810). The figure of Atlas, half-kneeling on a triangular base, supports on his shoulders and upraised arms a huge globe. The hinged cover opens to disclose an interior equipped for needlework; beneath the semi-circular tray is a work pouch and drawers. *Courtesy Parke-Bernet, from the collection of Walter P. Chrysler. (See page 359.)* ABOVE RIGHT: Carved mahogany stand, supported by chimeras, one of a pair (c. 1810); from a design in Thomas Hope's *Household Furniture*, plate 15, Fig. 1. (*See page 359.*) BELOW: Mahogany table inlaid with ebony and silver (c. 1810). Thomas Hope designed it for his house, Deepdene; it corresponds with plate 39 in his *Household Furniture. Courtesy Victoria and Albert Museum.*

the style in its more rational form, and show that he possessed a certain gift for adapting classical elements to the use of furniture, though in a much smaller degree than his friend Percier, the French architect and designer. The wilder extravagances of the style are illustrated in Sheraton's incomplete *Cabinet-Maker's Encyclopaedia* (1805) and George Smith's work entitled, *A Collection of Designs for Household Furniture and Interior Decoration* (1808).

Essentially the majority of designs belonging to this later phase show a somewhat disarranged imagination, while everywhere a disordered taste for symbolism ran wild. Extravagances half-archaeological and half-symbolic often exploited in the most incongruous positions had their counterparts in the French Directoire, but when the Imperial era arrived in France under the aegis of Percier and Fontaine these exaggerations were dropped and only the essence of the novelties retained. The Empire style had a symbolical meaning that was highly appropriate to Imperial France, but having no similar significance in England it simply could not be translated into good English. The novelties were never disciplined nor given sufficient uniformity in England to become a finished style. But, in any case, how could a style so archaeological ever have found favor with the English public? How could it ever have been rendered intelligible in ordinary households? Furniture as depicted by Hope could have but little vogue. In fact, Hope's *Household Furniture* was not well received by the critics, and a writer in the Edinburgh *Review*, 1807, criticizes the articles in general "as too massive and ponderous to be commodious for general use" and concludes by asking whether it is possible for pieces like those in the Egyptian room at Deepdene "to come into general use as articles of furniture till aldermen wear armour." In brief, there was no harmony between it and the manners of the time. This strange archaeological style was preserved in a haphazard fashion into the age of Victoria for want of knowing what to put in its place; there was, however, an increasing tendency toward coarseness of detail and clumsiness of proportion.

Apart from the archaeological style based upon a vernacular interpretation of classical ideals and the French Empire, which is the mainstream of Regency, the period included tributaries that contributed their quota to its miscellaneous character. English cabinetmakers did not entirely repudiate eighteenth-century English classicism, and some of them continued to produce furniture in this taste. In this respect they were not unlike French cabinetmakers working outside of Paris who went on quietly with the Louis XVI style. At this time some English designers once again renewed their interest in Chinese as well as Gothic art; the former no doubt owed something to the influence of the Prince of Wales. There was the Chinese drawing-room at Carlton House, illustrated by

Sheraton in his *Drawing Book,* as well as later alterations made at Brighton Pavilion. Characteristic of this taste were light chairs and tables made of soft wood, japanned and decorated with *chinoiseries;* others had their framework bamboo-turned. As a result of a growing romantic tendency, the Gothic style was again studied, having shown itself earlier in England in the 1750s. George Smith in his *Household Furniture,* in addition to designs "studied from the best examples of the Egyptian, Greek and Roman styles," also included specimens in the Gothic taste. A later publication brought out by Smith in 1826 represented Egyptian, Greek, Roman, Etruscan, Gothic, and Louis XIV styles, which also unconsciously shows how empty of invention the era had become—an unhappy omen for Victoria's reign.

The revived Gothic was partly inspired by the literary fashion set by Sir Walter Scott, which encouraged a considerable amount of domestic building in the "Gothic castle" style in the first quarter of the nineteenth century. Scott's baronial mansion, Abbotsford, which took more than a decade to build, was completed in 1824, with its ideas of medieval furniture, was typical of the taste and exerted wide influence. At this time the Gothic revival in furniture consisted largely in the introduction of an excessive amount of delicate and fanciful Gothic detail into structures that remained classical in form. The pieces were a travesty on medieval

OPPOSITE: Olivewood writing table, marked Wright and Mansfield, 104 Bond Street (c. 1810). It is decorated with an inlay of neo-classical motifs and Wedgwood plaques. *Courtesy Frank Partridge, Inc., New York. Photo Albert Waks. (See page 361.)* LEFT: Rosewood secretary mounted with gilt brass, labeled John McLean (c. 1810). It is provided with a fall-front writing drawer; the superstructure of brass shelves is frequently found at this time. *Courtesy Victoria and Albert Museum.*

furniture and presented a romantic fantasy with their interest toward the picturesque no less exotic than some of the *chinoiseries* originating in England in the preceding century. The early Victorians inherited the romantic Gothic along with their legacy of Regency classicism.

But to return to the mainstream of Regency, its archaeological character. One of the chief discoveries made by the new school of designers from their study of classical originals was that the Greeks and Romans had not limited themselves to purely rectilinear designs, but had freely used curves in their furniture, as in the typical Greek chair or *klismos* frequently represented in vase paintings. This chair with a very sloping back made of a broad crosspiece, very deep and fitting the shoulders and with graceful but strange legs which raked outward and curved like sabers (the so-called saber leg), was now copied by Sheraton and his contemporaries at the end of the eighteenth century. Sheraton also represented in his *Cabinet Dictionary* chairs with curving X-forms supports and armchairs with low backs round as a tower—ideas gleaned from classical models and made in France around 1790 by Georges Jacob from designs by David. The later Roman practice of enriching furniture with large-scale scrolls and volutes

363

was also imitated by the contemporary school of designers, as may be seen in chairs, couches, and sofas with scroll over backs. Sheraton's designs for Grecian couches with scroll over ends, which are an adaptation of the type associated with David's portrait of Madame Récamier, are most representative of Regency classicism. The couch was often designed with an armrest on one side occupying half the length. Equally characteristic is Sheraton's design for a Grecian sofa of lyre form distinguished by scroll over ends continuing the line of the seat rail. These three forms, the chair adapted from the Greek *klismos,* the lyre-form sofa, and the Grecian couch, characterized by sweeping curves and scrolls, are closely associated in America with the work of Duncan Phyfe.

Another distinguishing feature of Regency classicism is that designers once again enthusiastically adopted the Roman device of employing all kinds of animal forms as supports and terminals. The practice was reminiscent of the Palladian school of designers, but there can be no confusing the handling of them by the two schools. Realistically carved claw and paw feet, a medley of human and animal heads, sphinxes with upraised wings, dolphins, swans, chimeras, hocked animal legs, and eagles' heads characterized the new designs, while the ringed lion's mask and the lion monopodium composed of a head and chest continued by an enormous paw seemed to be everywhere.

At this period mahogany was supplemented by rosewood, while satinwood was still used, especially during the early years of the style. The pre-eminence of metal for decorating furniture established by the creators

364

OPPOSITE: Rosewood Grecian couch with brass inlay (c. 1810). It resembles with slight variations plate 49 (1803) in Sheraton's *Cabinet Dictionary*. The scrolled ends continue the line of the seat rail; outward curving legs finish in brass paw feet. *Courtesy Parke-Bernet.* LEFT: Rosewood library table with brass mounts (c. 1810); from a design in Thomas Hope's *Household Furniture*, plate 2. The gilt lion terminal legs rest on an incurvate quadrangular plinth. BELOW: Commode *à vantaux* veneered with rosewood (c. 1820). It is decorated with applied gilt brass female masks and an inlay of engraved brass, and mounted on carved gilt wood paw feet. *Courtesy Victoria and Albert Museum.* (See page 366.)

of the French Empire style was also observed in England, but English efforts in this direction were merely tentative and scarcely successful. Besides appliqués of paterae, water leaf, and other classical motifs, much of the carved detail was gilt or bronzed. Brass inlays of foliated patterns and stringing lines were in high favor. Of this practice Sheraton writes in his *Cabinet Dictionary* that "the present mode of inlaying with brass is more durable" than inlaying with wood "and looks well let into black woods of any kind." Silver was occasionally used as an inlay, alone or combined with wood; while inlaid stringing lines of wood were much in evidence. The graining or painting of furniture, in which a more costly wood is counterfeited in one of a less expensive kind, a process practiced in England since late in the sixteenth century, now came into wider use, being frequently recommended in nineteenth-century trade catalogues, as in the use of a soft wood grained to imitate rosewood.

Models for chairs provided by the earlier neo-classical designers were now considered hopelessly obsolete. The new school of designers was chiefly influenced by the more intense archaeological revival introduced in emulation of the French Directoire style. The variety of seats created at this time is much greater than might be imagined; in fact, the many attempts made at new combinations of lines for chairs is a distinctive feature of the epoch and some turned out to be real happy finds. Though broad simple lines were much sought after, they are by no means always straight; certain chairs have scarcely a single straight line in them. There is a noticeable emphasis on horizontal lines, while arms set high, giving a high-shouldered effect, is a prominent feature. In many instances the uprights of the chair back are given a pronounced scroll over, their profile forming a line the shape of an elongated S. Other backs are hollowed to shovel shape or into a half cylinder. Arms without armposts that end in huge open volutes resting directly on the tops of the legs were much favored, an arrangement that remained fashionable until the mid-nineteenth century. Front legs shaped in bold concave or saber curves are characteristic of the time; others are straight and tapering or perhaps formed as lion terminals. The back legs curved outward. Extant examples of Regency chairs by Thomas Chippendale, Jr. prove that he maintained the high standard of craftsmanship which had always distinguished his father's shop in St. Martin's Lane. In fact, all of his pieces are admirable examples of the less extravagant Regency taste.

Early in the nineteenth century, tables began to be affected by the classical revival based on the Empire style. The popular extension dining table was still usually made in sections which could be fastened together, each section being mounted on a turned pillar resting on four legs shaped in concave curves. Of this type, Sheraton writes, "The common useful dining tables are upon pillar and claws, generally four claws to each pillar,

366

ABOVE: Chair painted white and gold (c. 1800). The latticework splat supports an entablature ornamented with a musical trophy; it has saber front legs. *Courtesy Frank Partridge, Inc., New York. Photo Albert Waks.* ABOVE RIGHT: Chair decorated with a marquetry of various woods with brass stringing lines (c. 1795–1800). RIGHT: Mahogany armchair inlaid with brass (c. 1810–15). It has saber front legs. *Courtesy Victoria and Albert Museum.*

with brass casters. A dining table of this kind may be made any size, by having a sufficient quantity of pillar and claw parts, for between each of them is a loose flap, fixed by means of iron straps and buttons, so that they are easily taken off and put aside."

Social or wine tables were among the specialized varieties introduced toward the close of the eighteenth century. These were particularly suitable for the large consumption of liquor, typical of the period, that was indulged in when the meal was over. Wine was seldom served until after the food had been removed. Especially appropriate for this kind of protracted sitting and drinking were fireside tables of horseshoe form, averag-

368

OPPOSITE ABOVE: Mahogany pedestal dining table (c. 1800). It consists of a set of four pillar and claw tables with three leaves, of which three pillar and claw tables are shown. *Courtesy Parke-Bernet, from the collection of Mrs. Harrison Williams.* OPPOSITE BELOW: Mahogany wine table of horseshoe form (c. 1810). Two painted metal coasters are hinged to a brass rod. *Courtesy London Museum.* ABOVE: Satinwood sofa table inlaid with rosewood bandings and stringing lines (c. 1800–10). *Courtesy Frank Partridge, Inc., New York. Photo Albert Waks.*

ing around six feet in length; the two ends of the horseshoe-shaped top faced the fireplace. Because of the narrow surface of the top, the table was provided with metal coasters to hold the bottles, either hinged to a brass rod extending between the rear ends of the top or sliding in a well, while a net bag to hold biscuits was stretched across the open portion.

Another new form of table that became popular at the close of the century was the sofa table, distinguished by hinged drop leaves, supported in most cases by fly wooden brackets on the Pembroke principle. "They are," writes Sheraton, "used before a sofa and are generally made between four and six feet long and from twenty-two inches to two feet broad"; while the average height is about twenty-eight inches, the more practical type being equipped with frieze drawers. Their supports are typical of Regency classicism—a pillar and four claws, or shaped end supports, often of lyre form and occasionally of curving *X*-form mounted on splayed feet.

LEFT: Set of quartetto tables japanned black and gold (c. 1810). *Courtesy Parke-Bernet.* OPPOSITE ABOVE: Satin-wood commode (c. 1810). It has a bronze pierced gallery; the pilasters are mounted with bronze Egyptian heads and paw feet. *Courtesy Frank Partridge, Inc., New York. Photo Albert Waks.* (*See page 372.*) OPPOSITE BELOW: Low bookcase with pen and ink decoration on a black ground (early nineteenth century). The pilasters are mounted with Egyptian heads and feet of gilt bronze. *Courtesy Victoria and Albert Museum.* (*See page 372.*)

Nests of tables were also introduced toward the end of the eighteenth century. Sheraton in his *Cabinet Dictionary* describes them as quartetto tables, the proper number in a set being four; he writes that they are "a kind of work table made to draw out of each other and may be used separately and again inclosed within each other, when not wanted." On the other hand, George Smith in his *Household Furniture* finds them useful in drawing-rooms, where they "prevent the company from rising from their seats, when taking refreshments."

Since most of the Greek and Roman tables had round tops, many tables at this time are also round. For example, in addition to the popular and practical library and writing tables fitted below their large oblong tops with a row of frieze drawers, a considerable number were also made with revolving round or sometimes hexagonal or octagonal tops supported by a turned column resting on either four concave legs (the familiar pillar and claw support) or a solid base nearly always in the shape of a triangle with deeply concave sides mounted on paw feet. Tables of this type, now frequently called drum tables, were furnished with a row of frieze drawers; in others the frieze space was partitioned for books.

Pier tables with heavy rectangular tops and decorative center tables with round tops were greatly affected by the archaeological revival; animal sup-

ports, resting on thick bases, advocated by Hope were favored for these tables in the early nineteenth century. In distinct contrast were commodes and certain types of wall furniture, such as tall bookcases and cabinets, which often afforded excellent examples of the more ordinary Regency style, since to a large extent antique details, perhaps in the form of pilasters mounted with antique bronze heads, were simply applied to classical forms. For bookcases and the like brass trelliswork backed with silk curtains was often used in place of glazed doors. Of this practice, Smith writes that the silk backing "gives repose to the eye for nothing can distress the eye more than the sight of a countless number of books occupying one entire space." In high favor were low bookcases of elbow height. These were, according to Smith, "calculated to contain all the books that may be required in a sitting-room without reference to the library." They represented the current fashion in England for *meubles d'appui*, which enjoyed a great vogue in France. Also designed for the reception of books taken for present reading was the revolving bookcase with circular shelves. According to Ackermann's *Repository* for the year 1810, the problem of arranging books on a circular shelf was surmounted by inserting at regular intervals wedge-shaped blocks faced with a false book back or handled in any other decorative manner.

Mahogany revolving bookcase (c. 1800). It is fitted with compartment divisions in the form of triple-tooled leather book bindings, surmounting a drum table with two small drawers and a long double through drawer fitted at one end with a leather covered tablet on a ratchet support. *Courtesy Parke-Bernet, from the collection of Mrs. Charles E. F. McCann.*

372

American

It is easy to understand the common cultural ties existing between England and America when we realize that our ancestors were British subjects until they declared their independence in 1776. In fact, all the early settlers were of English origin except for a relatively small number, as the Dutch in New York, the Germans in southeastern Pennsylvania, and the Spanish in Florida. So it was only natural for the settlers and their descendants to look to England rather than to any other country for their forms of art. Of course we cannot disregard the role continental Europe played in molding American life and customs, but the vigor of English culture was such that it eclipsed and assimilated all other influences.

Although some settlers brought English furniture with them and later others imported it, most of the furniture was made in America by craftsmen who had learned the art of cabinetmaking in England before migrating to America, or by those who had learned the craft in America. The amount of furniture brought to America by the early settlers brings forth all kinds of estimates. This recalls Oliver Wendell Holmes' well-known lines about the Pilgrims embarking on the *Mayflower:*

> "With those that on the Mayflower came, a hundred souls or more,
>   Along with all the furniture to fill their new abodes,
>   To judge by what is still on hand, at least a hundred loads."

No matter how much furniture is supposed to have come over on the *Mayflower,* the earliest settlers cannot have brought much with them. They had to make what they needed, and using chiefly oak, maple, and pine they followed the contemporary styles, though necessarily simplified, as may be seen in Wallace Nutting's book *Furniture of the Pilgrim Century, 1620–1720.*

Whatever has been said about the salient features of English furniture styles essentially applies to American styles. The close similarity existing

373

between the work of these two countries can be largely attributed to the wide circulation of architectural publications, builders' handbooks, and pattern books of engraved ornament and designs for furniture. These pattern books were a great formative influence in the adoption of a new style in England and America; they created a high standard of knowledge among the craftsmen, making the eighteenth century a period of remarkable achievement. Copies of the various publications appeared in America often within a few years of their original issue in England. Extant examples of American cabinetwork show in many cases how closely these engraved plates with their plans and details were followed by American cabinetmakers. The rapidity and amount of success with which these fashions were absorbed in America were essentially about the same as in provincial England for cabinetwork representing the same social standards. This dependence on pattern books tended to give much of the important American cabinetwork a style common to all the colonies. Naturally many changes or variations occurred from the prevailing English styles according to the character of the region in which it was made. Through the medium of pattern books, American cabinetwork achieved a high level of design; American cabinetmakers produced many pieces notable for their formal and functional excellence and fine craftsmanship. In general, the work is more sober in design than its English counterparts, but this was due no doubt to an insufficient concentration of wealth in the big cities to purchase the more costly and ambitious pieces.

The early years in America were marked by the courageous struggle of the pioneers to convert a vast wilderness into a new home. There was the task of clearing the lands, sowing the crops, planting the vegetables, and raising cattle. Furniture in the earliest permanent homes was simply utilitarian. Gradually through their prodigious industry the colonists began to acquire wealth, for the land was rich in vast resources and they were slowly able to indulge in certain comforts and luxuries. Much of the wealth was concentrated in such cities as Boston, Newport, Philadelphia, and Charleston, which became important centers of colonial crafts.

Because America was settled by various classes of people, a noticeable difference existed in the kind and amount of furniture produced in the colonies. There were the poor Pilgrims and prosperous Puritans in New England, the affluent Dutch in New York, and the even more affluent Quakers in Pennsylvania and the wealthy settlers of the southern colonies. The Pilgrims made strong plain furniture, simple and crude in character, which was no doubt similar to the furniture they had used in England. On the other hand, the Pennsylvania colony from the time of William Penn fared much better and enjoyed many refinements which the colonists had been accustomed to in their former homes. Much of the fine furniture was made in that colony, and the leadership of Philadelphia has long been

Living room of the Paul Revere House in Boston. From left to right: maple and pine desk on frame (early eighteenth century); three-legged chair stained red (seventeenth century); oval-top gate-leg table of curly maple (c. 1700). *Courtesy the estate of Russell H. Kettell; from his book* Early American Rooms, 1650–1858.

recognized in cabinetwork from the days of William Penn to those of George Washington. The country house at Lansdowne of Governor John Penn, the Chews at Cliveden, the Logan family at Stenton, and the Powel house at 244 South 3rd Street, where many revolutionary patriots enjoyed the hospitality of Samuel Powel, Mayor of Philadelphia, 1770–80 (to mention but several), attest to the standard of refinement existing in this city. South of Philadelphia, the most flourishing province was Charleston, whose furniture eloquently reflects the cultivated taste of the plantation owners along the Ashley and Cooper rivers and in Charleston itself. The account book of the furniture maker Thomas Elfe, covering the years from 1768 to 1775, attests to the sophisticated life of that colony. Baltimore's role in American furniture history dates from the end of the eighteenth century. With Baltimore is connected the furniture of Annapolis, especially labeled pieces by John Shaw.

American furniture styles are frequently divided into two historical groups, colonial and federal. The former refers to the styles prevailing before and at the time of the Revolution, that is, through the Chippendale style. The latter denotes the styles in vogue after the federal government was established in 1789, or from Hepplewhite through American Empire. Essentially the earliest furniture brought to America or made in America was in the Early Jacobean style, and very little of it still exists; Late Jacobean pieces are slightly more plentiful. The types of furniture are few in number, comprising chiefly joined stools, chairs, tables of trestle and gate-leg construction, chests having their legs formed by the prolongation of stiles and sometimes fitted with one or more rows of drawers, and press and court cupboards. Turning was by far the favorite form of decoration; not only all the parts of chairs and the legs and stretchers of tables were turned, but balusters and spindles split down the center and oval bosses, often painted black to imitate expensive ebony, were glued on chests and

375

cupboards as ornament. Much carving was used for embellishing chests; in some instances the façade was entirely covered with carving, as for example the Hadley type of chest. The carving is generally flat and peasant-like rather than artistic; it was also frequently combined with applied ornament as on the so-called Connecticut chests. Of all the carved motifs, the tulip is the most common. It is endlessly repeated on Hadley chests and is also found on the two end panels of the front of a large class of Connecticut chests distinguished by a front and center panel carved with a pattern supposed to represent sunflowers. Typical early Pilgrim chairs are wainscot chairs with paneled backs, turned and spindled Brewster and Carver chairs, and slat-back chairs having turned members and horizontal slats in the back.

The William and Mary style, like all subsequent English styles, became fashionable in America about five to ten years after it was established in England. Hitherto the types of furniture in use in America had been few in number, but toward the close of the seventeenth century a greater variety of forms came into use. The new types were more convenient, more refined in form and decoration, as well as lighter than the heavy solid furniture that had previously been in common use. The era witnessed the introduction of new woods, notably walnut, and new processes of decoration such as veneering and japanning, while wood carving lost its primitive character and was lifted to a more artistic plane. The entire framework of chairs was still a popular subject for the turner's lathe, as well as the legs and stretchers of table. Upholstered furniture was not quite so scarce and wing chairs, called easy chairs in contemporary records, made their first appearance. The vogue for japanning reached America around 1700. Virtually all the japanned furniture done in a manner similar to that found in England with raised designs was made in New England, especially at Boston where at least as early as 1712 several cabinetmakers advertised in the newspapers that they specialized in japanning. There was the engraver and japanner Thomas Johnston, working around 1732–67, whose card states, "japanner at the Golden Lyon in Ann Street, Boston." Highboys were favorite pieces for japanned decoration.

The William and Mary period is notable for the introduction of highboys and lowboys, whose almost overnight popularity, destined to continue for more than a hundred years, had much to do with the rapid decline of chests after 1700. In fact their popularity retarded the development of chests of drawers, which were not too plentiful before the Chippendale period. Comfortable and convenient types of writing furniture were also introduced. There was the tall writing cabinet with a fall front and the slant-front bureau or desk over several rows of drawers which in the near future was to acquire an upper stage and become the secretary cabinet. Ball feet are typical at this time for these and other similar case pieces.

ABOVE: Late Jacobean two-drawer Hadley chest of oak (c. 1685) bearing the doubtfully valid inscription MARY ALLYNS CHISTT—CUTTE AND JOYNED BY NICH. DISBROWE. It is profusely carved with tulips and scrolling leafage. The two end panels of the upper frontal section are carved M and A respectively. BELOW: Late Jacobean two-drawer Connecticut sunflower chest of oak and pine (late seventeenth century). The three panels are carved with stylized tulips and sunflowers; the front is decorated with applied ebonized oval bosses, turned and split balusters and spindles. *Courtesy Parke-Bernet, from the collection of Luke Vincent Lockwood.*

ABOVE: William and Mary walnut lowboy (c. 1710). Its valanced frieze is provided with three drawers; the tapered legs with inverted cup-shaped cappings rest on a flat and scroll-shaped X-form stretcher mounted on ball feet. *Courtesy Wallace Nutting Collection, Wadsworth Atheneum, Hartford.* BELOW: William and Mary japanned highboy, made in New England, probably Boston (early eighteenth century). Its trumpet-turned legs rest on a flat, scroll-shaped stretcher mounted on globular feet. *Courtesy Metropolitan Museum of Art. Joseph Pulitzer Bequest Fund, 1940.* OPPOSITE LEFT: William and Mary Spanish-foot banister-back armchair of maple with pierced arched cresting, rush seat, block-and-turned front legs (c. 1700). *Courtesy Metropolitan Museum of Art. Gift of Mrs. Russell Sage, 1907. (See page 380.)* OPPOSITE RIGHT: Salamander type of slat-back armchair (eighteenth century). It is made of birch and is block-and-turned with rush seat. *Courtesy Metropolitan Museum of Art. Sylmaris Collection, Gift of George Coe Graves, 1930. (See page 380.)*

Gate-leg tables were in high favor; their stretchered, block-and-turned legs terminate in ball, or the so-called Spanish feet which scroll under.

The characteristic leg for this epoch is clearly seen on lowboys and highboys. It is a turned straight leg of baluster form beginning from a mushroom-shaped capping and tapering as it lowered to a flat, shaped stretcher, sometimes of X-form, which was inserted between the base of the leg and a globular foot; other tapered and turned legs are of the so-called trumpet variation, but they are less frequently found than those with the mushroom or inverted cup-shaped cappings. In comparing the two types of tapering legs, we find that both are trumpet turned; the lines of the former, with its mushroom-shaped cupping, are generally more pleasing. In chair design the height of the back is increased, and throughout the structure there is a noticeable emphasis on vertical lines. An arched cresting surmounting the top rail of the chair back is a typical William and Mary feature. Caning was more frequently used for the back panel and seat than upholstery. The turned parts of chairs were turned out of pieces of wood, square in section, and this square form was left untouched in places where the greatest strength was necessary, that is, at the joining points, resulting in what we term block-and-turned. In most cases this technical necessity resulted in a happy shape. Banister-back chairs having a back filled with vertical split banisters, or balusters were introduced

379

around 1700, and more often than not were given the popular arched cresting, solid or pierced. Turned banister-back and also slat-back chairs were commonly made of maple, a wood admirable for turning because it is strong and smooth. These chairs, provided with rush seats, remained popular for many years, especially in the country districts. Many are remarkable for their elaborate turnings and fine proportions. The slat back of the salamander type, with each slat consisting of two figures like notes of interrogation set one against the other lengthwise, is always a much sought-after model.

The William and Mary style was followed by the Queen Anne. From around 1710, certain features of the new style occasionally appeared in American furniture design and around 1720 it was fully established. The particular development of cabinetwork found in England in the three decades after the death of Queen Anne was seldom if ever found in America. Such phases as lion and satyr mask furniture were practically unknown. Furniture of a pronounced architectural character was also limited, though some examples of secretary cabinets displayed fluted pilasters or columns. The elaborate carved and gilt wood furniture in the taste of William Kent was unknown. The lack of this furniture is not difficult to explain, since in England it was found only in the great Palladian houses owned by the aristocracy. In America neither houses of such consequence nor such a class of society existed.

The Queen Anne style, which remained fashionable in America until the advent of Chippendale around 1755–60, brought to American furniture greater lightness and grace and a new concept of comfort; far greater attention was given to form and ornament. The typical Queen Anne splat-back chair provides a remarkable example of the newly awakened appreciation of form and comfort; the chair shaped to fit the body is one of the most graceful types ever made in America. Though carving was employed, beauty of surface was chiefly obtained by a careful choice of material and fine finish; an effective decorative use was made of figured burr walnut in veneers. The shell, sometimes a double shell, was the favorite motif; sunrise and sunburst carvings, such as on highboys and lowboys, were also favored and are often found on the same piece. The most fashionable wood was black walnut, a dark, close-grained wood admirable for fine carving and veneering. White walnut was not so important. Second only to walnut at this time were several kinds of maple, such as curly and bird's eye. Mahogany, which was introduced in the first quarter of the eighteenth century, was not employed on an extensive scale until around the middle of the century. Even after the virtues of mahogany were fully appreciated as a wood of great durability, rich color, and an ideal medium for carving, walnut was not entirely abandoned in some centers during the colonial period. For example, in Philadelphia numerous pieces in the fully devel-

LEFT: Queen Anne walnut chair with vase-shaped splat (c. 1745). The bracketed cabriole leg terminates in a cushioned club foot. It is one of a set originally owned by Edward Holyoke, president of Harvard College, 1737–69. *Courtesy Mabel Brady Garvan Collection, Yale University Art Gallery.* RIGHT: Queen Anne walnut settee with cabriole legs and trifid feet (c. 1735), made for Stenton, the home of James Logan at Germantown, Philadelphia. Described and illustrated in Wallace Nutting's *Furniture Treasury*, Fig. 1692: "Arm precisely the shape of that in the best wing chair. . . ." *Metropolitan Museum of Art. Rogers Fund, 1925.*

oped Chippendale style were made of walnut. Mahogany was destined to remain the most fashionable wood in America for almost a hundred years. In New England the use of cherry is frequent; no doubt its color made it a popular substitute for mahogany.

Queen Anne furniture can be recognized at first glance from that preceding it by the cabriole leg, which continued in fashion until it succumbed to the rectilinear neo-classic vogue around 1785. During this long period it figured predominantly on chairs and tables. In the Chippendale style, however, a straight quadrangular leg sometimes terminating in a plinth foot was often used as an alternative support. The principal terminal adopted for the cabriole leg on Queen Anne furniture was the Dutch pad or club foot in the form of a rounded and thickened disk extending forward from the leg and often having underneath the foot another disk or cushion called a shoe, serving as a protection to the foot. Other feet adopted include the trifid foot (also called drake or web foot), a kind of Dutch foot, but instead of being rounded, it has three points or toes, the snake foot so called because of its resemblance to the head of a snake and often used on tripod tables, the slipper foot an elongated Dutch foot and a Dutch grooved foot marked with several grooves. These feet, which all splay outward from the leg and usually have a "shoe," are primarily identified with Queen Anne cabinetwork. The ball-and-claw foot though it does occur on Queen Anne pieces, is essentially associated with the Chippendale style in America and is the principal terminal for the cabriole leg during that era, while the French whorl foot, as we have already seen, was used by Chippendale and Hepplewhite for certain "French" pieces. Before leaving the subject of feet, the bases of such Queen Anne case furniture as chests of drawers, chests-on-chests, secretary cabinets, and cupboards are mounted in most instances on straight bracket feet having straight corner edges. As in England, so in America, this type of bracket foot continued to be used to some degree throughout the eighteenth century. Numerous pieces represented in Hepplewhite's *Guide* are given straight bracket feet as an alternative to the then more fashionable French bracket foot having a corner edge curving slightly outward. As for Chippendale, the ogee bracket foot characterized by a corner edge in the form of a cyma curve with the convex curve at the top, or brackets in the form of very short cabriole legs, terminating in ball-and-claw feet, are typical for this general class of case furniture.

Throughout the Queen Anne period, many fine chairs, highboys, lowboys which served as toilet tables, all kinds of tables—rectangular tray-top tea tables, sideboard tables often with marble tops, card tables having a top one half of which folded over the other half, dining tables with drop leaves supported on swing legs, and corner tables sometimes called handkerchief tables with triangular tops—swinging toilet mirrors on box stands, tall chests of drawers mounted on frames, tester beds, and other pieces were made in America. Standing somewhat apart from the main evolution of chairs are Windsor chairs, the most notable of rustic varieties, which were first made in Philadelphia in the early part of the eighteenth century. Philadelphia Windsors were always highly esteemed; "Windsor chairs from Philadelphia" were frequently advertised in colonial newspapers. An advertisement in a Charleston newspaper (1784) inserted by Andrew Redmond mentions that he made "Philadelphia Windsor chairs, either armed or unarmed, as neat as any imported, and much better stuff." Corner cupboards, most of them movable, made their appearance around 1725 and are among the most numerous of the larger pieces; while chests-on-chests, a stately class of pieces, appeared first toward the end of the Queen Anne and continued through the Chippendale period.

The Chippendale style was in vogue in America from around 1755 to 1785 and came into full expression around 1760. It continued in fashion in America for some time after it was superseded in England by the neo-classic style of Adam, which had little effect in America until around

Three-back Windsor having a low back, intermediate hoop back, and comb cresting, from New England (eighteenth century). Described and illustrated in Wallace Nutting's *Furniture Treasury*, Fig. 2667: "Rare, Three Back. Seven spindles running through the three backs, all without bending." *Courtesy Parke-Bernet, from the collection of J. Stogdell Stokes.* BELOW: Drawing room of the Powel House in Philadelphia. From left to right: mahogany wing chair, Chippendale style from Philadelphia (c. 1770); tilt-top table, Chippendale style from Philadelphia (1760–75): portrait of Mrs. Margaret Willing Hare by Peale; pair of carved and gilt mirrors, Chinese Chippendale style from England (c. 1760); mahogany wing chair, Chippendale style from Philadelphia (c. 1770). *Courtesy the estate of Russell H. Kettell; from his book,* Early American Rooms, 1650–1858.

1785 when the Hepplewhite style became the prevailing fashion. Broadly speaking, in the Chippendale period the features of the Queen Anne style were retained, but a considerable amount of carved rococo ornament and to a much less degree Chinese and Gothic details were grafted on mid-eighteenth century American forms. Fine materials and consummate workmanship in conjunction with thoughtful and often masterly designs made the output of cabinetmakers working at such leading centers as Boston, Newport, New York, and Philadelphia during the Chippendale period of outstanding excellence and enduring merit.

In Philadelphia, the undisputed center of furniture making before the Revolution, the Chippendale style reached the acme of colonial achievement. The Philadelphia Chippendale style of highboys and lowboys, which have no counterpart in any other country, with their fully developed carvings mark the apogee of mahogany carving in America and are unsurpassed for their wealth of variety and elaboration in our country. Es-

Beng Randolph
Cabinet Maker
at the Golden Eagle in Chesnut Street
Between third and fourth Streets,
PHILADELPHIA,
Makes all Sorts of   Cabinet & Chair work
Likewise Carving Gilding &c   Performed in the Chinese
and Modern   Tastes

OPPOSITE: Philadelphia-style mahogany highboy (c. 1765–80). A scrolled pediment terminates in rosettes and centers a pierced cartouche. Quarter columns enrich the stiles. The
cabriole legs end in ball-and-claw feet. *Courtesy Winterthur Museum.* (*See page 386.*)
ABOVE: Benjamin Randolph's trade card, showing thirteen pieces of Chippendale-style
furniture; engraving by J. Smithers of Philadelphia (c. 1770). *Courtesy Library of Philadelphia. Philadelphia Museum of Art Photo.* (*See page 387.*)

sentially Philadelphia-style highboys are more richly carved models of the scrolled and in most cases bonnet-topped or hooded highboys. For example, the inner ends of the scrolled or swan-neck pediment terminate in rosettes; on the acroter is a light and graceful ornament, perhaps a pierced flame or cartouche, while finials surmount the two front corners. Beneath the elaborate cornice molding are spiritedly carved rococo vines and tendrils very often centering a carved shell; the stiles are enriched with quarter round fluted columns. The lower portion of the highboy, which is essentially similar to a lowboy, has centered in the lower row of drawers a shell flanked by rococo foliage; the gracefully valanced apron is enriched with carving and the cabriole legs with their realistically carved ball-and-claw terminals are richly carved with acanthus foliage.

Prominent among the many craftsmen working in the Philadelphia school were Thomas Affleck, who worked for Governor Penn at Lansdowne and

at his Sixth Street house, William Savery, Benjamin Randolph, credited
with the six famous sample chairs, of which one was a wing chair, Jonathan
Gostelowe, James Gillingham, Thomas Tufft, and John Folwell, who is
noted for making the case for the orrery by David Rittenhouse.

In the flourishing seaport of Newport a group of cabinetmakers unparalleled in the history of American furniture were the Townsends and Goddards, twenty in all, spanning three generations, closely related by inter-
marriage as well as by standards of excellence in craftsmanship. Their
technical skill has long been acknowledged in the singular block-front and
shell carved pieces, as well as in many notable examples of chairs, tables,
and clock cases. Block front reached its full development in America and is
no doubt the most distinctive contribution of American cabinetmakers to
furniture forms made of mahogany. Some pieces are plain block, but of
far greater interest are those carved with shells, the middle shell being

concave and flanked by convex shells. Block fronts occur on chests of drawers, chests-on-chests, secretary cabinets with slant fronts, kneehole writing tables or toilet tables and slant-front bureaux or desks. Of course the Townsends and Goddards were not the only makers of block-front pieces; many were made by other cabinetmakers in various parts of New England, but those with the strongest feeling of beauty are attributed to the Newport school.

Before leaving Chippendale, a word or two about several new forms and changes in some not so new ones. Of the new types introduced at this time, none were destined to enjoy greater popularity than the carved tripod tea tables with round tops. Of these the most highly esteemed are the pie-crust models with tilting and usually revolving circular tops, their outer edge skillfully carved in a series of curves. There were also china tables with rectangular tops and four legs and breakfast tables distinguished by hinged drop leaves supported on fly wooden brackets of the Pembroke principle. At this time chests of drawers were often given serpentine or reverse serpentine (also called ox-bow) fronts; slant-front bureaux or desks and secretary cabinets with slant fronts were in high favor and were also frequently serpentine-fronted. As for upholstered furniture, settees became more plentiful. American cabinetmakers produced many handsome settees with graceful serpentine-arched backs and outscrolled sides of the same height as the backs.

We have already seen in Europe how around 1760 the rococo gradually gave way to a newly awakened enthusiasm for classical design evoked by the discoveries at Pompeii and Herculaneum. In America the federal period marks the return to classicism. The first of the neo-classical styles to be embraced by American cabinetmakers was the Hepplewhite style, which remained in vogue until around 1800. This was to be followed by the Sheraton, Directoire, and American Empire respectively. There was in America as in England an overlapping and at times even an interlacing of the styles. This is especially true in certain Hepplewhite and Sheraton pieces such as sideboards in which the two styles can be so similar that it is difficult if not impossible to determine whether the article should be classified in the style of one or the other. Both styles employ straight tapered legs. Square legs frequently terminating in a spade foot are more closely associated with Hepplewhite, whereas legs turned round and reeded distinguish Sheraton pieces. Of course, projecting columns placed at the corners of a piece of furniture are identifiable only with Sheraton. This was one of Sheraton's favorite devices and he employed it on all types of furniture, even in tables, continuing the legs upward to the table top resulting in the distinctive outset rounded corners.

The Hepplewhite style as represented in American furniture is simple, rational, and elegant. In chairs, heart- and shield-shaped backs are par-

ABOVE: Chippendale mahogany settee with a serpentine back and outscrolled ends of the same height as the back, from Philadelphia (c. 1770). It has cabriole legs and ball-and-claw feet. *Courtesy Philadelphia Museum of Art.* ABOVE LEFT: Sheraton bow-front small sideboard of inlaid mahogany and satinwood, from Salem, Massachusetts (c. 1810). It illustrates one of Sheraton's favorite devices: colonnettes placed at the corners extend the entire height. *Courtesy Parke-Bernet, from the collection of J. A. Haskell.* ABOVE RIGHT: Sheraton bird's-eye maple work table, from New England (c. 1800). It is decorated with sprays of oak leaves and acorns painted in polychrome, and is provided with a frame for a work bag. The projecting corners above the ringed-turned three-quarter round stiles which continue to the turned and tapering legs is a distinctive Sheraton design feature. *Courtesy Parke-Bernet, from the collection of Luke Vincent Lockwood.* RIGHT: Hepplewhite shield-back mahogany armchair, with carving attributed to Samuel McIntire, from Salem, Massachusetts (c. 1795). It has quadrangular tapering legs and spade feet. The splat closely resembles a design in Hepplewhite's *Guide,* first edition, plate 2. *Courtesy Winterthur Museum.*

Hepplewhite serpentine-front sideboard of inlaid mahogany with original knife boxes, from New York (c. 1790–1800). It was presented by Chancellor Robert Livingston of New York (1746–1813) to Robert Fulton and his bride, a daughter of Walter Livingston, as a wedding gift. *Courtesy John S. Walton.* OPPOSITE ABOVE: Hepplewhite inlaid mahogany chest of drawers, labeled by Michael Allison (flourished 1800–23), from New York (c. 1800). A valanced base curves into French bracket feet. The top drawer centers an inlaid design. OPPOSITE BELOW: Detail showing of inlaid design. *Courtesy Metropolitan Museum of Art. Sylmaris Collection, Gift of George Coe Graves, 1931.*

ticularly associated with Hepplewhite. Upholstered settees, wing chairs, field beds with arched testers, shield-shaped toilet mirrors on box stands, sideboards, dining tables in two or more parts, Pembroke and card tables, secretary cabinets now frequently having a fall-front writing drawer in place of a slant-front lid, and serpentine or bow-front chests of drawers mounted on a valanced base curving into French bracket feet (a prime favorite base and feet at this time for all kinds of case pieces) are among the principal articles found in America in the Hepplewhite style.

Frequently inlaid on such pieces as desks and chests of drawers is an oval medallion enclosing a design of the American eagle, a popular patriotic design in the early days of the United States of America, which became the national emblem shortly after the adoption of the Constitution

in 1788. Not only was it inlaid on many articles, such as tables and desks, but it was also used as a carved ornament on mirrors and clocks. When used as inlaid decoration, the eagle often holds in its mouth a streamer on which appear a series of marks representing stars, or the stars are arranged in a chain-like manner above the eagle. Sometimes the stars indicate the number of states in the Union, but in some examples the number of stars is simply added to complete the design. Tambour desks distinguished by a low recessed superstructure equipped with sliding doors of tambour construction, the form no doubt inspired by the French *bonheur du jour,* are

among the most refined examples of late eighteenth-century cabinetwork. Extant examples labeled by John Seymour and Son, working in Boston, are notable.

The decoration of American pieces in the Hepplewhite style consisted chiefly of inlay and carving; the ornament, drawn from the classical repertory—festoons of husks or bellflowers, anthemion or honeysuckle, small rosettes or paterae—was employed with an admirable sense of fitness and carefully related to structural lines. Brilliant and expensive satinwood was favored for inlay in the finest late eighteenth-century pieces, while maple, holly, and tulip also figured in inlay work. Mahogany remained the king of woods. Veneering was of great importance, and many pieces such as chests of drawers relied entirely for their decorative effect on the rich beauty of contrasting veneers. Painted decoration, or japanning came into favor around 1790. Some cabinetmakers, especially in Baltimore, following the styles of Hepplewhite and Sheraton, employed this decorative medium with conspicuous success. Baltimore painted furniture of the Sheraton epoch is notable for its light graceful elegance. The painted decoration— landscapes with ruins, musical instruments, or floral compositions—is as refined as the carved or inlaid enrichment. Other means of decoration, which seemed limited in our country to Baltimore, were painted glass panels or plaques of classical figure subjects and flowers, especially bell- flowers, which were set into the frieze of tables, the doors of secretary cabinets, and the like.

OPPOSITE: Inlaid mahogany tambour desk, labeled by John Seymour and Son, Boston (1796–1805). The recessed superstructure is provided with two doors of tambour construction. It has quadrangular tapering legs. *Courtesy Winterthur Museum.* ABOVE: Sheraton mahogany secretary cabinet, from Baltimore (c. 1800). Inlaid with satinwood, holly, and ivory, it is inset with painted glass panels of classical figure subjects: Temperance and Justice adorn the two cabinet doors, left and right respectively. ABOVE RIGHT: Detail showing the painted glass oval panel enclosing the figure of Justice. *Courtesy Metropolitan Museum of Art. Fletcher Fund, 1934.* RIGHT: Sheraton mahogany armchair (c. 1800), attributed to Henry Connelly, Philadelphia cabinetmaker (1770–1826). The rectangular splat enclosing a lyre-shaped device closely resembles a design illustrated in Sheraton's *Drawing Book*, plate 36, Fig. 3. *Courtesy Parke-Bernet, from the collection of J. A. Haskell.* (See page 394.)

393

The Sheraton style, the final one to make its appearance in the eighteenth century, became increasingly popular in America after 1795. Every form of fashionable furniture from around 1795 to 1820 was made in the Sheraton style by Duncan Phyfe and other contemporary American cabinetmakers. In his *Drawing Book*, Sheraton showed a marked preference for rectangular forms, usually emphasizing vertical lines. Inlaid decoration was also favored on Sheraton pieces; inlaid ovals on the doors of sideboards and the like fulfilled their decorative purpose through their good proportions and skillful placing. The legs of Sheraton furniture depended almost exclusively on turnings; reeding was much used. "Reeding amongst cabinetmakers," writes Sheraton, "is a mode by which they ornament table legs, bed pillars. . . . It is much preferred to fluting or cabling in point of strength; and in look much superior to the latter, and almost equal to the former. . . ." Fine examples of reeding are found on chairs, settees, and legs of tables made by Duncan Phyfe and his contemporaries.

At this time one name stands out as a carver of great merit, the prominent architect and builder of Salem, Massachusetts, Samuel McIntire, 1757–1811. Though it is believed that he made a few pieces of furniture, he more often executed the carving on furniture made by others, such as the Sandersons, who were well-known Salem cabinetmakers. As for painted

394

OPPOSITE LEFT: Sheraton inlaid mahogany butler's sideboard (c. 1800). It has a fall-front drawer equipped as a desk in which the butler kept the accounts of his department in the household. *Courtesy Parke-Bernet, from the collection of George Horace Lorimer.* OPPOSITE RIGHT: Sheraton fancy chair, possibly by Thomas Ash, New York (c. 1820). It is painted red with pierced metal appliqués and gilt enrichments. *Courtesy Metropolitan Museum of Art. Rogers Fund, 1935.* LEFT: Directoire mahogany lyre-back chair, attributed to Duncan Phyfe, New York (c. 1815). The sweeping elongated S-shaped reeded uprights come to the top of the incurvate front legs; the lower portions of the legs are furred and end in lions' paws. *Courtesy Parke-Bernet, from the collection of J. A. Haskell.*

decoration, there is that large class of inexpensive open-back painted chairs with cane or rush seats, the so-called fancy chairs, probably the most popular painted chairs in America. The best of these were made from about 1800 in the Sheraton style; later they were made in the American Empire style until around 1845. Enriched with painted and, from around 1820, stenciled designs, the majority were painted black, while the decoration chiefly consisting of flowers and foliage was usually gilded. There are also the Hitchcock chairs made from around 1826 to 1843; almost always painted black, their polychrome and gilt decoration of fruit, flowers, and leaves possessed a singular lively and decorative quality.

The American Directoire style became current in America around 1805 and flourished for about ten or fifteen years. Its classical origin may be traced to the French Directoire, which was freely adapted in England by Sheraton in his *Cabinet Dictionary.* Thomas Hope also praised the new style in his book, *Household Furniture,* where we read: "Freedom now consolidated in France has restored the pure taste of the antique Greek for chairs." Representing the Greek Revival style in America is a chair of Grecian pattern, inspired by the Greek *klismos.* It has a back whose profile forms a line shaped like an elongated S, continuous with no visible break through the side rail up to the very top of the front saber or incurved legs—

ABOVE: Directoire mahogany lyre-form settee, purchased with a matching set of chairs by Henry McFarlan of New York City (1772–1830) from Duncan Phyfe (1818). It is richly carved with a drapery festoon. The elongated S-shaped reeded ends form a lyre: directly above the lion paw foot the leg is carved with a hairy shank. *Courtesy Parke-Bernet, from the collection of J. A. Haskell.* BELOW: Small Grecian couch of mahogany with an armrest, probably from the workshop of Duncan Phyfe, New York (c. 1810). It is carved and reeded, with outward curving reeded legs finishing in brass paw feet having casters attached. *Courtesy Parke-Bernet, from the collection of Norvin H. Green.* OPPOSITE: American water color drawing showing the shop and warehouse of Duncan Phyfe at Nos. 168–172 Fulton Street, New York (c. 1820). *Courtesy Metropolitan Museum of Art. Rogers Fund, 1932.*

one of the simplest, most elegant, and graceful chairs ever made in America. There is also the settee of lyre form with outward curving legs (sometimes called cornucopia legs) finished in brass paw feet having casters attached, and the Grecian couch, often with an armrest on one side extending more or less half the length, freely adapted from the one in David's studio made famous by the portrait of Madame Récamier.

The most celebrated exponent of American Directoire was the New York cabinetmaker Duncan Phyfe, 1768–1854, whose name soon will be or is now given to all fine furniture made from around 1800 to 1820 conforming to his refined, delicate taste, whether the pieces are in the prevailing Sheraton, Directoire, or Empire styles. Distinguished by excellent materials and craftsmanship, his pieces possess an elegant and graceful simplicity that appealed to the cultured public of his day as it appeals to us at the present time. Among the typical features of the Phyfe school are the fine lines of reeding, carved acanthus leafage on pillar and claw supports, realistically carved eagles, animalistic detail such as the hairy shanks on

Directoire mahogany chair with curving X-form supports and brass paw feet. It was purchased by the Pearsall family from Duncan Phyfe (c. 1810–15). *Courtesy Museum of the City of New York.* CENTER: Cartoon for silk damask (French, 1800–15). Fashionable decorative compositions were a source of inspiration for the stenciled designs ornamenting American cabinetwork. *Courtesy Cooper Union Museum.* BELOW: Empire mahogany couch with stenciled decoration, from New York (c. 1820–30). It has the popular cornucopia-shaped end ornamented with a cornucopia laden with fruit. *Courtesy Mabel Brady Garvan Collection, Yale University Art Gallery.*

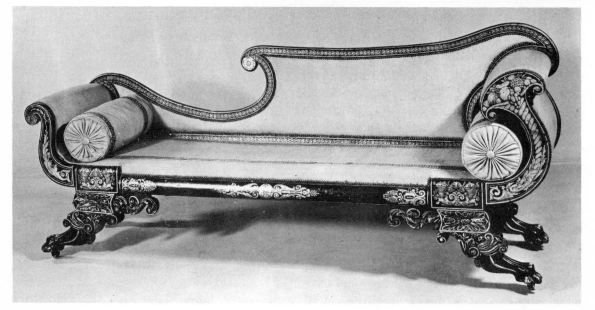

saber legs, lions' paws, elegant lyre standards and splats, carved waterleaf on saber legs, and occasionally curving X-form legs for chairs, stools, and settees, often listed in English catalogues as "Grecian cross-fronts."

In America the Empire style prevailed from around 1810–15 into the reign of Victoria. In fact, until the advent of the revived rococo toward the middle of the nineteenth century, there is little or nothing to distinguish the classical cabinetwork of the thirties from that of the forties. The principal difference is that from around 1830 the rapidly approaching decadence became evident in the coarsening quality of the work. An interest in Gothic detail was kindled in America in the thirties, and as late as the eighties Gothic was still represented in American furniture catalogues. Of course the Gothic Revival in America immediately brings to mind the architect Alexander J. Davis, 1803–92, who in the 1830s began to design Gothic country houses. But to return to the Empire style. American cabinetmakers enthusiastically adopted the Roman device of using all sorts of animal forms as terminals; the lion's paw was much in evidence on Empire sofas and couches where it was often combined with a boldly carved eagle-wing bracket and occasionally a foliage bracket. The Roman practice of enriching furniture with large-scale scrolls and volutes was also copied, such as for chairs, sofas, and couches. Decorative supports in the form of sculptured human figures were occasionally employed on console tables, such as those bearing the label of Charles Honoré Lannuier, a French *émigré* craftsman who was one of the leading exponents of the Empire style in New York. Gilded bronze mounts so characteristic of the French Empire were sometimes used; but much more often the carved wood ornament was gilded to simulate bronze. Round wood columns, a decorative feature of the French Empire, were in high favor in America and were often found on the façades of sideboards, wardrobes, chests of drawers, and similar pieces. The triumphant character, the essence of French Empire ornament, did not appeal to American cabinetmakers, who preferred other Empire motifs more appropriate to the young republic—eagles, fruits, flowers, foliage, and horns of plenty signifying the abundance of the new land.

Victorian furniture displayed no fresh source of inspiration, no unified style, but only a pattern of imitation drawn exclusively from the cult of past traditional styles. A notable amount of Victorian furniture, esteemed as examples of a local style, was produced from around 1840 to 1860 in the New York workshop of John Henry Belter. Typical of his work are ornate rosewood chairs and settees in the revived rococo taste with pronounced curves and elaborate openworked frames profusely carved with flowers, fruit, and foliage. In order to avoid shrinkage and to obtain strength, the wood was built up in several thin layers with the grain of the wood in every other layer running in the opposite direction, or laminated, as the method is called; it was then glued together and cut out.

LEFT: Revived rococo chairs of rose-wood made in the New York work-shop of John Henry Belter (c. 1850). The rear view shows his distinctive method of lamination. The chairs belong to a set of furniture used by Abraham Lincoln at Springfield, Illinois. *Courtesy Henry Ford Museum.* (*See page 399.*) BELOW: Parlor of the Roosevelt House, an accurate reconstruction of the original site of the birthplace of Theodore Roosevelt. From left to right: copper plate engraving after Raphael's *La Fornarina;* pair of upholstered rosewood sofas; gilded mantel glass. *Courtesy the estate of Russell H. Kettell, from his book,* Early American Rooms, 1650–1858. OPPOSITE: Carved walnut sideboard, made in Philadelphia by Daniel Pabst (c. 1868). Its prototype was the French Renaissance *dressoir. Courtesy Philadelphia Museum of Art.*

Of interest in the history of American furniture literature is a pattern book, *The Cabinet Maker's Assistant*, by John Hall, published in Baltimore in 1840. Arranged on forty-four plates containing 198 figures, it is believed to be the first completely illustrated furniture pattern book published in America. It is unfortunate that around 1840 the American Empire style had reached its lowest ebb, and, as one critic remarked, "This furniture shrieks its own agony to all observers." Numerous heavy, clumsy scrolls used as feet and massive curves characterize much of the work; apparently such distinguishing Empire features as round columns and animal feet were no longer in vogue, presaging the curvilinear fifties. In the sixties there was a predilection for Renaissance forms. The walnut cabinetwork made in the Philadelphia workshop of Daniel Pabst, such as sideboards inspired by French Renaissance *dressoirs* and center tables with tapering pillar legs joined with shaped stretchers reminiscent of Louis XIV, indicates this taste. Richly buttoned and tufted, draped, fringed, and corded upholstery work was still another feature. Some of these pieces with no trace of wood visible were masterpieces of the upholsterer's art. Moorish and Turkish chairs and divans figured in this taste.

Stylistic confusion continued throughout the century.

"As regards styles of furniture for various apartments in this day," write Williams and Jones in their book *Beautiful Homes* (1878), "it would appear almost fruitless to attempt the descriptions of varieties . . . there being such a vast number that a person about to furnish their house may chose ad infinitum ad libitum. . . . For dining-rooms, bed-chambers, sitting-rooms and halls, the quaintly simple English Gothic styles, after designs by Eastlake, are appropriate . . . in wood of various colors and kinds, embellished with illuminated designs in blue, scarlet and dead gold, arranged after medieval patterns. The curious oxidized rings, screws, hinges and locks give a massive appearance to some of the pieces. . . .

"The ebonized and highly ornamental furniture in imitation of the exquisite Japanese lacquered and inlaid work, Chinese papier-mâché, ormolu, gilded and painted fancy suites are highly esteemed for parlors and drawing-rooms, and can be so perfectly imitated that the great fear is, persons will be apt to overdo the matter and run into extremes that will tend rather to vulgar and pretentious display than to chaste and elegant adornment. . . .

"The 'cottage suites' of enamelled wood are exceedingly pretty, particularly for country houses or children's chambers. . . .

"The fancy for medieval furniture which is now the caprice of the wealthy people can be brought to impart a special beauty to the homesteads of the more humble housekeeper inasmuch as it is a style peculiarly adapted to the quaint rooms belonging to many of our country dwellings. . . . For parlors, drawing-rooms, or saloons, ebony (which may be so beautifully imitated) is the wood in special favor. . . . the ambitious housewife may have her entire parlor suite made of well-seasoned pine, after certain patterns which correspond with her peculiar taste, and proceed to ebonize and embellish after the true medieval style. . . ."

An interesting development dating from the 1880s, and for which we have cause to feel pride, is the work of the Associated Artists who followed the trail blazed by Morris and his followers. Launched as a guiding hand to improve taste in the arts of decoration and to restore an interest in them, it was a notable step forward. The group comprised Mrs. Candace Wheeler, 1827–1923; John La Farge, 1835–1910; Lockwood De Forest, 1850–1932; Samuel Coleman; and Louis Comfort Tiffany, 1848–1933. Mrs. Wheeler, in her book, *Yesterdays in a Busy Life,* 1918, relates how Mr. Tiffany approached her about the project. He said that he "was going into decorative art as a profession. Coleman and De Forest and I are going to make a combination for interior decoration of all sorts. I shall work out some ideas

I have in glass. De Forest is going to India to look up carved woods and Coleman will look after color and textiles. . . . It is the real thing you know; a business not a philanthropy or an amateur educational scheme. We are going after the money there is in art, but the art is there all the same. . . . you had better join us and take up embroidery and decorative needlework. . . ." We all know how Tiffany's wonderful experiments in glass iridescence were to culminate in the 1880s in the manufacture of favrile glass.

The painter and craftsman John La Farge, through his special talent as a lecturer and writer, exerted a fruitful influence on contemporary American thought. He made accessible and intelligible so much of the culture of Europe and the Far East that he had gleaned during his sojourn abroad in the late 1850s, where on different occasions he had come in contact with the Pre-Raphaelites. As early as 1863 he imported Japanese prints to America. In the 1860s La Farge turned to the design and manufacture of stained glass. His most brilliant contribution came in the 1870s when he introduced opaline glass. It is said that the idea for this glass, which was to make him famous, occurred to him when he noticed sunlight pouring through the cheap milky glass of a toothpowder receptacle. "La Farge's immediate effect upon his own generation," we read in Lewis Mumford's *The Brown Decades*, 1931, "was due to his aid in reawakening with H. H. Richardson the decorative arts."

He and the American architect Henry Hobson Richardson, 1838–86, were close friends and worked together on certain projects. Richardson also produced a considerable body of furniture designs, a fact seldom

Oak armchair designed by Henry Hobson Richardson for Woburn Library (1878). It embodies the honest methods of construction advocated by William Morris and his followers. *Courtesy Museum of Fine Arts, Boston.*

known by most of his admirers. Much of his furniture, however, was integral with the interior woodwork of the churches, libraries, and other public buildings he designed. Movable pieces still extant reveal their simple and sound construction; a great deal of these "golden oak horrors" are related to the contemporary furniture made by William Morris and his circle. Just as the past had been a source of inspiration but not of imitation to Morris, so it was to be with Richardson. This virtue is clearly expressed in Mrs. Schuyler Van Rensselaer's notable work on Henry Hobson Richardson published in 1888, where we read: "He studied precedents of ancient art with love and care but in no slavish indolatrous mood. He regarded them as starting points not patterns." Like Morris, Richardson was also trying to break the bonds of historicism, which permits us to examine his furniture as an aesthetic object, not as a social error.

A turn-of-the-century development—essentially an offshoot of the Arts and Crafts movement, of which we shall read much more in the following chapter—was the so-called Mission furniture, which in spite of its name was more American than Franciscan. This furniture, inspired by the rustic aspect of the English Cotswold group, featured severely straight and simple lines, vertical slat backs, "weathered oak" finish, and leather upholstery. In 1902 at the Turin Exhibition, where all Europe as well as America was represented, the furniture exhibited from England and America was obviously different from the fanciful extravagances of Art Nouveau and stemmed from the trail blazed by the Arts and Crafts movement. In the Grand Rapids *Record,* 1902, we read: "It is undeniable that the people of to-day desire their furniture plain, the popularity of the California and the so-called Mission effects furnishing abundant evidence of this taste."

Victorianism and the Arts and Crafts Movement

The Empire style and its English version, Regency, were the last consistent and recognizable styles before the flood gates were opened to a wave of imitative styles, each more ostentatious than the last, with which industrialism engulfed the luxury arts in the nineteenth century. From about 1830 practically all artistic industries had been subjected to the machine, and by the 1840s the marriage between the Industrial Revolution and the religious revival had been consummated and Victorianism was born. The arguments most frequently offered for rejecting Victorian furniture and furnishings are a general lowering of standards entailed in mass-production methods and a stylistic confusion destined to last throughout the century. The decline was a result of the breakup of the old order of society in the new age of industrialism. Such favorable attention as Victorian furniture is now receiving is chiefly directed to those outlandish and retrospectively picturesque pieces which seem by exaggeration to describe what we think of as Victorianism.

But apart from the routine everyday production and bizarre examples of the period it is essential before we judge Victorian design to have an understanding of the conflict destined to arise when mechanical mass production on a dominantly commercial scale laid its iron hands upon what had formerly been the exclusive province of the hand craftsman. The great industrial movement invaded the artistic world without any plan being made for its acknowledgment and accommodation. Because in England industrialism attained a high degree of importance at an early date, it was only natural that England was perhaps the first country in Europe to be concerned about the state of her arts and crafts in relationship to the influences now brought to bear on them. The story of adjustment to this new and perplexing turn of events—the theories and growth of principles to regulate the production of art manufacture

405

and design, the sincere and original expressions set forth by the designers who tried to determine the taste of the Victorian and subsequent Edwardian age—reveals that the entire period was characterized by amazing variety and vitality. It is on the work of these original designers, much of which was the result of a conscious revolt against popular taste, that this chapter chiefly concentrates; their degree of failure or success must be measured against the vastness of the enterprise. With the appearance of these individual reformers, a series of movements gradually crystallized which are significant in their own right, but when associated with the entire Modern movement acquire an even greater significance. It would be erroneous to consider these pioneers as working in complete isolation from public demand, or as wielding no influence on the standards of mass production. The far-reaching influence of Pugin and Morris has long been accepted, but it can equally be claimed that the furnishings of the period were in the end influenced not only by them but also by the work of others—whether it is the conventionalized arabesque of Owen Jones, the Anglo-Japanese taste of Godwin's furniture or Talbert's wallpaper, the sophisticated simplicity of Voysey or the Art Nouveau extravagances of Mackintosh.

Before considering the art theories and work of some of the leading individual reformers, it is helpful to look for a moment at the salient features of this epoch. The Great Exhibition of 1851, the first international exhibition ever held, affords an excellent understanding of Victorian tendencies and characteristics; even a cursory examination of the official catalogue of the Great Exhibition shows clearly the direction in which things were going. At first glance it becomes obvious that the copying and mixing of past styles of all countries and all centuries, accompanied by a straining after novelty in trivial details, is a striking characteristic. Not only did the Victorians freely copy and mix other styles, which was in itself to become a typical stylistic phenomenon, but their knowledge of them left much to be desired. Standing out in the general confusion is a marked emphasis on rich and elaborate carving of a sculpturesque quality; ornamental motifs from several styles were crammed together as if a horror existed for an empty space. The profusion of ornament was more often than not executed with a certain coarseness. The Victorians must have found it intoxicating to produce with the new tools the exuberant carving which, when done by hand on the costly models, was the hallmark of all fine furniture at this time. The typical Victorian dislike of plain surfaces is mirrored in the interiors, where everything is also packed and overcrowded with ornament, creating an atmosphere incredibly disturbing and very often of intolerable ugliness.

The age is distinguished by a strong pride in invention; the Victorians

"It would have been difficult to select any department of the Great Exhibition which could compare with Class XXVI (Furniture) as an evidence of our national prosperity. . . ." A contemporary comment on the Furniture Section. *Courtesy Victoria and Albert Museum.*

were delighted with their advance in scientific knowledge and technical skill. Thus, machine-carved ornament had many admirers, who considered it an achievement for the human mind to invent machinery that could do the same work as the hand in less than 100th of the time—and do it more perfectly. In many cases this pride in inventiveness supplanted aesthetic appreciation. For example, one could be proud of the imitation of one material by another—wood painted in imitation of mahogany, ebony, or marble; panels painted in imitation of inlaid wood; glass imitating various kinds of marble, semi-precious stones, lapis lazuli, and malachite that were used for decorative purposes, as in pietra dura. Frankly fascinated with these substitute materials, the originals of which were associated in the past only with wealth, the Victorians reveled in their display of commercial prosperity. (Ruskin branded imitative or substitute materials as well as machine-made ornament among his "deceits.")

There was a noticeable delight in new materials, the reproduction of things familiar in one material in another newly developed or unusual

407

Oak sideboard carved in the Renaissance style, designed by E. Prigot and made by Jackson and Graham, London. "The style of the work is a happy adaptation of the English revival of antique art most generally known under the name of Elizabethan. . . ." The Great Exhibition, 1851. *Courtesy Victoria and Albert Museum.* (*See page 406.*)

material—beds made of iron or brass, for example. At the fair, models of a brass rocking chair, armchair, and table were exhibited. Tubular metal furniture was already in existence; tables and chairs of hollow wrought-iron tubes were exhibited by Kitschelt of Vienna, who also exhibited a table cast in zinc. Though papier-mâché was far from being a new material, it was suddenly made available for furnishings on a large scale because of new patents. It was used not only for small pieces but even for chairs. Its use for furniture compares with our use of Bakelite and other plastics in furniture. Typical of the daring that characterized many of the exhibits was an entire piano of papier-mâché made by Jennens and Bettridge. A whole sideboard was made of gutta-percha, a material extracted from the sap of a Malayan tree. A new technique, though not a new material, was seen in a table by Michael Thonet of Vienna, the inventor of bentwood furniture, in which solid beechwood was bent under heat.

Because the Victorians loved novelty and gadgets, ingenious devices by which furniture was made to serve several purposes—from the functionally sound to the most futile—were improved and their number increased. There was a wide range of intelligently designed furniture for invalids, such as beds convertible into armchairs; while numerous chairs were designed on the principle later to be reintroduced by Le Corbusier and Marcel Breuer (Isokon chair) for daily use in a less formal age. For instance, William Ryan's reclining chairs, designed "so that the degree of inclination is regulated with facility by the weight of the body"——, J. M. and F. Brown's "patented suspensory chair, forming a couch or campbed and adapting itself to every movement of the body." The American Chair Company made a patent chair with an iron frame having centripetal springs and railroad-car seats "capable of almost universal movement."

Another outstanding feature of mid-Victorian design is the preference for broken outlines; straight lines were generally replaced by a medley of Regency scrolls, Louis XIV scrolls, and rococo curves—bulging and blurred at the same time. Even Gothic pieces were given a restless outline. Abundant protuberances and a peculiar top-heaviness stamp most of the furniture. Blown-up curves appealed to a prosperous, well-fed middle class whose tastes dictated the dominant flavor of the nineteenth century, just as the tastes of the eighteenth century were decreed by the aristocracy.

An overwhelming interest in ornament that tells a story or has an allegoric or symbolic meaning is another distinguishing feature of Victorianism. The Victorians by no means stand alone in their love of these and other ornament or in their reverence for the beauties of nature and their pleasure in its minute imitation; what is regrettable is their

ABOVE: The small retiring room reserved for Queen Victoria at the Great Exhibition, 1851, and first used by her on the opening day. *Courtesy Victoria and Albert Museum. (See page 409.)* BELOW: The "Daydreamer," easy chair in papier-mâché designed by H. Fitz Cook and made by Jennens and Bettridge. From the Furniture Section of the Great Exhibition, plate 151. *Courtesy Victoria and Albert Museum.* RIGHT: Armchair of Irish bog oak by A. J. Jones, Dublin, exhibited at the Great Exhibition. The arms are formed by wolf dogs. *Courtesy Philadelphia Museum of Art.*

lack of taste or style in exploiting these subjects. Examples might be quoted by the hundred. One, expressing the spirit of 1851, is the day-dreamer easy chair in papier-mâché made by Jennens and Bettridge, "decorated at the top," according to a description in the catalogue, "with two winged thoughts—the one with bird-like pinions, and crowned with roses, representing happy and joyous dreams, the other with leather bat-like wings—unpleasant and troubled ones. Behind is displayed Hope, under the figure of the rising sun. . . ." Another is the armchair of Irish bog oak exhibited by A. J. Jones of Dublin, which has armrests in the form of a sleeping and watching wolf dog, bearing the mottoes, "Gentle when stroked" and "Fierce when provoked" on their respective collars.

The purpose of the Great Exhibition was, in the words of Prince Albert, to present "a living picture of the point of development at which the whole of mankind had arrived . . . and a new starting point from which all nations will be able to direct their further exertions." For the first time the products of all nations were seen together for comparison. English industry made an excellent showing in many fields of manu-facture where technical advances counted, but in fields dominated by taste her products were unimpressive artistically. England had not been unaware of her obvious decline in design, and a spirit of reform had been in the air since the 1830s. In 1835 the first Parliamentary Com-mittee to examine the question of industrial design in England was es-tablished. Schools of design "to marry art to industry" and a reform group including such prominent men as William Dyce, R.A., Richard Redgrave, A.R.A., and the architect Matthew Digby Wyatt date from the late 1830s. These men worked chiefly to improve the standards within the accepted order of things.

Their approach offers a striking contrast to that of the remarkable English architect and designer Augustus W. N. Pugin, 1812–52, who, like Ruskin and Morris later, felt only fear and contempt for machinery. According to Pugin, who was one of the most important of the pioneers, there could be only one style and one faith, and with the publication of his influential *Contrasts* (1836) and his *True Principles of Pointed or Christian Architecture* (1841) he became the champion of a Catholic Gothic revival. Of course the Gothic revival, which on the continent is called neo-Gothic, had been in the air in England before Pugin arrived on the scene. Originally it was developed in close association with roman-ticism and the historical outlook. The early period is notable for its fanci-ful and picturesque romanticism, after which the non-classical style developed into a more scientifically archaeological phase. It was intensi-fied by an interest in restoration and, especially in England, where the style had its deepest roots, by strong religious movements to "Christianize" the architecture of churches. To Pugin and later to Ruskin, classical art and paganism were interchangeable. Thanks to Pugin, Gothic art was strongly represented at the Great Exhibition by the Medieval Court; this type of Gothic was reserved for sacred purposes and was different from the simple Gothic furniture he designed about that time for domestic use.

Pugin's great achievement rests in his writings, not in his work; as a theorist among Victorians his position is indisputable. The basis of his architectural doctrines is clear and sound. In *Contrasts* he writes that "the great test of beauty is the fitness of the design for the purpose for which it was intended"; while in *True Principles* we read that "all really beautiful forms in architecture are based on the soundest principles of utility." All ornament should be no more than the "enrichment of the essential composition." He despised the "glaring, showy and meretricious ornament" then in fashion. He scornfully attacked the trade Gothic furniture, on which "we find diminutive flying buttresses about an armchair; everything is crocketed with angular projections, innumerable mitres, sharp ornaments and turreted extremities. A man who remains any length in a modern Gothic room and escapes without being wounded by some of its minutiae may consider himself extremely fortunate." Pugin condemned all sham; he hated "the false notion of disguising instead of beautifying articles of utility," which was a typical Victorian failing. Many pieces at the exhibition were regarded as lovely because they did not look like what they were, and though the admiration of *trompe l'œil* is as old as art itself, the Victorians stretched the idea of disguise to incredible lengths.

There can be no doubt that the exhibition was a great stimulant to reform. The government made a new attempt for the improvement of industrial design and, under the leadership of Henry Cole, who was chiefly responsible for the exhibition, a Department of Practical Art was organized within the Board of Trade, though its name was changed after a year to the Department of Science and Art. A Museum of Manufactures was set up first at Marlborough House and then from 1851 onward at South Kensington. At Marlborough House Cole was brave enough to organize a Chamber of Horrors for displaying bad design. This short-lived project was described by Dickens in *Household Words* when Mr. Crumpet speaks, "I could have cried, Sir, I was ashamed of the pattern of my own trousers, for I saw a piece of them hung up there as a horror. I dared not pull out my pocket-handkerchief while anyone was by, lest I should be seen dabbling the perspiration from my forehead with a wreath of coral. I saw it all; when I went home I found that I had been living among horrors. . . ."

With regard to general education, the department fostered the founda-

The Medieval Court at the Great Exhibition, arranged under the supervision of A. W. Pugin. "The exhibitors . . . had in view the illustration of a style of decoration now almost totally neglected except in Roman Catholic churches. . . ." *Courtesy Victoria and Albert Museum.*

tion of the Museum of Ornamental Art, which opened at Marlborough House in 1852. (This museum may be regarded as the original ancestor of the Victoria and Albert Museum, for in 1857 it was transferred to the present location with the name of South Kensington Museum, which was changed in 1899 to Victoria and Albert.) It was hoped in this manner to improve the taste of the general public so as to make it demand a higher standard of design. Numerous writings were published in the years following 1851. Of these, none were to have as much influence throughout the remaining Victorian epoch as Owen Jones' *Grammar of Ornament* (1856). Yet, in spite of the work of the reformers, the standards of the International Exhibition of 1862 were as confused and the taste as uncultured as in the Great Exhibition. One important change lay in the Medieval Court, which represented the last of the religious Gothic and the introduction of a new medieval style of secular inspiration. Probably of most consequence were the items shown by Morris and Company; with these came the first impact on the public of Morris' ideas and the first nebulous beginnings of the Arts and Crafts movement.

413

Around 1850 the Gothic revival underwent a change. It was marked by a preference for earlier medievalism, with Norman and Byzantine architecture furnishing the models, and by a growing interest in polychrome, resulting no doubt from the findings of research into polychrome architecture as well as Byzantine architecture. The literary prophets for this period were John Ruskin, 1819–1900, and Viollet-le-Duc, 1814–79. Ruskin set forth his principal architectural ideas in *The Seven Lamps of Architecture* (1849) and *The Stones of Venice* 1851–53. The latter work, which extolls Gothic architecture in general and Italian Gothic in particular, contains one chapter, "The Nature of Gothic," in which he expressed some of his most important ideas. Ruskin held that Gothic art derived from a God-inspired nature; with love of nature and religion in their hearts and nature always before their eyes, these men worked with joy. It was this credo of joy in work, the belief in an integral concept of the unity of art and life, which Ruskin felt led to true art. In a word, art can only grow out of happy work, and since he believed that the joy of the creative process is not compatible with mechanical labor, he objected on principle to the entire system of mechanical production of any work in the arts.

It was through William Morris, 1834–96, who completes the triad of the Gothic revival in England, that the basic principles formulated by Pugin and developed by Ruskin acquired a new actuality. With Morris as a bearer of Ruskin's art theories, the dominant ideal became the desire to produce beautiful things and a hatred of modern civilization. He shared Ruskin's profound love for the Middle Ages and its relation to art and the artist; the consideration of architecture as the Mother or source of all the arts; he looked to nature as the main source of inspiration; he opposed every form of imitation; he demanded honesty of construction and genuineness of materials and his philosophy was founded entirely on the joy of the creative process. Though from Pugin to Morris the main principles in the development of theories for art manufacture remained the same, a very noticeable change occurred in furniture making and the decorative arts, stronger and more radical than in any other kind of art at this time. If we compare the large Gothic cabinet having wrought brass panels designed by Pugin for the Medieval Court at the Great Exhibition of 1851, or even the simple table with a pointed arch underbracing of about 1850, with furniture designed about 1860 by the architect Philip Webb, 1831–1915, it is easy to recognize an essential difference. In Webb's furniture, medievalism is reflected not in the ornamental details, but rather in the honest joinery and honest use of materials, in its simplicity and solidity. Freed from false values, it possessed the spirit of the Middle Ages according to Morris' standards, which were the basis of the Arts and Crafts movement.

414

ABOVE: Circular table of oak designed by Philip Webb (c. 1858–59), reputed to be the first piece of furniture he ever designed. *Courtesy Dr. D. C. Wren. Photo Victoria and Albert Museum.* RIGHT: Wardrobe, painted and gilt, with a scene from Chaucer's "The Prioress's Tale" (1858–59). Designed by Philip Webb and painted by Edward Burne-Jones as a wedding present to Morris, this was Burne-Jones's first completed oil painting. *Courtesy Ashmolean Museum, Oxford. Photo Victoria and Albert Museum.*

For Morris, trained as an architect and painter, it was a first-floor flat of three unfurnished rooms at 17 Red Lion Square, leased in 1857 by Morris and Sir Edward Burne-Jones, 1833–98, which marked his beginning as a designer and craftsman. Unable to buy any furniture characterized by good materials and sound joinery, Morris and his good friend Philip Webb in desperation designed the furniture themselves. They made rough sketches of the essential pieces and gave them to a local carpenter to execute. The Pre-Raphaelite painter Dante Gabriel Rossetti, 1828–82, described the furniture as being "intensely medieval . . . tables and chairs like incubi and succubi." There was a large round table "as firm and as heavy as a rock" and chairs "such as Barbarossa might have sat in." There was also a monumental paneled settle having above the long seat a cupboard portion with three paneled doors. Rossetti designed the oil paintings to decorate the panels. Love between Sun and Moon was the subject of the center panel, while the meeting of Dante and Beatrice in Florence and their meeting in Paradise provided the themes for the other two panels. A wardrobe designed by Webb was painted by Burne-Jones with subjects from "The Prioress's Tale" in Chaucer. These pieces illustrate the Victorian love for the telling of stories by things made for daily use.

The same experiment was repeated at The Red House, Kent, built in 1859 for Morris and his wife by Webb. Apart from the oak furniture, much of which was designed by Webb, tiles were designed and made to line the fireplace, cloth or paper for the walls, and glasses to drink out of. Care and originality marked the work; guided by principles drawn from a study of early art, it never sank into antiquarianism or to a slavish imitation of early forms, and in this work the joy of craftsmanship came to Morris to stay.

In 1861, the year after he moved into Red House, instead of a brotherhood of artists for which Morris had yearned during his days at Oxford, he organized a firm with offices at 8 Red Lion Square—Morris, Marshall, Faulkner and Co., Fine Art Workmen in Painting, Carving, Furniture and the Metals—whose object was to renew decorative art on a medieval basis. Here at Red House in almost rural surroundings worked William Morris, Philip Webb, the Pre-Raphaelites Sir Edward Burne-Jones, Ford Madox Brown, 1821–93, (who associated with the Pre-Raphaelites but did not join them) and sometimes Dante Gabriel Rossetti, as well as the expert mathematican Charles J. Faulkner; the seventh member was Peter Paul Marshall, originally an engineer but like the others vitally absorbed in arts and crafts. At Red House, in accordance with Morris' beliefs, simplicity, honest craftsmanship, and co-operation between artist and artisan became the watchwords.

For financial reasons, Morris moved his firm in 1865 to 26 Queen Square. In 1875 the firm was reorganized as Morris and Company, and in 1881 the workshops were removed to Merton Abbey at Hammersmith. From 1877 to the 1920s the firm of Morris and Company maintained showcases in Oxford Street; in 1940 it went into voluntary liquidation. From the 1870s the productions of the firm comprised practically every branch of applied art; it participated in international exhibitions and seemed to be having a marked influence on contemporary tastes and trends.

With the exception of a few very early pieces of furniture for his own use, it appears that Morris never designed furniture, and even those pieces are questioned by some. The firm produced the widely known rush-seated chairs adapted from models found on farms in Sussex and an armchair with an adjustable back bar, the so-called Morris chair. Morris' connection with the design of furniture, as far as it is known at the present time, was as a painter of legends or stories on cabinets and similar pieces. All the Pre-Raphaelites—Rossetti, Burne-Jones, William Holman Hunt, 1827–1910, and Madox Brown—designed furniture at some time in their career. Occasionally the painted decoration on such pieces as cabinets was a result of their composite talent. The name of Philip Webb, who designed almost all the early furniture produced by the

ABOVE LEFT: Ebonized beech chair, turned, with a rush seat. This is an example of the rush-seated furniture copied by Morris from a traditional Sussex chair, made in large quantities by Morris and Company from the 1870s onward. *Courtesy Victoria and Albert Museum.*
ABOVE RIGHT: Ebonized oak chair with an adjustable back, known especially in the United States as the Morris chair, though it was not designed by Morris. Made by Morris and Company from about 1866. *Courtesy Victoria and Albert Museum. (See page 416.)* BELOW: Rush-seated settee made by Morris and Company. *Courtesy T. Pevsner, Esq. Photo Victoria and Albert Museum.*

Morris firm, is associated with a particular type of austere and undecorated cottage or farmhouse furniture chiefly made of unpolished or ebonized oak, possessing an air of medievalism in its massive rectangular forms and depending for beauty on the value of good craftsmanship. To Webb, furniture was first of all a common tradition of honest joinery. It was this same care and interest in the use of materials and in good planning that laid the foundation for the revival in English furniture, which was to win the admiration of all Europe at the turn of the century. Charles Lock Eastlake also turned to unsophisticated vernacular furniture of his own country in his widely read book *Hints on Household Taste* (1868), which had great influence both in England and America. The furniture he favored was a vaguely traditional rural style based on early English forms, somewhat Elizabethan and Early Jacobean, uncomfortable, but marked by good materials and sound joinery. Like Morris, he tried to create something new but was still steeped in the flavor and principles of early times.

Morris, in his quest for the house beautiful, observes in *Making the Best of It* (1879) that in the house there should be nothing "for mere finery's sake or to satisfy the claim of custom"; and above all "have nothing in your houses," he recommends in *The Beauty of Life* (1880), "which you do not know to be useful or believe to be beautiful." Morris' taste in furniture as in most other matters tended to simplicity. Remain-

OPPOSITE: Oak cabinet inlaid with various woods designed by J. P. Seddon and made by Morris, Marshall, Faulkner and Co. (1862). It is painted with imaginary incidents in the honeymoon of King René of Anjou, as recounted in Scott's *Anna von Geierstein,* by Ford Madox Brown, Edward Burne-Jones, William Morris, and Dante Gabriel Rossetti. (*See page 416.*) ABOVE: Oak table designed by Philip Webb (c. 1870). The structural elements are strongly emphasized, a marked feature of his furniture. RIGHT: Oak sideboard, designed by B. J. Talbert and illustrated in his book, *Ancient and Modern Furniture,* 1876, plate 31; made by Gillow and exhibited in London in 1873. It has carved boxwood panels and metal hinges, bearing a Latin inscription translated as: "It is better to be summoned to a dish of herbs with love than to a fatted calf with hate." *Courtesy Victoria and Albert Museum.* (*See page 420.*)

ing in sympathy with the sturdy honest joinery traditions of medieval times, the furniture was to have, except for easily movable pieces such as chairs, considerable substance, a rich feeling of wood—not walking sticks. First there were to be only those pieces necessary for daily use, no more, no less; this "work-a-day furniture" was to be simple. But in addition there was to be what Morris called "state furniture," such as sideboards, cabinets, and the like made of choice materials and richly decorated for beauty's sake as well as for use. These should be enriched with carving, inlaying, and painting, for "they are," he says in *The Lesser Arts* (1877), "the blossoms of the art of furniture used architecturally to dignify important chambers and important places in them."

Expressing decorative symbolism by means of an inscription—that is, a text painted on or inlaid, which is a very medieval idea—was reintro-

419

duced by the Gothic revivalists. Pugin often placed an inscription both on ecclesiastical and secular objects. Bruce J. Talbert, 1838–81, who produced designs for furniture chiefly in the Gothic and Early Jacobean styles, followed this custom on a sideboard he designed in 1873, "while William Burges, 1827–81, wrote *"venez laver"* on a washstand made in 1880. Later among the artists of the Arts and Crafts movement the use of inscriptions was widespread. For instance, an oak cabinet painted in red and gold made by Ashbee's Guild of Handicraft in 1889 and shown by the Arts and Crafts Exhibition Society in 1899 bears this inscription: "A truth thats told with bad intent beats all the lies you can invent." "It is right it should be so, man was made for joy and woe and when this we rightly know, safely through the world we go." "Joy and woe are woven fine, a clothing for the soul divine, under every grief and pine runs a joy with silken twine." (From William Blake's *Auguries of Innocence.*) The use of quotations that aimed to convey a mood as well as to show the function of the furniture no doubt stemmed in part from the strong literary attitude which was widespread in England in the second half of the nineteenth century. This fashion for the use of texts on furniture was by no means confined to England. In the early 1890s the French designer Emile Gallé created a number of pieces which bear inscriptions, the so-called *meubles parlants* with quotations taken from Hugo, Maeterlinck, Ruskin, Morris, and others.

Among those who in their work gave life to the teachings of John Ruskin was the architect Edward William Godwin, 1833–86. He was active in the 1860s and 1870s, and his importance rests on his being a designer widely admired by the public of the day. Though Godwin started his career as a Gothic revival architect, he soon became cognizant of the aesthetic effect of Japanese art and was perhaps the strongest exponent in England of an influence stemming from that source. In 1862, which marks the first time Japan participated in a World Exhibition in London, Godwin furnished his house in 21 Portland Square, Bristol, in a simple Japanese style with plain colors and Japanese prints on the wall —and for this, according to his biographer, D. Harbron, "there was no contemporary precedent."

In the course of 1863 and shortly afterward Whistler completed his Japanese-inspired pictures, and, as William Rossetti, the brother of Dante Gabriel Rossetti, writes, "The Japanese mania began in our quarters towards the middle of 1863." Throughout the 1860s and right up to the 1890s the interest in Japan was stimulated by many books, pamphlets, and magazine articles. For example, there was Dresser's *Japan, Its Architecture, Art and Art Manufactures* published in 1884, while E. S. Morse's *Japanese Houses and Their Surroundings* appeared in 1886. Morse draws a delightful comparison between the "general nakedness"

Oak cabinet painted in red and gold, designed by C. R. Ashbee and made by the Guild of Handicraft (1889). *Courtesy Abbotsholme School, Rocester, Staffordshire, England.*

of the Japanese house and the "labyrinth of varnished furniture" he had been familiar with in America; the former with its "fresh air and broad flood of light limited only by the dimensions of the room" against the latter "perforated with a pair of quadrangular openings wholly or partially closed against light and air." Hand in hand with the fashion for Japanism was an interest of a more ephemeral kind for Turkish, Persian, Egyptian, Indian, and Moorish art.

Godwin as well as other contemporary designers saw in Japanese art, with its highly expressive line and color and its disdain of symmetry, a chance to break the bonds of historicism. They found in Japan a new unexplored world, an uncorrupted culture based on a different structure of thought. This revelation was to have far-reaching consequences. In short, Japan gave them the opportunity to discover what they were seeking; it was not the parent but the godparent of the Modern movement. Like

Morris and the reformists who prided themselves on imitating nothing, they looked to Japan for lessons not models, for inspiration not imitation. With respect to furniture, Godwin produced new forms which, with their light rectilinear structure combined with a carefully calculated balance of form, were conditioned by oriental precepts. In his book *Art Furniture, with Hints and Suggestions on Domestic Furniture and Decoration* (1877), Godwin includes numerous pieces of furniture in what he calls Anglo-Japanese, all distinctive for the same rectilinear construction. The fact that a Japanese house has no furniture was unimportant to Godwin. He realized that Japanese aestheticism preached the gospel of simplification as no other country did.

Thus either directly or indirectly may be attributed to the influence of Japanese art certain trends in furniture design which were to set their seal on the style of the 1890s, such as an interest in simple and rectilinear structure, a feeling for the light and airy, a more sparing use of ornament which when used contrasted effectively and clearly with the smooth surface that forms the background, and perhaps above all the value of the elegant and refined use of line. This change is mirrored in two pieces of state furniture

OPPOSITE: Sideboard of ebonized wood, with silver-plated fittings and inset panels of "embossed leather" paper, designed by E. W. Godwin and made by William Watt (c. 1877). The light, rectangular construction shows Japanese influence. LEFT: Coffee table of ebonized wood designed by E. W. Godwin and made in numbers by William Watt from about 1868. *Courtesy Bristol City Art Gallery. Photo Victoria and Albert Museum.* BELOW: Cabinet on an oak stand, designed by Philip Webb (1861) and painted by William Morris with scenes from the legend of Saint George. *Courtesy Victoria and Albert Museum.* (*See page 424.*)

designed by the Morris firm, both of which adhered to Morris' golden rule on luxuriousness—that is, luxury is permitted "if it is done for beauty's sake, and not for show." One, a cabinet designed by Webb in 1861, is medieval in spirit; it is massive and its façade is painted with pictorial scenes from the legend of St. George. The second, also a cabinet, was designed by the American architect designer George Jack, 1855–1932, in 1893 after he had been chief furniture designer to Morris and Company for about three years. The medieval feeling is gone; the lines are noticeably lighter and more refined and the façade is decorated with foliage marquetry treated in a conventional manner.

Godwin's importance in the Aesthetic movement of the 1870s and 1880s, which like the Pre-Raphaelite movement was an expression against the current Philistinism, has always been fully acknowledged. Founded and built on the axiom, *l'art pour l'art,* or art for art's sake, the aesthetes tried to make out that the only thing in life worth taking seriously was aesthetic satisfaction. The aesthetes were enchanted by the artistic charm of Japan, the medievalism of Morris, the ideals of Ruskin, the elegance of Wilde, and the free treatment of artistic ways of expression followed by Whistler. It was the mannerisms and affectations of the aesthetes as a group that brought down on them the good-humored bantering of George Du Maurier in *Punch* and the ridicule of Gilbert and Sullivan in their light comic opera *Patience* (1881). The symbols of the movement—the lily (purity) the peacock (beauty), and the sunflower (constancy)—were much in evidence in decorative art until the "crash" of 1895—the trial of Wilde at Old Bailey, which banished him to oblivion. Although these symbols and other manifestations of the movement—"blue and white," or Nanking ware introduced from Paris to London by Whistler, consciously disposed fans, spidery bamboo chairs, and wickerwork furniture of all kinds from palm stands to bookcases—are what one principally associates with it, there can scarcely be any doubt that in spite of everything that might be said against it, the force of the movement did much to promote a general interest in art and design.

The fashion for research into the antique and the cultivation of the past in the nineteenth century brought with it a tendency that was to grow into a respect and desire for furniture of early times—at least for furniture before the age of industrialism, or before 1830. Of course a taste for collecting whatever art can call rare and singular is as old as art itself. We have already had the opportunity to observe how from the time of the Renaissance princely houses were furnished with worthy collections of rare medals, manuscripts, precious marbles, statues of porphyry and oriental alabaster, and other priceless treasures. By 1860 or earlier the taste for collecting eighteenth-century French furniture had become fairly widespread among a small but wealthy group; while the seal of fashion

Writing cabinet mounted on a stand decorated with a marquetry of foliage and trailing vines treated in a conventional manner. It was designed by George Jack and made by Morris and Co. (1893). *Courtesy Victoria and Albert Museum.*

on eighteenth-century works of art was set by the wholehearted support given by Empress Eugénie to the exhibition of works of art associated with Marie Antoinette held at the Petit Trianon during the Paris Exposition Universelle of 1867. Soon the fashion for collecting ceased to be the exclusive prerogative of the rich and was avidly pursued by the middle class.

The taste for antiques referred to in contemporary writings as "a modern freak of fashion" grew by leaps and bounds. Though various reasons are offered to explain the antiques craze, one excellent reason is that the Victorians were snobs; in fact they invented the term. It was Thackeray who gave it its present significance. Snobbery does not flourish in a rigid society like that of the eighteenth century, where everyone could tell a duke by the star of some order on his coat, but only in a fluid society where a prosperous and rising middle class presses on the heels of an established aristocracy. It is a defense mechanism, a snobbish longing for an old established background which has sold countless ancestor portraits. Because antiques became a profitable business, the forger entered the field; almost overnight the manufacture of antiques became a modern industry. Even apart from the practice of faking, the desire to furnish with "genuine antiques" has other sinister aspects. For example, to some people age became a test of beauty; they reasoned that, if it is old, if it is really

425

antique, it must be beautiful. They never heard of the fundamental precept that beauty is not determined by age. There was also a general belief that in antiques or their reproduction lay the only road to good taste. This belief was chiefly conditioned by unfortunate experiments in new design, at that time by Art Nouveau. Since then, owing to some original work worthy only of a Chamber of Horrors, the idea has not been cast to limbo. The main argument against the practice of reproduction is that it retards the development of design. Imitation should go no further than to honor the lesson set by craftsmen of previous centuries, that is the lesson of original creation. To invest our work with the mental richness of the past is prudent, but progress in design can never result from servile copying.

No one expressed this idea more succinctly than Charles Callahan Perkins, 1823–86, the noted American lecturer and art critic, an influential friend of the arts of design when in a lecture delivered in 1872 he observed that "it may be questioned whether it is desirable to copy the architectural forms of past times, with which modern habits and manners are necessarily out of keeping. To this it may be answered that if we repeat them slavishly we do wrong, but if we imbue them with a new spirit, and thus make them in some sense our own, we do the next best thing to the originating of forms peculiar to ourselves."

To the doctrines of Morris expressed in thirty-five lectures delivered between 1877 and 1894 on social and artistic questions, to his ability to master the working details and the handling of each craft he took up, and to his dynamic personality which inspired his helpers and followers may be attributed the influence which in the 1880s brought into existence a series of craftsmen's and designers' associations. This influence was the Arts and Crafts movement, which motivated the long and tedious journey away from historicism. The Century Guild formed in 1882 by A. H. Mackmurdo, 1851–1942, and Selwyn Image, 1849–1930, was followed in 1884 by the Art Workers' Guild, with Walter Crane, 1845–1915, and Lewis F. Day, 1845–1910, as its leading originators, and in 1885 by a smaller organization, The Home Arts and Industries Association, which was especially interested in rural crafts and in which Mackmurdo was also actively engaged. The comprehensive title Arts and Crafts, signifying the arts of decorative design and handicraft, came into general use when the Arts and Crafts Exhibition Society was founded in 1888 with men like Day, Crane, and Heywood Summer.

The Arts and Crafts movement, which in the words of Morris was "to help the conscious cultivation of art and to interest the public in it," encouraged a number of architects, such as W. R. Lethaby, 1857–1931, Voysey, Ashbee, Gimson, and the Barnsleys, to design furniture; it even encouraged a most notable example in the furniture trade itself, Sir Ambrose Heal, 1872–1959. It is erroneous to believe that all the members of

426

Oak cupboard inlaid with ebony and satinwood, designed by Lewis F. Day and shown at the first Arts and Crafts Exhibition (1888). It is decorated with *grisaille* paintings of the Signs of the Zodiac. *Courtesy Victoria and Albert Museum.*

these organizations subscribed completely to the Ruskin-Morris school of thought. There were a number of designers, such as John Sedding, 1837–91, and Christopher Dresser, 1834–1904, who as the heirs of the industrial-minded pioneers of 1851 adopted a commercial attitude to their work and designed for machine production. But unfortunately for the growth of industrial design in England they welcomed the machine only half-heartedly; they acknowledged it only because they felt it was futile to rebel against the inevitable, while the real pioneers of the Modern movement are those who from the start stood for machine art. True to innate English conservatism, Morris and those who came after him refused any drastic break in tradition. Nevertheless, it is invariably recognized that the Modern movement was built on the results which Morris and the English school had achieved from 1860 up to the mid 1890s, when the initiative passed from England to America and the continent, and

LEFT: Turned ash slat-back chair with a rush seat, designed and made by Ernest Gimson. He learned to make traditional turned ash chairs in the late 1880s while he was articled to John D. Sedding, architect and designer. *Courtesy Victoria and Albert Museum.* RIGHT: Cabinet and stand of ebony inlaid with mother-of-pearl, designed by Ernest Gimson and made at the Daneway House Workshops (1908). *Courtesy City of Leicester Museum. Photo Victoria and Albert Museum.*

after a short period to Germany. The Werkbund, composed chiefly of young architects and craftsmen, was set up in Germany in 1907. To this group the horror of the machine was unknown. (The Design and Industries Association, established in England in 1915, was to acknowledge the program developed by the Werkbund and state in its *Journal* in 1916 that it was "accepting the machine in its proper place, as a device to be guided and controlled, not merely boycotted.")

The attitude to the machine of the English school was certainly responsible for many beautiful things, especially in furniture, presented by the Arts and Crafts Exhibition Society from 1888 to 1914. The original work of such men as Gimson, Scott, the Barnsleys, Walton, Ashbee, and Voysey was frequently exhibited on the continent, where it was much admired for its good taste and reticence; in Italy, names such as the *Stile*

428

Liberty and *Stile Inglese* were given to the work of the Arts and Crafts style and showed that its influence was considerable abroad. Once again England became a leader in artistic cabinetwork. It must be confessed, however, that this extremely simple and constructive style of furniture, which provided the impetus for the development on the continent just after the turn of the century, was scarcely known to the general public, who were entangled in the craze for antiques and reproductions and, to a lesser extent, in the extravagances of Art Nouveau propagated by the Paris Exposition of 1900. In the work of Gimson, Heal, and Voysey, this Arts and Crafts style acquired an elegant and sober quality.

Ernest Gimson, 1864–1920, together with the Barnsleys (Sidney, 1865–1926, and Ernest, 1863–1926), wishing to get away from the center of modern civilization, a very "medieval" idea, retreated in the early 1890s from London to the quiet village of Gloucestershire in the Cotswolds, where it seems craftsmanship survived with more vigor than in other parts of England. The Cotswold school of furniture designers was the link between the English rural traditions of craftsmanship and the ideas of William Morris. They were guided by the principles of Morris in their designing and they practiced them in their workshops. Though Gimson never actually executed any of his designs and made nothing himself except the turned ash chairs, he worked closely with his craftsmen. Simplicity of form, soundness of construction, and an unerring judgment in the selection of woods used are the chief characteristics of Gimson's work. The sound oak furniture made by the Barnsleys clearly acknowledges their debt to Webb and foreshadows the more rustic side of the Cotswold movement. In 1902 Gimson and Ernest Barnsley opened workshops at Daneway House, Sapperton. The partnership was of short duration, lasting only a year or two, because the latter returned to practice as an architect. Sidney Barnsley, who never participated in the venture, maintained a small workshop nearby. After Gimson's death in 1920, the Daneway House workshops were closed, but craftsmen to this day keep his traditions alive in the Cotswolds. The unquestioned leader of these craftsmen is Edward Barnsley, b. 1900, son of Sidney Barnsley, whose workshop at Petersfield has produced furniture inspired by the best traditions in English design.

In 1888 the architect Charles R. Ashbee, 1863–1942, founded his Guild and School of Handicraft, which he moved from London to Chipping Campden, in the Cotswolds, in his desire to revive handicraft. Perhaps because he recognized the hopelessness of the struggle against the forces of modern industry, he wrote in his last book that "modern civilization rests on machinery and no system for encouragement or the endowment of the teaching of the arts can be sound that does not recognize this," which is one of the basic premises of the Modern movement.

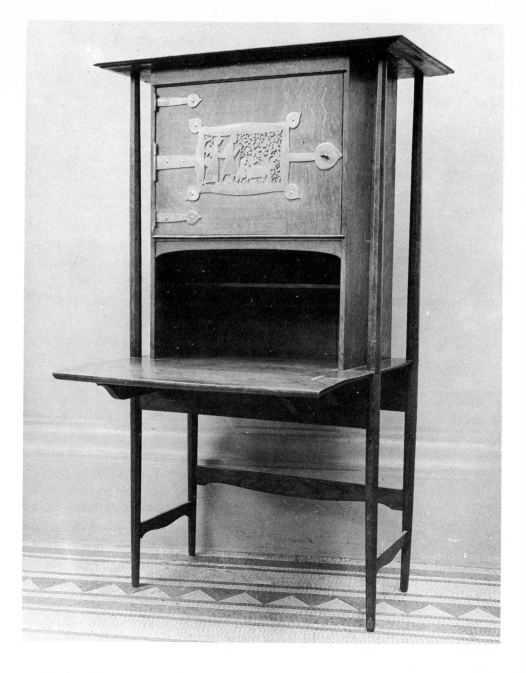

Charles Francis Annesley Voysey, 1857–1941, generally regarded as the most important designer before and at the turn of the century, demonstrated his versatility in the crafts—wallpaper, textiles, and furniture—at the Arts and Crafts Exhibition Society of 1896. Some of his work, as the *Studio* pointed out, was at the same time the most original and the most reticent at the exhibition. The same review continued: "It is especially good that his influence which tends to simplicity and severity should be made prominent at this time." His furniture, like the interiors of the

OPPOSITE: Oak desk with brass hinges and mounts designed by C. F. A. Voysey (1896). The influence of Japan is evident. LEFT: Oak chair designed by C. F. A. Voysey (1896). The simplified hearts in the splat of the chair back are a typical Voysey feature. *Courtesy Victoria and Albert Museum.*

houses he designed, was light and airy and plain, revealing the importance of Japanese influence on his work. Voysey realized that simplicity was not easy to achieve; he expressed this idea in an incomparable phrase, "Simplicity requires perfection in all details while elaboration is easy in comparison with it." He said, "Let us begin by discarding the mass of useless ornaments and banishing the millinery that degrades our furniture and fittings." The uncluttered character of his interiors inspired continental designers. It was, in the words of Van de Velde, "as if Spring had come all of

431

a sudden." The simple beauty of his work furnished the initial inspiration for such English and Scottish designers as Charles Rennie Mackintosh, 1868–1928, M. H. Baillie Scott, 1865–1945, and George Walton, 1867–1933.

The furniture made in Glasgow in the 1890s by the Scottish architect Mackintosh was the most original of any at this time. Because his furniture forms, especially his chair backs, as well as his decorative motifs, were markedly elongated, giving them something of an eerie quality, the group of designers working with Mackintosh were christened the "Spook school" in England. But we shall read more about Mackintosh and the Glasgow school in the following chapter. Furniture designed by the Glasgow architect George Walton owes something to the Glasgow school, but much more to the English school. His furniture forms, pleasantly simple, reveal a penchant for constructive elements and an economy of ornament. The English architect Baillie Scott, whose work combined sound craftsmanship and a fresh approach, was perhaps the best known of all English designers on the continent, particularly in Germany where he had decorated the palace of the Grand Duke of Hesse at Darmstadt. One of his favorite devices was to decorate the flat surfaces of his basically simple but rather massive forms of furniture with elaborate stylized natural motifs, executed in relief, in colored woods, mother-of-pearl, ivory, and pewter.

432

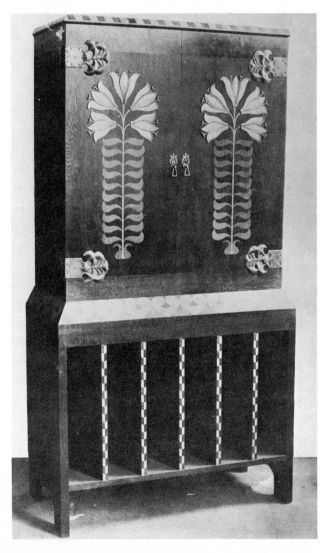

OPPOSITE: Entrance hall of Voysey's house, The Orchard, Chorley Wood, Buckinghamshire (1900). It contains typical Voysey features such as the strong contrast of verticals and horizontals, simple oak furniture. *Courtesy Cooper Union Museum.* ABOVE: Table and armchair designed by George Walton (c. 1897–98). LEFT: Oak music cabinet decorated with colored inlays and metal relief, designed by M. H. Baillie Scott and made by the Guild of Handicraft for the Grand Duke of Hesse (1898). *Courtesy Victoria and Albert Museum.*

433

Oak writing table designed by Arthur Mackmurdo in 1882. *Courtesy William Morris Gallery. Photo Victoria and Albert Museum.*

There was also the work of the architect Arthur Mackmurdo, 1851–1942, one of the leading personalities of the Arts and Crafts movement, who, though less important than his friend Voysey, occasionally revealed a fresh and imaginative approach to design. The carved back of a chair he designed in 1881 with its swirling composition of flame-like leaves anticipated the ornament associated with Art Nouveau by about a decade. Mackmurdo's best designs were his simplest; his most original designs were entirely without ornament, depending for their beauty on the strong contrast of verticals and horizontals.

As we look on this long period covering almost a century, it is obvious that from the time of the Gothic revival a great deal of trouble had been taken to move away from a dry historicism and a servile series of period revivals. Through men like the Pre-Raphaelites, Morris, Webb, Cole, Godwin, Dresser, Day, Lethaby, Gimson, Voysey, and a host of others, a simple, sober style of furniture, essentially rectilinear, had been evolved on traditional grounds, based on an honest use of materials and honest principles of joinery. In ornament, imitation that reproduced the world of flowers with minute attention to naturalistic detail was gradually discarded, passing by way of stylization to simplification. It is easy, therefore, to appreciate that in England the continental Art Nouveau with its flexible and sinuous lines and floral decoration was like seed falling on stony ground. Walter Crane refers to it as "that strange decorative disease known as l'Art Nouveau." As we shall shortly see, after the enthusiasm for Art Nouveau had dimmed on the continent, the sober and austere aspects of this English furniture which Van de Velde praised in his *Die Renaissance,* 1903, for its "systematic discarding of ornament" were zealously cultivated and developed until they became revolutionary ideas.

With all its faults, the Victorian age was an age of progress and of outstanding men who furnished the initial source of inspiration for the international style of the twentieth century. Without the English impetus, the subsequent creative work in Europe and America seems unthinkable. We should regard the emergence of the diverse and often faltering efforts of the pioneers as most fortunate. In their work we see their hopes to make a fresh start. No matter how deeply Morris regretted the death of the past, he held to the belief, as he writes in *The Lesser Arts* (1877), that "all the change and stir about is a sign of the world's life . . . it will lead—by ways, indeed, of which we have no guess—to the bettering of all mankind."

Art Nouveau
and Its Corollaries

Another movement which evolved about the same time as the Arts and Crafts and the Modern movements was Art Nouveau. It had no credo and sought its way in very diverse directions. Though Art Nouveau extended itself into all realms of artistic activity, it belongs first and foremost to the decorative arts. Like the Arts and Crafts movement, it possessed the merit of reviving handicraft; it was the style of the individual designer, who, following in Morris' footsteps, relied on the work of men's hands and not on the machine. As this new international movement gradually spread and achieved notable success as the style of fashion and the *avant-garde,* it was given a legion of names in the various countries, each name suggesting a somewhat different view. Among the designations generally applied in derision were *Paling* (eel) *stijl* in Belgium, *Style Nouille* (vermicelli) in France, and *Schnörkelstil* (flourish style) and *Bandwürmstil* (tapeworm style) in Germany. The French author Edmond Goncourt, aware of its streamlined elements, gave the new style the celebrated sobriquet "Yachting Style"; while the average French citizen frequently dubbed it *Style Métro,* referring to the decorative subways of the Métro stations designed by Hector Guimard, 1867–1942. In Italy the name *Stile Floreale,* if it is regarded as referring to the entire plant form—blooms, leaves, stems, and roots—and not to its blooms alone, summarizes if not always visually at least conceptually the kind of organic expression that was always aimed at and rather often attained. *Stile Liberty,* after the firm of Liberty and Company in London, was still another name frequently used by the Italians. At that time, according to Arthur Liberty himself, "the name Liberty was the quintessence of fashion in London." This name, as we learned in the preceding chapter, had already become identified with the renaissance in English art manufacture which came into existence with Morris. But because the two movements appeared together at the exhibitions of the decorative arts held on the continent, and their dif-

436

Detail from a buffet by Eugène Gaillard (1900). The "whiplash" curves convey the sense of powerful movement, a marked feature of Art Nouveau. *Courtesy Museum of Decorative Art, Copenhagen.*

ferences were not too clear at that time, a confusion of terms occurred.

In Germany, Art Nouveau quickly acquired the term *Jugendstil,* taken from a ribald and lively periodical, *Jugend,* first published in Munich in 1896, in which Otto Eckmann, 1865–1902, charmed his readers with floral Art Nouveau vignettes. To explain the title for this new weekly magazine, the editors wrote in the preface, "We want to call the new weekly *Youth.* This really says all we have to say." The English, not realizing how much they had contributed in graphic design through the work of such men as Aubrey Beardsley, 1872–98, and never really taking part in the full-bloom movement, called it Art Nouveau. In Austria this new style was known as *Secessionsstil* or *Sezessionsstil,* a term deriving from the union of radical Viennese painters and sculptors established in 1897 under the name of *Wiener Sezession.* The Scots, who certainly influenced the Viennese school, called their corollary the Glasgow School, while in Spain it was named *Modernismo.*

In the early days in France the commonest designation was simply Modern style. But after S. Bing, a native of Hamburg, who had previously been interested in Japanese art as a connoisseur, dealer, and publisher, opened his first shop, Maison de l'Art Nouveau, at 22 Rue de Provence in Paris in December 1895, the name Art Nouveau took root. An amusing description of the orange-colored sign on the front of Bing's shop is given

437

by the editor of *Revue des Arts Décoratifs*. "Above two enormous sun orioles with their round discs violently exaggerated without taste and style can be read these two words with their delightful modesty: art nouveau." As the French molded their own version out of Art Nouveau, the name became the customary one in France, and except for the German-speaking countries, which kept the name *Jugend*, the term Art Nouveau was finally accepted in the majority of countries. The name easily entrenched itself, because there was little agreement on principles among the contemporary innovators other than a general desire to break with the past and to protest against the traditional and the commonplace. Little did Bing realize that his shop was destined to become the focal point and Paris the main center of the new style. Of the shop and its name, Bing wrote: "At its birth Art Nouveau made no claim to rising to the distinction of a generic term. It was simply the name of an establishment opened as a meeting ground for all keen young artists anxious to demonstrate the modernness of their tendencies."

Art Nouveau was not an isolated and peculiar phenomenon. It was already nascent in the Gothic revival and the Arts and Crafts movement; it even continued into the foundation of the Bauhaus, 1919. Art Nouveau, at its height from about 1895 to 1905, appeared in full bloom around 1900 and may be placed midway between historicism and the emergence of the Modern movement; it was the product of a wide social reaction that marked the close of one period and the start of a new one. The innovators resolutely turned away from the beaten track and, in an effort to gain a new footing, freed themselves from tradition and conscientiously pursued novelty. It was but a step to the exaggerated or sensational, in this case the extravagances of Art Nouveau.

No doubt Art Nouveau's most important contribution to the art of interior decoration was to re-establish a sense of unity in interior design. To conceive of the room and its contents as a unified whole was perhaps the one characteristic found in each of the national interpretations of the new art. An anti-historical attitude was as much a marked feature of Art Nouveau as was its striving for unity. But Art Nouveau, which was acclaimed in Europe and America as new and revolutionary in its emphasis on the use of decorative form, line, and color and rich in symbolic meaning, was never entirely free from the bondage of the historical past. The style shows certain traditional features—in particular Gothic, rococo, and baroque. Each in its way contributed to mold Art Nouveau; Gothic contributed theory, rococo its application of asymmetry, and baroque its plastic conception of form. Art Nouveau also found timely inspiration in the highly linear and colorful art of Japan and emancipation from the bondage of symmetry and the Greek Orders. The fluidity and technical achievements of the East are everywhere apparent in it. Then, too, the marked in-

438

A drawing for the dining room of the Castel Orgeval by Hector Guimard (1904–5). *Courtesy Cooper Union Museum.*

dividuality the new style evinced in the various countries is due in part to a special interest in particular traditions. There was, for example the influence of Celtic art on the Glasgow school and of rococo art on the Nancy school. This can scarcely be surprising, for the history of art shows that men have always allowed the past to enrich and stimulate their creative energy, even when there is a conscious effort toward innovation.

Much of Art Nouveau furniture has an aspect of novelty that makes it seem unrelated in the chain of furniture history. To free themselves from the past, the designers scattered accepted principles of design to the wind. They were scarcely aware of the nature of materials; wood was twisted into bizarre shapes, and metal writhed in tortuous curves inspired by the flowing interlacings of Nature—for, on the whole, the style is based on Nature, not only in ornamental development but in structural conception,

439

and this is one of the keys to the understanding of it. In reality the attitude of most Art Nouveau designers toward Nature as the main source of inspiration was a characteristic mid-Victorian idea, of which John Ruskin was the leading exponent. It was in Art Nouveau that the culmination of Nature as an aesthetic expression reached its climax. Sensuous, undulating lines of growth twine and spread across the structure, taking complete possession of it. Chairs and tables seem as if they were molded in a taffy-like substance. Straight lines are erased wherever feasible, while natural structural divisions are no longer definable, flowing into one another to maintain as continuous a linear movement as possible. Happily, Nature is less extravagant than many of Art Nouveau's interpretations of it. On the other hand, Art Nouveau at its best, rich in linear rhythm, reveals a harmony of line which places it side by side with cabinetwork made in the eighteenth century.

The Turin Exhibition in 1902 marked the climax as well as the crossroad of Art Nouveau. Though a number of artists adopted the style and continued to use it up to the years preceding the First World War, it was clear to everyone that the style was already on the decline. Shortly after 1902, the main artistic development of furniture tended toward simplicity, with less emphasis on decoration and more on structural function. The deepest reason for the sudden demise of Art Nouveau was the rumblings of a new movement—the Modern—which was slowly evolving in Germany and Austria, where English influence was especially strong. All the time that Art Nouveau was in vogue, the names of a group of English artists —Walter Crane, Voysey, Image, Baillie Scott, Walton, Ashbee, and several others—were repeatedly mentioned on the continent. It was not their contribution to the development of ornamentation that attracted the wide interest but rather their constructive principles, a rational feeling for form and its fitness. The early rejection of Art Nouveau becomes understandable when we comprehend that in this style the continental artists first turned their attention to ornament. They believed decoration necessary; the problem was to find a suitable form for it and in finding it they felt they would have a style. Gradually, however, when they realized that the solution to the stylistic problems of the nineteenth century, which new materials and social tasks had created, lay in the constructive principles, that is, simplicity of form and honesty toward materials and working processes—ideals which the Arts and Crafts fought for—the leading artists abandoned Art Nouveau in order to give their creative energy to a wide movement promoting these ideas. Decorative problems were relegated to a subordinate role; their interest centered on new shapes.

The new style became the most firmly established in France and retained its popularity there the longest. Inasmuch as rococo and neo-rococo achieved their apogee in France, it is hardly surprising that the most

ABOVE LEFT: Revolving music stand by Alexander Charpentier (1901). The standard resembles the stalks of a plant, and gives a very good idea of the structural conception based
on nature. *Courtesy Musée des Arts Décoratifs, Paris. Photo Mella.* ABOVE RIGHT: Carved
pearwood tripod table by Hector Guimard, from the architect's house in Paris (c. 1908).
The supple curves of the molded frame flow into one another with great refinement.
BELOW: Carved ashwood writing table by Hector Guimard, from the architect's house in
Paris (c. 1903). The structure has an endless rhythmic flow, while the frames of the panels
give a branch-like effect. *Courtesy Museum of Modern Art, New York. Gift of Mme. Hector
Guimard.*

LEFT: Carved ashwood screen by Emile Gallé (1900). The skillful disposition on a wood ground of the inlaid and applied ornament representing vines and flowers allows it to be fully appreciated. RIGHT: Work table of ash and walnut, carved and inlaid with a floral marquetry, by Emile Gallé for the Paris Exhibition of 1900. It bears the inlaid inscription TRAVAIL EST JOIE. *Courtesy Victoria and Albert Museum.*

important influence of rococo on Art Nouveau occurred in this cultural area. In the 1880s neo-rococo appeared for the second time in France in the nineteenth century, in a somewhat coarser form, together with the neo-baroque of the 1880s. Even when it became the fashion in the last decades of the century to decorate each room in its own style—perhaps a Louis XVI drawing-room, a Louis XV lady's bedroom, a Renaissance library, and a Louis XIV entrance hall—in a broad sense, Louis XV was the dominant trend. As for the influence of baroque on French Art Nouveau, the plastic conception was so important to some designers, such as Majorelle and André, that they actually modeled prototypes of their furniture in advance. The creator of the most characteristic fusion of baroque and Art Nouveau in France was Guimard, as can be seen in the iron grillwork of the Métro stations in Paris.

Two distinct centers of Art Nouveau developed in France—one in Paris around Bing and his shop and the other in Nancy under the aegis of

Emile Gallé, 1846–1904, who was committed to several branches of art industry. He was one of the most interesting of all Art Nouveau designers, as well as France's outstanding naturalist. It is in Nancy that we find the closest affiliations between rococo and Art Nouveau. In the eighteenth century, during the reign of the Polish King Stanislaus, 1735–66, this university town had been transformed by rococo façades and sinuous grillwork into a veritable maze of linear fantasies. When the Bourbon king Louis XVIII, 1815–24, was returned to power after Napoleon I's downfall, the earliest neo-rococo furniture was made at Nancy and flourished until it was supplanted by Napoleon III's neo-classicism in the 1860s. When the artistic revival of the 1890s took place, the artists who lived at Nancy were once again stimulated by their rococo background, which they fused with the new style.

Less fascinating, but among the most characteristic of Art Nouveau's artistic personalities, is Nancy's other celebrated furniture designer, Louis Majorelle, 1859–1926, who, as well as Eugène Vallin, 1856–1925, Emile André, 1871–1933, and Jacques Gruber, continued Gallé's furniture tradition, which was floral and markedly plant-inspired. Gallé's forte was inlay work, varying from plant motifs to inscriptions, the latter providing a literary touch of a symbolic nature. (In the preceding chapter we have already met with the fashion for inscriptions on furniture, *meubles parlants*, as they were called in France.) His furniture designs adhered to a greater or lesser extent to the French stylistic traditions, while the nature-inspired decoration without particular stylization was inclined to spread over the entire surface, enclosing it in a floral embrace. A feature Gallé employed in much of his furniture, especially in smaller pieces, was to change the actual structure into stalks or branches that sprang up and developed into blossoms and flowers. In contrast to Gallé, the furniture of Majorelle reveals a greater degree of unconventionality, being less bound by tradition and more plastic in conception; the main characteristic of his work is the dynamic line. Shortly after Gallé's death in 1904, the Nancy school declined.

In contrast to the Nancy school, Parisian Art Nouveau is lighter, more refined, and austere. The Nature-inspired decoration is more stylized, occasionally even abstract, and frequently confined to small areas. Unlike the Nancy school, where the artists followed in Gallé's footsteps, the Parisian artists were entirely individual personalities, each presenting his own form of Art Nouveau. Apart from the Big Three who worked for Bing—Georges de Feure, 1869–1928, Eugène Gaillard and Eugène Colonna—there were such other well-known representatives as Charpentier, Aubert, Selmersheim, Plumet, and Guimard, the last-mentioned being the most prominent French architect working in the new style. This group produced

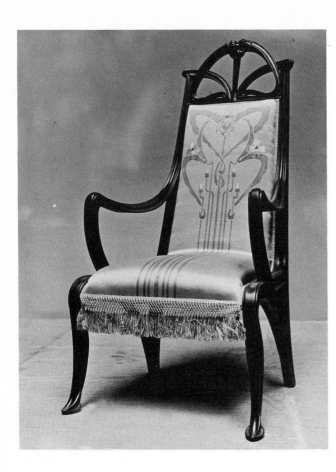

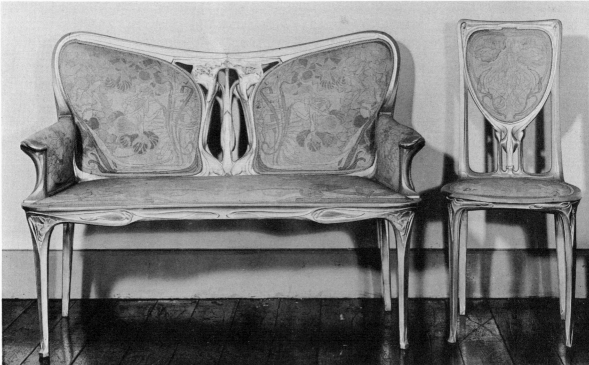

OPPOSITE ABOVE LEFT: Walnut armchair stained green by Louis Majorelle (1900). The piece illustrates his talent for sculptured, smoothly flowing silhouettes. OPPOSITE ABOVE RIGHT: Veneered cabinet enriched with carving and marquetry, signed L. Majorelle, Nancy (1900). *Courtesy Victoria and Albert Museum.* OPPOSITE BELOW: Settee and chair of carved and gilt wood by Georges de Feure (1900). *Courtesy Museum of Decorative Art, Copenhagen.* ABOVE LEFT: Walnut buffet by Eugène Gaillard shown at the Paris Exhibition (1900). The carved ornament is characterized by dynamic movement. *Courtesy Museum of Decorative Art. Copenhagen.* ABOVE RIGHT: Palissander chair by Eugène Colonna (1900). BELOW LEFT: Chair by Eugène Gaillard (c. 1908). This illustrates the trend toward classical form. *Courtesy Musée des Arts Décoratifs, Paris. Photo Mella. (See page 443.)* BELOW RIGHT: Palissander table by Eugène Colonna (1900). *Courtesy Metropolitan Museum of Art. Edward C. Moore, Jr. Gift Fund, 1926.*

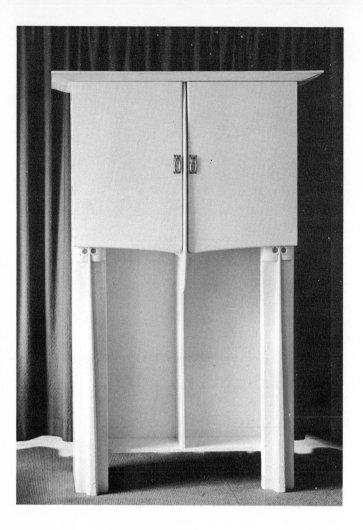

Cupboard of white enameled wood by Charles Rennie Mackintosh, exhibited at Turin Exhibition (1902). *Courtesy University of Glasgow.*

some of the finest examples of Art Nouveau furniture. After the Exposition Universelle in Paris in 1900, when French artists were confronted with the extravagant excesses of the style, they made a subtle retreat and returned to a restrained form of Art Nouveau which was more in harmony with French period furniture. This final phase of simplification in which the lines of furniture became straighter was of short duration. Before 1910 a simplified and modernized classicism, especially in the direction of Directoire and Empire, came into vogue, presaging the revolution in design of the 1920s.

The English corollary of the continental Art Nouveau had its center in Glasgow with the architect and designer Charles Rennie Mackintosh, 1868–1928, as its most powerful exponent. The other three artists who, with Mackintosh, comprise the Glasgow group—"the Four" as the group was frequently called—were Herbert MacNair and the MacDonald sisters, Margaret, 1865–1933, and Frances, 1874–1921. Margaret married Mackintosh; Frances married MacNair. The Scottish school is the result of a great many interesting trends—the Celtic revival with its nationalistic spirit, the Pre-Raphaelites and the symbolical and literary tendencies, the rectangu-

446

larity of Japanese work. Like his architecture, Mackintosh's furniture is often straight-lined, markedly linear, and makes much decorative use of structural elements. We have come to associate with the Scottish school very simple pieces of furniture with broad plain surfaces contrasted with comparatively small areas of rich pattern. Moldings are dispensed with to increase the effect of the large smooth surfaces. Typical of this style, with its linear and symbolic features, is a severely plain, white-enameled, rectilinear cupboard designed by Mackintosh around 1902. The projecting cornice devoid of moldings is notably simple. When the cupboard doors are opened, a kind of decoration with a marked tendency to verticalism is revealed, which is so characteristic of the school. Against a pearl-gray background stands a strange slender elongated figure of a woman wrapped in a white robe, holding in her outstretched arms a pink, ball-shaped rose, whose form vaguely evoked the natural form from which it was derived. The decoration is inlaid with opaque colored glass, in white, dark blue, and pink.

Because of the unusual shapes of his furniture, displaying little or no traces of tradition, Mackintosh earned a name for himself as a designer of

447

unorthodox furniture. His chairs with extremely tall backs, often six feet, six inches high, characterized by oval insets, the pierced patterns of squares or crescents admirably exemplify his peculiar inventiveness. Angular and rigid as his chairs were, with either tall or low backs, they looked and undoubtedly were uncomfortable. Mackintosh had an aversion to rich and heavy upholstery; even his easy chairs were sparingly upholstered. (Overstuffed furniture is conducive to a heavy look, which Mackintosh was determined to avoid.) The light and airy quality of Mackintosh's interiors reveals the importance of Japanese influence on his work and is reminiscent of Voysey's designs for interiors with their sense of spaciousness engendered by sparse furnishings. This new spirit of furnishing, in which there was hardly anything in the room, against the former overcrowding, is of especial significance to the Modern movement. Mackintosh's sprightly linear style—the interplay between verticles and horizontals and their decorative value, the square and the circle for ornamental purposes—stimulated the Austrian artists far more than did the fashionable floral experiments of the French. In the capable hands of Josef Hoffmann the square became a most fashionable motif around 1900.

OPPOSITE LEFT: Oak chair by C. R. Mackintosh for his apartment at 120 Main Street, Glasgow (1900). This illustrates his decorative use of structural elements. *Courtesy Museum of Modern Art, New York. Gift of the University of Glasgow.* OPPOSITE RIGHT: Oak chair by C. R. Mackintosh (c. 1900). *Courtesy Kunstgewerbemuseum, Zurich.* OPPOSITE BELOW: Dining room for the house of a connoisseur by C. R. Mackintosh (1901). *Courtesy Museum of Modern Art, New York. Photo Pevsner.* BELOW: A part of the drawing room at 120 Main Street, Glasgow, by C. R. Mackintosh (1900). Panels of clear and white glass decorate the white enameled bookcase. The general whiteness of the room creates a feeling of freshness which is never monotonous because of the free use made of bright spots of color in the ornaments. Around the room in the deep frieze rail, pairs of richly designed purple panels are set and decorated with colored stones. The hanging lamps at the four corners of the room are made of silver profusely set with purple glass ornaments. *Courtesy Cooper Union Museum.*

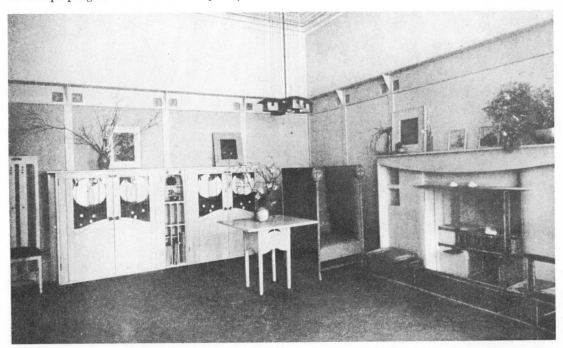

RIGHT: Settee by Chris Wegerif, founder of the Arts and Crafts in The Hague (c. 1900). BE-LOW: Oak chair by H. P. Berlage (c. 1895). *Courtesy Municipal Museum, The Hague, Netherlands.* OPPOSITE: Casa Battló by Antonio Gaudí in Bar-celona illustrates a complete fu-sion of neo-baroque and Art Nouveau (1907). *Courtesy Mu-seum of Modern Art, New York.*

Though in some of her Arts and Crafts originations England helped to mold Art Nouveau she did not participate in the movement. In Holland the extravagances of Art Nouveau also failed to materialize. Heeding the precepts of the English Arts and Crafts movement, the Dutch evolved a more sober style in which interest centered on the construction problems and not the decorative. Furniture designed by the Dutch architect H. P. Berlage, 1856–1934, with its simple lines and rectilinear construction, exemplifies this trend. The results of Berlage's attempt to lay the foundation for a new style became evident twenty-five years later at the Paris Exposition of Modern Art held in 1925. Furniture at the exposition designed by the Dutch architect Gerrit Rietveld, b. 1888, kept the integrity of the flat rectangular plane advanced by Berlage. Rietveld was one of the leading exponents of De Stijl, a movement flourishing in Holland from around 1917 to 1929. Theories advanced by Stijl artists, which opened a new era of interior decoration, continue to provide the fundamental formal aesthetic of much modern design.

Art Nouveau may be seen with remarkable clarity in Spain in the extraordinary architecture and furnishings of the Catalonian architect Antonio Gaudí y Cornet, 1852–1926. With religious intensity and rare imagination he successfully brought together most of the style elements of the nineteenth century—neo-Gothic, neo-rococo, neo-baroque, and the most fanciful naturalism—into a decorative, rhythmic whole. His chairs and interiors, with their markedly plastic shapes, their flowing, undulating lines,

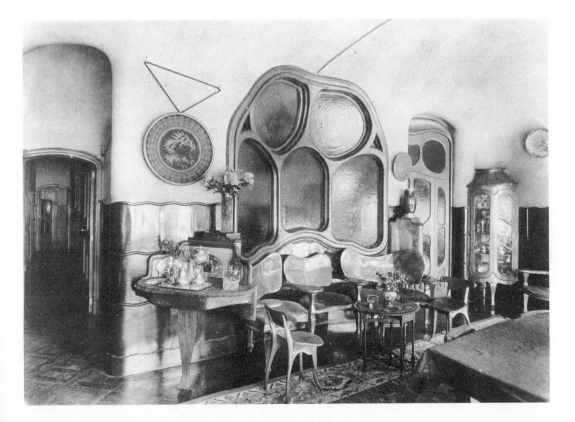

admirably exemplify his style. Anyone who has seen his Casa Milá at Barcelona, or even a photograph of it, appreciates that he is one of the most imaginative of artists.

Just as the neo trends—baroque and rococo—clearly influenced Art Nouveau in France, so they influenced Art Nouveau in Belgium, the country generally regarded as the epicenter of the new style. Belgian Art Nouveau, however, with its plastic and noticeably three-dimensional treatment, presents a far more heavy and ponderous impression of the new art than any that appeared in France, while the ornament in the hands of the Belgian designers was presented in an abstract manner.

Victor Horta, 1861–1947, Belgium's most important architectural figure at the turn of the century, was the first to achieve a fully developed mastery of the new style. It is usually agreed that Horta launched the new style in his now celebrated house designed for Professor Tassel, No. 6 rue Paul-Emile Janson, Brussels, completed in 1893. Compared with Horta's dynamic and plastic forms, the work of the architect and furniture designer Gustave Serrurier-Bovy, 1858–1910, who was inspired by the Arts and Crafts movement, is refreshingly simple. In contrast to the sophisticated elegance of Gallé and Majorelle, Bovy's furniture is tinged by a note of rusticity that has much more in common with England. English influence is evident in the constructive striving, the simple unpainted wood, and the lack of decoration. A marked feature of Bovy's style, but one not borrowed from England, are the slightly curved supports always placed diagonally, giving the effect of a series of arches, which he freely placed where they were or were not needed. These slightly arched trusses were adopted and transformed by Van de Velde to become one of his most characteristic design principles.

Both aspects of Belgian Art Nouveau—the dynamic and plastic and a constructive striving—are represented in the work of Henri Van de Velde, 1863–1957, who has been considered the creator and theoretical founder of Art Nouveau, quite apart from the role he played in the Modern movement. Deeply absorbed in the doctrines of Ruskin and Morris, he was probably the most prolific writer of Art Nouveau and the leading theoretician among the men of the 1890s. Van de Velde, a gifted painter, made his debut as a decorative designer in 1893. To Van de Velde the line was everything; and as a result of his conscious striving for line it is felt too much in almost all his furniture. Typical of his style is the undecorated furniture, depending for its strength and beauty on the movement of the lines, which he designed for the first house he built, at Uccle, near Brussels, completed in 1896. In all his furniture Van de Velde continued his struggle to find beauty in the fitness and eloquence of the line. In 1899 he left Belgium and in 1901 accepted an invitation from the Grand Duke of Saxe-Weimar to head the Weimar School of

452

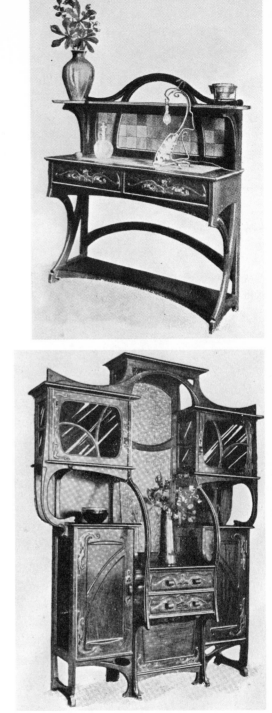

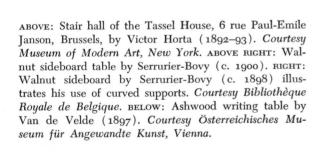

ABOVE: Stair hall of the Tassel House, 6 rue Paul-Emile Janson, Brussels, by Victor Horta (1892–93). *Courtesy Museum of Modern Art, New York.* ABOVE RIGHT: Walnut sideboard table by Serrurier-Bovy (c. 1900). RIGHT: Walnut sideboard by Serrurier-Bovy (c. 1898) illustrates his use of curved supports. *Courtesy Bibliothèque Royale de Belgique.* BELOW: Ashwood writing table by Van de Velde (1897). *Courtesy Österreichisches Museum für Angewandte Kunst, Vienna.*

453

Arts and Crafts, the immediate predecessor of the Bauhaus, which was opened under the tutelage of Walter Gropius in 1919 in the building designed by Van de Velde.

With Van de Velde, who introduced Belgian Art Nouveau to Germany, we approach the cultural phase in Germany and Austria, both countries being latecomers on the scene. Germany was in 1900 almost entirely under the spell of Art Nouveau, enjoying unbounded exuberance of ornamentation as she had done so often in the earlier centuries—in late Gothic, baroque, and rococo. The *Jugend* style had two principal centers, one in Munich and a second somewhat later at Darmstadt, where the Grand Duke Ernst of Hesse had his residence. The furniture designed by the members of the Munich school is markedly constructive; its wealth of joints, curving ribs, struts, and the like is reminiscent of the furniture of Serrurier-Bovy and Van de Velde.

A milestone in the history of Art Nouveau was marked in 1899 when the Grand Duke of Hesse invited seven designers to live as a group in an artist colony at Mathilde-Höhe. Among those accepting the invitation were Peter Behrens, 1868–1940, the leading figure in the Munich group,

454

and Joseph Maria Olbrich, 1867–1908, who was among the founders of the Secession in Vienna, thus bringing together the two schools. The colony was officially opened in 1901 with an exhibition called A Document of German Art. Instead of the customary temporary buildings designed for an exhibition, it was the colony's permanent houses that were under consideration. The work of Behrens, the only member who had designed and furnished his own house (Olbrich had designed the other buildings while the other members shared in the design of the rooms), was in marked contrast to the elegant and imaginative Olbrich. In Behrens' own house, which was his first building, little *Jugend* remained. The dining-room shows a hardening of the tender curve of Art Nouveau, while the bedroom indicates the direction that Behrens was to follow.

After a brief but golden interlude, *Jugendstil* was renounced by the leading designers. In the first years of the twentieth century the group of seven artists, who comprised what is generally called the Munich school—Otto Eckmann, 1865–1902, Richard Riemerschmid, 1868–1957, Hermann Obrist, 1863–1927, Bernhard Pankok, b. 1872, August Endell, 1871–1925, Bruno Paul, b. 1874, and Behrens—had already seen beyond

455

the purely decorative aspects in favor of more rational construction. Stimulated by the work of the tireless writer Hermann Muthesius, 1861–1927, they experimented with construction and function, thereafter working more on the principles of the contemporary English designers. To simplify designs, to create new shapes became their main interest. Riemerschmid's furniture around the turn of the century is occasionally so simple and modern in appearance that it can easily be supposed to date from the 1940s. The rapidity with which the outstanding artists abandoned *Judendstil* is apparent in an observation made by a critic describing the interior-decoration exhibition in St. Louis in 1904: "The sins of the *Jugend* style have been completely overcome."

Finally a few words about the Austrian version of Art Nouveau, to which the term Secessionist was applied, a name which signifies its independent and even rebellious character. The Secession style was almost entirely concentrated in Vienna and is irrevocably connected with Otto Wagner's two pupils, the architects Josef Hoffmann and Joseph M. Olbrich. Although the early work of the Secessionists included designs for interiors in the curvilinear manner, they moved away from what is usually associated with the idea of Art Nouveau because their solution to the style problem—to start entirely anew, which they had in common with all Art Nouveau originators—was so different.

This, of course, brings up the question of Mackintosh's connections with the Viennese school. The similarity existing between the two schools is a much discussed subject; complete accord is still to be reached. It seems safe to conclude, however, that if the influence was not direct, at least at the start it offered a stimulus to the artists of the Secession. Ashlers-Hestermann wrote about the work of Mackintosh displayed at the annual exhibition in Vienna, 1900: "These rooms were like dreams . . . —verticals everywhere. Little cupboards of rectangular shape with far-projecting top cornices, smooth, not of visible frame-and-panel construction; straight, white, and serious-looking . . . decoration like a gem, never interfering with the contour. . . . The fascination of these proportions, the aristocratically effortless certainty with which an ornament of enamel, colored glass, semi-precious stone, beaten metal was placed, fascinated the artists of Vienna who were already a little bored with the eternal solid goodness of English interiors. . . . As against the former overcrowding, there was hardly anything in these rooms, except that, say, two straight chairs, with backs as tall as a man, stood on a white carpet and looked silently and spectrally at each other across a little table. . . ." The stylistic mannerisms of Mackintosh, however, represented only a deviation from the general development in Vienna. As early as 1901 in *Das Interieur,* a Viennese critic described the work of Mackintosh as "quite decadent (*recht dekadent*)."

456

Mahogany armchair by Richard Riemerschmid (1899). *Courtesy Museum of Modern Art, New York. Gift of Dunbar Furniture Corporation of Indiana.* BELOW: Drawing for the bedroom of the Comtesse Esterhazy at their palace, Saint-Abraham, Hungary, by the Viennese Secessionist Joseph Urban (1872–1933). A fine example of Viennese Art Nouveau, this drawing was exhibited at the Water Color Club, Vienna, in 1900. The ornamentation has fixed limits: it never overflows. Everything is subordinated to a strict ornamental order. *Courtesy Cooper Union Museum.*

This brings us to the heart of the Secession style in furniture design and interior decoration. Both Hoffmann and Olbrich, who were architects, were more interested in constructional problems than in ornament. The simple geometrical ornament, the square and the circle, which they developed in the late 1890s was sparingly employed and was subordinate to a strict ornamental order in an entity comprising simple planes. The simpler relationships of flat surfaces, such as Hoffmann preferred, showed the way to the next generation's stylistic ideals of undecorated geometric form. Hoffmann favored the square motif arranged in twos or threes or in rows horizontally or vertically. Owing no doubt to Hoffmann's influence in the following decade, squares enjoyed a great vogue in Vienna and in large sections of Europe. Olbrich adopted as his favorite ornament the circle—circles in rows or in clusters, circles enclosing flames.

To sum up, as a result of the work of Hoffmann, Olbrich, and others, such as the architect Adolf Loos, 1870–1933, who is reputed to have said, "Ornament is a crime," Vienna quickly gained world recognition as one of the most progressive centers of the new movement in Europe.

OPPOSITE ABOVE: Antechamber in the house of Dr. S. Herrn, designed by Josef Hoffmann. It exudes a Mackintosh atmosphere. (*See page 456.*) OPPOSITE BELOW: Dining room in the house of Dr. S. Herrn, designed by Josef Hoffmann. This gives a very good idea of the many ways in which Hoffmann introduced the square motif in his interiors. BELOW: Enameled furniture for a child's room designed by the architect Wilhelm Schmidt. It is decorated with simple geometrical motifs, especially a lavish use of miniature squares. *Courtesy Cooper Union Museum.*

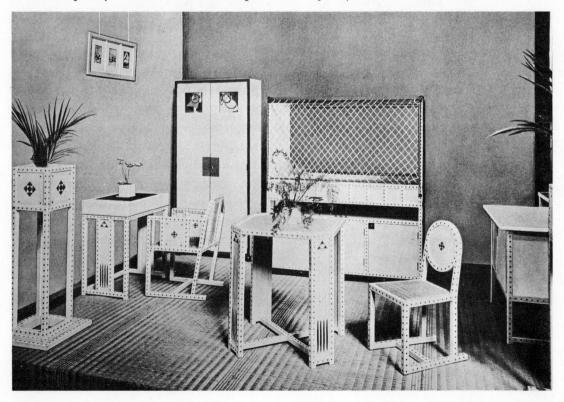

LEFT: Sideboard decorated with vertical bands of intarsia representing stylized fish, by Koloman Moser. Exhibited at the famous Sezession, Vienna (1900). RIGHT: Inlaid cabinet designed by Rosa Krenn in the school of Josef Hoffmann, made by Karl Adolf Franz, Vienna (1912). *Courtesy Österreichisches Museum für Angewandte Kunst, Vienna.*

Even before 1900, Vienna had charted a course which bypassed Art Nouveau and had created her own style, which was to lead directly to the Modern movement with its completely new stylistic ideals. "To try to find beauty in form instead of making it rely on ornament," a principle recommended by Loos in a series of articles that appeared in newspapers and magazines in 1897–98, protesting against the extravagances of Viennese Art Nouveau, was spread across Austria and Europe through the Wiener-Werkstätte, an organization founded in 1903 by Hoffmann in conjunction with Koloman Moser, 1868–1916, and others.

The Modern Movement
and the Twentieth Century

TO WORLD WAR I

As we approach the Modern movement, it is not difficult to question the selection of the name because all movements are modern when they begin. The term, however, has been universally recognized for the trend that was to become the basis for the philosophy and artistic ideals of the twentieth century. The Modern movement—which unhesitatingly removed all ornament and permitted a constructional form to emerge emancipated from petty structural conceits, paying full attention to the qualities of the material and honesty in the use of it—no less than the movements that preceded it, came into existence in response to certain definite problems. The objects made at this time are an expression of a mode of thinking and feeling—an essential part of the age itself.

The Modern movement is an unfolding story—starting as a protest against the intolerable ugliness of the Victorian home, through a phase of oversimplification and a predilection for geometrical shapes (the tide of functionalist modern: the square, spare, bare period), and progressing to an era which shed its clinical attitude and stopped talking about the house as "a machine for living" to the freer, more aesthetic designs of today.

Many who deride Modern and greet it with hostility would be surprised to learn how much of the teachings of the movement—a preference for clean lines, for satisfying proportions, for the rejection of useless ornament—has already entered their lives and helped mold their tastes and preferences.

The mainspring of progress in the technique of manufacturing furniture lies in introducing new materials and new methods and evolving appropriate designs for them, such as the metal tubes Breuer bent into springy supports and the similar spring-support principle that Aalto

461

adapted to curved strips of laminated wood. Out of new materials and new methods, new and strange forms will come. Let us accept them; let us, at any rate, be adventurous. History has taught us that some extravagant designs originally ridiculed have in time become the basis for a popular fashion. The great majority of furniture made today is of wood, which has dominated cabinetmaking from ancient times. It is joined in virtually the same manner as has been employed for hundreds of years, because there are still few substitutes for mortise, tenon, and dowels.

Morris' teachings revealed that it was essential in a civilized community for everyone to have pleasant things to use. If Morris was correct in thinking that the machine could never emulate the work of human hands, the solution was to learn what the machine could do, for it was obvious that manufacture could not be organized upon any other basis. Some designers, awakening to the potentialities of the twentieth century and the marvels of modern industry, shared the feeling that industrial design and the products made by the machine might be as legitimate a form of artistic expression as those made by human hands. Henri Van de Velde, 1863–1957, lecturing on the beauty inherent in machines, maintained, "The powerful play of their iron arms will create beauty as soon as beauty guides them." Hand in hand with a strong belief in the machine was an appreciation for designs of a classically pure perfection—to simplify or to eliminate decoration and to preserve the qualities inherent in natural materials. The American architect Louis Sullivan, 1856–1924, in his *Ornament in Architecture,* 1892, contends that "ornament is mentally a luxury not a necessity," and that we would benefit aesthetically "if we should refrain entirely from the use of ornament for a period of years in order that our thoughts might concentrate acutely upon the production of buildings well formed and comely in the nude." He points out in the same article that "organic ornament should be the phase to follow the removal of all ornament." In an organic system, the ornament seems a part of the surface that receives it, rather than an addition to it, resulting in a peculiar sympathy between ornament and structure which is absent in the case of the latter.

The Viennese architect Otto Wagner, 1841–1918, observed in 1894 that a new style consonant with our modern requirements would stress "horizontal lines . . . great simplicity and an energetic exhibition of construction and materials." Also from Vienna were the forceful words of the architect Adolf Loos, 1870–1933, who declared that "the lower the standard of the people, the more lavish are its ornaments. To find beauty in form instead of finding it in ornament is the goal toward which humanity is aspiring." The Greeks of our culture, according to Loos, were the engineers; he looked to them to translate the geometric forms of classical Greek art to the machine. Briefly, classical form restated. These ideals were expressed in a more comprehensive manner by Frank Lloyd Wright, 1869–1959, Sullivan's most illustrious pupil, in his manifesto, *The Arts and Crafts of the Machine,* 1901. As Nikolaus Pevsner writes in his *Pioneers of Modern Design,* 1949, these five men (Van de Velde, Sullivan, Wagner, Loos, and Wright) were "the first architects to admire the machine and to understand its essential character and its consequence on the relation of architecture and design to ornamentation. . . ."

Undoubtedly the credit for the propagation of these ideas must be given to German writers and architects. Foremost among the German writers is Hermann Muthesius, 1861–1927, who served as a connecting link between the English styles of the 1890s and Germany. As an ardent advocate of reason and simplicity in architecture and art, he soon became the recognized leader of a new trend toward *sachlichkeit,* a development which followed the short-lived *Jugendstil* in Germany. The term *sachlich,* which has no English equivalent, but means "relating to the thing itself," became the slogan for the ever-expanding Modern movement. Reasonable *sachlichkeit,* relationship to the thing itself, is the quality Muthesius extols in the English Arts and Crafts, while from the modern designer he asks for "perfect and pure utility, creation for use."

Other partisans of *sachlichkeit* called for the making of practical, undecorated furniture in smooth, polished, lightweight forms as a boon to housewives; for wide horizontal windows and "floods of light." Some of the earliest results of this campaign were revealed at an exhibition of industrial art in Dresden, 1906, where the Deutsche Werkstätten showed their first quantity-produced (therefore less expensive) and machine-produced furniture of modern design. The next hurdle the German industrial designers overcame was the standardization of parts; their first modern unit furniture—an idea originating in America, where it was introduced for bookcases—was shown in 1910. It was designed by Bruno Paul, who like some of the best German architects furnished industrial designs for the Deutsche Werkstätten. Since the Deutsche Werkstätten did not object to a touch of tradition, the new furniture, developed from the spirit of the machine, was as a whole neat and comfortable, of a simple classical character but with all gingerbread omitted. These features, which were not revolutionary but reasonable, popularized the new furniture in Germany and brought about a change of taste throughout the country.

Similar ideas to those held by the Deutsche Werkstätten guided the activities of the Deutsche Werkbund established in 1907 to coalesce the various individual experiments into a recognized world-wide style. This association, comprising manufacturers and designers, was formed to promote high standards of craftsmanship and industrial design by encouraging a closer co-operation among architect, designer, manufacturer, and workman. From the beginning, this group felt no horror of the machine. They believed that the machine was after all but a more powerful kind of tool which if properly directed could achieve a beauty of its own. The program developed by the Werkbund—the acceptance of the machine in its proper place—was adopted by other countries. There arose the Austrian Werkbund established in 1910, the Swiss Werkbund in 1913, the English Design and Industries Association founded in 1915, while the Swedish Slöjdsförening was organized anew into a Werkbund toward the end of World War I.

But the controversial problem confronting the industrial designers—where the emphasis should be placed in the future, on standardization or individualism—was not settled until, at the Werkbund Exhibition at Cologne, 1914, Van de Velde and his ideas of individualism yielded to Muthesius, the standard-bearer for the opposite camp. It was the model factory at this exhibition, by Walter Gropius, b. 1883, the most unyielding German innovator, who considers himself a follower of Morris, Van de Velde, and the Werkbund, that cast the die. This factory, showing as never before the exciting architectural potentialities of new materials—steel, concrete, and glass—in contrast to buildings employing traditional methods and materials—wood, brick, and stone—won the day and the future for Muthesius. From the efforts of a relatively small group of men of remarkable talent, then, Morris and his followers—Voysey, Mackintosh, Van de Velde, Loos, Behrens, Wright, Gropius, and the other architects and artists—our visual ideas were raised out of the morass of late Victorian historicism, the imitation of the hackneyed forms of earlier times, onto the level of honesty, fitness of purpose, and contemporary expression. The bridge between the nineteenth and twentieth centuries had been spanned, which brings our narrative to the time of the two great wars.

THE INTER-WAR PERIOD

In the immediate years before World War I, modern designers were becoming increasingly aware of the challenge of an industrialized society and the vivid beauty of engineering, whose celebrated monument was the Eiffel Tower. On the other hand, familiar influences—the lightness and spaciousness learned from Japan, the ideal of honesty in materials and construction but now transferred to new conditions—appeared more urgent than ever before. World War I brought dynamic changes in people's lives and thoughts. The younger generation who survived it emerged with a hatred of war, and they instinctively tended to blame the older generation for the horrors they suffered. The time was ripe for a change and changes there were, as modern designers focused their interests on industrial materials and processes. A new, very powerful synthesis of modern design ideals sprang up and became embodied in the work of artists' groups in various European countries, as in Holland, Germany and France. By 1920 modern designers were developing three elements heretofore kept in the background—the acceptance of mass production, a predilection for geometric shapes, and the forms and materials of engineering.

In 1919 the Germans opened a new school under the tutelage of Walter Gropius to teach experimental methods of designing for the machine. This school, whose influence has been pre-eminent, was called the Staatliches Bauhaus. It was to become for more than a decade a focal point of creative energy in Europe as well as a storm center of propaganda for and against the machine until it was abolished by the National Socialists in 1933. Essentially the Bauhaus was a workshop and a school. The students were urged to explore industrial materials and processes, to experiment freely and boldly, but always to keep in mind the purpose their design should serve; that is, form should follow function, creation for use. Their functional solutions were expressed in geometric forms influenced by the Stijl movement flourishing in Holland from around 1917 to 1928. Among the Bauhaus innovations were the employment of metal tubes in the design of furniture, highly polished surfaces made interesting by textures rather than by decoration, and stacking furniture designed to facilitate storage. Many Bauhaus designs were acquired by industry for mass production; although most of their products were made by hand, the precision and clarity of their geometric contours imbued them with a machine-made appearance. This was an important consideration for early modern designers. The theories for which the Bauhaus stood are often summarized in the slogan of functionalism. The emphasis on functionalism was so great as to suggest that all furniture made throughout the ages was hopelessly non-functional. Nevertheless, the doctrine of functionalism brushed away much Victorian clutter and in certain ways has considerably simplified our lives.

It was at the Bauhaus in 1925 that Marcel Breuer, b. 1902, a student at the school from 1920 to 1924, invented the first tubular-steel chair. In his cantilevered chair he applied a new design principle by substituting a double S-shaped support for the conventional four legs. The metal tubes, bent into springy supports, gave comfortable resiliency.

One of the great innovators of chromium-plated steel furniture was Ludwig Mies van der Rohe, b. 1886, who succeeded Walter Gropius as director of the Bauhaus. His sleek Barcelona chair, which entrusts the sitter's weight to cantileverage, has become a classic. Like all Mies's furniture, it requires faultless hand craftsmanship to produce, paradoxically,

465

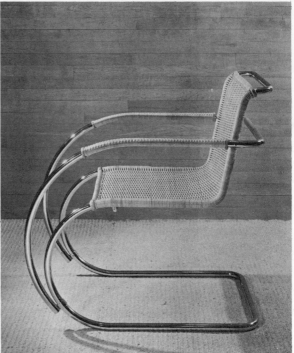

ABOVE LEFT: Chair designed by Marcel Breuer (1925). This version of the cantilevered tubular-steel chair is the model for thousands of variations seen all over the world. *Courtesy Museum of Modern Art, New York. (See page 465.)* ABOVE RIGHT: Armchair of chrome-plated tubular steel and cane, designed by Mies van der Rohe (1927). *Courtesy Laverne International Ltd., New York. (See page 465.)* LEFT: Barcelona chair of chrome-plated steel bars designed for the German Pavilion at the International Exposition at Barcelona (1929) by Mies van der Rohe. *Courtesy Knoll Associates.* OPPOSITE: Living room at Tugendhat House, Brno, Czechoslovakia, by Mies van der Rohe (1930). *Courtesy Museum of Modern Art, New York.*

its machine-made look. Described by its admirers as "pure," this steel chair with supporting leather straps and tufted leather cushions received its name from the International Exposition held at Barcelona, 1929, where Mies's pavilion for the German government won world acclaim. The best qualities of Mies's work—economy of line, beauty of proportion, and extreme precision—are revealed in this chair.

Both Mies and Breuer, in their wish to represent very elegant interiors of their own day, turned their backs on the interiors of bygone times

with their infinity of little pieces. Furniture with gleaming steel tubes, designs limited to simple geometrical forms, proportions which are nearly always right because of the faultless equilibrium of balanced masses, and the axiom "the less is more" imbued their rooms with an air of sobriety, of formal austerity. None of these elements offer any very varied resources to designers, but when interpreted by hands less skillful or stripped of space and rich materials, the interiors acquire a barren air, the air of poor relations, but at any rate of relations.

It was at this period that the tide of functionalist modern reverencing the influence of Germany—that is, all this geometric purity in design, which has in it something abstract, something purely rational—had its brief moment. Need we ask, is geometry in design new? We have already become acquainted with it in the Louis XVI style, a society that loved simplicity and reason, but their geometric shapes were always softened by moldings and the abundant grace of ornament. Again we meet with simple lines, pure contours, and correct shapes in the Empire style, a style of uncompromising geometry. In this style no ornament ever availed

467

ABOVE: Study and living room at Tugendhat House, Brno, Czechoslovakia, by Mies van der Rohe, 1930. *Courtesy Museum of Modern Art, New York.* (*See page 467.*) OPPOSITE: State bedroom at the Vanderbilt mansion, Hyde Park, New York (c. 1898). The balustrade and columns recall the *lit de parade.* (*See page 470.*)

to mitigate the block-like or box-like shapes which pleased the eyes of that generation. In fact, from the days of antiquity Western culture has traditionally chosen geometric shapes in preference to non-geometric forms; their superior beauty lies in their rational appeal. Plato, in the *Philebus*, declares that when he speaks of beauty of form he means "straight lines and circles, and the plane or solid figures which are formed out of them by turning-lathes, rulers and measures of angles; for these I affirm to be not only relatively beautiful, like other things, but they are eternally and absolutely beautiful." It was inevitable, however, that a reaction set in against the cold simplification of forms of the 1920s and early 1930s, which only admits as much comfort as is compatible with its abstract notions of pure beauty. From around 1933 many designers returned to some extent to freehand curves and forms overlooked since the beginning of the twentieth century.

While Gropius and his group were organizing the Bauhaus, most people in America were enamored with the past. Antiques and reproductions routed any vestige of pioneering from the drawing-room. The quest for

antiques was no longer confined to a few; in the brief span of about two decades shopping for antiques in all seasons, from Duveen to dark and squalid shops, had become one of the most popular American pastimes. In the 1920s even department stores—the Jordan Marsh Company, Marshall Field, and John Wanamaker, to mention but several—put in large stocks of antiques to lure the collector. The occupants of the White House were not unaware of the significance of American antiques. President Coolidge in 1925 appointed a commission to collect for the White House specimens of the work of our early American cabinetmakers, which it was hoped would "create a still deeper and more abiding interest and respect for the work of our forefathers."

Everyone in the trade was busy making reproductions. There was a comfortable number of relatively small cabinetshops, such as Karcher and Rehm, Vollmer, Pottier and Stymus, Kimbel or Alavoine, where copies of the original work were faithfully reproduced to the most minute detail. Great houses built by wealthy Americans were furnished with carefully selected reproductions to convey a continental atmosphere, a much sought-after look. Italian Renaissance and French interiors provided the chief source of inspiration, as is shown in the Vanderbilt mansion at Hyde Park built by the illustrious firm of McKim, Mead and White in 1896–98.

The elaborate furnishings of this mansion were chosen with care and taste by Stanford White, Ogden Codman, and other noted decorators. In order to give an air of authenticity to the state bedroom of the Louis XV period, a balustrade was placed around the state bed in the manner of the French *lit de parade*.

Now let us glance at ordinary reproductions made for the great majority of Americans. How do they compare with the costly examples? In the mass-production furniture trade during the first quarter of the twentieth century the increased use of machinery was chiefly devoted to making atrocious copies of period pieces matched only by the poor quality of materials. A considerable part of this "machine art" was in the "Borax" class, so-called because hawkers of that cleanser offered premiums, and the word became associated with "extra" values which commercial furniture factories frequently offered in words or in "extra" large forms, "extra" carvings, "extra" glossy finish. As we shall see a little later, the era of quality reproductions made for commercial distribution was initiated in the 1930s.

Aside from brief flirtations, the first real interest in modern furniture in America was inspired by the Paris Exposition, which was to bring into existence the style known as Art Moderne. But before we consider the Paris Exposition, which was a resounding success, let us discuss briefly an important change in interior design that developed in France after World War I. The eye level of the room dropped; furniture was accordingly designed to be appreciated from this lower perspective. Sofas and chairs supported on legs no more than three inches in height, occasional tables no higher than chair seats, beds frequently no more than a mattress placed on a dais, and huge cushions (perhaps the most fashionable of all seats) are typical of this taste. Credit for this vogue is often accorded to Paul Poiret's artistic discovery of Morocco, with its long, low sofas, *tabourets,* thick carpets, and absence of chairs. Others regard it as a Japanese influence, the influence of the Japanese house with its rooms designed to be seen by persons sitting on the floor. Whatever the source, the fashion for a lower living level was accepted, and at the conclusion of the war the low horizon was adopted in the design of French interiors.

In France a quarter of a century had elapsed since Art Nouveau, and in the meantime modern art had arrived. The French realized that the time had come to conform to the requirements and conditions of present-day life, to harmonize the decorative arts with current tastes and new architectural concepts so that the atmosphere of the home should reflect in a reasonable and convincing manner the age we live in. All too long French decorative art had been restricted to the making of single objects of artistic interest, surely very precious, but not in step with modern industrial development. By encouraging her designers to adapt new designs to the possibilities of machine tools, to industrialize in the best sense of the word without sacrificing artistic quality, the French hoped to inject new life into her own arts, thereby considerably spreading their use. Relying on the French reputation for luxury craftsmanship, her aim was to create a new style that could play an important role in the new order of things. The outcome was the Exposition Internationale des Arts Décoratifs covering more than seventy acres along the right bank of the Seine, which opened in May 1925. The exposition stood for modern decorative and industrial art; this is clearly conveyed in a paragraph which excluded from the exposition "copies, imitations, or counterfeits of ancient styles." All industries were represented, since the most simple and everyday objects are capable of being made with as much beauty as articles of luxury.

More than twenty countries participated in the exposition, and though America did not exhibit (neither did Russia nor Germany), American furniture manufacturers and designers attended in the thousands. The exposition as a whole was a demonstration of the results of that transition period which had its inception in England in the nineteenth century. The principle article in *L'Illustration* describing the exposition emphasized the profound influence of William Morris and his followers on continental design. It is not possible to describe the furniture because each designer expressed himself freely and fearlessly. In a general sense some designers showed a self-conscious breaking away from tradition; others carried on the various formulas of their classical training, while a third category worked out their personal ideas without regard for those of their contemporaries. However, in spite of individual aberrations, the furniture was related to the great program laid down by William Morris—in its determination to belong to its own times, to reject anachronisms, to bring more beauty into everyday life. To a large extent the furniture was fundamentally the product of a new arrangement of old "studio properties," in which the designers recognized their first necessity was to break with the older ornamental traditions.

"There are many clever decorators in Paris but comparatively few specialize in this new field," stated *The Upholsterer*, July 1925. "Of course Jacques Ruhlmann is preeminent. His work is remarkable. . . . Many of the tables are no higher than the chair seats. It is one of the characteristics of this New Art. [Apart from Ruhlmann there is] the work of a very progressive young organization, Süe et Mare, some of whose pieces have just been acquired by the Metropolitan Museum of Art . . . these two firms . . . best typify the last word in New Art." But the French art of 1925 called New Art, or Art Moderne was not strictly new. If we reflect a little, we must admit that the elements of the style—a predilection for geometric forms and a marginal interest in the "nature" forms popular in Art Nouveau, but now considerably refined, were not after all such unheard of novelties in the history of French furniture. Art Moderne, un-

ABOVE: Ebony writing table mounted in gilt bronze designed by Louis Süe and André Mare for the Paris Exposition (1925). LEFT: Ebony writing chair designed for the writing table above. *Courtesy Metropolitan Museum of Art. Edward C. Moore, Jr. Gift Fund, 1925. (See page 471.)* BELOW: Cabinet of macassar, ebony, and ivory, designed by E. J. Ruhlmann (1925). *Courtesy Metropolitan Museum of Art. Edward C. Moore, Jr. Gift Fund, 1925.* OPPOSITE: Salon designed by Süe and Mare for the Paris Exposition (1925), showing the writing table in context. The seating level has been lowered noticeably. *Courtesy Cooper Union Museum.*

consciously indeed, for it cherished a fine contempt for the furniture. Art Moderne, unconsciously indeed, for it cherished a fine contempt for the furniture that went before it, merely took up the old French classicism. It fastened by instinct on the point where an earlier generation had stopped; but now it was interpreted according to the ideals and philosophy of the twentieth century—a whole new attitude of mind. So once again the old visibly influences the new, the new the logical outcome of it.

Ruhlmann, whose work exercised a wide and beneficial influence on interior decoration in France, was one of the first with the courage to conceive and carry out works that were entirely rational in construction, relying for their beauty mainly on the general harmony and balance of lines. Some of his chairs, as well as some of his sideboards and cabinets, have the legs partly included as part of the body of the piece itself, a device inaugurated by Ruhlmann and since much imitated. "Ruhlmann's simple and sumptuous art," *The Studio,* 1926, observes, "has been greatly aided in its success by the remarkable clearness, precision, economy and sobriety of the forms to which modern machine production has accustomed us." But furniture so conceived required beauty of material, beauty of execution. Ruhlmann appreciated these values from the outset. He was especially fond of exotic woods—amboina, macassar, ebony, amaranth,

473

Chair of macassar and ebony designed by E. J. Ruhlmann (1925). *Courtesy Metropolitan Museum of Art. Edward C. Moore, Jr. Gift Fund, 1925.* (*See page 473.*) BELOW: Corner of a salon designed and executed by Ruhlmann for the Paris Exposition (1925). The armchair and settee recall the style of the First Empire. OPPOSITE ABOVE: Bedroom for a woman, designed by Maurice Dufrène for the Paris Exposition (1925). The semi-Venetian mirror and "vanity" became indispensable bedroom properties. OPPOSITE BELOW: Bedroom for a young woman, designed by René Gabriel for the Paris Exposition (1925). This type of bedroom suite became a model for the mass-produced modernistic bedroom of the 1930s in the United States. *Courtesy Cooper Union Museum.*

and tulipwood—from which he obtained exquisite effects, ornamenting them with ivory marquetry which never wandered beyond the limits of good taste. The same sureness of touch was evident in Ruhlmann's interiors, which were remarkable for their sense of space, for the broad lines of their compositions. The Hôtel d'un Collectioneur at the exposition was entirely furnished and decorated by him. "He does not," we read in *The Studio*, 1926, "like so many others force himself to appear 'modern' but is so instinctively."

In contrast to Ruhlmann's work, extravagant excesses and arguable tastes marked much of the work at the exposition, which passed at the

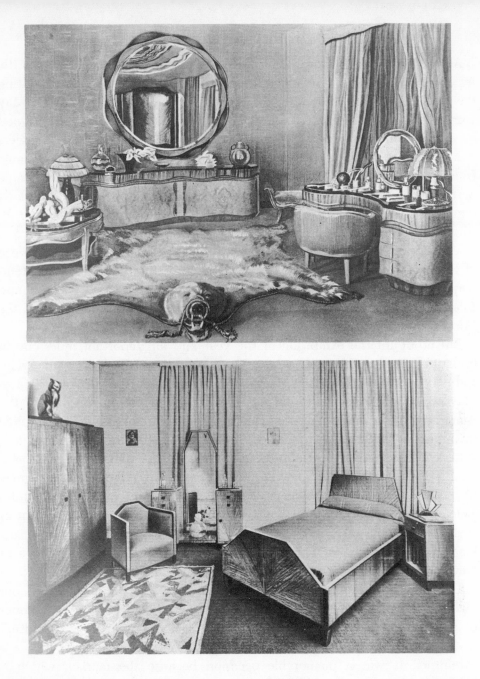

time for the latest word in French decorative art. Was this the effect of the mania for modern or merely an irresistible desire to do something that had not been done before? However this may be, in less than five years after the exposition the French moderated modern. "By degrees," *The Upholsterer*, December 1929, reports, "they abandoned and are still abandoning the unusual which is meaningless and they are divorcing Art Moderne from the principles of Cubism, Futurism, and the various other *isms* of art development with which it has become associated in the public mind. They are striving for an elegant simplicity that shall successfully symbolize the current age."

As the department stores in France—Bon Marché, Galeries Lafayette, Au Printemps, to mention several—were the main source for acquainting the public with Art Moderne, so they were to be in America. In May 1927, R. H. Macy sponsored a New Art show at which furniture designed by Paul Frankl, Jules Bouy, John Helmsky, and other modern designers was exhibited. Frankl's so-called skyscraper furniture, deriving its name from the architecture which influenced it, was designed on severely simple perpendicular lines with all superfluous ornament removed. In the following year numerous department stores, such as Lord and Taylor and B. Altman, sponsored exhibitions of Art Moderne furnishings. The Lord and Taylor exhibition was entirely a French interpretation of the style; the work of Ruhlmann was conspicuous. At the Altman exhibition held in September, which displayed the work of the French designers Ruhlmann and Jules Leleu, a new source of inspiration—Chinese domestic furniture of the Ming dynasty—was introduced in a breakfast room by C. B. Falls.

But no doubt the exhibition of the year and an important milestone in promoting modern in America was the International Exposition of Art in Industry sponsored by R. H. Macy and held in their store from May 14 to May 26. Its purpose was to encourage further interest on the part of the American public and the American designers in modern art as applied to industrial design and to present examples of the best European and American schools so the public might appraise the entire picture. Three hundred exhibitors were selected. Such famous architects and designers of modern as Josef Hoffmann of Vienna, Bruno Paul of Germany, Jules Leleu of Paris, and Giovanni Ponti of Milan created rooms in the spirit of their national art. Included among the American exhibits was a city apartment by Kem Weber of Los Angeles, a living-room by Eugene Schoen of New York, while Lescaze of New York created a penthouse studio.

Heeding the admonition, "Be not the first by whom the new is tried, nor yet the last to lay the old aside," American designers created a fair number of pieces showing Art Moderne influence at the January 1928 furniture market of the Grand Rapids Market Association, an association with 450 exhibitors. It was a memorable occasion because the market, which is held semi-annually, celebrated its 100th birthday. In honor of the occasion a panorama of furniture covering the past fifty years had been arranged—rooms with marble-topped dressing tables and monumental black walnut beds riotous with carving, furniture of the "golden oak" period, of the "mission" period, the "arts and crafts" period, and the polychrome fashion which swept the country some years ago. As for the Art Moderne furniture, the ubiquitous vanity with its cubes, planes, and great round looking-glass, the so-called semi-Venetian mirror, was the most modern of all modern. At the summer market of the same year Art Moderne attained the peak of its sudden popularity.

In the next few years an undercurrent of protest, which had never ceased to make itself felt from the birth of modern in America, grew more lively. Critics waxed indignant at the so-called "corruption of taste," and justifiably so when we consider the jukebox, or jazz-type modernistic which was really cleaned-up "Borax." Then, too, it was about this time in the early 1930s that steel furniture, especially the tubular type, had its brief hour of fashion—bred in the wake of Breuer, Mies, and the Swiss-born architect Charles Édouard Jeanneret, called Le Corbusier, b. 1887. The latter's famous dictum, "the house is a machine for living," is as enigmatic as Mona Lisa's smile. *The Upholsterer,* March 1932, states: "The bulk of what the modernistic school creates is either mediocre or downright absurd . . . [but] it still has a healthy following in this country and abroad."

It can hardly be surprising that at the Chicago Century of Progress Exposition, 1933, modernistic furnishings in harmony with the ultra-modernism of the fair were given prominence. It was, however, a modified modernistic; functional, conservative, and distinctly removed from the bizarre Art Moderne of the past. In the ensuing year a fleeting caprice of modern—classic modern—with more emphasis on classic and less on modernistic was introduced to dispel the sameness, the heavy dull monotony that hovered over modern. It was hoped that classic modern, which was mostly white and gold, would scatter to the four winds the "clinical" look—a look so strenuously resisted by the general public. In 1937 a new "homey" look, a crafted expression for modern, was forecast by Widdicomb with its new collection of Swedish modern by Carl Malmsten.

After more than a decade of much effort, uncertainty, and setbacks, the Modern movement gained a firm grip in America. For a clearer understanding of modern design in the 1930s we have to thank the continuous showings at the Museum of Modern Art, New York, founded in 1929, and the exhibitions of industrial art held at the Metropolitan Museum of Art. First inaugurated in 1917, the fifteenth exhibition, held at the Metropolitan in 1940, revealed that modern design had made considerable progress in its brief lifespan. The New York World's Fair, as well as the Golden Gate Exhibition in San Francisco, both held in 1939, climaxed the upsurge of modern. Swedish modern enjoyed a great vogue after its spectacular success at the World's Fair in New York, while the exhibition at San Francisco brought into focus a growing recognition of the regional independence of architecture and design on the West Coast. An informal type of living, with patios, became admired; the seed of the ranch house was sown. Briefly, the ranch-house stampede had arrived to vie for honors with the Cape Cod house, preferred to all others from the 1920s.

Gilbert Rhode, d. 1944, one of the prominent names in all that was progressive in furniture, expressed his views on the progress made and the future trend of modern in an article appearing in *The Interior Decorator,*

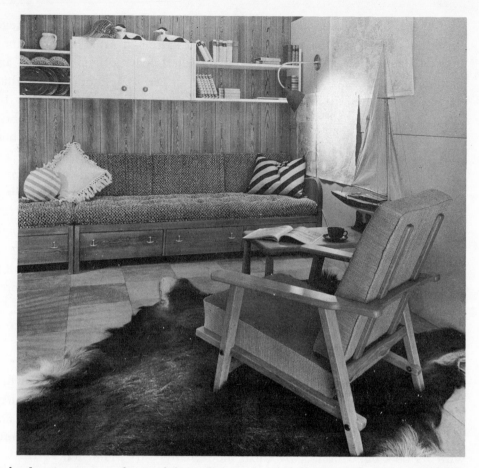

Weekend sitting room in the Swedish Pavilion at the New York World's Fair (1939). The furniture was designed by Elias Svedberg. *Courtesy Nordiska Kompaniet, Stockholm.* (*See page 477.*)

January 1940. "It is only about ten years ago that the first severe straight-lined furnishings eschewing all decoration and making much ado about 'functionalism' appeared on the American scene. . . . That this style did not satisfy the needs of human beings is manifest in the many attempts to find something with more emotional content. The abortive attempts that came under the head of neo-classic, or modern classic, were gropings in this direction; in the latest of these efforts euphemistically called Swedish Modern we at least find a solution more nearly suited to our American way of life. But now for the first time we see a maturing that can be called all our own. It is no mere accident that so many of the designers, who ten years ago began with the pure 'international style,' are now designing in a 'humanistic' manner that admits a place to the past as well as to the present, and to the emotions as well as the mind. . . ."

But before we continue our story about the developments after World War II, let us briefly discuss Scandinavian modern furniture, in particular that of Sweden, the birthplace of Scandinavian modern. The general public first became acquainted with Swedish modern on a considerable scale at the exhibition held in 1930 at Stockholm. Simplicity and unpretentiousness, directness and usefulness transmitted to craft materials and techniques are its notable virtues. An engaging honesty has been the hallmark of Swedish furniture of the past. In the eighteenth century, when French influence was pre-eminent, the Swedish craftsmen gracefully and intelligently blended this influence into a native Swedish style which received appropriately enough, during the latter part of the century, the name Gustavian, in honor of the great charmer king, Gustavius III, 1746–92. It can hardly be surprising that under Napoleon's Marshal Bernadotte, 1763–1844, who became king of Sweden in 1818, the country had a special affinity for Empire, in particular Biedermeier. The plain but agreeable, wholesome and homey quality of Biedermeier was to have a formative influence on Swedish modern. The debasement in taste which everywhere accompanied the advent of industrialism was also felt in Sweden, where handicraft and the homecraft movement were recruited in the crusade against the machine.

This emphasis on handicraft naturally widened the gap between it and industry; on the other hand, it laid the groundwork for the international reputation of Swedish arts and crafts. Handicraft flourished in an unprecedented manner in Sweden until 1923, the year the Stockholm Town Hall was completed. From that time onward Swedish efforts were directed more and more into the channels of industrial design, for the Swedish had learned toward the end of World War I that their house-furnishing products made in industrial factories employing designers had received world-wide praise for superior design. As the movement toward aesthetically improving machine-made products gained momentum in the 1920s, the Swedish, steeped as they were in handicraft tradition, believed and practiced that beauty and quality can be achieved only through the close cooperation of the furniture architect, as he is called in Sweden, and the manufacturer. The latest phase in the program for raising the quality of industrial products has been directed toward developing mass-produced articles of a high standard, but within a price range acceptable to the general public. Working within the framework of a general scheme for the control of manufacture to meet the physical and aesthetic needs of the general public and not special classes, more emphasis is placed on the natural beauty of the wood (its fiber texture and color) and form—briefly, aesthetic consideration of designs tempered by economic and social conditions.

It is interesting to note here the English Utility Furniture Scheme, a social experiment brought into existence by the extreme shortage of timber caused by World War II. The interesting feature of this wartime control was a definite and conscious effort to improve design. Through it the public became accustomed to a much better and simpler type of design than was

Armchair of laminated bent birch plywood with black canvas webbing and a white lambskin slip cover, designed by Bruno Mathsson (1940). *Courtesy Museum of Modern Art, New York, Edgar Kaufmann, Jr. Fund.* BELOW: A combination of separate units made of teak and pine (c. 1956). *Courtesy Nordiska Kompaniet, Stockholm.* OPPOSITE: Dining corner designed by Carl Malmsten (1951). *Courtesy The American Swedish News Exchange.* (See page 482.)

available before the war. Of course permanent government control of design in any consumer trade is scarcely likely to be beneficial.

The Swedish prefer to think of Swedish modern not as a style but as a movement predicated on the conception of the role of furniture in modern life. A movement capable of endless development and adaptability to all conditions guided by a fundamental idea—the human form and the ar-

rangement of the interior so as to give the individual the greatest freedom for his activities in a harmonious environment within the walls of his home. There can be little doubt that Swedish designers have not lost sight of this idea. The typical Swedish modern chair is especially shaped to the human form, as few chairs have been since early times. Their comprehensive unit system of furniture allows the individual to build up the exact accommodations he requires, to arrange it in a number of ways and to rearrange it easily in another quite different room, or, if necessary, even another house. Moreover, an additional unit can be purchased to cope with a demand for more space without discarding any of the units already purchased. Among other advantages, Swedish units are purchased flat in a cardboard package and can be assembled at home. They can be taken apart again for packing, so that an entire houseful of furniture can be put in a relatively small van.

Although Swedish modern has such prominent designers as Carl Malmsten, Elias Svedberg, Karl Bruno Mathsson, and Captain G. A. Berg, generally regarded as the apostle of contemporary Swedish, it is in the tradition of anonymous furniture. In this respect as well as in its standards of usefulness and sparse simplicity, it is not unlike Shaker furniture. Mathsson occupies a singular position for his laminated wood-frame chairs, which he has been continually developing and refining for a period of over twenty

481

years. Many Swedish pieces of graceful and modest design, such as chairs displaying with remarkable clarity the separation of frame and upholstery, chairs with spindled backs, wood seats, and finely turned legs and stretchers, cane-paneled low cupboards and slender sideboards, have been a fruitful influence on American furniture. In fact it is true to say that the influence of Swedish modern has become one of the essential parts of the furniture we like to think of as American.

FROM WORLD WAR II TO THE PRESENT

The progress made by the Modern movement is clearly portrayed in chairs, which reveal the character of a period more fully than any other piece of furniture. The chair has always been, if only by reason of necessity, the undisputed queen of domestic furniture. But now in this age of simple interiors, of disappearing wall space, built-in storage cupboards or furniture that behaves as if built-in, such as sectional storage and seating units, the chair has become even more important. All ingenuity is brought into play to design chairs having agreeable silhouettes, relative transparency, portability, durability, and comfort. As we cannot pass all chairs in review, let us first describe a few models which represent achievements in technologically inventive furniture. As true products of the machine, these chairs have, and properly so, strongly marked characteristics of their own, quite different from handworkmanship but not necessarily inferior.

First are the light bentwood chairs, an invention of a Rhinelander, Michael Thonet, 1796–1871, who devoted his talents to inventing durable, portable, and economical chairs. His earliest successful experiments were in a material we now call bent plywood. Instead of gluing a thin strip of veneer to a wood frame, he built up, sandwich fashion, strips of veneer of proper thinness which he steamed in a mold and then cut out his designs. Thousands of miles away in New York, Belter was working on much the same principle—lamination—in his ornately carved rosewood chairs. Prince Metternich of Vienna became acquainted with Thonet's bent plywood chairs and invited him to live in Vienna, an invitation Thonet accepted. Thonet continued his experiments. In 1856 he perfected a process by which solid lengths of beechwood could be steamed and bent to form long curved rods. He used Carpathian beech because of its singular tight parallel grain; other woods not possessing this quality are apt to splinter at the point of greatest strain. Bentwood made it possible to produce chairs without complicated carved joints and contours, paving the way for the first mass production of standardized furniture. One piece of bentwood could be used to form both the open back and the rear legs, as, for example, the popular "Vienna" café model. Countless thousands of bentwood chairs, one of the lightest, strongest chairs ever designed, have been sold through-

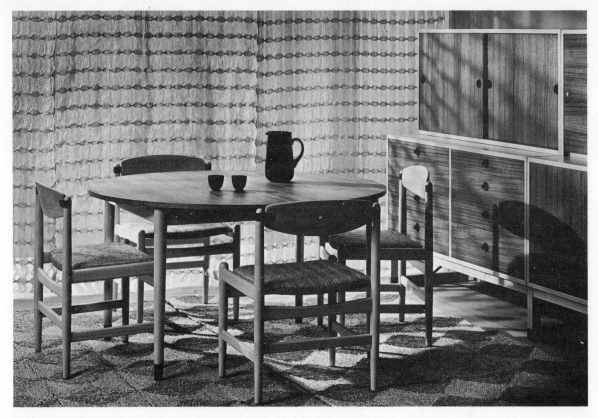

Dining-room furniture of teak and pine, designed by Börje Mogensen (c. 1956). The chairs have flexible crest rails. *Courtesy Nordiska Kompaniet, Stockholm.* BELOW: "Vienna" café chair of bent beechwood designed by Gerbruder Thonet (1876). *Courtesy Museum of Modern Art, New York.* RIGHT: Water color by William Leroy Jacobs (1869–1917), showing the universally popular "Vienna" café chair. *Courtesy Cooper Union Museum.*

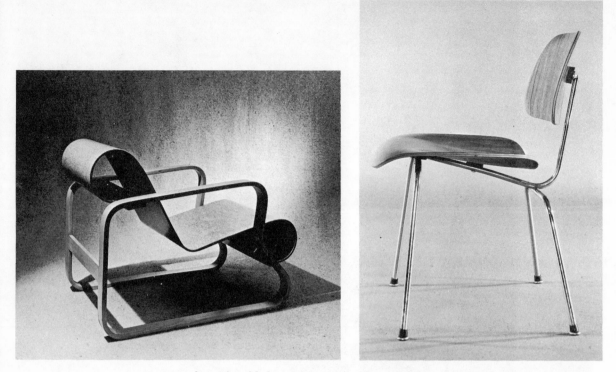

LEFT: Lounge chair of molded and bent birch plywood designed by Alvar Aalto (c. 1934). *Courtesy Museum of Modern Art, New York. Gift of Edgar Kaufmann, Jr.* RIGHT: Chair of molded walnut plywood, metal rod, designed by Charles Eames (1946). OPPOSITE LEFT: Armchair of molded plastic reinforced with Fiberglas, enameled black wire, designed by Charles Eames (1951). OPPOSITE RIGHT: Chair with back, seat, and base formed of wire painted black, designed by Charles Eames (1951). The slip cover is made of gray plastic. *Courtesy Museum of Modern Art, New York. Gift of Herman Miller Furniture Company.* (*See page 486.*)

out the world. Some of Thonet's designs for chairs achieved a simplicity that made them especially attractive to twentieth-century designers. Le Corbusier selected one bentwood chair for buildings he designed in the 1920s, because, in his own words, it "possesses nobility."

Next we come to the invention of tubular steel furniture, which we have already considered in Part II of this chapter. Breuer, one of the outstanding names in the history of modern furniture, is best remembered for his cantilevered tubular steel chair with its double S-shaped supports, while Miës's name is indelibly associated with his Barcelona chair. Following the lead of German designers, the Finnish architect Alvar Aalto, b. 1898, famed for his sanatorium at Paimio, adopted the similar spring-support principle used by Breuer in his tubular steel furniture to bent laminated plywood. Though the patent for this material is reputedly traced to the time of the Civil War in America and has been in general use for decades for seats in public conveyances, Aalto was the first to apply the principle to modern domestic furniture design. Using native birch, he not only designed a number of laminated plywood chairs and stools but also invented some of the methods for making them. He also experimented with curving plywood to fit the human shape. In 1934 he introduced a chair having a

continuous seat and back bent in sweeping curves and formed from a single sheet of plywood, suspended within a bent cut-out plywood frame. The chair was ingeniously designed so that the curves made use of the natural springiness of plywood.

Even though new materials were used in their manufacture, these chairs still employed traditional methods of shaping individual pieces and then joining them in different ways. Now we come to chairs whose plastic or plywood seats are made in much the same manner that the body of an automobile is stamped out by a die press. In this manner the back, seat, and arms can be made in one piece. This technique was used by Charles Eames, b. 1907, and Eero Saarinen, 1910–61, for a molded plywood chair entered in the Organic Design competition conducted by the Museum of Modern Art in 1940. Their entry won, and even though their molded plywood chair never went into production, the era of the molded chair had arrived. It was only after World War II that independently Eames and Saarinen each produced molded chairs, Eames of plywood and plastic and Saarinen of plastic.

In 1945 Eames, one of America's most genuinely industrial architect-designers, introduced his shock mounted chair, with its two separate pads of molded plywood serving as a back and seat and its skeleton-like steel tubing frame. Making use of the springiness of both tubular steel and laminated plywood, this chair with its rubber shock mounts electronically welded to the wood and steel is a notable product of machine technology. Though Eames's furniture is known and used around the world, it is this comfortable, flexible, and almost indestructible chair that the general public remembers whenever Eames's name is mentioned. Apart from Eames's molded plywood chair and his 1951 version of a molded plastic shell chair, he introduced a molded wire mesh chair in 1951, though metal mesh is not a new material. His more recent designs include a unique cast aluminum group. It is interesting to compare Eames's wire shell chair with the wire chair by the Italian-born sculptor Harry Bertoia, b. 1915, which came out in 1952. In spite of a superficial likeness, the two chairs are fundamentally different. One basic difference is that Eames's seat cradle is supported on legs, while in Bertoia's chair the seat cradle is suspended by triangular side braces over the base. "This suspension of the seat cradle," we read in *Interiors,* October 1952, "gives the chair flexibility, automatic adjustment to two positions by means of an effortless shift of body weight."

With the rapid development of plastics it was only a matter of time until designers would turn to plastic molded shells. In 1946 the architect-designer Saarinen introduced a molded plastic shell armchair. The capacious molded shell, upholstered in foam rubber and provided with loose seat and back cushions, was held up cradle fashion in a skeleton-like tubular steel framework mounted on four conventionalized steel legs. This skillfully designed easy chair, in which the average person can sit comfortably in a variety of positions, offered such pleasant protection to the sitter that Florence Knoll, b. 1917, the architect-trained designer for whom the chair was designed, popularly dubbed it the "womb chair."

Saarinen, who always designed imaginatively and soundly within the new aesthetics that the machine demands and allows, achieved a great triumph in his chalice-like pedestal chair introduced in 1957. It was designed with a single stem and base in place of the customary four legs. In contrast to the other molded chairs, that is, plastic, plywood, or wire mesh, where the distinction between the shell and supports is quite apparent, this chair presents a more truly unified design whereby the seat and supports, the two essential parts, seem to be of one and the same material. In this instance the seat is a molded plastic shell reinforced with Fiberglas, while the stem and base are of spun aluminum. It is interesting to note that up to this time no chair has been designed that is produced entirely from one piece of folded or pressed material.

Finally, but not in the same category, a few words about the Hardoy chair adapted from a folding wood and canvas chair used by Italian officers in North Africa during the Libyan campaign. This non-folding adaptation having a metal rod frame and leather was done by three Argentinians, Antonio Bonet, Juan Kurchan, and Jorge Ferrari-Hardoy. It turned out to be one of the most inexpensive and practical of all easy

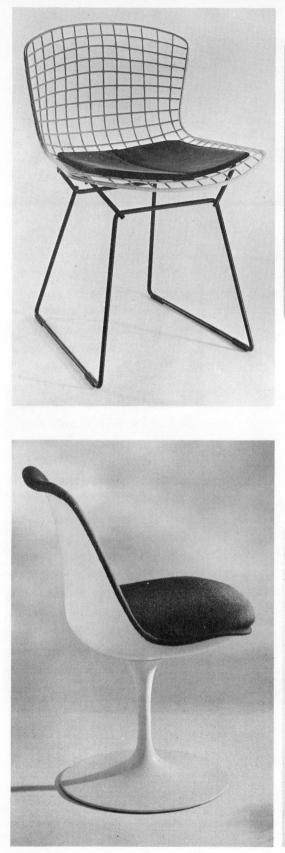

ABOVE LEFT: Chair of chrome-plated steel wire, designed by Harry Bertoia (1952). *Courtesy Museum of Modern Art, New York. Gift of Knoll Associates.* ABOVE RIGHT: "Womb" chair and ottoman, designed by Eero Saarinen (1946). This molded plastic shell with a tubular steel framework is upholstered in foam rubber. BELOW LEFT: Pedestal chair designed by Eero Saarinen (1957). The molded plastic is reinforced with Fiberglas and supported on an aluminum pedestal base. *Courtesy Knoll Associates.* BELOW RIGHT: Hardoy chair, designed by Antonio Bonet, Juan Kurchan, and Jorge Ferrari-Hardoy (1938). A metal rod frame supports a leather slip cover. *Courtesy Museum of Modern Art, New York. Edgar Kaufmann, Jr. Fund.*

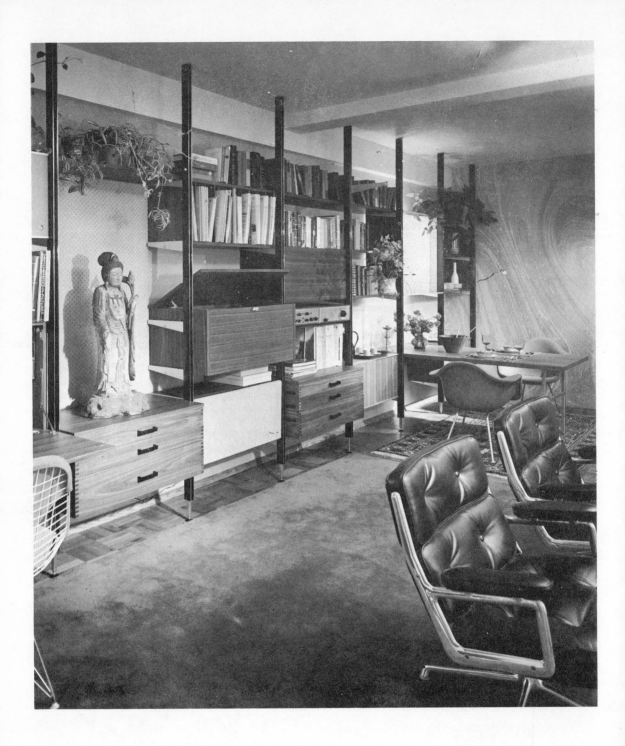

Comprehensive storage system, designed by George Nelson. In addition to storage space for books, records, linens, it contains a dining table and a writing table. In the right foreground are two pivot lounge chairs designed by Charles Eames. *Courtesy Herman Miller. Photo Paul Hyde.*

488

chairs and illustrates so well how the machine has been put to economical and aesthetic use. Of somewhat unorthodox construction, it is nothing more than a continuous metal frame on which the four pocket-like ends of a length of leather are slipped over the two uprights of the back and the two front corners of the seat.

Apart from these examples of chairs, there are certain practical ideas and functional innovations, such as storage walls, room dividers, demountable partitions, and modular case furniture, virtually unknown in 1940, which are found in every kind of interior today. These ideas can be attributed to the industrial designers who are a phenomenon of the United States unparalleled elsewhere. Of this group of designers the architect-industrial designer George Nelson, b. 1908, is outstanding. A substantial part of Nelson's designs are furniture "systems" rather than individual items of furniture, for example, his basic storage component system comprising ready-made drawer, shelf, and door components to be fitted into a custom-built frame, or his comprehensive storage system of floor to ceiling poles on which can be suspended a wide selection of drawers, desk, shelf, table, door, and panel components plus accessories. The storage wall system, set up as a wall or against one, conveniently provides the storage space formerly handled by a bookcase, cupboard, desk, chest of drawers, and the like.

After treating in a very brief fashion several of the leading industrial designers and how they have put the machine to economical and aesthetic use, let us glance for a moment at the other extreme—an increasing appreciation of handicrafts. We are all aware of the fact that in great heavily industrialized nations such as America the machine has shut one by one the little workshops from which so much simple beauty had issued to spread its boon among the homes of the unpretentious. But in the last several decades America has witnessed an aroused interest in handicrafts in their traditional form, an awareness of that all but lost delight in the making of the thing itself. As William Morris expressed it in *The Art of the People,* 1879, "An art which is to be made by the people and for the people, as a happiness to the maker and the user." We are primarily indebted for this renaissance of craftsmanship in America to the American Craftsmen's Council, a non-profit organization founded in 1943 by Mrs. Aileen Vanderbilt Webb. More than 125 of the leading craft organizations in America are affiliated as members with the council, whose aim is to provide education in the crafts and to stimulate public interest in and appreciation of the work of handcraftsmen. Under Mrs. Webb's dynamic leadership, the council conducts the Museum of Contemporary Crafts in New York, founded in 1956, and *Craft Horizons* Magazine. As part of the program to find new horizons of expansion for the American craftsman, the council maintains a close relationship with America House in New York, the lead-

ing marketing outlet for craftsmen in America. The council also has a similar relationship with the School for American Craftsmen, originally founded by the council in 1945 and now a division of the Rochester Institute of Technology.

The council, following the trail blazed by Morris, has within the new order of things enforced a respect for the handmade product and secured recognition for the individual designer-craftsman or artist-craftsman. Although only history can assess its true significance, it does beyond a doubt keep alive the flame of fine handworkmanship. The fact that the council is more concerned with how to create conditions for art to grow rather than how to create the forms of that art is an excellent augury for the success of its work.

Among the outstanding figures in the field of design for handmade furniture are Wharton Esherick, b. 1889, and George Nakashima. Inspired by the tradition of fine hand craftsmanship, these men work with a full appreciation of materials and the needs of today.

It is by no arbitrary choice that in discussing the great wealth of modern

OPPOSITE: Interior of the house of George Nakashima, designer-craftsman, at New Hope, Pennsylvania. The furniture he designed is in complete harmony with the rustic simplicity of its surroundings. *Courtesy George Nakashima. Photo Ezra Stoller.* ABOVE: Corner of a room, the furniture and interior made by M. Bega (c. 1950). The chair at the far right was designed by Gio Ponti. *Courtesy Altamira.*

wood furniture made in the 1940s and 1950s—lying between the two extremes already noted, the industrial designer and the designer-craftsman—we are led to treat of influences stemming from Italy, the Far East, and Scandinavia, in the case of the latter, particularly Denmark. Let us begin with Italy. In the years following World War II, modern Italian architecture and furniture attracted great interest. Its admirers acclaimed it as the second Italian Renaissance, a fact more than partly true, for the essential characteristics harked back to Italian art that had flourished since earliest times. Looking handcrafted and sculptured to pinpoint delicacy, the new furniture was a mélange of the antique, baroque, and rococo with a drop or two of German Bauhaus and French *moderne* cloaked in a playful, ingenious Italian guise. A marked characteristic of the new furniture, which had been developed by a group of Italian architects around Milan, was the floating look. For example, the legs of chairs that had formerly extended from the seat frame to the floor were now cut off in midair. Beneath the truncated legs a concealed stretcher supported the "floating" seat. Table legs were treated in a similar fashion; indeed, with

491

typical Italian fecundity, all kinds of ideas, such as contrasting colors and materials, shelves and edges narrowed to knife-blade thinness, were employed to achieve an appearance of relative weightlessness. Needless to say, this sculpturesque and light appearance had profound significance in America. It presaged the doom of the heavy block-like look which up to that time meant modern in America. In a word, from earthbound to airborne.

It is interesting to note here the extent to which the contemporary furniture made in Italy and, as we shall soon see, also in Denmark reflects the experiments of modern architecture. Especially in chairs the designers have broadly interpreted the weightless look of modern buildings by trying to minimize the strength it takes to support a relaxed human being. This recalls one of Le Corbusier's characteristic architectural devices—the lifting of the main part of a building off the ground by columns of distinctly sculptured character. This feature occurs in his classic *chaise-longue*.

Also deserving consideration is the influence of the Far East. The year 1948 was a great year for orientalism in America, especially at Grand Rapids. Ever since the days of the East India Company, the West has been

enamored with China, so remote in place and time. But it has always been the exotic—dragons, peacock feathers, towers with turned-up roofs, gnarled branches of willow trees, humpy bridges, and outlandish rocks—that has enchanted us. Less than three decades ago our description of domestic furniture used by the well-to-do Chinese around 1500–1600 would conform to the so-called Mandarin modern—ornately carved with pagodas and choked with mother-of-pearl. It is unfortunate that the early Chinese furniture made by cabinetmakers who sought to find a deeper richness— not a richness emanating from extraneous detail and superficial brightness —remained virtually unknown to us for more than 300 years.

Perhaps our first and best opportunity to study this furniture was in Gustav Ecke's splendid portfolio, *Chinese Domestic Furniture,* published in Peking, 1944. Dr. Ecke's book, however, would not have filled the vacuum with such conspicuous success were it not for the drawings illustrating the principles of Chinese joinery, which is unique. This joinery had never been investigated technically until Dr. Ecke made a thorough study of the subject in furniture repair shops in Peking. In this volume he has presented a scholarly record of his findings, which is of immeasurable value to students and designers. Some time after the publication of Dr. Ecke's book, we were given an excellent opportunity to see a collection of Chinese domestic furniture made in the Ming dynasty. The collection belonged to and was made by Dr. George N. Kates, curator of Oriental Art at the Brooklyn Museum, during his sojourn in China. It was displayed at an exhibition held at the Brooklyn Museum. In March 1946, *Interiors* re-

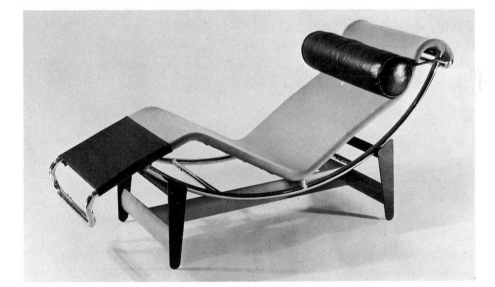

OPPOSITE: A modern design by the French designer Gustave Gautier (1956). *Courtesy French Embassy, Press Division, New York.* ABOVE: Reclining chair made of chrome-plated steel tubes, and painted oval steel tubes and sheets, designed by Le Corbusier (1927). The seat frame can be adjusted to any angle; it is perhaps the most relaxing chair that has ever been designed. *Courtesy Museum of Modern Art, New York. Gift of the Manufacturer, Thonet Frères, France.*

viewed the exhibition; the rest of the story we know. Hollis Baker persuaded Dr. Kates to come to Grand Rapids to supervise a collection of Chinese furniture.

Early Chinese furniture can be compared in beauty only to the furniture of ancient Greece. No period styles made in Europe possess the timeless beauty, the serenity, strength, and simplicity of this furniture with its deep feeling for the nature of wood. The structural honesty, an unerring instinct for line, flawless proportions, the carved decoration (what little there is), which is so integral a part of the construction, give this cabinetwork an almost pristine severity that is in accord with the finest classical traditions. It is beyond doubt that these qualities have and more importantly continue to have great influence on contemporary furniture design in America. Apart from the line-for-line reproductions and adaptations, this early Chinese furniture has also inspired a notable group of rawhide-bound rattan furniture designed by Eleanor Forbes and introduced by the McGuire Company in 1954. The sculptured quality of this rattan group contributes considerable interest to modern interiors.

When we think of the Far East we must constantly take into account the influence stemming from Japan. Not the influence from her furniture, for she has little or none, living as she does on mat level, not the influence from a form of exoticism as she appears in *Madame Butterfly*, but the influence emanating from her traditional culture—a feeling for the light and airy, an interest in simple and rectilinear construction, an understanding of the value of the elegant and refined use of line which equals an economy of line. These aesthetics, part of the concept of shibumi, are sometimes successfully translated into the form language of contemporary furniture designed in America, imparting a distinctly Japanese flavor. In such pieces, rectilinearism plays an important role and has become an essential decorative element. We have already seen in the nineteenth century how Japanese influence added lightness and spaciousness to the ideals of Morris and his followers. Guided by these principles, the furnishings of the earliest rooms in a modern sense, such as those by Mackintosh or Voysey, were simple, airy, and honest about every material and method of construction. To us who admire the classic excellence of Japanese culture, and in view of the spectacular build-up it has been receiving in the West for many a year, our hope is that it can add to the depth of culture in America.

Danish designs have exercised perhaps the greatest single influence on American interiors and furnishings. Indeed, modern Danish furniture, which retains the sparsely seasoned flavor of contemporary Swedish design, has become almost as familiar in the American home as the Boston rocker. Its transatlantic success appears to rest on two Danish virtues—a graceful practicality and livability, a simple and natural vocabulary of

ABOVE: Rosewood armchair, Ming Dynasty (c. 1600). *Courtesy Collection of Mrs. H. Batterson Boger. Photo Taylor-Dull.* BELOW: Rosewood cupboard in four parts, Ming Dynasty (c. 1600). When more cupboard space was required additional parts were added. *Courtesy Collection of C. Wendell Carlsmith. Photo Honolulu Academy of Arts.*

495

form that looks handmade. For this reason it mingles easily with such perennial American favorites as the pine furniture of New England, Pennsylvania farmhouse, or the furniture made by the Shakers.

The groundwork for light, modern Danish furniture was laid in the 1930s when Danish cabinetmakers employed the leading designers in Copenhagen to free them from the mire of derivative styling. In this period the architect Kaare Klint, 1888–1954, through his appointment in 1924 to lead the newly created class in furniture design at the Royal Academy's School of Architecture, exercised great influence. "It can hardly be wrong to say," we read in Esbjørn Hiort's *Modern Danish Furniture*, "that Klint was the first Danish furniture designer who founded his system on a purely rational basis." His emphasis on function, however, was accompanied by an innate Danish pride in handicraft traditions. Toward the end of the 1940s, as a result of the fruitful collaboration between designers and cabinetmakers, a few simple types of furniture had been created which were to become the nucleus for a more industrialized production.

As an example of these models, we can take the teakwood chair with open arms designed by the architect Finn Juhl, b. 1912, for the cabinetmaker Niels Vodder. The practical elegance of this chair with its sensitively molded, sculptured frame and its sparsely upholstered back and seat aroused great admiration. As is clearly revealed in this chair, Juhl particularly likes to emphasize the separation between seat and frame—an ingenious way of shedding weight. The carrying structure is emphasized as one thing and the seat and back are just surfaces to give rest. To divide a chair into components is one of Juhl's characteristic design principles. Some of his case pieces, such as chests of drawers, reveal a similar independence between the drawers and frame. It is well to mention here that Danish armchairs as a rule are not overstuffed or even entirely upholstered. The use of sparse upholstery as well as cane or rush, which frequently replaces the upholstery, gives a general impression of light and airiness.

Another example is the well-known chair designed in 1949 for the cabinetmaker Johannes Hansen by Hans Wegner, b. 1914, which he simply called "the chair." It was inspired, according to the designer, by a Chinese child's chair having a solid splat and an arched horseshoe-shaped crest rail, a typical Ming design, in the Copenhagen Museum. Wegner rarely employs the "floating" device—having the back and seat suspended or held away from the frame—a device associated with Juhl and freely adopted in America after his work became more widely known. Though the two examples of chairs by Juhl and Wegner are handmade, they became, as well as several variants of these types, the basic models for numerous chairs produced by industrial methods. Danish industrial art, however, is chiefly produced in small factories; the borderline between

LEFT: Cupboard unit, designed by Paul McCobb. In this piece rectilinearism is an essential decorative element. *Courtesy Paul McCobb.* (*See page 494*). RIGHT: Armchair designed by Finn Juhl for the cabinetmaker Niels Vodder, 1945. *Courtesy Danish Society of Arts and Crafts and Industrial Design. Photo Erik Hansen.*

handwork and industrial methods is more flexible. While the basic frames and other uniform parts are machine made, a great part of the working processes—for example, the sculptured or plastic shaping of the arms and tapering legs, the intricate joinings and soft oil rubbing—are by hand.

The "Danish mania" began in our quarters almost from the day Edgar Kaufmann, Jr., of the Museum of Modern Art, New York, returned from Europe in 1948 with photographs of Finn Juhl's chairs. In the course of the 1950s this fashion gathered impetus, culminating in an exhibition of the Arts of Denmark which opened at the Metropolitan Museum of Art on October 14, 1960. "The exhibition," wrote James J. Rorimer, the late director of the Metropolitan Museum, in the foreword of the exhibition's catalogue, "developed momentum gradually after Edgar Kaufmann, Jr., in 1958 asked whether the Metropolitan Museum of Art would consider having an important exhibition from Denmark." The interest in Danish furniture led not only to a collection designed by Finn Juhl for the Baker Company and introduced in 1951 but more importantly it created among American designers a new respect for the treatment of wood—that is, its

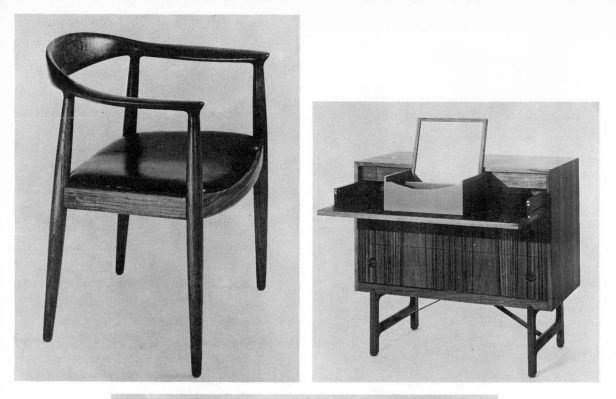

structural and decorative possibilities when woods of various colors and grains are combined.

Since 1950, there are a few factories in Denmark based purely on industrialized methods, in which such materials as light metals and artificial materials such as plastics are employed exclusively in the same manner as in the manufacture of automobiles and such household appliances as refrigerators. The stringent simplicity that characterizes this furniture is clearly revealed in two chairs in upholstered plastic, "the egg" and "the swan" designed by Arne Jacobsen in 1957, or in the steel chairs combined with leather or wicker, reminiscent of Mies's steel furniture, by Paul Kjaer-

OPPOSITE LEFT: Armchair of teak designed by Hans W. Wegner for the cabinetmaker Johannes Hansen (1949). (See page 496.) OPPOSITE RIGHT: Toilet table of teak designed by Madsen and Larsen (1960). OPPOSITE BELOW: Writing table of teak designed by Madsen and Larsen (1960). *Courtesy Georg Jensen, Inc., Collection of Just Lunning.* ABOVE LEFT: "The Egg," designed by Arne Jacobsen for the manufacturer Fritz Hansens (1957). ABOVE RIGHT: "The Swan," designed by Arne Jacobsen for the manufacturer Fritz Hansens (1957). *Courtesy Fritz Hansens, Inc., New York.*

holm, who won the Grand Prix for these chairs at Milan's tenth Triennale, 1957. Their formula for design—to simplify form and at the same time make it more expressive, to achieve a complete harmony between form and material—augurs well for their new endeavors. These two polarities in Danish design—the handcrafted, sculptured quality in wood and the new international expression in modern materials with austere linear lines reflecting Bauhaus traditions—continue to win new admirers in America each year.

In addition to influences stemming from Italy, Scandinavia, and the Far East, the form language of contemporary American furniture is gleaned from a mélange of cultural elements which the world has produced from the time of the Pharaohs to the clean lines of architectural modern. From this harvest of ideas American designers have been most consistently influenced by an appreciation of the craftsmanship traditions of our forefathers—the careful selection of the materials, the beautiful exactness of the joints, the meticulous execution of the carving, the veneering, and the finish. Nothing whatever is lacking in this honest workmanship of early days, whether it was done by such celebrated American cabinetmakers as Affleck, Randolph, or Savery for well-to-do people or by unknown cabi-

499

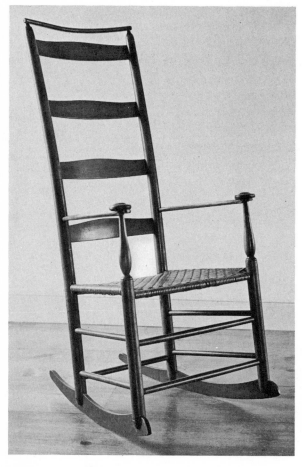

ABOVE LEFT: Chair of steel and wicker designed by Paul Kjaerholm (1957). *Courtesy Danish Society of Arts and Crafts and Industrial Design.* (*See page 498.*) ABOVE RIGHT: Breakfast table designed by Edward Wormley. The model is easy to use with late-eighteenth-century English furniture. *Courtesy Dunbar Company.* LEFT: Shaker rocking chair with a shagging rail over which was dropped a length of material. *Courtesy Shaker Community, Inc. Hancock, Massachusetts.* (*See page 502.*) OPPOSITE: Corner of a room in Edward Wormley's New York apartment showing furniture he designed for the Dunbar Company. The light and airy quality is reminiscent of Voysey's work. *Courtesy Edward Wormley. Photo J. Alex. Langley.* (*See page 502.*)

netmakers for people of less affluence. The merits of Shaker furniture—honest joinery, extreme simplicity, durability, lightness—have also been a wholesome influence on contemporary American work.

Now that we have a comprehensive idea of our contemporary furniture and the atmopshere in which it is being shaped we are indeed fortunate to have a comfortable number of designers, from such well-known names as Edward Wormley, Paul McCobb, T. H. Robsjohn-Gibbings and Jens Risom, to mention but several, to those with names less familiar but whose work possesses the same engaging honesty, the same graceful inventiveness. Imbued with a classic simplicity, this contemporary furniture reflecting the clean lines of modern architecture may be mixed with period styles. But it calls for taste and tact to choose from among the contemporary and period furniture the pieces that have sufficient affinities to come together without clashing.

After treating contemporary furniture, let us briefly discuss reproductions of the period styles whose hallmark is now authenticity. Most of the reproductions are copied exactly from antiques, chiefly museum antiques. Some of these copies such as from Colonial Williamsburg or the Henry Ford Museum are made under the supervision of staff members of each respective museum. Apart from the dowel-for-dowel reproductions, certain models are available in adaptations. These versions, smaller in scale and less costly, manage to preserve their authentic look. This seems to be an appropriate place to comment on the important role played by the Baker Company of Grand Rapids, which has been responsible for some of our best reproductions. The era of authentic reproductions with fine finishes began in 1931, when Baker launched the Connoisseur group comprising quality reproductions of English period styles. Up to that time practically all the reproductions had a factory look unless they had been for the main part made by hand in relatively small cabinetshops. Once the trend for authentic reproductions had been established, and more importantly the public bought them in depression years, other manufacturers began to plan similar groups. A few years later, for example, the Johnson Company offered an American Museum collection. In these quality reproductions mechanization is less advanced; the furniture looks like the work of the craftsman and in part it is.

In the field of reproductions, the American homemaker's first choice has always been the American past—three centuries of American furniture from the unpretentious farmhouse to the elegant Georgian, which is as useful and livable today as when it was first made. Then follows perhaps that large collection of European furniture notably from France and more recently from Italy which we in America call provincial in answer to the American taste for charming simplicity. Of this class of furniture, the Louis XV style has enjoyed the greatest vogue. This is because a very ordinary

Dining room of the Richard Davis residence, Wayzata, Minnesota, Philip Johnson, architect (1954). The interior emphasizes a closer relationship between indoors and outdoors, an influence from Japan which has changed our ideas about furnishings. *Courtesy Philip Johnson. Photo Ezra Stoller.* BELOW: Living room in the Philip Johnson Glass House, New Canaan, Connecticut, Philip Johnson, architect (1949). Furniture of the twentieth-century architectural school is shown against the natural background of earth, sky, and trees. *Courtesy Philip Johnson. Photo Alexandre Georges.*

Living room of an Essex, Connecticut, residence, Ulrich Franzen, architect. This gives an excellent idea of the twentieth-century architectural school of furniture in context. *Courtesy Ulrich Franzen. Photo Robert Damora.*

piece of Louis XV furniture is often a perfect feast for the eye, merely by the beauty of its lines and its harmony of silhouette. The eighteenth-century English styles—Queen Anne, Chippendale, Hepplewhite, and Sheraton—always have an extensive following. At the present time English Regency made in the nineteenth century is enjoying considerable popularity, no doubt because it takes kindly to the proximity of contemporary pieces. For the same reason French Directoire and Empire proclaim an affinity for the classical simplicity of our best contemporary furniture.

The really important thing about furniture is not whether it is hand-made or machine made, old or new, but that it should be first-rate at the time it is made—first-rate in material, in design, in workmanship. An appreciation of these qualities is not a natural gift. It can be learned and it is best learned by looking critically at furniture possessing these qualities. It is surprising how soon the eye begins to reject the inferior.

A last question arises; is it necessary to furnish in one style or is it permissible to have a mixture of furniture? The question has been strongly debated and each side has its staunch supporters. It is true that if we are not entirely confident in our taste, we are less apt to err if we stay within the limits of one style. But on the other hand such a rigid rule affords less scope for our individual taste, less opportunity to express our personality. It resolves itself into a matter of taste and tact. Two pieces of different styles may seem to be made for each other; they are different but get along well together. This is the story of many happy marriages.

What of the future? The prophet's is a thankless task because he is so rarely right except when his theme is "woe." Furniture designers of the future, as those of the past, will always go beyond conventional standards to explore a more adventurous world for a broader, richer "contemporary" style. There should be no reluctance to interpret the richness of the past. The best of tomorrow's furniture will always show conclusively that loyalty to tradition and a sound knowledge of the great historic schools of design need not impede inventive ability nor hinder the free expression of a strong personality. The best of tomorrow's furniture will always reflect in a logical and reasonable manner the age we live in. Above all, it will always translate the eternal aspiration of all mankind, toward that which is lacking in daily life and that which completes it, those rudiments of aesthetic enjoyment that our sensibility craves and that no mere utilitarian progress can replace.

BIBLIOGRAPHY

Note: The bibliography has been selected to include two or perhaps three indispensable works for each subject. The selection was chiefly determined by three requirements: fuller lists including references to periodicals, etc., to serve for further research; the most recent theories and information; and availability.

ANDREWS, EDWARD DEMING, and ANDREWS, FAITH. Shaker Furniture. New Haven, 1937.

ASLIN, ELIZABETH. Nineteenth Century English Furniture. New York, 1962.

BJERKOE, ETHEL HALL. The Cabinetmakers of America. New York, 1957.

BODE, WILHELM VON. Italian Renaissance Furniture. English translation by Mary E. Herrick. New York, 1921.

BOE, ALF. From Gothic Revival to Functional Form. Oslo, 1957.

BOGER, LOUISE ADE. The Complete Guide to Furniture Styles. New York, 1959.

BOGER, LOUISE ADE and BOGER, H. BATTERSON. The Dictionary of Antiques and the Decorative Arts. New York, 1957.

BRACKETT, OLIVER. English Furniture. Illustrated. A Pictorial Review of English Furniture from Chaucer to Queen Victoria. Revised and edited by H. Clifford Smith. London, 1950.

BRITISH MUSEUM. A Guide to the Greek and Roman Antiquities in the British Museum. Sixth edition. London, 1928.

BURCKHARDT, DR. JACOB. The Civilization of the Renaissance in Italy. Vienna, 1937.

BURR, GRACE HARDENDORFF. Hispanic Furniture, with examples in the collection of the Hispanic Society of America. New York, 1941.

BYNE, ARTHUR and BYNE, MILDRED STAPLEY. Spanish Interiors and Furniture. 2 vols., New York, 1921.

CARTER, HOWARD and MACE, C. C. The Tomb of Tut-Ankh-Amen. London, 1923.

Catalogues van Meubelen en Betimmeringen Rijksmuseum. Amsterdam, 1952.

CESCINSKY, HERBERT. . English Furniture from Gothic to Sheraton. Michigan, 1937.

Collection de L'Art Régional en France. (A Survey of French Provincial Furniture) Le Mobilier Lorrain, Charles Sadoul; Le Mobilier Basque, Louis Colas; Le Mobilier Breton, Paul Banéat; Le Mobilier Provençal, Henri Algoud, Le Mobilier Bas-Breton, Jules Gauthier; Le Mobilier Alsacien, Paul Gélis; Le Mobilier Bressan, Alphonse Germain; Le Mobilier Normand, Léon le Clerc; Le Mobilier Auvergnat, Jules Gauthier; Le Mobilier Flamand, V. Champier; Le Mobilier Vendéen et du Pays Nantais, Jules Gauthier. Paris, 1924.

CORNELIUS, CHARLES OVER. Furniture Masterpieces of Duncan Phyfe. New York, 1925.

DICKINSON, GEORGE. English Papier-Mâché. London, 1925.

DOWNS, JOSEPH. American Furniture (Queen Anne and Chippendale Periods) in the Henry Francis du Pont Winterthur Museum. New York, 1952.

DOWNS, JOSEPH. A Handbook of the American Wing, by R. T. H. Halsey and Charles O. Cornelius. 7th edition revised by Joseph Downs. New York, 1942.

ECKE, GUSTAV. Chinese Domestic Furniture. Peking, 1944.

Egyptian Museum, Cairo. A Brief Description of the Principal Monuments. Government Press, Cairo, 1956.

FÉLICE, ROGER DE. Little Illustrated Books on Old French Furniture, 4 vols. Vol. I, French Furniture in the Middle Ages and under Louis XIII, translated by F. M. Atkinson, London, 1923. Vol. II, French Furniture under Louis XIV, translated by F. M. Atkinson, New York, 1923. Vol. III, French Furniture under Louis XV, translated by Florence Simmonds, New York, 1920. Vol. IV, French Furniture under Louis XVI and Empire, translated by F. M. Atkinson, New York, 1921.

FOX, PENELOPE. Tutankhamun's Treasure. London, 1951.

Frick Collection Vol. IX, French Furniture of the 18th Century. New York, 1955. Vol. X, French Furniture of the 18th Century. Objects in Ormolu. New York, 1955. Vol. XI, Renaissance Furniture, Oriental Carpets, English Silver. New York, 1956.

GOMBRICH, ERNST HANS JOSEF. The Story of Art. New York, 1954.

HAMLIN, TALBOT FAULKNER. Architecture Through the Ages. New York, 1940.

HEAL, SIR AMBROSE. London Furniture Makers, From the Restoration to the Victorian Era, 1660–1840. London, 1953.

HIORT, ESBJØRN. Modern Danish Furniture. New York, 1956.

HORNOR, WILLIAM MACPHERSON. Blue Book of Philadelphia Furniture, William Penn to George Washington. Philadelphia, 1935.

HOWARTH, THOMAS. Charles Rennie Mackintosh and the Modern Movement. New York, 1953.

JOURDAIN, MARGARET and ROSE, T. English Furniture, The Georgian Period, 1750–1830. London, 1953.

JOURDAIN, MARGARET and EDWARDS, RALPH. Georgian Cabinet-Makers. Second edition, London, 1948.

JOURDAIN, MARGARET. Regency Furniture, 1795–1820. Revised and enlarged edition, London, 1948.

KETTELL, RUSSELL HAWES. The Pine Furniture of Early New England. New York, 1929.

KETTELL, RUSSELL HAWES. Early American Rooms. Portland, Maine 1936.

KIMBALL, FISKE. The Creation of the Rococo. Philadelphia, 1943.

LENNING, HENRY F. The Art Nouveau. The Hague, 1951.

LESTER, MARGON. Construction of American Furniture Treasures. New York, 1949.

LICHTEN, FRANCES. Decorative Art of Victoria's Era. New York, 1950.

LOCKWOOD, LUKE VINCENT. Colonial Furniture in America. 2 vols., Third edition, New York, 1926.

LONGNON, HENRI and HUARD, FRANCES WILSON. French Provincial Furniture. Philadelphia, 1927.

LYON, I. W. The Colonial Furniture of New England; a study of the domestic furniture in use in the 17th and 18th centuries. Boston, 1925.

MACQUOID, PERCY and EDWARDS, RALPH. The Dictionary of English Furniture from the Middle Ages to the Late Georgian Period. Revised and enlarged by Ralph Edwards. 3 vols., London, 1954.

MADSEN, STEPHAN TSCHUDI. Sources of Art Nouveau. English translation by Ragnar Christophersen. New York, 1956.

MILLER, EDGAR GEORGE, JR. American Antique Furniture. 2 vols., Baltimore, 1937.

MOLINIER, EMILE. Royal Interiors and Decorations of the 17th and 18th Centuries. 5 vols., Paris, 1902.

Museum of Modern Art, New York. Introduction to Twentieth Century Design from the Museum's Collection. Edited by Arthur Drexler and Greta Daniel. New York, 1959.

Museum of Modern Art, New York. Art Nouveau. Edited by Peter Selz and Mildred Constantine. New York, 1959.

Museum of Modern Art, New York. What Is Modern Design? by Edgar Kaufmann, Jr. New York, 1950.

MUSGRAVE, CLIFFORD. Regency Furniture. New York, 1961.

NUTTING, WALLACE. Furniture of the Pilgrim Century, 1620–1720. Revised edition. Massachusetts, 1924.

NUTTING, WALLACE. A Windsor Handbook. Saugus, Massachusetts, 1917.

NUTTING, WALLACE. Furniture Treasury. 1st and 2nd vols., 1928. 3rd vol., 1933, Massachusetts.

ODOM, WILLIAM M. A History of Italian Furniture from the 14th to the Early 19th Centuries. 2 vols., New York, 1918.

PEDRINI, AUGUSTO. Italian Furniture; interiors and decoration of the 15th and 16th Centuries. London, 1949.

PEVSNER, NIKOLAUS. Pioneers of Modern Design, from William Morris to Walter Gropius. New York, 1949.

PEVSNER, NIKOLAUS. High Victorian Design. Ipswich, Great Britain, 1951.

RICHTER, GISELA MARIE AUGUSTA. Ancient Furniture; A History of Greek, Roman and Etruscan Furniture. Oxford, 1926.

ROGERS, JOHN C. English Furniture. Revised and enlarged by Margaret Jourdain. London, 1950.

SALVERTE, FRANÇOIS, COMTE DE. Les Ébénistes du XVIII Siècle, Leurs Oeuvres et Leurs Marques. Paris, 1927.

SALVERTE, FRANÇOIS, COMTE DE. Le Meuble Français d'après les ornemanistes de 1660 à 1789. Paris, 1939.

SCHMITZ, DR. HERMANN. The Encyclopedia of Furniture. New York, 1957.

SINGLETON, ESTHER. Dutch and Flemish Furniture. London, 1907.

SPELTZ, ALEXANDER. Styles of Ornament, from Prehistoric Times to the Middle of the XIX Century. Translated from the second German edition. Revised and edited by R. Phene Spiers. London, 1910.

STONE, LOUISE HAWLEY. The Chair in China. Toronto, 1952.

STRANGE, THOMAS ARTHUR. French Interiors, Furniture, Decoration, Woodwork and Allied Arts, 17th, 18th, and 19th Centuries. London, 1907.

STRANGE, THOMAS ARTHUR. English Furniture, Decoration, Woodwork and Allied Arts, 17th, 18th, and 19th Centuries. London, 1901.

SYMONDS, ROBERT WEYMSS. Masterpieces of English Furniture and Clocks; a Study of Mahogany and Walnut Furniture. London, 1940.

TEAGUE, WALTER DORWIN. Design This Day. American Edition, 1946.

The Conant-Ball Furniture Company. A catalogue of Cape Cod Maple. Gardner, Massachusetts, 1939.

The Dunbar Furniture Company. A catalogue of contemporary furniture. Berne, Indiana, 1956.

The Herman Miller Furniture Company. A catalogue of furniture designed by George Nelson, Charles Eames, Isamu Noguchi and Paul Laszlo. Zeeland, Michigan, 1948.

UPJOHN, EDWARD MILLER; WINGERT, PAUL S.; MAHLER, JANE GASTON. History of World Art. Second edition revised and enlarged. New York, 1958.

VERLET, PIERRE. French Royal Furniture. New York, 1963.

Victoria and Albert Museum. English Furniture Designs of the Eighteenth Century. Peter Ward-Jackson. London, 1958.

Wallace Collection Catalogue on Furniture. Text with historical notes by Francis Watson. London, 1956.

WATSON, FRANCIS. Louis XVI Furniture. London, 1960.

WETTERGREN, ERIK. The Modern Decorative Arts of Sweden. English translation by Tage Palm. Malmö Museum, 1926.

INDEX

510

Leleu, Jules, 476
Lemon wood, 217
Lepautre, Jean, 115
Lepautre, Pierre, 100
Lescaze, 476
Lescot, Pierre, 85
Lesser Arts, The (Morris), 419, 435
Lessing, 46
Lethaby, W. R., 426
Levasseur, 96
Liberty, Arthur, 436
Library bookcase, 342–43
Library steps, 300–1
Library tables, 269–71, 287, 352, 365, 370
Liguria, 34
Linen-fold motif, 21, 23–24, 58, 67, 221–23
Lion monopodia legs, 12, 15, 204, 364–66
Lion motif, 16, 81, 87, 202, 271, 273–74, 276–77, 282, 287
Lion paw feet, 36, 173, 395–96, 399
Lit: à colonnes, 107, 137, 152, 180; *à dome,* 211; *à la duchesse,* 137, 180; *à la polonaise,* 137, 165, 180–81; *clos,* 151–52; *de parade,* 107–8, 468, 470; *de repos,* 193; *en batteau,* 196–97, 210–11
Lock, Matthias, 285–86
"Long-sytte bordes," 243
Loos, Adolf, 459–60, 462, 464
Lord and Taylor department store, 476
Lotus plant motif, 2, 8
Louis XIII style, 71, 82, 87–94
Louis XIV style, 43–44, 74, 95–115, 170; and American, 401
Louis XV style, 64, 121–50, 502, 504; and American, 470; and Art Nouveau, 442; and French provincial, 150–54; revival of, 217
Louis XVI style, 46, 64, 155–86; and French provincial, 151; Italian, 48; and Sheraton, 340, 346–47
Louis XVIII, 214
Love seat, 135
Love motifs, 119
Lowboy, 254, 376, 378–80, 382
Lozenge motif, 167, 187, 197
Lyre-forms, 16, 54, 56, 178–79, 183, 210, 213, 219, 306–7, 317, 349, 364, 369, 393, 395–97
Lyre motif, 345

Macassar, 472–74
McCobb, Paul, 497, 502
MacDonald sisters, 446
Macé, Jean, 96
McIntire, Samuel, 394
Mackintosh, Charles Rennie, 406, 432, 446–49, 456, 459, 464
Mackmurdo, Arther H., 426, 434
MacNair, Herbert, 446
Macy's department store, R. H., 476
Maggilioni, Guiseppe, 46
Mahogany: Adam, 316, 318, 320; American, 380–81, 383–84, 386–87, 389–90, 392–96, 398; Art Nouveau, 457; Biedermeier, 219; Chippendale, 287–90, 293, 295–96, 298; Early Georgian, 269, 274, 276–77, 281; Empire, 202, 204–5, 209–10, 212–14; first chair of, 178; first use of, 132; Hepplewhite, 325–26, 331–32, 334–36; imitation, 407; Louis XV, 123, 132, 150; Louis XVI, 161–63, 165–67, 170, 172–73, 178, 185–86; Regency, 364, 369, 372; Restauration, 217; Sheraton, 345–46, 352–55; William and Mary, 255
Majorelle, Louis, 442–45, 452
Making the Best of It (Morris), 418
Malmsten, Carl, 477, 480–81
Manchettes, 119, 135, 177
Mandarin motif, 293
"Mannerist" tradition, 38
Maple, 217, 373, 378–80, 389, 392
Marble decoration, 33, 85, 87, 134, 158; imitation, 407
Marble-top tables, 109, 112, 165, 198, 213, 271–72, 281
Mare, André, 471–72

Marie Antoinette, 173, 184
Marot, Daniel, 74, 102, 109, 247, 250, 252–53, 255
Marotesque chair, 76, 250
Marqueteurs, 96
Marquetry: Adam, 315; *à la reine,* 167; Art Nouveau, 442, 445; Boulle, 96–101, 111, 114–15, 173; Chippendale, 288, 290; Dutch, 77–78; floral, 77–78, 91, 141, 143–49, 235–37, 245, 288, 290; French school of, 96; Hepplewhite, 324, 326, 330, 332; Italian, 40, 46; ivory, 474; Late Jacobean, 235–37, 245; Louis XIV, 96–101, 111, 114–15; Louis XV, 132–33, 141, 143–49; Louis XVI, 157, 164, 167, 169–70, 174; modern, 474; Morris, 424–25; pictorial, 132–33, 170–71, 290; polychrome, 77–78, 91, 132–33, 236, 290, 324; Regency, 367; seaweed, 249, 255–58; Sheraton, 353; wood, 96–97, 367
Marquise, 135
Marshall, Peter Paul, 416
Martin brothers, lacquer by, 131
Mask motif, 38, 81, 87, 99, 101, 247, 271, 273–74, 276, 281
Mathsson, Karl Bruno, 480–81
Mazarin, Cardinal, 95–96
Mazarine Commodes, 114–15
Medallion motif: Adam, 304, 307, 311–12; American, 390–91; Elizabethan, 221–22; Empire, 206; French Renaissance, 79–80; Henri II, 83; Hepplewhite, 324, 329–30, 336; Louis XIV, 114; Louis XVI, 167, 173, 176–77
Medallion-shaped chair back, 136, 161, 175–77
Medieval Court of Great Exhibition, 412–14
Medieval furniture, 17–28. *See also* Gothic
Meissonier, Juste Aurèle, 122, 283
Menuisiers-ébénistes, 125–26
Menuisiers en sièges, 124
Méridienne, 197, 210–11
Metal furniture, 59, 409, 465, 477, 493
Metropolitan Museum of Art, 477
Meubles d'appui, 149, 372
Meubles parlant, 420
Michelangelo, 30, 37
Middle Ages. *See* Gothic; Medieval
Mies van der Rohe, Ludwig, 465–68, 477
Migeon family, 124
Military motifs, 173, 181, 194, 205
Miller, Sanderson, 296
Mirrors: Adams, 312, 316–17, 320–22; American, 383; cheval, 214, 355–57; Chippendale, 284–85, 290; Early Georgian, 270–71, 282; girandole, 316; Hepplewhite, 327; Louis XIII, 88; pier, 320, 322; Roman, 15; semi-Venetian, 474–76; Sheraton, 355–57; toilet, 84, 246, 254, 264–65, 326–27; wall, 255–56. *See also Trumeau*
Mission furniture, 404
Modernismo, 437
Modern movement, 421, 427, 429, 440, 449, 460–505; American, 476–78, 412, 485–505; Chinese, 492–95; Danish, 494, 496–99; French, 470–76; German, 465–68; Italian, 491–92; Swedish, 477–83
Mogensen, Börje, 483
Molded furniture, 484–87
Molding, decorative: Adam, 304; Empire, 202; François I, 79; French provincial, 150, 152–54; Italian, 36–38; Louis XIII, 92; Louis XIV, 104, 115; Louis XV, 128–29; Louis XVI, 163
Monnoyer, Jean Baptiste, 97, 105
Montigny, 96
Moorish influence, 49–50, 53, 57–60
Moroccan influence, 470
Morris, William, 402–4, 406, 413–19, 422–24, 426–27, 429, 435, 471, 489
Morris chair, 416–17
Morris and Company furniture, 416–19, 424–25
Morse, E. S., 420–21
Mortise, 18
Mosaicists, 96
Moser, Koloman, 460

515

519